MORE PRAISE FOR *HOMELANDS*

"Tremendously enjoyable.... Thoughtful, honest, open, self-deprecating."
—Dominic Sandbrook, *Sunday Times*

"From the 'miracle' of 1989 to the return of state thuggery, readers could
hardly wish for a wiser guide to the continent's triumphs and travails."
—*Financial Times*

"Garton Ash is a clear-headed chronicler of the Continent [and]
Homelands is an engaging read."
—*Irish Times*

"There are historians of Europe who remain detached from the messy
realities of the continent's present. And there are commentators who
are immersed in that present but lack the historical knowledge to truly
understand it. No figure better unites both disciplines than . . . Timothy
Garton Ash. His history of the continent's 'overlapping timeframes of
postwar and post-Wall' is rich with originality and memoiristic details."
—Jeremy Cliffe, *New Statesman*

"A fluent and authoritative account."
—*Literary Review*

"A beautiful new book.... *Homelands* is a synthetic, personal retrospective . . . yet it is far more than a compendium of illustrative vignettes
and well-told stories. . . . It provides essential analytical overviews of
all the salient events of European unity and division."
—William Collins Donahue, *Commonweal*

"*Homelands* is an illuminating and accessible work on a mammoth
subject: Europe.... A stunning combination of memoir, reportage
and history."
—Lucy Popescu, *Camden New Journal*

"Beautifully written and full of perceptive detail and personal observations.... In his astute reflections on the arc of European history since
the Second World War through to the return of major war in Ukraine
in 2022, Garton Ash does not let his aspirations for Europe obscure the
enormous challenges it faces today."
—Hanns W. Maull, *Survival*

T0000012

TIMOTHY GARTON ASH

Homelands

A Personal History of Europe

Yale UNIVERSITY PRESS
New Haven and London

For D, T & A

First published in hardcover in 2023 in the United States by Yale
University Press and in the United Kingdom by The Bodley Head,
which is an imprint of Vintage and part of the Penguin Random
House group of companies. First published in paperback in 2024 in
the United States by Yale University Press and in the United Kingdom
by Vintage, part of the Penguin Random House group of companies.

Maps by Bill Donohoe.

Yale University Press books may be purchased in quantity for educational, business, or promotional use. For information, please e-mail
sales.press@yale.edu (U.S. office) or sales@yaleup.co.uk (U.K. office).

Printed in the United States of America.

Library of Congress Control Number: 2023930094
ISBN 978-0-300-25707-6 (hardcover : alk. paper)
ISBN 978-0-300-27672-5 (paperback)

10 9 8 7 6 5 4 3 2 1

Contents

To write the genuine history of present-day Europe:
there is an aim for the whole of one's life.

Leo Tolstoy, *Diaries*, 22 September 1852

It is quite true what philosophy tells us, that life must be
understood backwards. But then one forgets the other
principle, that it must be lived forwards.

Søren Kierkegaard, *Journals*

States and frontiers in 1972. Places marked in *italics* play a special role in this book.

Europe during the
Cold War

FINLAND
Helsinki

SEA

Moscow

SOVIET
UNION

Warsaw

AND

Lviv

VAKIA

Budapest

GARY

ROMANIA

Belgrade

Bucharest

SLAVIA

BULGARIA

BLACK SEA

Sofia

Tirana

ALBANIA

Ankara

GREECE

TURKEY

Athens

IRAN

Knossos

IRAQ

CYPRUS

SYRIA

EAST
BERLIN

WEST
BERLIN

Berlin Wall

States and frontiers in 2023. Places marked in *italics* play a special role in this book.

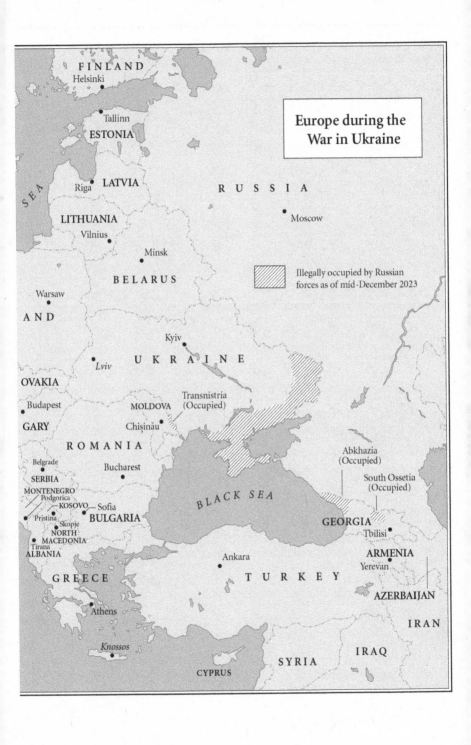

Europe during the
War in Ukraine

Illegally occupied by Russian
forces as of mid-December 2023

FINLAND
Helsinki

Tallinn
ESTONIA

SEA

Riga   LATVIA

RUSSIA

Moscow

LITHUANIA
Vilnius

Minsk

BELARUS

Warsaw

AND

Kyiv

OVAKIA

Lviv   UKRAINE

Budapest

GARY

MOLDOVA

Transnistria
(Occupied)

Chisinău

ROMANIA

Abkhazia
(Occupied)

Belgrade

Bucharest

SERBIA

South Ossetia
(Occupied)

MONTENEGRO
Podgorica
KOSOVO   Sofia

BLACK SEA

GEORGIA

Pristina
Skopje   BULGARIA

Tbilisi

NORTH
MACEDONIA
Tirana
ALBANIA

ARMENIA
Yerevan

GREECE

Ankara

TURKEY

AZERBAIJAN

IRAN

Athens

Knossos

IRAQ

SYRIA

CYPRUS

Prologue: Our time

In a small front room, amid the unfamiliar smells of Gauloise tobacco smoke and strong black coffee, I sit with my French host family staring at a small black-and-white television screen. I am fourteen years old, on a school exchange, and helping to translate. '*Armstrong il dit: un petit pas pour moi, un grand pas pour l'humanité!*' Soon a shadowy figure in a spacesuit is taking weightless leaps across the surface of the moon, a scene entirely familiar to me from the Tintin book *Explorers on the Moon*.

It's hard to recover a sense of just how remote continental Europe was to an English schoolboy in 1969. I won't say that France seemed as far away as the moon, but it was everything the English have traditionally packed into the word 'foreign'. Over there they eat frogs, ride scooters and have oodles of sex. Whatever you do, don't drink the water. Reaching the town of La Rochelle, on the Atlantic coast, had involved a seemingly endless journey by bus, tube, train, ferry (violently seasick), train and bus again. My brand-new, stiff-backed, very dark blue British passport had been closely examined and stamped at the frontier post. In my pocket, I nervously fingered some crisp, enormous French franc notes. To telephone home was a complicated procedure that involved wrestling with an operator down a crackling landline in bad French ('*Peut on reverser les charges?*').

Twenty years later, I was at a dissident rally in Budapest, signing copies of a Hungarian-language edition of my essays about central Europe. It was that year of wonders, 1989. Freedom and Europe – the two political causes closest to my heart – were marching forward arm in arm, to the music of Beethoven's ninth symphony, heralding a peaceful revolution that would open a new chapter of European and world history. No part of the continent was 'foreign' to me anymore. Living the paradox that encapsulates what it is to be a contemporary European, I was at home abroad.

So much at home, in fact, that one of my Hungarian friends turned to me, as we walked back through the warm, sensual streets of Budapest, and exclaimed, 'You must be descended from Scholem Asch!'

'No,' I replied, slightly taken aback.

'Then how come you're so interested in central Europe?'

As if a genetic explanation were somehow required for being emotionally involved in another part of Europe.

Our identities are given but also made. We can't choose our parents, but we can choose who we become. 'Basically I'm Chinese,' Franz Kafka wrote in a postcard to his fiancée. If I say 'basically I'm a central European' I'm not literally claiming descent from the central European Yiddish writer Asch, but declaring an elective affinity.

Since my birthplace is Wimbledon, England, I was indubitably born in Europe and therefore, in that rudimentary sense, born a European. Mapmakers, all the way back to Eratosthenes some 2,200 years ago, have always placed Britain in Europe, a region counterposed to Asia and Africa in what is probably the oldest continuous mental subdivision of the world. So long as there has been a geographical notion of Europe, our vaguely triangular islands have been part of it. But I was not 'born a European' in the stronger sense of being brought up to think of myself as one.

The only time my mother referred to herself as a European was when she reminisced about her youth in British-ruled India, where she was born a daughter of the Raj. 'As a European,' she told me, happily recalling some romantic months spent as a young woman in New Delhi at the end of the Second World War, 'one went out riding early in the morning.' In India, the English called themselves Europeans. Only back home do they still often like to deny a truth that seems self-evident to anyone looking at them from Washington, Beijing, Siberia or Tasmania.

I never heard my father talk of himself as a European, even though his formative experience had been landing on a Normandy beach with the first wave of British troops on D-Day and fighting with the liberation armies all the way across northern Europe, until he quietly, exhaustedly welcomed VE (Victory in Europe) Day in a tank somewhere on the north German plain. One of his favoured Conservative prime ministers, Harold Macmillan, supposedly remarked of the legendary French president Charles de Gaulle that 'he says Europe and means France'. But that was equally true of Englishmen of my father's ilk. When they said Europe they meant in the first place France, as the English had done for at least six centuries, since the Hundred Years' War shaped the national identities of France and England, each against the other.

For my father, Europe was definitely foreign and the European Union was one of those 'knavish tricks' that our national anthem calls upon patriotic Brits to frustrate. I once gave him a large chocolate euro for Christmas and he promptly devoured it, gnashing his teeth with theatrical delight. A lifelong, active Conservative, in his old age he briefly, to my horror, defected to UKIP, the UK Independence Party. Had he still been alive in 2016, he would undoubtedly have voted for Brexit.

I feel myself blessed by historical luck to have grown up in England, a land that I love; but that geographical fact did not make me a European. I became a conscious European some time between that first schoolboy inhalation of Gauloise tobacco smoke in 1969 and signing books in revolutionary Budapest in 1989. My diary for Friday 12 August 1977 records an evening spent in a West Berlin pizzeria with Karl, an Austrian 'electrician, film guide and taxi driver', whom my toffee-nosed twenty-two-year-old Oxford graduate self describes as 'a recognisably civilised fellow European'. (Wouldn't do to have an uncivilised pizza companion, would it?) Still and all, a *fellow* European.

This book is a personal history of Europe. It's not an autobiography. Rather, this is history illustrated by memoir. I draw on my own journals, notebooks, photographs, memories, reading, watching and listening over the last half-century, but also on the recollections of others. So when I say 'personal' history, I don't just mean 'my own'; I mean history as experienced by individual people and exemplified by their stories. I quote from my conversations with European leaders where this helps to illuminate the story but also from many encounters with so-called ordinary people, who are often more remarkable human beings than their leaders.

I have visited or revisited some places to see for myself, as journalists do. I have also drawn on the best primary sources and most recent scholarship, as historians do. Unlike in the reportage and commentaries I wrote as things happened, here I make full use of the benefit of hindsight. Hindsight, they say, is 20:20, and although the view from the early 2020s is far from perfect, some things have become clearer.

I always strive to be accurate, truthful and fair, but I make no claim to be comprehensive, impartial or objective. A young Greek writer would paint a different Europe, as would an elderly Finn, a Scottish nationalist, a Swiss environmentalist or a Portuguese feminist. Europeans can have multiple homelands, but no one is equally at home in all parts of Europe.

If our places are different, so are our times. Some of my Polish friends, for example, were operating 'underground' during a period of intense repression in the early 1980s, using assumed names, furtively changing apartments at night and sending coded messages, for all the world like members of the Polish underground resistance to Nazi occupation during the Second World War. On one trip to visit them, I noted in my diary: 'departure from Heathrow: 1984, arrival: 1945'. Different generations may inhabit different times even when they live in the same place. My 2023 is not my students' 2023. Everyone has their own 'our time'.

Thus, if there are today some 850 million Europeans – using a broad geographical definition of Europe, including Russia, Turkey and the Caucasus – then there are 850 million individual Europes. Tell me your Europe and I will tell you who you are. But even that framing is not wide enough. Identity is a mix of the cards we are dealt and what we make of them. It's also a mix of how we view ourselves and how others view us. Europeans, who have a strong tendency to self-congratulation, need also to see themselves through the eyes of non-Europeans, especially in the very large portion of the world that has experienced European colonial rule.

Yet while we all have our own personal eras and our own Europes, they are located within shared timeframes and spaces. Today's Europe cannot be understood without going back to the period that Tony Judt encapsulated in the title of his history of Europe since 1945: *Postwar*. But overlapping and in some important ways superseding that postwar framing is post-Wall Europe – the one that emerged following the fall of the Berlin Wall on 9 November 1989, the demise of the Soviet Union in December 1991 and the end of the Cold War division of our continent into two hostile blocs. In what follows, I offer both a personal account and an interpretation of Europe's history in these overlapping timeframes of post-war and post-Wall.

Europe's post-Wall period was not one of uninterrupted peace. It was punctuated by the bloody disintegration of former Yugoslavia in the 1990s, terrorist atrocities in many European cities, Russia's aggression against Georgia in 2008, its seizure of Crimea in 2014 and the subsequent, ongoing armed conflict in eastern Ukraine. Nonetheless, for the majority of Europeans this period could also be described as the Thirty Years' Peace. That came to an end with Russia's full-scale invasion of Ukraine on 24 February 2022, starting a war on a scale and of a horror not seen in Europe since 1945. And 1945 is where our story must begin.

Destroyed
(1945)

Westen

'He came in the late afternoon, the Englishman,' says Heinrich Röpe, a sturdy Lower Saxon farmer with a face the colour of rhubarb. As we walk along the tranquil, grassy banks of the River Aller he shows me the spot next to his family's timber-framed home where British troops threw a temporary metal bridge across the water one day in April 1945. 'Montgomery crossed here!' he exclaims, with more than a hint of local pride. As a five-year-old boy, little Heini stood on tiptoe to peer through the window, watching the khaki army go by.

I have come to the now prosperous village of Westen (the name means West), in the middle of the north German plain, on account of three grainy black-and-white photographs. They show a group of British army officers watching a game of cricket. One of them is my father, aged twenty-six. He has noted on the back, in his characteristic forward-sloping hand, that the photos were taken in June 1945 in Westen, which his gun troop occupied at the end of the Second World War. For Dad, who had spent the best part of a year since D-Day fighting through France, Belgium, the Netherlands and Germany, seeing comrades wounded and killed around him, a quiet game of cricket must have been anything but ordinary. I study the tense face of a young man I never knew who would become the old man I loved. What was going through his mind?

Looking more closely, I notice in the background a woman with a toddler on her knee. Beyond her are several other children in civilian clothes. One boy has bright blond hair and high-waisted trousers held up by braces. Germans. How did it look to them, as they sauntered among the strange foreign soldiers playing this strange foreign game?

Might I find someone in Westen who remembered a few details of that time?

So here I am, on a sunny spring day, sitting in a handsome eighteenth-century redbrick building that now serves as a communal museum and meeting place. Round a large wooden table in front of me are twelve elderly men and women and they remember . . . everything. Everything – and perhaps a little more.

'For me, as a Hitler Youth,' Albert Gödecke begins, arrestingly, 'it was completely clear that Adolf Hitler would win the war.' He believed it right up until the moment he met his first Tommy. (All self-respecting Westeners speak of the British forces in the singular, as 'the Englishman' or 'the Tommy'.) Fortunately, Albert spoke some English, so he said to the Englishman, 'Please sir . . .'

Heinrich Müller, a thickset old farmer with a head like a giant pumpkin, had actually been a Wehrmacht soldier, fighting on the Eastern front, until he was wounded. Now the Tommy stormed into his family farmstead in Westen and demanded, in broken German, '*Warum Du nicht Soldat?*' ('Why you not soldier?'). The Wehrmacht veteran pulled up his trouser leg and showed his wound.

Some thirty young Germans died in a hopeless defence of Hitler's front line on the east bank of the Aller. I walk down the rows of small, rectangular tombstones in the village cemetery, looking at the names and birthdates: Gerd Estemberger, aged seventeen; Wilhelm Braitsch, seventeen; Paul Jungblut, seventeen. Rudyard Kipling's epitaph for a raw recruit springs to mind:

> On the first hour of my first day
> In the front trench I fell.
> (Children in boxes at a play
> Stand up to watch it well.)

Meanwhile, German refugees had doubled the population of Westen from around 600 to more than 1,200. Some had come from Hamburg after the terrifying Anglo-American bombing raids known as Operation Gomorrah, which resulted in at least 900,000 people fleeing the pulverised city. Another group had been moved – 'in Adolf's time', as Albert puts it – from Bessarabia to Pomerania, and subsequently fled before the advancing Red Army 'with 140 horses'. I like the farmerly precision of the horse-count. Then there was an even larger trek of Germans fleeing for their lives from Silesia, which Stalin, Churchill and Roosevelt had decreed should be given to Poland.

Helga Allerheiligen is one of those refugees from Silesia. A neat, petite woman who looks much younger than her eighty years, she takes up the story, helped by her husband Wilhelm. Yes, she came from Breslau (today Wrocław) 'in a cattle cart, with just three suitcases'. Her family was housed in the neighbouring village of Hülsen, in a camp previously used for Polish forced labourers. 'You should have seen the awful mess the Poles left those barracks in,' she confides in me later, with just a hint of old prejudice.

These German refugees were not welcomed by the locals, and certainly not as partners for their sons: 'Westen men should marry Westen girls.' But fortunately, the British troops organised dance evenings. The British soldiers 'wanted to get together with the German girls', explains Helga. At one such dance, in the pub in Hülsen, she met a fine young Westener called Wilhelm Allerheiligen. Wilhelm's father was appalled: 'She doesn't bring anything with her!' But love will have its way. So here they are, a whole lifetime later, remembering those good old, bad old days.

Her mention of the British troops organising dances 'to get together with the German girls' leads me to another question: did relationships ever develop with British soldiers? A long pause, then one of the men says teasingly: 'Are you looking for relatives in Westen?'

When we break up for coffee and home-made cakes, I show my father's cricket photos to the two Heinrichs. Do they have any idea where these might have been taken? They put their sturdy heads together. Why of course, they exclaim, that's the road to Wahnebergen, and look here, that's the telegraph pole at Nocke.

Could someone show me the place? Jan Osmers, the youngest of the group, volunteers to help. We jump into my rented Volkswagen and in no time there it is: unmistakably the meadow in the photos, with the telegraph pole in the same place. I stand ankle-deep in the sweet-smelling long grass and hear in my mind's ear the sounds of that cricket match on a warm summer afternoon all those years ago: 'Good shot, sir!' 'Howzat!'

Jan, a slim figure with tousled silver hair and tinted spectacles, is the local historian. The proud inheritor of a windmill that has been in his family for five generations, he has written a detailed, carefully researched chronicle of Westen's history. He is just a couple of years older than me and we hit it off at once.

From the cricket meadow we drive to the *Steinlager*, the camp where forced labourers were housed in the neighbouring village of Döverden. In what is now known as the *Steinsiedlung* (the wartime camp became a post-war estate), solidly constructed barrack huts have been turned into modest, one-family bungalows, with neat lawns and small cars in the driveways. One bungalow flies the Stars and Stripes on a tall flagpole.

Many of the Nazis' forced labourers in this area lived with the farmers for whom they worked, while those farmers' sons went off to kill their labourers' relatives in Hitler's war. But the Poles, Russians, French and Belgians billeted in the *Steinlager* worked in the nearby Eibia gunpowder factory which, among other things, manufactured a primitive chemical weapon. Jan and I drive into a dense, coniferous forest in Barme, where the remains of this death factory can still be glimpsed amid the fir and pine trees. An abandoned works railway line leads directly to the plant and a still operational branch line runs close by. Railway lines – those varicose veins of Nazi evil, carrying poison, slavery and death to every corner of occupied Europe.

In the Barme forest you are already close to the heart of darkness, but you will be closer still if you turn off the main road back to Hanover and follow the signs to Bergen-Belsen. Here, just a few days after crossing the Aller, my father's fellow soldiers were confronted with horrors that few Brits had even dimly imagined. All around them they saw 'living skeletons with haggard yellowish faces' and smelled the 'stench of putrefying flesh'.

Maltreatment, starvation and disease stripped survivors of the last shreds of human dignity. Alan MacAuslan, a medical student working with the British forces, recalled:

> I looked down in the half light, and saw a woman crouching at my feet. She had black matted hair, well populated [with lice], and her ribs stood out as though there were nothing between them ... She

was defecating, but she was so weak that she could not lift her buttocks from the floor, and as she had diarrhoea, the yellow liquid stools bubbled up over her thighs. Her feet were white and podgy from famine oedema, and she had scabies. As she crouched, she scratched her genital parts, which were scabetic too.

A Czech prisoner, Jan Belunek, told his liberators that he had seen corpses with their hearts cut out, and watched another prisoner 'sitting beside one of such corpses . . . eating flesh that I have no doubt was human flesh'.

Dead bodies were now stacked high upon each other displaying, as one British officer recorded, 'every trick that rigor mortis can play with the human countenance, every freakish posture that a sprawling human skeleton, thrown down at random, can assume'. If you visit the Bergen-Belsen memorial today, you can see original documentary film of captured camp guards ordered to wrench those naked, rigid corpses off lorries and drag them into mass graves, while camp survivors shout abuse at them in all the languages of Europe.

In just one day spent driving around what is today a prosperous and peaceful corner of north-western Europe, I have been transported back into our continent's darkest hour. Those ghosts are waiting there for you, just a conversation away. For every Helga, Albert and Heinrich, for every British soldier like my father, for every French, Polish or Russian forced labourer in the *Steinlager*, for every inmate of Bergen-Belsen, there were millions more.

Hell

Human beings have never succeeded in building heaven on earth, even – perhaps especially – when they have tried. But they have repeatedly built hell on earth. In the first half of the twentieth century, that is what Europeans did to their own continent, as they had in earlier centuries to other people's continents. No one else did it for us. This was European barbarism, done by Europeans to Europeans – and often in Europe's name. You cannot begin to understand what Europe has tried to do since 1945 unless you know about this hell.

'One death is a tragedy, one million deaths is a statistic.' Even leaving aside the difficulty of establishing precise figures, the mind is soon numbed by the numbers. Shall I tell you that some 18,000 people died in Bergen-Belsen in just one month, March 1945? Or that there were nearly eight million forced labourers in Germany at the end of the war? Or that some ninety-three per cent of living space in Düsseldorf was uninhabitable after the Allied bombing of the city? Or that Belarus lost some two million people out of a pre-war population of around nine million, with another three million or more displaced?

In a book that hauntingly applies to twentieth-century Europe the label that nineteenth-century European imperialists slapped on Africa, *Dark Continent,* Mark Mazower estimates that 'close to 90 million people were either killed or displaced in Europe between 1939 and 1948'. This means that roughly one out of every six Europeans was either killed or displaced. That is before we even get to the further millions who were merely starved, stricken by disease, raped, tortured, crippled, paupered, frozen, reduced to prostitution, orphaned, humiliated, degraded, widowed, psychologically scarred for life – let alone the long-term effects on their children and children's children.

As the Old Testament observes, the iniquity of the fathers is visited upon the children 'unto the third and fourth generation'. When I investigated the lives of the Stasi officers who had spied on me in East Germany in the late 1970s and early 80s, first reading their own Stasi personnel files and then interviewing them in depth, I was forcibly struck by the fact that all but one of them had grown up without a father. The fathers had died or disappeared in the war. As I talked to them it became clear to me how this had made them psychologically vulnerable to the appeal of the father state. Tens of millions of children all over Europe grew up without a father after 1945, and their mothers without a husband.

There were different circles of this hell. The rich generally did not starve, but an aristocratic background was no defence against penury. Depending on the date, it was better to be German or Hungarian than French or Dutch, then vice versa, but usually worse to be a Slav and worse still be Roma or Jewish. The inferno had a distinct geography. If you were in a neutral country, such as Switzerland, Sweden or Ireland, you avoided the worst horrors. Military losses, wartime bombing and post-war austerity imposed great suffering on Britain – my brother's second name, Brian, honours my father's best friend, killed in the war. The most terrible horrors were in the eastern half of the continent, in what Timothy Snyder has memorably called the bloodlands.

In the village cemetery in Westen, next to the small square gravestones of those German child soldiers who died on the banks of the river Aller in April 1945, is a memorial tablet that reads:

> *Ihr Findet Sie*
> *Wo Ihr Nach Ihnen Fragt*
> *Im Osten Gefallen*
> *Im Westen Beklagt*
> (You shall find them
> Where you ask after them
> Fallen in the East
> Lamented in the West)

Lamented in the West – and in this village called West. Since this was a farming village well supplied with timber for firewood, there was not the famine and cold endured in most big cities, especially in the East. In the course of the liberation of western Europe, some British soldiers committed atrocities, including summary executions and vicious beatings, but there was nothing like the mass rape and brutality that the Red Army wreaked on German civilians. Albert, the former Hitler Youth, kindly assures me that in Westen the English were 'very calm and matter-of-fact'. But then, the British had not suffered what Russians, Ukrainians, Belarusians and other east European peoples who served in the Red Army had suffered at German hands.

Osten

After an accident of personal history has taken me to the village of Westen I find myself wondering if there was a village called Osten, meaning East. Sure enough, there were three of them in the pre-1914 German Reich, and one is now Przysieczyn in western Poland. So here I am sitting in Przysieczyn, at another wooden table with another group of elderly men and women who, like their German counterparts in Westen, remember everything (and perhaps a little more).

A retired Polish schoolteacher dramatically holds up a battered, blackened French army metal water bottle, a present from a French soldier to his Polish fellow prisoner in a German prisoner-of-war camp. An old farmer remembers seeing the bodies of dead Germans lying around in the woods in early 1945. Red Army Cossack cavalry had gone hunting for them. But before that there had been the murder of 103 Poles by the SS in those same woods, following the German invasion in September 1939. And the mass deportation of Poles to the east.

The squat, yellow-walled building in which we sit in Przysieczyn had been the *Polenschule* (school for Poles) under Nazi occupation. Only German children had been allowed to attend the regular primary and secondary schools in the local town, Wągrowiec. Polish kids were compelled to travel out to primitive schools like this in the surrounding villages, where they were not allowed to speak Polish and received only elementary education in German until the age of twelve, when they had to go to work. After all, they were to be a subject race.

I meet Zbigniew Orywał, a hale and hearty former Olympic athlete in his nineties, who was a pupil at that Nazi 'school for Poles'. He recalls that no more than two Poles were allowed to walk together on the street under the German occupation. His father used to slip out at night, despite the curfew, to buy food from local farmers. If the Germans had caught him, he would have been shot on sight. Most of the Germans fled as the Red Army drew near in early 1945, taking the wagons and the horses. (Here, as in Westen, horses figure prominently in the conversation.) And he, too, remembers Red Army soldiers finishing off the few Germans who remained.

The Wągrowiec area illustrates the madness of those years, in which not just millions of men, women and children but whole countries were shunted around against their will like cattle. The region had been Polish for centuries until Prussia took it over by force in the first partition of Poland in 1772. As a result, it became part of united Germany after 1871. After the First World War, it became Poland again; in 1939, Germany again; in 1945, back to Poland. At the end of our conversation round the table in Przysieczyn, the former village mayor, a delightful, sturdy countryman called Jan Kaniewski, presents me with a large cardboard roll. Opening it, I find a wartime German map of the region preserved by his father, with every place name given in German: Wągrowiec is Eichenbrück and Przysieczyn, Osten. He tells me his father never mentioned the existence of this map until after the end of communist rule in 1989.

During the German occupation, nearly half the Polish population of Wągrowiec was deported, mainly to Nazi-occupied Polish territory to the east but also to do forced labour in places like Westen. The Poles' businesses and farms were usually taken over by Germans, many of them from the eastern parts of the German Reich. Adam Mesjasz, for example, a loquacious old farmer's son, recalls that when he was three years old, on 11 February 1941, his entire family was kicked out of their farmstead and loaded onto a freezing train to be transported to the east. Their farm was taken over by a 'Baltic German'. When Adam's family came back on Easter Day 1945, the Baltic Germans had fled westward – taking all the *horses*, he emphasises.

Mesjasz also has something to show me, a large book wrapped in brown paper. It turns out to be a photo album called 'Adolf Hitler: Photos from the Life of The Führer' – the Führer reading the newspaper, the Führer patting delightful blond children on the head, the Führer mobbed by adoring women – each photo carefully collected from some kind of subscriber serial and glued into the intended place in the printed volume by a local German farmer. Adam and his colleagues had found it hidden under the floorboards of a farmhouse when they were doing renovation work in the 1970s. A household ghost.

Those local Germans, some of whose families had lived there for generations, also fled in early 1945 and most of them settled in the Lüneburg area of north Germany, not far from Westen. Many of their farms in what was now again the Wągrowiec area were taken over by Poles who had, in their turn, been forcibly removed from Poland's eastern territories, now incorporated into Stalin's Soviet Union. Some of the Poles who drove Helga Allerheiligen, the old lady in Westen, out of the formerly German city of Breslau (today's Wrocław) had themselves been expelled 'with just three suitcases' from their equally long-settled and beloved homelands in what is now Ukraine or Belarus. Here was Europe's mad carousel of involuntary displacement.

The vengeance wreaked by advancing Soviet troops on Germans, guilty and innocent alike, was not confined to summary executions and plunder. An eyewitness reported that when the Red Army reached the Baltic port of Danzig (today's Gdańsk), 'Nearly all the women were raped – among the victims were old women of sixty and seventy-five and girls of fifteen or even twelve. Many were raped ten, twenty or thirty times.' The men were often forced to watch. 'Men nowadays all seem to have shrunk,' says Maria in Rainer Werner Fassbinder's film *The Marriage of Maria Braun*. German men, that is.

In Immanuel Kant's home town of Königsberg, then being forcibly transformed into the Soviet city of Kaliningrad, a young doctor, Hans von Lehndorff, heard women who were being subjected to endless brutal rapes cry out to the Red Army soldiers: 'Shoot me! Just shoot me!' 'Oh,' Lehndorff exclaims, 'how many envious looks the dead must endure!' All across devastated Europe there were innumerable suicides.

When Lehndorff and his remaining compatriots were finally driven out of their nearby East Prussian homeland by the new Polish authorities, the noble doctor told his fellow Germans, 'the [Polish] local councillor here says he's sorry we have to leave our homeland in this way. But he can't change it, because our people earlier did the same thing to the Poles – and that is unfortunately true.'

It is futile to try to reckon these sufferings off against each other, in a kind of moral double-entry bookkeeping. The poet W. H. Auden captures the essential truth:

> I and the public know
> What all schoolchildren learn,
> Those to whom evil is done
> Do evil in return.

In all this panorama of horror, with its endless variations of torment resembling nothing so much as Hieronymus Bosch's depictions of hell, what most pierces the heart is the children: orphaned, abandoned, abused, traumatised. In the neighbourhood of Westen, the babies of forced labourers were taken from their mothers during the war and kept in crude orphanages – two of them converted pigsties and another a stables. Many of the infants died. Those who survived were psychologically scarred for life. Immediately after the war, English nurses were astonished at the behaviour of Jewish children who had survived the concentration camps. If a child went missing from the group, the others would say quite matter-of-factly: 'Oh, he's dead'. To them, that was normality.

Zero, recurring

The idea that 1945 was Year Zero for Europe contains a truth and two traps. The important truth is that for most Europeans there was some moment when they said: 'That horror is at last over; let's now start to rebuild a better place from the rubble.'

The first trap is to take this as a starting point without regard to Year -1 or Year -10, the years that led to this point. You cannot understand the horrors inflicted on innocent Germans in 1945 unless you know what was done by Germans to other Germans, starting in 1933, and then to other Europeans, starting with the annexation of Austria and parts of Czechoslovakia in 1938. For the peoples of the Soviet Union, the brutality was there from the very beginning of Soviet rule, in 1917. At least eight million people died in the Russian civil war, which lasted into the early 1920s, and close to four million more in the Ukrainian famine at the beginning of the 1930s. To understand these developments, in turn, you need to go back at least to 1914, and the causes, course and legacy of the First World War. Some of the disputes between states and peoples that re-emerged in the period after 1989 had origins that can be traced back to the dissolution of the pre-1914 Ottoman and Austro-Hungarian empires and the peace settlement imposed by the victorious Allies at the end of that war.

The second trap is to assume that all Europeans had the same Year Zero – that is, 1945. For southern Italy, Year Zero was 1943, following the Allied invasion. For much of eastern Europe, it began in 1944, as the Red Army swept forward, but definitely did not end in 1945. In Ukraine and Poland there was fierce fighting between communist and anti-communist forces, and between Poles and Ukrainians, well into the late 1940s. Yugoslavia and Greece saw equally ferocious struggles, with British forces supporting communist partisans in Yugoslavia while other British forces suppressed communist partisans in Greece.

There was no bright line separating hot war from cold war. Austria only became securely part of the West with its state treaty in 1955. In Estonia, the extraordinary 'Forest Brothers' went on fighting the Russian occupation from their camouflaged woodland hideouts well into the 1950s. The last surviving Forest Brother, August Sabbe, died when the KGB tried to arrest him in 1978. Across the Soviet Union, the vast network of camps that came to be known as the Gulag (from the Russian acronym for Main Administration of Camps) continued to inflict the torments described by Aleksandr Solzhenitsyn in *The Gulag Archipelago*. The Gulag was officially closed in 1960 but special detention centres for political prisoners survived well into the 1980s.

From the mid-1950s onwards, the oppression and brutality endured by most people in the Soviet bloc was less extreme than it had been in the 1930s and 40s. But as the Czech dissident playwright Václav Havel kept pointing out, the 'peace' experienced by people living in a country like Czechoslovakia was not comparable with the peace enjoyed by citizens of France, the Netherlands or Belgium. It was punctuated by the Soviet invasions of Hungary in 1956 and Czechoslovakia in 1968, as well as the declaration of a 'state of war' in Poland in 1981, and it was pockmarked by everyday police repression.

Nor was this simply an east–west divide. Portugal and Spain continued to live under fascist dictatorships, so their Year Zero only came with the end of those dictatorships in the mid-1970s. Perhaps more accurately, they had two Year Zeros. Greece fell under the military rule of the Colonels in 1967 and only re-emerged in 1974.

Walking up the East German part of Friedrichstrasse a couple of days after the Berlin Wall was breached on 9 November 1989, I met a man who declared euphorically '28 years and 91 days!' – the exact time his family had been stuck behind the Wall. He told me he'd just seen a handwritten poster that declared: 'Only today is the war really over'. For the societies of the Soviet-dominated eastern half of Europe, 1989 was their second Year Zero.

No sooner had we said 'goodbye to all that' than all that came back with a vengeance in former Yugoslavia. War. Ethnic cleansing. Rape as a weapon. Concentration camps. Terror and lies. I will never forget sitting in Sarajevo in 1995 with a magazine editor who talked expansively about the time 'after the war', occasionally turning away to feed a primitive stove with sawn-off chunks of old furniture. For a moment, I thought he was referring to post-1945; then I realised that for him 'after the war' meant post-1995.

As I write, a major land war continues in Ukraine, launched by Vladimir Putin with a full-scale invasion in February 2022 and prosecuted by Russian armed forces with indiscriminate brutality. When people there can eventually say 'after the war' they will mean post-2024, or whenever the war finally ends. That will be yet another Year Zero. In Europe, zero is a recurring number.

Of fathers and fatherlands

While we drive from the cricket field in Westen to the forest of Barme, Jan and I talk about our fathers. Jan's father served in the Waffen-SS, the combat arm of the Nazis' dreaded SS. Afterwards, Helmut Osmers hardly ever talked about the war, except to say 'it was a hard time'. He loathed the British, who had interned him for more than two years after 1945, in a camp where he was not kindly treated. Tragicomically, his antipathy to all things British extended even to the Beatles. Years later, he had been appalled when, in one of the great gestures of post-war Europe, West German Chancellor Willy Brandt fell to his knees in Warsaw in 1970, at the monument to the heroes of the Warsaw ghetto uprising. 'That he bows down before the *Poles*!' the old Waffen-SS man had exclaimed.

After fighting on the Eastern front, Helmut Osmers had been stationed in Normandy with the 10th SS Panzer Division, which fought fiercely to stall the British advance following the D-Day landings. He once told his son that of 120 men in his company, only thirty had survived. So Jan's father might easily have killed my father, or mine his. A veteran of the ferocious hand-to-hand fighting in the bocage, the densely wooded and hedgerowed Normandy countryside, recalled seeing the corpse of a British soldier who had been

> run through the middle of his body by a German rifle and bayonet which had pinned him to a tree. At the same time, [the bayoneted British soldier] had reached over . . . and plunged his dagger into the middle of his opponent's back. The two had died at some time during the night but in daylight could be seen propping each other up.

It could have been our fathers. One of Dad's wartime anecdotes was of how, somewhere in the bocage not far from Bayeux, he found himself just the other side of a thick, high hedge from a German tank. He could distinctly hear the tank commander barking orders in German, but fortunately neither of them could see through the hedge. He always remembered that near-death moment.

My father had what in the Britain of my childhood was referred to as 'a good war'. (Is there any other European country where people would talk of 'a good war'?) At about 7.30 a.m. on D-Day, 6 June 1944, Captain John Garton Ash landed with the first assault wave of the Green Howards on King section of Gold Beach and scrambled up towards a landmark in the small Normandy town of Ver-sur-Mer that they knew as 'lavatory pan house', because of the shape of its driveway on the aerial reconnaissance photos, and then on to take the German artillery emplacement beyond. Months of hard fighting followed. Corpses and dead cows lay scattered in the fields.

As a forward observation officer for the artillery, he would advance with the front line of the infantry and climb up to the highest observation point – often a church tower – in order to radio back the most accurate firing instructions to the guns behind. The enemy would soon guess that someone was up there. In November 1944, after some especially fierce fighting, he wrote home to his parents:

> I know when we used to go on holiday we always looked round lots of churches, but one thing in the future, never ask me to look at a church tower. They have an unfortunate way of being knocked down violently and frequently.

This unfortunate habit of church towers was even mentioned in the citation for his Military Cross.

The war was the defining experience of Dad's life. Like the veterans of Agincourt invoked by Shakespeare's King Henry V ('This story shall the good man teach his son'), he would often tell us anecdotes of his wartime service: the one about the German tank, for example, or how, while occupying the little village of Westen, his troop received orders to search for and confiscate all uniforms. Next morning a delegation from the village knocked on his door: Could they please have the local firemen's uniforms back? Perhaps my father was the officer who ordered Jan's father – in summer 1945, Helmut Osmers was hiding in the family windmill in Westen, having burned the SS tattoo off his upper arm with hydrochloric acid – to be detained and sent to a British internment camp, generating his lifelong Anglophobia. But Dad never told me that story.

The British gunners whiled away the dreary months in Westen, as they waited impatiently to begin the rest of their lives, by refashioning 25-pounder artillery shells into heavy metal ashtrays. Dad carefully preserved his and it now has a place of honour on the mantelpiece in my study. 'Artillery shells into ashtrays!' may be less poetic than 'Swords into ploughshares!' but this ashtray has the untrumpable advantage of reality.

My father's anecdotes remained firmly within a very English vein of semi-humorous understatement. As with most Englishmen of his generation, there was so much he just never talked about, even when I sat down to interview him about his wartime experience near the end of his life. Yet occasionally, in those last years, when he was well into his nineties, he would mention that he had slept badly.

Why?

'Oh, you know, thinking about things I saw in the war.'

What were those 'things' exactly? Being English, old school, stiff upper lip, he would never say. But among the personal papers I found when he died in 2014 was a flimsy carbon copy sheet, one of many reminiscences of shared actions written by former comrades-in-arms. 'Snow – blood red snow –,' begins this report by an Irish officer, 'a Company and a half of the 13th Para Battalion, obliterated on the start line . . .' Dead friends. Corpses in the fields. Mangled body parts stuck in the hedges. Perhaps there were also split-second decisions for which my father still rebuked himself? Why didn't I help that man there? If only. In the same folder, he prayerfully preserved his correspondence with the widows and mothers of soldiers who had fallen while serving in his gun troop.

Nearly seventy years on, in the second decade of the twenty-first century, those memories still kept him from his sleep. As Dad lay awake at night in Roehampton, a leafy corner of south-west London, so surely did old men of other nations lie awake in Naples, Marseille, Kraków and Dresden, afflicted by cognate memories and cousin ghosts. Like radiation, evil has such a long half-life.

The memory engine

Personal memories, starting with those from the hell that Europeans made for themselves on earth, are among the strongest drivers of everything that Europe has done and become since 1945. I call it the memory engine. Take Bronisław Geremek, for example, a key figure in Poland's struggle for freedom in the last decades of the twentieth century and one of the great Europeans of our time. He carried deep inside him enough memories for three lifetimes, including early experience of the lowest circles of hell. Towards the end of his life, Bronek – as close friends knew him – recalled in filmic detail the following scene from his early life.

It is 1942. In a tram rattling through Nazi-occupied Warsaw sits an emaciated, half-starved ten-year-old boy. Bronek. He is wearing four sweaters, yet still he shivers despite the August heat. Everyone looks at him curiously. Everyone, he is sure, sees that he is a Jewish kid who has slipped out of the Warsaw ghetto through a hole in the wall. Luckily, no one denounces him, and a Polish passenger warns him to watch out for a German sitting in the section marked *'Nur für Deutsche'* ('Germans only'). Amazingly, after recovering his health in the care of family friends, he returns to his parents inside the ghetto, then escapes a second time by slipping away from a funeral procession to the Jewish burial ground. So Bronek survived, while his father was murdered in a Nazi extermination camp and his brother sent to Bergen-Belsen, the camp liberated by British soldiers.

Having escaped the horrors of the ghetto ('the world burned before my eyes'), he was brought up by his mother, who had also managed to escape, and a Polish Catholic stepfather, whose surname he took – Geremek, instead of the Jewish Lewertow. The teenage Bronek served as an altar boy and was taught by an inspiring priest in the Sodality of the Blessed Virgin Mary. So he had also, in his bones, Europe's deep and defining Christian heritage. Then, at the age of eighteen, he joined the communist party, believing it would build a better world. Eighteen years later, stripped of his last illusions by the Soviet invasion of Czechoslovakia in 1968, he resigned from the party in protest and returned to his professional life as a mediaeval historian. But politics would not let him go.

I first encountered him during a historic occupation strike in the Lenin Shipyard in Gdańsk in August 1980, when the leader of the striking workers, Lech Wałęsa, asked Geremek to become an adviser to the protest movement that had just been christened Solidarity. Over the subsequent decade I would visit him whenever I got the chance. As he puffed away at his professorial pipe, he shared with me his historically informed analysis of the decline of the Soviet empire, even as he and his comrades in Solidarity helped turn that decline into fall in 1989.

Ten years later, Geremek was the foreign minister who signed the treaty by which Poland became a member of NATO. When I visited him in the foreign ministry, I spotted on his mantelpiece a bottle of a Czech vodka called Stalin's Tears. 'You must have it!' he exclaimed. 'A Polish foreign minister can't keep Stalin in his office!'

After being instrumental in steering his beloved country into the European Union, he became a member of the European parliament. Tragically, but in a way symbolically, he died in a car accident on the way to Brussels. Bronisław Geremek believed in the project of building a better Europe with every fibre of his being.

Geremek's story is unique, but the basic form of his Europeanism is typical of several generations of Europe-builders who made our continent what it was at the beginning of the twenty-first century. When you look at how the argument for European integration was advanced in various countries, from the 1940s to the 1990s, each national story seems at first glance very different. But dig a little deeper and you find the same underlying thought: 'We have been in a bad place, we want to be in a better one, and that better place is called Europe.'

Many and various were the nightmares from which Europe's nations were trying to awake. For Germany, it was the shame and disgrace of the criminal regime that murdered Bronek's father. For France, it was the humiliation of defeat and occupation; for Britain, economic and political decline; for Spain, a fascist dictatorship; for Poland, a communist one. Europe had no shortage of nightmares. But for people in all these countries, the basic shape of the pro-European argument was the same. That shape was an elongated, exuberant pencilled tick: a steep descent, a turn, and then an upward line ascending to a better future. A future called Europe.

Among the founding fathers of what is now the European Union were what one might call 14ers, still vividly recalling the horrors of the First World War. The 14ers included the British prime minister Harold Macmillan, who would talk with a breaking voice of the 'lost generation' of his contemporaries. After them came 39ers like Geremek, indelibly shaped by traumas of war, gulag, occupation and Holocaust. How could that not also be true of the French politician Simone Veil, who survived Auschwitz and Bergen-Belsen?

Then there were the 68ers, revolting against the war-scarred generation of their parents, yet some of them also having first-hand knowledge of dictatorships in southern and eastern Europe. Each generation had its long tail: post-39ers like Helmut Kohl, for example, just too young to fight in the Second World War but nonetheless defined by it, and post-68ers like me. After the 68ers came the 89ers, in their late teens or early twenties as they witnessed the velvet revolutions of 1989 that ended communism in Poland, Hungary and Czechoslovakia, the fall of the Berlin Wall and the subsequent dissolution of the Soviet Union.

We must certainly beware of turning the history of post-war Europe into a fairy tale in which wise, virtuous heroes learn from their experience of hell to create heaven. The true history is full of states pursuing their national interests, decaying empires, devious power plays, sharp-elbowed business lobbying, diplomatic trade-offs, personal ambitions and, last but certainly not least, the historical luck that Machiavelli says is half the explanation of most things that happen in politics. Yet somewhere in there, across four generations, was the memory engine, hard at work in millions of European minds and hearts.

So we travelled hopefully towards that better future called 'Europe'. The trouble starts once you arrive in the promised land. By the second decade of the twenty-first century we had, for the first time ever, a generation of Europeans who had known nothing but a peaceful, free Europe consisting mainly of liberal democracies. Unsurprisingly, they tended to take it for granted. (Those who grew up in former Yugoslavia, or countries such as Ukraine, Belarus and Russia, were important exceptions.) This new generation may be called the post-89ers or, to borrow a vivid term from post-apartheid South Africa, the Born-Frees.

Memories of things you have personally seen and heard, enjoyed or endured, are an incomparably powerful motivating force. But direct personal memory is not the only way in which knowledge of things past can be transmitted. Thus, for example, D-Day was an important moment for me, even though it happened eleven years before I was born. A single personal encounter with a veteran or survivor can be life-changing. And then there is the work of historians, novelists, journalists and filmmakers, who try to bring alive the dead for the sake of the living. The Auschwitz survivor Elie Wiesel called this process 'a memory transfusion'. The gamble of civilisation is that we can learn from the past without having to go through it all again ourselves.

Divided
(1961–1979)

Curfew

The Europe in which I came of age in the early 1970s was no longer in ruins, although its city streets had many ugly new concrete buildings where older ones had been bombed, like an old boxer revealing a mouthful of ill-matching false teeth. The continent's defining characteristic was no longer that it was destroyed but that it was divided between 'East' and 'West', two blocs headed by their respective superpowers, the Soviet Union and the United States. While these two camps were not actually fighting each other on European soil, they were still locked in what was accurately called a Cold War. Most of the dividing lines between them went back to the end of the Second World War, but the most famous symbol of the Cold War, the Berlin Wall, had only sealed off West Berlin from East Germany on 13 August 1961. When what was originally a crude barrier of barbed wire and breeze blocks was turned into a solid wall, the East–West divide was literally set in concrete. To most of those who grew up behind it, it seemed it would last for ever.

Fascinated, I set out to explore this divided Europe as soon as I left school. I began in the West. In the autumn of 1973, aged eighteen, I was working on a converted troopship, the SS *Nevasa*, carrying British schoolchildren around the Mediterranean. On Saturday 17 November 1973 we visited the island of Crete. My journal records that during a tour of the extraordinary Bronze Age archaeological site at Knossos I had been 'wondering about dictatorship. Then 4 pm CURFEW. 1,000 students herded back to ship. All because of student riots in Athens. That is dictatorship!'

'Student riots' is not how I would put it today. In fact, the student occupation of the Athens Polytechnic was a pivotal moment in the history of the military dictatorship imposed six years earlier, after a coup by a group of officers who came to be known around the world as 'the Colonels'. While an improvised shortwave radio station (dubbed 'Radio Station of the Free and Fighting Students, The Free and Fighting Greeks') blasted out 'The Bells Will Ring' and other thrilling liberation songs by Mikis Theodorakis, the students occupying the polytechnic demanded 'Bread–Education–Freedom' and daubed the walls with slogans such as 'Power to the people', 'Down with the army' and 'Sexual freedom!'. Another graffito said simply 'May '68', and this protest was the slightly delayed Greek political manifestation of the distinctive generation of 68ers who would transform the social and cultural life of Europe. One leading anarchist protester, known as Aretoula, is said to have scrawled 'Long live the orgies!' 'Where? I wish this had happened!' an ageing former student activist would sadly confide to a historian many years later.

But in the night of 16/17 November, the liberation circus was brought to an abrupt and bitter end. Regime snipers killed some twenty-four civilians in streets around the polytechnic. A tank crashed through the main gate, crushing the legs of a female student, Pepi Rigopoulou, and producing the defining photographic image of these events. Then the Colonels imposed a curfew right across the country, even on the island of Crete 300 miles away, where it surprised our shipload of British schoolchildren. So my eighteen-year-old self was not wrong to exclaim 'That is dictatorship!' Five days later, we saw buses full of troops in the main squares of Athens.

Europe of the Dictators is the title of a book about the 1930s, but in 1973 much of our continent was still a Europe of the dictators. If we include the European republics of the Soviet Union, then some 389 million Europeans lived under dictatorships whereas only 289 million lived in democracies. (Turkey, with a further thirty-seven million people, was somewhere in between the two forms of government.) Most of those dictatorships were communist-ruled states behind what, already in 1946, Winston Churchill had dubbed the Iron Curtain, cutting off the eastern half of our continent.

Closest to the 1930s, however, in both spirit and historical continuity, were the right-wing dictatorships of southern Europe. The Greek Colonels banned long hair, mini-skirts and the study of sociology. António

Salazar, a former lecturer in accountancy and deeply conservative Catholic, ruled Portugal from 1932 until his death in 1970. In the 1930s, he had expressed admiration for Italy's fascist dictator, Benito Mussolini. His all-pervasive political police are described by one historian as 'similar to, if not trained by, the German Gestapo', with informers in every village and office.

In Spain, General Francisco Franco, who finally emerged victorious from a long, brutal civil war in 1939, ruled until his death in 1975. During the war, Franco had been photographed with a framed picture of Adolf Hitler on his desk. Even in the early 1970s, Franco's closest associates, including his wife, Carmen Polo, and his personal doctor, Dr Vicente Gil Garcia, would still raise and straighten their right arms in the fascist salute popularised by Hitler and Mussolini. As the SS *Nevasa* carried us from Crete to Athens on 20 November 1973, Franco was attending a memorial mass for the fascist hero and founder of the Falange party José Antonio Primo de Rivera. News photographs show the Generalissimo – as Franco was modestly known – walking down steps in the monumental Valley of the Fallen, wearing the paramilitary uniform of the National Movement. Francoist flags were waved and the crowd sang the Falangist anthem 'Cara al Sol'. Just pause for a moment and imagine Italy being ruled by an aged Mussolini until 1975.

Both Salazar and Franco adapted to changing external circumstances, embracing the Western allies as it became clear that Hitler and the Axis powers would be defeated. After all, fascists hated communists too. Portugal even became a founding member of NATO in 1949. In the early 1970s, these were weakened authoritarian regimes, but still nasty enough.

As a twenty-three-year-old British university graduate, Jonathan Keates went to teach English language and literature in the Portuguese city of Porto in 1970. Rather to his bewilderment, one of his classes insisted on inviting him to a picnic among the vineyards and olive groves of the Douro valley. Jonathan, today a distinguished author and passionate European, recalls:

> No sooner had we started to eat than, one by one, members of the group began telling me, in English, about the various crimes and

outrages committed by the regime. Some of them had relatives and friends who had fallen foul of the police, some knew of people who had been tortured or else sent to prison camps in the Cape Verde islands, others spoke of the disadvantages they had suffered for being suspected of subversive opinions or activities. Now and then one of them got up and walked to the edge of the field, looking carefully over its dry-stone walling – you never knew, after all, who might be listening, even in a remote olive grove. Little chips came off my British complacency then and there.

Even after the Portuguese dictator's death, the post-Salazarist People's National Action won 150 out of 150 available seats in the National Assembly in 1973. Following the murder of a student by the secret police the previous year, repression had intensified. There were 476 political prisoners in Portugal, of whom 187 were students. The punishment for a man who murdered his adulterous wife, or her lover, or both of them together, was merely exile from the district for six months.

Then there was Greece. A few months after I stumbled into the Colonels' curfew, I was sharing a room with a young Greek I knew only as Giorgos, in the picturesque little Bavarian town of Prien am Chiemsee, where we were both meant to be learning German. His parents would regularly send Giorgos large cardboard boxes of pistachio nuts, apparently fearful that a diet of Bavarian beer and Weisswurst might irreparably damage his health. He had grown up in a villa in Kifisia, a wealthy northern suburb of Athens, but one of his uncles had been a partisan captain during the war and had become a communist. 'Why?', little Giorgos once asked him. The old partisan replied that he had not fought in the mountains for five years to clear Greece of the Germans just so it might become 'a colony of the Americans'.

Another uncle had been a communist organiser in the port of Piraeus. As his front door bell rang on the night of the Colonels' coup in 1967, he escaped out the back. He spent two years in hiding, moving conspiratorially from house to house, just like my friends in Poland under martial law. His wife came to live with Giorgos's family in their nice bourgeois villa. Sitting on the terrace of an evening, they would sometimes see flashlights among the trees at the end of the garden, as police searched for the red in the flower bed. 'Shall we offer our friends some coffee?' the family would joke.

Giorgos told these stories vividly, over Bavarian beer and Greek pistachios, but he was not himself very political. While I was earnestly diving into Friedrich Nietzsche and Thomas Mann, he dedicated his evenings to canoodling with the girls at the local disco to the strains of the current hit song, 'Black Madonna'. This schmaltz-dripping number addressed a beautiful girl sitting tearfully by a river under the stars. If she stayed with him tonight, the Yugoslav-German singer Bata Illic explained, with an irresistible twirl of his flared trousers, 'then already tomorrow the sun will shine for you and me'. Again and again came the refrain which remains stuck in my head to this day, like a stray fishbone in the throat, '*Es ist nie zu spät . . . Schwarze Madonna*' ('It's never too late . . . Black Madonna'). Although the thought did not occur to me at the time, as I wandered around the little town in my own hideous brown flared jeans, the ubiquity of this song was an illustration of rapidly advancing secularisation in western Europe. Even in conservative, Catholic Bavaria, the disco hit of the day could revolve around a man trying to cajole a 'Black Madonna' – a figure representing the mother of God, venerated by Christian Europeans for centuries as a 'virgin most pure' – into having unmarried sex on their first encounter.

Such a blasphemy would never have been broadcast on state-controlled radio and television in Salazar's Portugal or Franco's Spain, and probably not in conservative, Church-dominated Ireland. In the early 1970s, songs banned by the censor in Franco's Spain included the Beach Boys' 'Good Vibrations' ('completely erotic sentiment', wrote the censor, 'song alludes to sexual arousal'), Aretha Franklin's 'Rock Steady' ('the lyrics and rhythm of the music incite one to move one's hips'), Elton John's 'Tiny Dancer' ('disrespectful sentiment') and John Lennon's 'Imagine'. Sonia Cuesta Maniar, a Spanish history student who has helped me with this research, cannot find any trace of 'Black Madonna' being banned. But she tells me that her grandparents, Ricardo and Julia Cuesta, remember how nervous they were coming back from West Germany, where they were so-called *Gastarbeiter* (guest workers), and crossing the Spanish frontier with 'Black Madonna' playing on the car's radio. Nervous because they were returning from a free country to a dictatorship.

Giorgos took the Colonels fairly lightly, but for many young Greeks, Spanish and Portuguese the experience of these dictatorships and the struggle against them would shape their political commitments for life. It was the fuel in their memory engines. Several of them would be influential in European politics well into the early twenty-first century. Maria Damanaki, for example, who had been the chief announcer of the student radio station in the Athens Polytechnic protest, became Greece's European Commissioner between 2010 and 2014.

The president of the European Commission in which Maria served was the Portuguese politician José Manuel Barroso. On the wall of his office in the Berlaymont building in Brussels he had a framed photograph from a June 1970 number of the French colour magazine *Paris Match*. It showed the body of Salazar lying in state in a candlelit coffin, with a white dwarf from what at that time was still the Portuguese colony of Angola standing to one side and, on the other, a black giant from Portugal's other main African colony, Mozambique. The caption read: 'This photo is not taken from a film by [the Spanish film director Luis] Buñuel'. Barroso recalls that seeing this picture in *Paris Match* at the age of fourteen was his moment of political awakening. It showed him just how grotesque and backward his country looked to that modern Europe beyond the Pyrenees. A year or two later, his favourite high school teacher came into class with a sticking plaster on his head – the result, the teacher explained, of a beating by the riot police. By the age of 18, José Manuel was a Maoist activist – a.k.a. 'Comrade Veiga' – at his university in Lisbon, Maoism being the anti-authoritarian leftism of choice in Portugal. He would subsequently describe 25 April 1974, the day the post-Salazar dictatorship was overthrown in the 'Carnation Revolution', as 'the most important day of my life'.

Javier Solana, who in 1999 became the EU's first High Representative for Foreign and Security Policy, would never forget how, at the age of seventeen, he used to visit his older brother Luis in Spain's notorious Carabanchel prison – 'on Thursdays and Sundays', he recalled. Luis was active in a student group linked to the banned socialist party. He paid for his courage with two years' imprisonment, after being interrogated and beaten by Franco's security police. Luis' example helped inspire his younger brother to become involved in clandestine socialist politics, which led to Javier himself being expelled from Madrid's Complutense University in 1963. After years in the United States, where he was inspired by the civil rights movement and protests against the Vietnam War, Solana would return to become a leading figure in the still illegal socialist party in Spain in the early 1970s.

Spain, Portugal and Greece in the 1970s popularised a term that was to echo down the next fifty years: transition. The word 'transition' would come to be used as shorthand for 'transition from dictatorship to democracy', a phenomenon subsequently seen in many countries in Latin America; in parts of Asia and Africa; in central, eastern and south-eastern Europe after 1989; and an outcome hoped for (often in vain) by liberal Europeans like me in other parts of the world, such as North Africa and the Middle East after the Arab Spring of 2010–12.

In southern Europe, that transition was inseparable from another: towards membership of what by then was often called simply the European Community. Greece was hurried into the Community in 1981, less than seven years after the fall of the Colonels. It made a difference that Greece was seen by a generation of still classically educated European leaders as the cradle of European civilisation. 'One does not say no to Plato,' French president Valéry Giscard d'Estaing haughtily instructed an official in the European Commission. Plato-less Spain and Portugal had to strive and thrive for more than a decade until they finally joined in 1986.

For southern Europeans such as Barroso and Solana, the struggle for freedom, democracy and Europe was one and the same struggle. To arrive in 'Europe', meaning the European Community, was to consolidate the transition to democracy. Freedom meant Europe and Europe meant freedom. This is a way of thinking quite alien to most Brits, with their different historical experience. For an Englishman like my father, England stood for freedom and Europe was a threat to it. But it is entirely familiar to many other Europeans.

Most people in the Republic of Ireland, for example, experienced joining the European Community in 1973, at the same time as Britain, as an enhancement of their freedom and independence. The Irish writer

Fintan O'Toole recalls how a new phrase, 'we're into Europe', entered Irish English in the early 1970s, and it meant 'things are good'.

> 'How are things?' you'd ask, and the reply would be 'Ah sure, we're into Europe.' Or, 'Isn't it a grand day?' someone would say, and you'd answer, 'Oh, it is, sure we're into Europe.'

The same was true for most central and east Europeans after the Berlin Wall came down. Poland consciously learned from the example of Spain, as it set out on its own double transition, to democracy and to 'Europe'. These two nations, Spain and Poland, each an imperial power in the sixteenth and seventeenth centuries, each with a proud aristocratic heritage, each deeply shaped by the Catholic Church, also had in common a complex relationship to Europe. At different stages in their history, well into recent memory, each was at once defiantly insistent that it belonged to Europe – always had, always would, Europe unthinkable without it – and equally insistent that it must now return to Europe. But how can you return to somewhere you already are? This apparent paradox is dissolved as soon as we recognise that Europeans use the word Europe in a bewildering variety of ways, to the confusion of outsiders and often enough of themselves.

Europes

Perhaps France alone has never doubted that it is in Europe. In fact, France has a tendency to think that it *is* Europe. In the Normandy town of Courseulles-sur-Mer, hard by the D-Day beaches, there is a memorial that reads: '*Le 6 Juin 1944 les forces alliées libèrent l'Europe*' ('On 6 June 1944 the Allied forces liberate Europe', using the historic present tense), adding that Charles de Gaulle landed here on 14 June. Well, they liberated France so obviously they must have liberated Europe.

Belgians, Dutch and Luxembourgers seldom question that they belong to Europe. Some Germans, however, had serious doubts in the aftermath of two world wars and the Nazi dictatorship. When Thomas Mann told an audience of Hamburg students in 1953 that they should work towards a European Germany rather than a German Europe – a formula often repeated after German unification in 1990 – the clear implication was that Germany had not been properly European under Hitler. The history of Europe is unthinkable without Italy, from ancient Rome to the Treaty of Rome that created the European Economic Community in 1957. Yet in the early twenty-first century, after a hope-filled time when some Italians made a single word of *Italianieuropei*, Italian populists denounced 'Europe', meaning the EU and especially the eurozone, for imposing needless suffering on the Italian people.

All other European countries have a long history of existential uncertainty about their full belonging to Europe. The Polish historian Jerzy Jedlicki called his study of nineteenth-century Poland *A Suburb of Europe*. In Antonio Tabucchi's wonderful novel about Portugal under Salazar, *Declares Pereira*, we find the following exchange between

Pereira, who is the editor of the cultural page of an evening paper, and his friend Silva:

> Silva ordered trout with almonds and Pereira ordered a fillet steak à la *Stroganoff* with a poached egg on top. They started eating in silence, then after a while Pereira asked Silva what he thought about all this. All this what?, asked Silva. What's going on in Europe, said Pereira. Oh don't bother your head, replied Silva, we're not in Europe here, we're in Portugal.

Early in 1991, I sat in a hotel in prosperous, modern Stockholm, talking to Carl Bildt, then the leader of Sweden's liberal conservative Moderate Party and soon to be prime minister. I was startled when this tall and decided man, with a physique and nose vaguely reminiscent of de Gaulle, told me that he wanted Sweden to 'return to Europe'. What, *Sweden* needs to return to Europe? For too long, he explained, socialist governments had imagined their neutral, non-aligned country as being closer to the 'Third World' than to Germany or France. Now Sweden must return to its European roots and join what would soon be called the European Union. Which it did in 1995.

Most of us have had the mildly disconcerting experience of conversing in a small group where another person has the same first name as you. 'Lucy must have views on that,' someone says, and as Lucy opens her mouth she realises it's the other Lucy they are referring to. It's like that with Europe, only worse, because there are at least four different Europes at this table.

Otto von Bismarck, the statesman who united Germany in 1871, once dismissively wrote in the margin of a letter from a Russian statesman: '*Qui parle Europe a tort. Notion géographique.*' ('Whoever talks about Europe is wrong. Geographical notion.') But even as a geographical notion, Europe has no clear frontiers to its east and south. Most geographers agree on a conventional border running down the Urals mountains in western Russia, across the Caucasus (but where exactly in the Caucasus?), then westward across the Black Sea, through the Bosphorus and in a very squiggly line across the Mediterranean until you emerge into the Atlantic. Although the cartographical division between Europe, Asia and Africa is one of the oldest in geography, the arbitrariness of such supposedly bright lines is illustrated by Ayşe Kadioğlu, a Turkish academic who lives on the European side of the Bosphorus in Istanbul but works at a university on the Asian side: 'I commute between Europe and Asia every day.'

To the east and south, Europe does not end, it merely fades away, somewhere between Moscow and Vladivostok, between Istanbul and Erbil, across the Maghreb and the Levant. For the ancient Greeks and Romans, the idea of a clear divide between the northern and southern shores of the Mediterranean would have seemed ridiculous. To travel around what the Romans called the Mare Nostrum (our sea), as I did in the SS *Nevasa* in 1973, from Dubrovnik to Tangier, Santorini to Palma and Istanbul to Ceuta, was to encounter European history on every coast and island. Yet in 1987, when Morocco applied for membership of the European Community, it was swiftly refused permission even to become a candidate. Article 237 of the Treaty of Rome says that 'any European state' can apply, but the responsible European Commissioner in Brussels, Claude Cheysson, explained that Morocco was 'not geographically part of Europe'. Turkey, however, a majority Muslim country, and one against which Christian Europe had defined its identity for several centuries, was accepted as a candidate for EU membership in 1999. I defy anyone to explain how Turkey is unambiguously European and Morocco unambiguously not.

The next Europe at the table is a historical core Europe, roughly coinciding with the territories once ruled by Charlemagne. Were you to inject most Europeans with a truth serum, they would admit to feeling instinctively that Rome, Paris and Charlemagne's capital of Aachen (Aix-la-Chapelle to the French, Aquisgrán to the Spanish, Akwizgran to the Poles) are somehow more intensely, completely, unambiguously European than, say, Uzhorod or Tirana. Yet you will articulate any such distinction at your peril, since it immediately sparks in other Europeans a nervous bridling at any suggestion that we [fill in the name of your people] are not one hundred per cent European. What do you mean, not so fully European? We are more so, in fact, than those arrogant French!

There are good reasons for this touchiness. There is a long history of west Europeans treating the eastern part of the continent as exotic, backward, vaguely barbaric and not completely European. This is a kind of intra-European Orientalism. Such civilisational condescension reaches the point of parody in the work of the conservative Swiss historian Gonzague de Reynold, who flatly stated that 'Western Europe and eastern Europe are . . . not equally civilised' and 'European civilisation is . . . the work of western Europe.' He described western Europe as *l'Europe européenne*, thus implying that the rest of Europe is somehow non-European. Even in our own time, being European is often silently equated with being civilised.

Here is the third Europe, the Europe of culture and values, a well-dressed but distinctly two-faced character. The face that Europe presented to the rest of the world for centuries frankly and self-confidently asserted its own cultural superiority: white, Christian, usually male, summoned by God to bring civilisation to 'savages' and true religion to 'infidels'. Even as France was leading the creation of the European Economic Community in the 1950s, it was fighting brutal wars to preserve its overseas colonies. Most Europeans now view this colonial past as dim and distant, yet there it is, as recently as 1970, in that grotesque photo of Salazar in his coffin, flanked by white dwarf from Angola and black giant from Mozambique. Angola and Mozambique only became independent from Portugal in 1975.

To this day, a Tintin-loving child may still stumble on these colonial attitudes in a book called *Tintin in the Congo*. In the version that you can order with one mouse-click from Amazon, our pint-sized journalist hero takes a class in a missionary school in the Belgian Congo, repeatedly receiving no answer from rows of visibly perplexed small black children to the question 'What does 2+2 equal . . . ?' In the 1930s original of this classroom scene, which the Belgian artist-author Hergé later revised, Tintin said: 'Now I'm going to talk to you about your homeland: Belgium!'

Yet the other face of this third Europe radiates an aspiration towards the highest ideals. One day in the 1990s, Bronisław Geremek and I were walking together down the long, echoing, white-painted corridors of the parliament of a now-independent Poland, when he suddenly stopped, stroked his beard and said with quiet passion: 'You know, for me, Europe is something like a Platonic essence'. Europe, in this sense, is identified with a set of values such as freedom, democracy, peace, dignity and human rights. It can also be understood as a higher end-state or goal, what the ancient Greeks called a *telos*, to which we aspire and against which we measure our progress. As the French philosopher of international relations Pierre Hassner and I debated the future of Europe over lunch in the early 2000s, he sighed: 'Yes, I suppose you're right: Europe will not come to pass.' ('But Pierre,' I replied, 'you're in it!') In this prescriptive, idealist sense of the word, Hitler, the Holocaust and the genocidal massacre of Bosnians at Srebrenica in 1995 can be regarded as 'not European', although they undoubtably were European in a descriptive, empirical sense.

The fourth Europe at this already raucous table is that of the institutional organisation of European states. For most Europeans, that now means the European Union, but it was not ever thus. What emerged from the original founding meeting of post-1945 European unification, a congress held in The Hague in 1948, was an institution called the Council of Europe. It most directly embodies the post-war aspiration to build a better Europe, a more 'European' Europe, of freedom, democracy, the rule of law, respect for human dignity and human rights. It has given us the European Convention on Human Rights, whose implementation is adjudicated by the European Court of Human Rights in Strasbourg. If, as a citizen of one of the more than forty-five countries that belong to the Council of Europe, you cannot obtain redress in your country's domestic courts for a violation of one of the rights defined in that convention, you can take your case to the Strasbourg court. That's a great thing. Yet almost nobody talks any more about the Council of Europe. It's like a gentlemanly elder brother, in a slightly frayed tweed jacket, who watches from his country house as his thrusting younger brother, European Union, makes his way in the big city, appropriating, without acknowledgement, some of his best ideas. That impudent sibling has even stolen his flag, the twelve yellow stars on a blue background, which was originally designed for the Council of Europe.

The complications do not end there. Madeleine Albright, the Czech-born US Secretary of State in the administration of Bill Clinton, once gave me a copy of the diagram her staff had drawn up showing all the overlapping European organisations, with their confusing acronyms.

'We call it', she told me with a smile, 'the Euromess.'

The most wide-cast net in the Euromess is that of the Organisation for Security and Co-operation in Europe, whose members include Russia, Kazakhstan (which proudly boasts a chunk of territory west of the Ural mountains), Turkmenistan, Tajikistan, Canada and the United States. Yet when all these intricacies are acknowledged, what most people now mean when they refer to this fourth, institutional Europe is the European Union that will turn seventy in 2027.

All these Europes are present at the table, like people with the same first name, yet they are often talked about in the same breath, as if there were just one Lucy and not four, going on fourteen. For pedestrian clarity, one should really stop every time the word is mentioned and specify Europe (sense 1a) or Europe (sense 3b). Yet that would still miss the Europe that means most to most of us: the continent of personal experience.

Being there

Europe in our time differs from all earlier Europes thanks to one revolutionary change: the exponential growth of mass travel and communication since the 1960s. To be sure, upper-class young Englishmen in the eighteenth century would make the Grand Tour, visiting selected cultural splendours on the road to Rome. By the late nineteenth century, middle-class tourists from more prosperous countries would visit nearby European countries, often using newly built railway lines. The British tourist was a familiar figure of fun in continental caricatures. Early-twentieth-century European gentlemen – sometimes accompanied by their ladies – encountered each other socially at spas, country houses and racecourses, before meeting again in mortal combat, like the aristocratic German and French officers in *The Grand Illusion*, Jean Renoir's magnificent film about the First World War. First they shot pheasants together, then they shot each other.

Yet for most of European history, well into the twentieth century, most Europeans would never have visited another country, unless it was to do military service during a war, to emigrate because they couldn't get enough to eat on their parents' farm, or because they were forced out of their homes by a pogrom or other act of ethnic cleansing. For many who lived in rural areas, the mental horizon was not even the nation or state; it was the immediate neighbourhood, at most the region. Asked about their identity, peasants in the eastern borderlands of Poland, Ukraine and Belarus sometimes answered that they were *tutejszy*, meaning simply 'the people of here'. Travel meant riding your horse-drawn cart to market in the local town. Recalling the first post-war decade, one of those sturdy old Lower Saxon farmers in the village of Westen told me: 'No one then thought of Europe. Europe came much later.'

Then, suddenly, millions of Europeans were travelling to each other's countries: by train, by ferry, by coach, by car, by twin-propeller plane and, from the 1960s onwards, by jet. In the mid-1970s, a better-paid blue-collar worker in the western half of the continent could probably afford a Fiat 500, a Mini, a Volkswagen Beetle or Golf (the latter first produced in 1974), or a Citroën *deux chevaux* (literally 'two horses', referring to its two-horsepower rating for tax purposes). Each of these cars would become an icon of popular culture. Most still existed in modernised versions fifty years later.

By 1973, Spain had more than thirty-four million foreign visitors, roughly one for each permanent inhabitant. For the first time ever, 'Europe' became for most Europeans a personal, direct experience, embodied in real places and faces; interesting new sounds, sights, tastes and smells; a vista, a seaside restaurant, a beautiful girl or handsome boy, once encountered, never forgotten. In case memory did fade, there were now cheap cameras, such as the Kodak Instamatic, cine cameras and then camcorders, making possible the home movie. Soon there were also cheap and widely available audiocassettes, on which you could carry back in your hand luggage the sounds of Mikis Theodorakis, the Beatles, the incomparable Juliette Gréco or even, God help you, 'Black Madonna'. If you had made friends in another country, you could keep in touch with them by airmail letter (on flimsy blue paper, intriguingly folded, like origami), by increasingly affordable telephone call, and soon via that ultimate pinnacle of technological sophistication, the fax machine.

At the Congress of The Hague in 1948, the grand Spanish intellectual Salvador de Madariaga declared: 'When Spaniards say "our Chartres", Englishmen "our Cracow", Italians "our Copenhagen" and Germans "our Bruges" . . . Then Europe will live.' Back then, it was just a dream. But mass travel turned this dream into reality in a more material, pedestrian way than de Madariaga probably had in mind. People could say 'our Chartres' or 'our Copenhagen' because they had been there and cherished personal memories of the place.

Before I landed on the moon in La Rochelle, we had gone on a family holiday to revisit the Normandy beaches on which my father had landed in 1944. Our green and white Hillman Super Minx car (never an icon of popular culture) was loaded into the belly of a squat, toad-like ferry plane and we flew with the car to Cherbourg. Then we drove eastward along the French coast, Dad taking enormous delight in reproducing, as closely as possible, all the hardships of a military campaign. Tea was brewed, very slowly, on a tiny paraffin stove in chilly, windswept fields. So far as my brother Christopher and I can recall, contact with the locals was kept to an absolute minimum, and mainly consisted in friendly mutual incomprehension. Back home in Roehampton, extraordinary Heath Robinson preparations were made to set up, in a darkened room, a projector and screen on which we watched, with frequent technical interruptions, blurred and crackling eight-millimetre celluloid footage of ourselves brewing tea in chilly, windswept fields.

In the summer of 1973, I drove with a school friend down the course of the Rhine and into darkest Bavaria, camping in muddy fields, living off bread and sausage, and viewing the historic sites, from Charlemagne's octagonal church in Aachen, which I first visited on my eighteenth birthday, through the great cathedrals of Cologne, Worms and Speyer, to the university town of Heidelberg, where I noted aerosol-sprayed graffiti denouncing a 'reactionary Prof. Brückner'. Pausing only to send a telegram home – yes, a *telegram*, like a character in a 1930s black-and-white film – and fortified by a campsite diet of *Blutwurst* (black sausage) and Buddenbrooks, I sampled the aesthetic delights of Bavaria, including mad King Ludwig's fairy-tale castle of Neuschwanstein, until eventually we came, as almost our last stop, to the former concentration camp of Dachau. '*Harrowing* photos of conditions, torture etc and the effect on individual people,' I noted in my schoolboy hand, 'but despite the quote from Santayana ("Those who cannot remember the past are condemned to repeat it"), despite the grimness and horror of it all, despite the stark declaration on the monument outside ("Never again"), the main reaction visible on the faces of the tourists was incomprehension.' 'Now,' I concluded, rather sententiously, we needed a writer or TV programme 'to make present-day atrocities *impinge* upon the lives of everyone'. Sententious, but not wrong.

In the autumn of that year, it was on to that converted troopship, the SS *Nevasa*, gleaming white in the Mediterranean sunshine and dedicated to opening British schoolchildren's eyes to the glories of Europe. It did not always succeed. One letter home, recalled on an SS *Nevasa* nostalgia website, began: 'Dear Mum, I wish you were here instead of me.'

But for some of the children this was an eye-opening experience, even a life-changing one. Helen Buchanan, who went on that same cruise in 1973 as a thirteen-year-old from Falmouth High School in Cornwall, tells me it gave her a lifelong appetite for travel. When she got home, she told her mother about the soldiers on the streets of Athens. She also remembers the 'scarey' experience of 'being stared at' by what she calls 'the gentlemen' on the streets of Mersin in Turkey. But Santorini and Crete were so wonderful, she couldn't wait to go back.

Kaleidotapestry

So there we were, sheltering from the sun in one of the reconstructed courtyards of the Palace of Knossos on Crete, shortly before the Colonels imposed their curfew. The year was 1973 CE, but archaeological evidence shows that there was already a palace here in 1973 BCE. Europeans often go weak at the knees when confronted with the totemic '4,000 years' of Chinese history, but we Europeans have our own 4,000 years.

By the middle of the second millennium BCE, Knossos was an elaborate urban settlement, with perhaps as many as 100,000 people living in dwellings around the palace and a theatre that seated some 400. The palace itself had well-lit chambers decorated with frescoes, labyrinthine halls, anterooms and corridors; it also had bathrooms, toilets, a drainage system, and larders in which oil, wool, wine and grain were stored in giant pots. Its inhabitants traded around the Mediterranean, from Egypt to Spain. One of the languages found scratched on clay tablets is an early form of Greek.

This was 'Europe's first city'. It was also the putative dwelling place of the mythical woman from whom our continent takes its name. Europa was a beautiful princess in what is now Lebanon who mounted a handsome and apparently gentle snow-white bull. This was a mistake, for the bull turned out to be Zeus, the lubricious chief of the Greek gods. He carried her off across the eastern Mediterranean to the island of Crete. There she gave birth to three sons, including Minos, later King Minos, after whom Arthur Evans, the British archaeologist who first excavated Knossos, named the Minoan civilisation. Glorious frescoes of bulls, with people jumping balletically around and over them, were found in the excavation and can be admired in the nearby Heraklion museum.

It was not those frolicsome bulls that fascinated me, however, but one small fresco of a young woman, elegantly dressed and coiffed, with pale skin, lips picked out in red, and large, dark oval eyes under strongly highlighted, arched eyebrows. I have her image before me as I write, in a colour illustration to the original guidebook I bought at Knossos in 1973. Not for nothing is she nicknamed 'la Parisienne'. With those dark oval eyes she looks as if she has stepped out of a painting by the early-twentieth-century artist Marc Chagall.

This, too, is characteristic of the European experience. It is not just that we live atop so many layers of history, as if on an archaeological site, with the Cretan layers being among the oldest. As Europeans, we live in a densely populated multiverse of recurrences and anticipations, conscious cross-references and unconscious echoes, so that beside what the German philosopher Ernst Bloch called 'non-simultaneity' (departure from England: 1984, arrival in Poland: 1945) there is a countervailing simultaneity, telescoping centuries and even millennia. In Cologne cathedral you can see an exquisite small crucifix made of wood. The heavy fingers of the hands of Christ nailed to the cross, the starkly cut, melancholy curves of the face, the stylised, straight lines of hair and loin cloth – all suggest a work of modernism, perhaps by a pupil of the early-twentieth-century German sculptor Ernst Barlach. But this crucifix dates from the tenth century CE. It is ten centuries young.

The temporal cross-hatching becomes even more intricate when one recognises that because of changing taste, commercial development and the destruction wrought by the Second World War, much of the old is in fact new. In Warsaw, I would seek out Bronisław Geremek in his small apartment in Piwna St, at the heart of the Old Town. As we sat in his tiny study, its dark wooden bookshelves crammed with works of mediaeval history, a single ray of sunlight from the window illuminating professorial beard and pipe, it felt a little like visiting Goethe's Dr Faust in his 'narrow chamber'. But none of this apparently old building was actually old. In 1944, after crushing the Warsaw Rising of non-communist Poles who wanted to liberate their own capital, German forces had razed the entire city on Hitler's orders, in an act of cultural barbarism. In a riposte of cultural defiance, Polish architects, artists and skilled workmen drew on historic paintings and drawings to reconstruct the entire old town, brick by brick, lintel by lintel, including that house on Piwna St. The old was new, the new was old. It has been suggested, with only slight poetic exaggeration, that the oldest things in Warsaw are probably the trees in the Łazienki park.

My journals for the decade after my visit to Knossos contain a staggering list of places visited – today Mycenae, tomorrow Florence, the next week, Paris – commenting on endless churches, palaces, sculptures and paintings admired, books read, plays, operas and films watched. Yes, I was a culture vulture. Yet even today, after fifty years of constant travel and study, I know that I have turned only a few pages of a vast tome. Europe, the real Europe, not the two-dimensional, black-and-white 'Europe' of British political debate, is a *Gesamtkunstwerk*, an all-embracing work of art, to borrow a term from Richard Wagner. This artwork has been created not by one megalomaniac composer but by millions of hands over thousands of years, and is constantly being remade. It comprises not just the familiar elements of traditional high culture but also fashion, food, drink, sport, popular music and local customs; the characteristic smells of a Mediterranean island, a Scandinavian fjord, a windswept Atlantic coast and a crowded Italian restaurant; fifty subtly different ways of being a man or a woman, or of embracing some other sexual or gender identity; intricate, polychromatic local histories, all the way down to that of individual buildings. Ten thousand pages would scarcely begin this book of the real Europe. Every place on every visit is a new chapter.

What metaphor can begin to do justice to this variety? Palimpsest? Millefeuille? Patchwork quilt? The best I can come up with is a combination of kaleidoscope and tapestry: a kaleidotapestry. Europe is a tapestry in the sense that it has been worked over by many hands to produce a single unique picture – a street scene, perhaps, or a landscape, or an event such as the Palio, the inter-communal horse race in the main square of Siena that was first recorded in 1239 and still takes place annually. But it is a kaleidoscope inasmuch as the same colourful pieces are constantly reappearing in new combinations: the recurrent visual grammar of church, castle, marketplace and town hall; allusions to Rome, elements of the Gothic, Baroque, Jugendstil or 1960s brutalism; leitmotifs like the minotaur, sirens or the Madonna and child; cafés of every possible shape and kind; the Greek coffee that is so curiously like Turkish coffee, cabbage in endless gastronomic variations. Everywhere you find touches that are unique, or what in many European languages is called 'typical', alongside others that are strikingly familiar. Stand for the national anthem of Liechtenstein and you find yourself listening to the tune of 'God Save the Queen'. The same but different, different but the same. All this adds up to that characteristic European experience, perfectly summed up by my French-Greek-British friend Kalypso Nicolaïdis as 'being at home abroad'.

When Thomas Mann spoke to Hamburg students about 'European Germany' in 1953, he explained that the rich tapestry of European history was one of the main reasons why, at the grand old age of seventy-eight, he had decided to return to the 'old earth' after fifteen years living in the United States. Life in Europe, he said, is 'narrower in space but broader in time'. Mann's elegant formulation turns on a questionable assumption, rarely if ever challenged in his period, that historical 'time' in the Americas only began with European settlers and colonisers. In celebrating Europe's multi-layered heritage we are always in danger of falling back into sweeping claims about the uniqueness and inherent superiority of European civilisation.

Both China and India can point to memory sites that are as old and multi-layered as any in Europe. Just visit the Confucius temple in Beijing, with its stone tablets showing the names of more than 50,000 successful candidates in the imperial civil service exams across seven centuries. Or contemplate the edicts of the third-century BCE Indian king Ashoka, now graven in a metal tablet on an imposing boulder outside the National Museum in Delhi. Obviously, there are historical features that distinguish Europe from China or India – the extent to which political and legal authority was dispersed among many centres, for example, and an international church independent of any state. It's important to identify them. But there is no need to insist on the uniqueness, let alone the inherent superiority, of our part of human civilisation. We only need to decide what we value in our particular heritage – what we should reject, what cherish, preserve and enhance – just as Chinese and Indians will do with theirs.

Hamlet and the Yellow Submarine

Europeans speak in tongues. Many tongues. According to a leading specialist, estimates of the number of languages in Europe range from sixty-four to 234. None of us can speak them all but to understand Europe it does help to speak more than one.

Our continent has a strong strain of linguistic nationalism. As early as 1682, the German philosopher Gottfried Wilhelm Leibniz found embedded deep in the German language 'our way of living, of speaking, of writing, yes even of thinking'. His thought was developed by other German writers such as Johann Gottfried Herder, who saw the *Volksgeist,* the spirit of a people, embodied in a specific language. This in turn was taken up by Slav scholars who crystallised out distinct tongues from a spectrum of Slavonic dialects and set the newly codified languages fast in foundational dictionaries and works of literature. Later, influenced by yet more German philosophers, linguistic nationalists began to demand self-rule and eventually their own sovereign states. This process of political and territorial separation, which began in the early nineteenth century, continued into our own time.

In besieged Sarajevo in 1995, I met a writer called Alija Isaković who had worked for ten years on his *Dictionary of Characteristic Words of the Bosnian Language*, first published in 1992, as Yugoslavia began to disintegrate. 'Our language is our morality,' declared his preface, 'and it does not require any special effort to explain the concept of *the Bosnian language.*' He approvingly quoted a Croatian scholar who argued that 'giving a language the name of the people who speak it expresses something simple and obvious in itself: there exists a people, and that people has its language'. What followed was a lexicon giving Bosnian literary

49

references for around 7,000 words, some of them genuinely distinctive and often of Ottoman origin, others simply variants of familiar terms (Europa/Evropa, ethos/etos). So against those who claimed that Bosnian was merely a dialect of Serbo-Croatian, Isaković insisted that it was a language. What's the difference? Max Weinreich, a Russian Jewish linguist, liked to say that 'a language is a dialect with an army and navy'.

By the end of the disintegration of Yugoslavia, in the early twenty-first century, the original logic of linguistic nationalism was almost reversed. Two centuries earlier, the logic had been 'we speak a different language so we need a different state'. By the time Montenegro declared independence in 2006, it was 'we have a different state so we must speak a different language'. Out of what had been known for most of the twentieth century as Serbo-Croatian came four supposedly distinct national languages: Croatian, Bosnian, Serbian and Montenegrin. (Following the same logic, there should be languages called Canadian and NewZealandese.) Although Serbian and Montenegrin use the Cyrillic as well as the Latin alphabet, all four are variants of the same South Slavic language. As a Croatian friend of mine quipped: 'I never knew I spoke four languages!' An official interpreter from Serbian to Montenegrin would be a character from the theatre of the absurd. When people from those four parts of former Yugoslavia meet nowadays, they understand each other perfectly, speaking what many of them call simply 'our language'.

But what is the equivalent 'our language' for other Europeans, most of whom have genuinely different and mutually incomprehensible mother tongues? A first answer, attributed to the Italian scholar and writer Umberto Eco, is 'the language of Europe is translation'. This is not just a matter of functional translation like that done by the interpretation service of the EU among all its official languages. There is also something deeper, a shared vocabulary of symbols, myths, archetypes and quotations.

Shakespeare's *Hamlet* is the ultimate exemplar of translation as the language of Europe. The Prince of Denmark figures in the literature and imagination of every European language – the same but different, different but the same. In Polish there is a verb *hamletyzować* (roughly: to hamlet), meaning to dither in agonised indecision over a big choice, and a noun derived from it, *hamletyzowanie*. A Polish literary critic, Jacek Trznadel, wrote an entire book on Hamlets in Polish literature.

Tsar Paul I became heir to the Russian throne because his father was assassinated by his mother's lover, uncannily echoing Shakespeare's plot. When, as a young royal on his grand tour, Paul was received by the Holy Roman Emperor Joseph II, his considerate host cancelled a scheduled performance of *Hamlet*, apparently because the lead actor had suggested that there would be two Hamlets in the theatre that night. The Russian poet Maksimilian Voloshin wrote that *Hamlet* 'is a prototype of those tragedies that are experienced by the "Slavonic soul" when it lives through disintegration of will, senses and consciousness'.

'Germany is Hamlet!' wrote the German liberal poet Ferdinand Freiligrath in 1844. He meant that, like Shakespeare's prince, his compatriots were constantly doubting and dithering, instead of rising up to avenge the murdered father's spirit, which Freiligrath identified with 'buried freedom'. In 1949, Thomas Mann argued that in Goethe's view 'not only Germany, all of Europe is Hamlet' – and Fortinbras, the foreign leader who comes in to sort out the bloody mess at the end of the play, 'is America'. Hamlet might also, it seems to me, be a good avatar for the European Union, whose characteristic approach to many big decisions is to dither for a long time and then settle on neither alternative. In short, to hamlet.

Next to translation, the second European answer to the challenge of linguistic diversity is for individual Europeans to speak several different languages: polyglottery as an antidote to polyglossia. In the early twenty-first century, Eurobarometer opinion polls found that more than half the Europeans living in member states of the EU said they could speak at least one language other than their mother tongue 'well enough in order to be able to have a conversation'. Exactly a quarter of those Europeans declared in 2012 that they could converse in at least two foreign languages. Top of the class were the Luxembourgers, Latvians and Dutch, while the British were predictably close to the dunce's corner. But then, those tongue-tied Brits could rely on four out of every ten non-British EU citizens to speak some English. No other language came close.

From the time of the ancient Roman empire, across two millennia, the foundational common language of educated Europeans was Latin. Knowledge of it waxed and waned. Many wrote Latin badly and spoke it worse. But it was always there, well into the twentieth century.

In 1939, Clement Attlee, the leader of Britain's Labour Party, sponsored a German Jewish child, Paul Willer, to come with his mother to England, and took the boy into his own home. Willer had no English and the Attlees no German, so Attlee's daughter Felicity became the family interpreter. She and Paul communicated in Latin.

I probably belong to the last generation of Europeans for whom Latin was considered an essential part of elementary schooling. In a desperate attempt to make the ancient language of European civilisation seem relevant to an eleven-year-old in 1966, our teachers gave us cartoon strips in which trendy-looking young people in leather jackets rode around on motorbikes, speaking Latin. We found this risible.

Only once have I put my rudimentary knowledge of Latin to conversational use. The first time I visited Warsaw, in 1979, I found in the cloister of St Antony's church a memorial tablet on which the place and date of death was given as 'Katyn, 1940'. Simple as that inscription might seem, it was in fact explosive. All the communist regimes of the Soviet bloc were still officially insisting that the thousands of Polish officers murdered by Stalin's executioners in Katyn in 1940 had actually been killed by invading German forces in 1941. In Russia or Poland, you could lose your job as a journalist or teacher for saying otherwise. Shamefully, even the British government still officially declared that the facts of the case were unclear, although no reputable historian had any doubt who was responsible. So this simple inscription was silently rebuking a big lie. As I stood there, a Polish monk approached me, and I pointed to the date. Excitedly, he took me by the elbow and led me to another memorial plaque for a Pole who died in 'Katyn, 1940'. At the time, I had not yet learnt Polish and the monk seemed impervious to the English, French and German that I tried in quick succession. Then I had a brainwave. 'Fortis est veritas,' I said, 'et praevalebit!' ('Truth is strong and shall prevail!'). His eyes lit up with delight.

That was my first and last conversational use of Latin. Today's Latin is English. When a Bulgarian orders his cappuccino in a French coffee shop in Helsinki, he does so in Euroenglish. English was of course, as its name helpfully indicates, originally the language of the English. But it spread across Britain's overseas empire and became the language of the succeeding superpower, the United States. As a result – and perhaps also due to the relative ease of learning it to an elementary level – a stripped-down version of English is now the leading world language. It has been called Globish or Worldspeak. The language with the most native speakers is Chinese but English is spoken by more people for whom it is not their mother tongue.

The curious effect of this for us, the English, is that our English has become a dialect of itself. Václav Havel, the Czech dissident playwright turned president, once told me: 'You know, there are three kinds of English. There's the English that Czechs speak with Italians or Brazilians with Hungarians – there one understands one hundred per cent. There's American English, of which one understands about fifty per cent. And then there's the English spoken by the English, of which one understands nothing.' Since the English typically lower their voices at the end of phrases and leave a huge amount either understated or completely unsaid, I could see his point. So I silently agreed.

Europe's linguistic mélange contributes much to the discreet charm of Europe in our time. Who would have thought that a television drama about Danish coalition politics would become popular across the continent? Yet the TV series *Borgen*, named after the castle in central Copenhagen that houses Denmark's parliament, government and supreme court, is utterly riveting. Part of its appeal lies precisely in hearing the softly abrupt cadences of the Danish language – '*Tak!*', '*Undskyld!*' – while understanding from the subtitles what the characters are saying.

Next to the names of Cristiano Ronaldo, Zinedine Zidane and a few other legendary European footballers, the cultural reference points shared by the largest number of Europeans are probably pop songs performed in English. On a cold grey evening in the small grey town of Bruntál, in Czech Silesia, a British film crew and I went looking for a drink. Nothing seemed to be open. The words 'ghost town' would suggest somewhere more lively. Then, buried deep in an inspissated concrete shopping complex, we found one tiny bar, its dirty plate-glass window lit by a single flickering neon strip lamp. Inside, at a rickety Formica table, sat three Czechs, clearly well away after many beers and singing their ample bellies out. One played the guitar. In the absence of a drum, another tapped out the rhythm with a large bent metal spoon on his large, bald head. His cranium was apparently hollow, for it gave out an astonishingly loud sound. We ordered large beers. I exchanged a few words in Czech with the jolly trio. But how was wider social contact to be established? The Beatles, of course. Fred Baker, our British-Austrian film director, gently seized the guitar and with a professional nod to the drummer struck up 'Yellow Submarine'. 'We all live in a yellow submarine . . .' we roared in ragged unison. Knock, knock, knock, went the drummer's spoon on his loudly echoing pate. '. . . yellow submarine, yellow submarine. We all live in a yellow submarine, yellow submarine . . .' It was a moment of perfect pan-European sodality.

As was traditional for British schoolchildren, the first foreign language I learned was French. I still find it the most beautiful spoken language in the world. Then, thanks to my fascination with recent German history and Thomas Mann, it was on to German, learnt very systematically at the Goethe Institute in Prien am Chiemsee, alongside my pleasure-loving Greek friend Giorgos. Unlike French or Italian, German does not have a worldwide reputation for elegance, but it can be both beautiful and profound. I have loved the language ever since. In my twenties, inspired by the dissident movement in Poland, I added Polish. With every language I learned, I became a bit more European, more capable of seeing myself as another – to use a fine formulation of the French philosopher Paul Ricoeur – and more detached from the solid monolingual certainties of my father's England.

With French, German and Polish I gained access to the three major families of European languages, Romance, Germanic and Slavic, so could branch out to at least a newspaper-reading knowledge of Italian and Spanish, Dutch, Czech or Slovak. To the acute embarrassment of our young sons Tom and Alec (Tomek and Alik in Polish), on our family travels around the continent I would happily throw myself into the local language, with appropriate gesticulation. I undoubtedly made a fool of myself many times, but the willingness to have a go, even with just a few mispronounced words of the other person's language, is itself a gesture of mutual recognition, a token of Europeanism, and usually appreciated as such.

Yet even as we celebrate this linguistic diversity, we must recognise that it divides Europeans both geographically and socially. In the second decade of the twenty-first century, a period of nationalist populism, we discovered that one of the deep divides running through European societies roughly coincided with that between the half who spoke more than one language and the other half who did not. The former probably went to university, lived in cities or prosperous towns and travelled around the continent, happily conversing in another tongue; the latter not. Populist political entrepreneurs such as Nigel Farage in Britain mobilised the latter against the former by saying in effect: 'They, the cosmopolitan liberal elites, have Europe. Europe is only good for them, not for you. The nation is for you.' In the 2020 presidential election in Poland, the propaganda machine of the ruling populist party actually made it an argument against the liberal, pro-European opposition candidate Rafał Trzaskowski that he spoke five languages. Thoroughly unpatriotic, obviously.

Being able to live, study and work in your own language is so fundamental to human flourishing that it is widely construed as a human right. And poetry, as the saying goes, is what gets lost in translation. So, to a significant degree, is politics. After ten years' experience of high politics, as president first of Czechoslovakia then of the Czech Republic, Václav Havel liked to expound his theory that politics is like theatre. Both, he explained, are concentrated, intensified life.

Havel was surely right. The most gifted politicians are also actors, stage managers and writers. What would Britain's Second World War have been without the language of Winston Churchill, who deservedly won the Nobel Prize in Literature? Impossible to imagine post-war France without the rhetoric of Charles de Gaulle. West German Ostpolitik would have moved few hearts were it not for the inspirational phrases of Willy Brandt, most of them written, as I discovered when I studied his private papers, in green felt-tip pen. Havel, too, had a particular liking for the green felt tip – green, he said, is the colour of hope – and his own speeches shaped our imagination of post-communist Europe.

National politics is theatre, and nowhere more so than in Washington. Europeans follow the soap opera of American politics more closely than they do our supposedly all-European politics in Brussels, let alone the national politics of other European countries. In fact, America remains one of the few things that all Europeans have in common, alongside pop music and football. What most Europeans see of the political process in Brussels, by contrast, has all the drama of a dishwasher instruction booklet. A character in *Borgen*, the Danish TV series, says: 'In Brussels, nobody hears you scream.' I would add: 'Brussels does not sing.' The European Union comes closest to communication that touches hearts as well as minds in the sight of European flags fluttering besides national ones and, thanks to Beethoven, in the sound of the European anthem. But it's no accident that there are no official words to that anthem. Music and the flag may unite us; in language, we remain stubbornly divided.

Rome

E pluribus unum – from the many, one – is the well-known Latin motto on the Great Seal of the United States. *In varietate concordia* is the little-known Latin motto of the European Union, originally translated as 'unity in diversity' and now officially rendered as 'united in diversity'. To which even the most sympathetic observer might respond: I see the diversity, but where's the unity? Linguistically, the answer lies in polyglottery and translation. Politically, it depends on the fluctuating will of Europeans to act together. Historically, it begins with a single word: Rome.

'All roads lead to Rome' says a proverb that goes back to a twelfth-century French monk. Taken literally, this refers to the road system of the ancient Roman empire, in which all distances were measured from a single point in the Forum in Rome, marked by a monument called the golden milestone. You can get an impression of this extraordinary network from a map known as the Peutinger table. Copied by a thirteenth-century monk from a fourth-century CE original, this is a strip nearly seven metres long, charting some 112,000 kilometres of roads across the Roman world. Like modern route maps, it depicts selected features in stylised form: rivers in dark blue, roads as red lines and, dotted along them, with distances marked in Roman miles, coloured miniature buildings, of which some of the largest are spas. Aquis Sestis is Aix-en-Provence, Aquinco is Budapest, Aquas Aureanas is Kırşehir in today's Turkey, and so on. Like a modern tourist, the fourth-century traveller could plan ahead at which hotel or Aquibnb to spend the night.

Taken metaphorically, 'all roads lead to Rome' means something like 'whatever you do, you'll end up there'. For Europe, the most important meaning is somewhere between the literal and the metaphorical. Thomas Mann told those post-war Hamburg students that being back in Rome after a long absence reminded him of the 'millennial perspective' of Europe and filled his heart with 'a melancholy remarkably similar to pride'. Goethe wrote to his friends that he counted the day he entered Rome in 1786 as 'a second birthday, a true rebirth', because 'the whole history of the world attaches itself to this place'.

'History of the world' was a Eurocentric exaggeration but Goethe found the perfect words to describe the relationship of European history to Rome: it 'attaches itself' to it. It is not just that a great deal of what has historically constituted Europe was already there in the late Roman empire. It is not just that Rome never entirely disappeared in territories over which it once held sway. It is that even peoples and territories that were never any part of the ancient Roman empire were fascinated by it, studied it, claimed its heritage and tried to reproduce it, in every sense of the word reproduction. History and mythology, tradition and the invention of tradition, are inextricably intertwined.

A conventional version of this story would say that Graeco-Roman and Judaeo-Christian civilisation came down to us through Rome, and there is much truth in that, as well as some inevitable oversimplification. (For a now-multicultural continent, with a large and growing Muslim population, it is helpful to recall that classic texts of Greek philosophy were saved for us by Arab scholars and librarians.) Interned behind barbed wire by Poland's Soviet-backed regime in 1982, Bronisław Geremek divided his time between thinking about a strategy for the democratic opposition in Poland and reflecting on the mediaeval emergence of Europe. As a scholar, he had no doubt that it was the marriage of Rome and Christianity, *Romanitas et Christianitas*, that gave birth to the late mediaeval idea of Europe from which our own is descended.

Crucially for Europe's subsequent development, this Roman Catholic Church (the clue is in the name) would reach across numerous territories in which it was, at least in principle, independent of the local secular power. The Catholic Church was the world's first international NGO. But for much of eastern and south-eastern Europe, the Christian heritage came through the eastern Roman empire, known to us as Byzantium, centred in Constantinople and styled the 'second Rome'. I once had an opportunity to meet the Oecumenical Patriarch Bartholomew I, archbishop of Constantinople and customarily regarded as the most senior of Orthodox divines, in his dark, old-fashioned office in Istanbul. As our small delegation warily sipped a drink that seemed to consist entirely of liquid white sugar, the aged, white-bearded, bespectacled patriarch quietly welcomed us to a place 'where we have been for some 1,700 years'. Although just a few thousand Orthodox Christians are left in Istanbul, for the hour of that brief encounter we were in Constantinople.

Christianity was for many centuries the largest element of unity in all Europe's diversity. I have before me a map entitled Europa Polyglotta, made by a German cartographer in 1730. Visually, it is a complete mess, with tiny lettering in different languages covering the entire land surface of Europe and most of the seas around it, like the scribblings of a mad professor. But look more closely and you see that in all these thirty-three languages, whether in the Latin, Cyrillic, Greek or other alphabet, what is written is the same sentence: 'Our Father who art in heaven, hallowed be thy name'.

When the European Union established a convention to write a 'European constitution' at the beginning of the twenty-first century, there was a lively debate about whether to include Christianity in the preamble to that constitution. In the end, it referred only to 'drawing inspiration from the cultural, religious and humanist inheritance of Europe'. There was by now a large proportion of non-believers in many western European countries – nearly half the Dutch, for example, and more than a third of Swedes. Some of the most passionate 'pro-Europeans' were also convinced atheists. Whereas the founding fathers of the European project in the 1950s often invoked Christianity, this new generation believed passionately that the values of the European Union should be derived not from Christianity but from the heritage of the seventeenth- and eighteenth-century European Enlightenment and the Scientific Revolution that paved the way for it. The truths that this Europe upheld should be empirical, scientifically verifiable, fact-based truths, not the revealed Truth of religion. Humanist truths; not articles of faith but principles of reason. On this new map of Europe the shared motto, translated into all languages, would not be 'Our Father who art in heaven' but rather the advice the eighteenth-century German philosopher Immanuel

Kant gave in his seminal essay on Enlightenment: *Sapere aude!* (Dare to know!)

Yet even a deeply committed atheist must recognise the historical reality that without Christianity there would be no Europe as we know it today. Characteristically, even this underlying unity is criss-crossed with divisions. Christian Europe is divided by the great schism between the Western and Eastern rites, Roman Catholic and Orthodox. One Orthodox scholar slyly suggests that Roman Catholic is a contradiction in terms, since Catholic means universal. It is divided, as well, by the post-Reformation split between Catholic and several varieties of Protestant. In the 1860s, a Scottish nurse travelling on the continent with the author Robert Louis Stevenson found the French to be 'very nice people' but deplored the fact that they were living 'under the reign of the man of sin'. She meant the Pope. At my very Protestant boarding school, Sherborne, in the 1960s, I was reliably informed that boys at a rival, Catholic school, Downside, were exhorted to new heights of sporting savagery by cowled monks beating large drums at the end of the rugby field. Well within living memory, in several European countries, a 'mixed' marriage was one between a Catholic and a Protestant.

The mindsets of past faiths, like the doctrines of dead economists, shape even those who no longer believe in them. As the Israeli scholar Shlomo Avineri once observed, a Jewish atheist, a Catholic atheist and a Muslim atheist disbelieve in a different God. When Germans talk about debt they use the word Schuld, which also means guilt and comes heavy with Lutheran connotations of sinfulness. Today's continent is still haunted by the Christian churches' fraught, guilt-laden relationship with the Jews of Europe and long, deep-seated antagonism to Islam.

So is Europe united in diversity? Yes, but also divided in its deepest unities. For the same is true of its imitations of Rome. This Europe-defining habit began immediately after what is conventionally called the fall of the Roman empire. In 500 CE a Gothic warrior king, Theoderic, paid a triumphal visit from his own capital of Ravenna, itself the former headquarters of the imperial army, to Rome. He stopped first at the church of St Peter's, which housed the tomb of the leader of Christ's apostles, then addressed the still-existing Roman Senate and 'promised that, with God's help, he would uphold inviolably everything that previous Roman emperors had decreed'. There followed a traditional imperial progress, circus games for the populace and the distribution of food – the proverbial 'bread and circuses'.

Three hundred years later, in 800 CE, a Frankish warrior king, Charlemagne, was crowned emperor by the Pope in Rome, thereby asserting that the true 'second Rome' was headquartered in the West, not in Constantinople. Charlemagne then had inscribed on his seal the words 'the renewal of the Roman Empire'. Thus began the Holy Roman Empire, known in German as the Reich and probably the most underrated polity in European history. Adolf Hitler boasted that his would be a 'thousand-year Reich', but whereas his Third Reich lasted just twelve years, this first Reich actually did last a thousand years. It was finally terminated only in 1806, when the last Holy Roman Emperor, Francis II, abdicated, becoming merely Kaiser Francis I of Austria. Voltaire, with the cleverness of a newspaper columnist, quipped that it was neither holy, nor Roman, nor an empire. Yet for centuries, to most of its subjects, it was all of those things.

You can still feel something of the mystique of the Holy Roman Empire if you attend a High Mass in Charlemagne's own church in Aachen, as I did for the first time in 2017. As you approach the cathedral along a narrow courtyard, notice the ancient Roman stones reused in the high wall to your left. Entering the building through a magnificent pair of bronze doors that date from around 800, you reflect that Charlemagne himself must have walked through these doors. Passing a third-century BCE statue of a she-wolf, such as might have suckled Romulus and Remus at the mythical founding of Rome, you find yourself in the original church, also completed around 800. With its octagonal shape, stacked galleries, colour-banded arches and golden-grounded mosaics it feels as much Byzantine as Roman Catholic. A major influence on its design was the church of San Vitale in what had become, after Theoderic's time, the Byzantine 'exarchy' of Ravenna. Stones and marble from Ravenna were probably used in the original construction.

As usual in Europe, some of the old is in fact new – restored or elaborated since the nineteenth century. Yet on the first-floor gallery you can see the actual throne, made of slabs of Roman marble, upon which the 'Roman German' kings were crowned from the tenth to the sixteenth centuries. (The king became emperor only after the Pope had done the honours in Rome.) Above your head, shimmering through the incense, are candles on a huge circular candelabra, made at the behest of the twelfth-century king and emperor Frederick Barbarossa – he who still slumbers deep in the Kyffhäuser mountain in Thuringia, waiting for the European Council to call him when they can't reach agreement on the next EU budget.

Turning to the high Gothic choir section to the east, you look beyond a gold-fronted altar to an elevated, beautifully worked golden shrine containing (and this seems to be true) the bones of Charlemagne. To the side of the altar, magnetically drawing the eye, there stands a superb cross made for his son Lothar, encrusted with gems and precious stones, and having at its centre an original Roman cameo of the Emperor Augustus. The censers swing, the incense whirls around the gold, gems and candles. From the gallery above comes the sound of a choir singing, in Latin of course, *'Agnus Dei, qui tollis peccata mundi, miserere nobis'* ('O lamb of God, who takes away the sins of the world, have mercy upon us'). You are in 2017 and you are in 1217. You are in Rome, in Ravenna, in Byzantium – and in North-Rhine Westphalia.

A royal road of European history leads from Rome through Ravenna and Aachen to the thousand years of the Holy Roman Empire, and thence to its successors. After the end of the Cold War division of Europe, in the 1990s, Bronisław Geremek told me he wanted to persuade the French, Germans and Italians – who are, loosely speaking, heirs to the territories carved out for Charlemagne's three sons – that Europe should now be Ottonian rather than just Carolingian. In other words, like the dynasty founded by Otto I, the tenth-century Holy Roman Emperor, it should embrace east central Europe. As Geremek explained to a mainly German audience on receiving the Charlemagne prize in Aachen in 1998, Emperor Otto III's meeting with the Polish king Boleslaus at the tomb of the martyred St Adalbert in Gniezno in the year 1000 was 'an important date in European history'. It's no accident that the Polish and Czech words for king, *król* and *král*, derive from Karl – that is, Charlemagne. The German 'Kaiser' and the Bulgarian and Russian 'Tsar' are versions of 'Caesar'.

In 1027, King Cnut, by then ruler of much of what is now Scandinavia as well as England, travelled to Rome to attend the coronation of King Conrad II as Emperor by Pope John XIX. 'I would have you know', he wrote to his English subjects, while heading back to Denmark, 'that there was a great gathering of nobles there at the Easter solemnity with our lord Pope John and the Emperor Conrad . . . who all gave me a respectful welcome and honoured me with magnificent gifts.' One recognises immediately the slightly insecure boastfulness characteristic of leaders from the less self-evidently central parts of Europe. 'Everybody in Brussels, Berlin and Paris treats us with enormous respect' is the message back home of so many national politicians to this day. What was it British prime minister John Major, that latter-day Cnut, liked to say in the 1990s? Oh yes, Britain is 'at the heart of Europe'.

An even bolder historical claim was made in Russia. Some time after the fall of Constantinople to the Ottoman Turks in 1453, the Russian ruler Ivan III married Sofia Paleologue, niece of the last Byzantine emperor, and established a sumptuous court in Moscow on the Byzantine model. His Orthodox ideologues then developed the theory that Russia was 'the Third Rome' – both religious and imperial successor to Byzantium's 'Second Rome'. As the monk Filofei of Pskov wrote to Ivan III: 'thou art the sole Emperor of all the Christians in the whole universe . . . For two Romes have fallen, the Third stands, and there shall be no Fourth.'

How wrong he was. There had already been at least three Romes and a fourth, fifth and sixth were to follow. Of remakes of the hit movie *Rome* there would be no end. When Napoleon crowned himself Emperor of France in 1804, he used two crowns: a golden laurel wreath, recalling ancient Rome, and a replica of Charlemagne's crown. Pope Pius VII attended the ceremony in Notre Dame cathedral and read the very text used by Pope Leo III when investing Charlemagne just over 1,000 years before. The next year, Napoleon crowned himself king of Italy, now using the Iron Crown of Lombardy, which had been worn by every Holy Roman Emperor since Frederick Barbarossa. So by the time the Holy Roman Empire was formally brought to a close in 1806 there was already a new would-be-Roman boss on the block.

So it goes on. Mussolini used the fasces of ancient Rome as a symbol of his fascism. His 'il Duce' moniker was derived from dux, the Latin word for a military commander of a region in sixth-century Italy. He described Italian fascism as an heir to the 'universal civilisation' of ancient Rome. Adolf Hitler told dinner companions in his wartime headquarters that the Roman Empire was 'the only really great state-political formation in history'. If only Rome had not weakened itself by adopting Christianity, he said, channelling vulgarised Nietzsche, it could have defeated the Huns and we might have seen a quite different Europe. German emperors such as Charlemagne and his successors were so bold, 'when one thinks how often these men rode over the Alps'. Their empire always looked south, he reflected, not east. And in March 1942, as his own armies, like Napoleon's, were getting bogged down in the Russian winter, he mused that perhaps in a thousand years' time some dotty schoolteacher might say: 'What that Hitler did in the east was, to be sure, well intended, but in the end complete foolishness – he should have gone south.'

When post-war democratic leaders of western Europe decided to form a European Economic Community, where did they choose to sign the founding treaty? Rome, of course. The signing ceremony on that rainy Monday in March 1957 resounded with references to ancient Rome. 'No place could be better suited than the Eternal City to be the precious witness of our hopes,' declared Paul-Henri Spaak, a Belgian politician counted among the founding fathers of the European Union. 'It is in Rome, the former capital of the ancient world,' said Joseph Luns, the foreign minister of the Netherlands, 'that the political, legal and social foundations of our present civilisation were brilliantly laid. Likewise, today in this same Rome, we are laying the foundations for a new Europe that we hope will be united, strong and prosperous, as it once was under that imperial Rome of the Caesars.' Konrad Adenauer, the founding Chancellor of the Federal Republic of Germany, more cautiously observed that 'the great common heritage, to which the city of Rome forever bears witness, is at once a warning and a hope'.

In the late 1960s, when I first travelled to the continent, the European Community was still largely coterminous with Charlemagne's empire in 800. Only in 1973, with the accession of Britain, Ireland and Denmark to this sixth or seventh Rome, did the non-Carolingian barbarians start entering Charlemagne's garden. But we barbarians too, in our own peculiar ways, had looked back to and imitated Rome.

The Roman question is, to this day, Europe's core political conundrum. It is the conundrum of unity and diversity. 'How will Europe do best?' each generation asks. Some say 'more unity, more Rome!' This is the tenor of a thousand Brussels speeches. 'No,' others reply, 'more diversity, less Rome!' It's not imitating Rome, they argue, but on the contrary what the historian Walter Scheidel calls the 'Escape from Rome' that gave our continent its dynamism. Extending an old thesis that Europe's diversity is the historical key to explaining its unprecedented economic take-off, Scheidel argues that it was 'post-Roman polycentrism', by contrast with the centralised unity of Asian empires, that made Europe the birthplace of modernity: 'Without polycentrism, no modernity.' Yet he also raises the question whether this would have been equally true had there been no Rome in the first place. A Rome from which to escape but also of which to dream.

Unity and diversity are Europe's yin and yang, its thesis and antithesis, forever seeking their elusive synthesis. Push too hard for unity and the forced union starts to fall apart. Push too hard for diversity and Europeans end up fighting each other. Eventually someone comes marching in to clean up the internecine mess, like Fortinbras at the end of *Hamlet*. (Tomorrow's Fortinbras may be Chinese.) The Holy Roman Empire lasted so long precisely because it combined a deep, unifying mystique with what the historian Peter Wilson calls 'a framework sustaining local and particular liberties and . . . respecting diversity, autonomy and difference'. In negotiating those differences, Wilson goes on, 'success usually depended on compromise and fudge. Although outwardly stressing unity and harmony, the Empire in fact functioned by accepting disagreement and disgruntlement as permanent elements of its internal politics.' If that sounds familiar, I take it as a sign of hope, not despair, for the future of today's European Union.

Cold War West

European unity still seemed a pipe dream in the 1970s, since Europe was split down the middle. In the summer of 1975, aged twenty, I travelled to Berlin, the divided centre of a divided continent. Spending money I had earned working as a gardener in a public park, I made the long, overnight train journey across the flat north German landscape that my father had traversed in such different circumstances three decades before. My diary records a 'volatile Turk', dressed in orange and blue denim, delivering a late-night harangue against imperialism in general and English imperialists in particular, and a Pole making amorous advances to an 'unbelievably innocent' seventeen-year-old English schoolgirl who wanted to be a ballet dancer. Then, exhausted, I slept.

That sleep probably explains why there is no description of my first crossing of the Iron Curtain – in this case, the frontier between West and East Germany – and a second crossing, from East Germany into the weird enclave of West Berlin, which was entirely surrounded by the Berlin Wall. Although the Wall was officially described as the 'anti-fascist protective wall', everyone knew it was built not to prevent the fascists of West Berlin from getting out into the surrounding East Germany but to prevent the people of East Germany from escaping into West Berlin. That 'island in the red sea' had been sealed off fourteen years previously, on 13 August 1961, and by now the Wall was a formidable fortification, consisting of several walls, watchtowers, fences, anti-vehicle ditches and a 'death strip' of raked sand.

Europe has a long history of divisions, many of them involving labellings of 'West' and 'East'. This latest divide, however, was dictated not by those European powers that had fought over the heartlands of Europe from Caesar's time to Hitler's but by two nuclear-armed 'superpowers' engaged in the Cold War – a term used by George Orwell already in 1945. Between 1914 and 1945, Europe had torn itself apart in what Churchill called a new Thirty Years' War. The Soviet Union and the United States shared the part of Fortinbras, picking up the pieces. The Russian empire had long been a major player in European affairs. The United States was, in its origins and culture, a kind of New Europe across the seas. Yet neither the Soviet Union nor the United States could be described unambiguously as a European country.

Europeans had spent centuries dictating terms to people in faraway countries. Now the boot was on the other foot. Or rather, it was simultaneously on both feet – for in 1945 the overseas empires of the British, French, Dutch and Portuguese were still largely intact. France was bloodily suppressing a popular protest in Algeria on the very day victory was declared in Europe. So Europe was in a strange double condition: part colonised, part coloniser; still kicking others, but also being kicked. The oldest of all the European overseas empires, that of Portugal, was only finally dissolved, in Angola and Mozambique, around the time of my first visit to Berlin.

The arbitrary lines now drawn across the map of Europe had lifechanging consequences for the people who found themselves on the wrong side. Take Steinstücken, for example. In 1787, a village called Stolpe, out in the countryside south-west of Berlin, acquired a parcel of farmland separate from the main settlement. At the end of the nineteenth century, Stolpe and the residential part of that exclave – now called Steinstücken – were incorporated into the leafy parish of Wannsee, which in turn became part of Greater Berlin in 1920. When, in the summer of 1945, the United States, the Soviet Union, Britain and France agreed the final lines for the division of Hitler's capital into occupation sectors, they drew them along the borough boundaries of Greater Berlin. So Steinstücken, all twelve hectares of it, would belong to the American sector and hence to what would become, after the three Western sectors were effectively merged, West Berlin.

When East Germany sealed off West Berlin in August 1961, Steinstücken became its own miniature West Berlin, a tiny island of 'the West' in the middle of 'the East'. Although it was less than one kilometre by road from the main part of West Berlin, the US military created a rudimentary helicopter landing place for soldiers to be flown into the exclave. The square now contains a helicopter monument and there is even a helicopter-shaped climbing frame in the local children's' playground. But never mind the American soldiers, who could fly out and be in Texas the next day. Think of the people who actually lived there. Which side of the street your house was on decided which world you were in.

Here was the new front line between 'West' and 'East'. Arriving in Berlin for the first time, I was thrilled by the sense of a place where world history was being made. Much of the excitement came from not knowing in which direction that history was heading. I was like someone who, without consulting any tables, dives into the deep water of a cove notorious for its strong and treacherous tides. As you swim, you feel the swirl of powerful currents around you but you don't know whether they are carrying you landward or pushing you out to sea.

With hindsight – a gift that illuminates, but also obscures – it seems clear that the tide was flowing in the direction of democracy, the West, freedom and greater European unity. Greece, Spain and Portugal were beginning the transition from dictatorship to democracy. Britain, displaying its famous common sense, voted in a referendum in 1975 to remain in the European Community. The strongest support came in England and from Conservatives, the fiercest opposition from Labour and Scotland. Even my Eurosceptic father voted to remain in 'the common market'.

In the same year, the Belgian prime minister Leo Tindemans submitted a 'Report on European Union' to the European Council, as the decision-making council of heads of government of the nine member states was now called. He recommended that the European Community should become a Union, with direct elections to the European parliament, a common monetary and economic policy, free movement of people without frontier controls and a more closely co-ordinated foreign policy – thus anticipating much of what would come to pass over the next forty-five years. Meanwhile, the leaders of six major industrial democracies – the United States, France, West Germany, Italy, Britain and Japan (a member of the 'West' for these purposes) – met at an informal summit in the château of Rambouillet, south-west of Paris. The next year, Canada would be added to this select group, creating what we still know as the G7. Liberalising economic reforms would produce a new dynamism in west European economies.

Across the Iron Curtain, by contrast, the Soviet bloc was entering a period of economic and political stagnation. A few days before I took the train to Berlin, an international political declaration that came to be known as the Helsinki Final Act was signed in the Finnish capital. It was the product of a long negotiation between the Soviet desire for formal recognition of its dominant position in eastern Europe (only ambiguously conceded in the February 1945 Yalta agreement), the US policy of detente and the West German variant of detente known as Ostpolitik, forever associated with the name of Chancellor Willy Brandt.

The 1975 agreement started a 'Helsinki process' of review conferences. This contributed to a new political dynamic in countries like Poland, Hungary and Czechoslovakia, with dissidents citing the Final Act's endorsement of human rights, and its specific promotion of human contacts, to justify and reinforce demands addressed to communist rulers who had signed that treaty. With hindsight, one can draw a straight line from Helsinki to the end of communism in countries that would subsequently join NATO and the European Union, enlarging the key institutions of the Cold War West. Eventually what had been called the Conference on Security and Co-operation in Europe would become the Organisation for Security and Co-operation in Europe that we know today.

Thus a history textbook might summarise the story. But there was nothing inevitable about this development. Even a metaphor such as 'the turn of the tide' is misleading, since it suggests a natural, unstoppable process. Many intelligent and well-informed people at the time thought things were heading in the opposite direction. In that grand château of Rambouillet, leaders like Helmut Schmidt, Brandt's successor as West German Chancellor, and French president Valéry Giscard d'Estaing stared gloomily into their hors d'oeuvres, fearing that the knock-on effects of a dramatic increase in the oil price – the 'oil shock' – two years before would weaken the West as much economically as it was already weakened politically.

The United States appeared utterly compromised by the fateful combination of the Vietnam War and the Watergate scandal. The totemic capitalist city of New York had almost gone bankrupt. The US Secretary of State, Henry Kissinger, worried that Portugal, having thrown off its right-wing dictatorship, was about to go communist. Kissinger warned the new Portuguese foreign minister Mario Soares that he risked being like Alexander Kerensky, the Menshevik leader in the first phase of the Russian revolution who was soon swept away by Lenin's more radical Bolsheviks. Soares mildly replied that he certainly didn't want to be a Kerensky, to which Kissinger shot back, 'Neither did Kerensky.' In Portugal's former colony of Angola, forces backed by Cuba and the Soviet Union did in fact prevail over those supported by the United States. The Italian Communist Party won more than a third of the vote in the 1976 election, close behind the Christian Democrats, and seemed to be on the rise.

Both Italy and West Germany were shaken by left-wing terrorist attacks, including murders of prominent industrialists and politicians. In Italy, the Red Brigades kidnapped and killed former Christian Democrat prime minister Aldo Moro. When I visited a club on a lake in West Berlin, one of my new-found friends told me: 'You know, this place was recently bombed by the RAF.' For a moment, I wondered why the Royal Air Force would do that. Then I realised he was referring to the Red Army Faction, the far-left terrorist group also known as the Baader–Meinhof gang. Right-wing Germans felt that the very existence of their less than thirty-year-old democracy was threatened by the revolutionary left. Left-wing Germans believed their democracy was endangered by a repressive overreaction from the right. One day I sat in a West Berlin courtroom, witnessing a trial of RAF terrorists. The next I watched *Germany in Autumn,* a grim, moody collage made by leading West German filmmakers, intimating that the Federal Republic was on the verge of something like fascism.

In April 1978, I actually had lunch with an old fascist. I don't mean a fascist in the loose way those filmmakers used the term. I mean Fascist with a capital F, for in the 1930s Sir Oswald Mosley had been the leader of the British Union of Fascists. At the Mosleys' small but grandiose Napoleonic-era house in Orsay, modestly called the Temple de la Gloire,

I was received by his wife Diana, one of the famous Mitford sisters. I found her ice-cold. The company included a Catholic monsignore, in darkest black, several vaguely upper-class Brits and someone my diary describes as 'the rather seedy, but courtly, sole Frenchman present'. At one point he asked Mosley what we were talking about at our end of the table. My diary continues:

> 'Nous disons', O.M. thunders down the table, in French as English as Churchill's, 'Nous disons que le Marxisme est totalement fini!' ('We are saying that Marxism is totally finished!')

And then I comment on 'the extraordinary spectacle of this aged and isolated king over the water, surrounded by his court, proclaiming with supreme self-confidence the death of that creed under which 2/5 of the world's population at present live'. It was not communism but fascism, I thought, that was *totalement fini*. (Forty years later, we discovered that fascism was back, not least in Vladimir Putin's Russia. The kaleidoscope never stops turning.)

The Helsinki Final Act, celebrated by posterity as a historic catalyst of east European liberation, was excoriated by Aleksandr Solzhenitsyn, the recently exiled author of *The Gulag Archipelago*, as an act of shameful Western capitulation. Many central and east European dissidents agreed with him. Soviet leaders saw Helsinki as a triumph, securing the formal recognition of the post-1945 settlement that they had long desired. Alarmists declared that the East was winning the Cold War. Even the cautious, level-headed historian J. M. Roberts would write, in the first edition of his *History of the World*, published in 1976, that the Soviet Union now had 'a scientific and industrial base that matches that of the United States' and the United States 'was no longer the top dog she had been even ten years before'. The World Bank Atlas solemnly recorded that in 1975 per capita income in East Germany had overtaken that in Britain. A few years later, the French writer Jean-François Revel published a book called *How Democracies Perish*.

From the safe harbour of posterity it is tempting to exclaim: 'How absurdly mistaken they all were!' – and in one sense, that would be right. This is not how things turned out. But in another and perhaps more important sense, that would be entirely wrong. It was precisely the fact that Western politicians and intellectuals in the 1970s saw, indeed over-estimated, the weaknesses of Western democracies and the strength of the competition from the Eastern bloc that led the West to raise its game at home and abroad. One might even say that the West won the Cold War because it feared it was losing it. The contrast with the early 2000s is instructive. At the turn of the millennium, giddy with success and seeing no major systemic rival, the West became complacent and hubristic. Just look what happened next.

In the early 1980s, an intensification of the Cold War followed this cold shower of fear. At the time, people talked about the end of detente and a 'second Cold War', a term that has made its way into the history books. But the original Cold War had never ended. For both sides, detente was the continuation of Cold War by other means.

Not that most people woke up every day thinking they were at war. For many west Europeans of my generation, the division along the line of the Iron Curtain had become almost like a fact of physical geography. They accepted as normal a world of two blocs led by two nuclear-armed superpowers. If you pressed them, they would acknowledge that the front lines of 'the West' were arbitrary and that it was not nice for those stuck on the other side. Yet some of the most obvious hardships had been ameliorated – Steinstücken, for example, now had a stretch of road connecting it directly to West Berlin. Anyway, most west Europeans did not go east. When I went to live permanently in Berlin, in the summer of 1978, I was astonished how many West Berliners never crossed to the eastern part of their own city at all. They lived with their backs to the Wall. In their mental geography, Tuscany and Provence were closer than Saxony or Thuringia. Siberia began at Checkpoint Charlie.

Politically, too, many west Europeans were content with this state of affairs. A French novelist remarked: 'We love Germany so much we are glad there are two of them.' When I interviewed the British Foreign Secretary, Douglas Hurd, some two months after the Berlin Wall came down, he breezily looked back on a system 'under which we've lived quite happily for forty years'. I had to point out that people on the other side had not lived under this system quite so happily.

Why did my twenty-year-old self not accept this division as normal?

What drew me ineluctably to 'the East'? Was it the intensification of the Cold War? A typically English taste for travel and adventure? Too many spy novels? I didn't read much John le Carré at that time but I devoured everything by Graham Greene. A few years later, in my early twenties, I nearly became a British spy but (thank heaven) decided to preserve my independence as a political writer, or what I grandiloquently called 'a spy for the truth'. Was it a sense that my father and grandfather had fought in their wars and this was to be mine? A war all the more attractive, of course, for being unlikely to get you killed or maimed. Somewhere in that cocktail of youthful motives there was also a strong desire that people less fortunate than me should gain more of the freedom I enjoyed. Looking back, I find that I had an idealised, rose-tinted picture of Britain such as could be kept intact only by a privileged white Englishman who spent much of his time abroad. Today, I view the country of my birth more critically.

Human motives are always mixed. We all unconsciously reflect the spirit of the time and place in which we grew up. Only years later do we unearth some of the hidden causes that led to our actions. In the end, what matters is what we do.

Friedrichstrasse, East

In late August 1975 I crossed for the first time into East Berlin, negotiating the concrete labyrinth (shades of Knossos) that was the underground frontier crossing at the Friedrichstrasse railway station. I noted every detail: the 'rather bewildered crowd hanging on the guttural shouts emitted by the loudspeakers', the compulsory exchange of five West German Deutschmarks into five lightweight East German marks, handed out in a sealed plastic packet. To my consternation and delight, I was singled out by a 'grim-faced official' who conducted me 'past a chained doorway, down a flaking ochre-painted corridor, to a small flaking ochre-painted room – a table, two chairs, a naked light bulb . . .' There followed 'a fantastically detailed and earnest examination' of everything in my suitcase and all my pockets, including my pocket diary, cheque book, Barclaycard and library tickets. "Are you a student?", "Where?", "What do you study?" "History," I said. Then he walked me to the doorway and the chain fell behind me.' The minotaur had let me into the East.

Naïve and full of Cold War clichés though I was, I had sufficient detachment to observe that this experience was 'comically' like one's over-excited expectations of crossing the Iron Curtain. For the next five years, in the intervals between studying history in Oxford and Berlin, I pursued a kind of self-made apprenticeship in life under communist rule. I travelled through Yugoslavia, then took a 'progressive tour' to the still Stalinist state of Albania – this being the only way you could get in. Our pre-departure instructions said that hair had to be cut short for this 'progressive' trip. My group included seven Marxist-Leninist teachers from Leeds and a former imperial policeman called Mr Godsave, who

74

told me he was there to 'get to know the enemy'. As our coach returned to our foreigners-only hotel, which was surrounded by a high wire fence, like a camp, our guide intoned: 'As you say in your country: East, West, home's best!' Subsequently, I drove for seven weeks through the entire Soviet bloc, from East Berlin to Sofia, the rough roads wreaking havoc on the delicate Italian suspension and wheel alignment of my hopelessly impractical dark blue Alfa Romeo.

Based in West Berlin from 1978, I travelled constantly to the East. Living in East Berlin in 1980, I drove all over East Germany. But I often dashed back through the Wall to see friends in West Berlin – profoundly conscious, every time, that my East German girlfriend would be imprisoned, if not shot, if she tried to do the same. As a British citizen coming by car, I had to use the frontier crossing on Friedrichstrasse that we all called Checkpoint Charlie. That was actually the name of the US checkpoint, by now a small hut that one usually drove past without formalities. In the East German checkpoint, by contrast, a bleak assemblage of portakabin-like structures in the middle of the complex of fortifications we called the Wall, I often spent half an hour being 'controlled'. As I write, I have beside me a pile of my old dark blue British passports, their pages filled with East German frontier stamps and Soviet bloc visas. There were so many stamps that I kept having to get a new passport.

If I close my eyes, I can still summon back to my nostrils the smell of plastic wood, cheap cleaning liquid, damp boots and sweaty armpits in the passport control cabin. I must have spent hours staring at the only decorative element, a thick, wall-mounted perspex sheet, on which was written in red letters:

> *Bertolt Brecht*:
> Great Carthage
> fought three wars.
> It was still powerful
> after the first,
> still habitable
> after the second.
> It was nowhere to be found
> after the third.

With time, the frontier guards got to recognise me. 'You look pale,' said one avuncular type. 'You should spend more time in the sun, like me.' A young female frontier guard could not refrain from making frequent references to 'Frau Tatscha', who she obviously found darkly fascinating.

Later, much later, I would meet that Mrs Thatcher and other prominent figures of the time – Helmut Schmidt, Valéry Giscard d'Estaing, Erich Honecker. Tolstoy argues in *War and Peace* that our leaders do not actually make the history they and the historians think they make. They are puppets laughably unaware of their strings. This seems to me wrong. As Tolstoy's compatriot Mikhail Gorbachev would demonstrate, important people sometimes really are important – although not half as much as they generally like to think. But the gift of my apprenticeship was to get to know the 'other Europe' through the eyes of men and women who appear in no history books.

We were as close in time then to 1945 as we are now to 1989. In a hotel restaurant in the Romanian town of Braşov, I heard a couple speaking Yiddish. I initiated a conversation with the banal but always useful question: 'Where are you from?' 'Poland originally, then Melbourne and now Israel.' Herman was a Polish Jew who had somehow survived four years in Nazi camps. On 15 April 1945 – he would never forget that date – he had been liberated from Bergen-Belsen by British forces. Pursuing the theme of my doctoral research, I asked whether he had experienced solidarity or even acts of resistance in the camps? 'Look,' he replied, 'we weren't people, we were numbers.'

At an art gallery in East Berlin, I met a highly cultured, white-haired German Jewish lady who had become a communist as a very young woman in 1930s Berlin. With her husband, also a communist, she had escaped from the Third Reich to find refuge in the Soviet Union. He had fallen victim to one of Stalin's purges and spent years in the Gulag camps, where his health was ruined, while she had been put to work in a labour battalion. 'An intellectual Mother Courage', I wrote in my journal. Years later I would discover, with profound sadness, that she had informed on me to the Stasi.

One of the mechanics who struggled to keep my Alfa Romeo going on the rough roads of the East turned out to come originally from the

Memelland, now the Klaipėda region of Lithuania. His mother, like so many other German refugees, had lost her life on the long, desperate flight westward from the advancing Red Army. He did not know his real name, those of his parents, or even his true date of birth. In the orphanage, he was simply assigned a birthday – April 12.

In my local corner-pub in Prenzlauer Berg, a district of East Berlin now gentrified but then grey and gritty, I got talking to a burly young guy wearing a University of California T-shirt. Having established to his satisfaction that I really was an English history student and not a Stasi nark, he told me his story. His parents lived in West Berlin, but on the night the frontier was sealed in 1961, he, aged three, had been sleeping over with his grandparents in East Berlin. The communist authorities refused to let him rejoin his parents. Occasionally, his dad would still come to visit, in a shiny Mercedes, bringing him presents from the glittering West. Hence the T-shirt.

To my surprise, I found that more of an older, pre-war Europe survived under the supposedly revolutionary communist regimes than under the supposedly reactionary democracies of western Europe. Communism, not least through its slower economic development, had a paradoxically conservative effect. At the most trivial, this was to be seen in the decayed grand hotels of central Europe, the Bristol in Warsaw, the Paříž in Prague, the Gellért in Budapest, with their elaborate restaurant menus containing items like 'Turtle Soup "Lady Curzon"'. ('*Why* turtle soup "Lady Curzon"?' my notebook rather absurdly asks.) Not that most of these delicacies were actually available. Handing me a menu in the Romanian town of Timişoara, a waiter confided: '*Es sagt sehr viel aber gibt sehr wenig*' ('It says a great deal but there is very little').

In the old German-built towns and villages of the Banat and Transylvania, which in the 1970s still had a substantial German population, I found myself walking through a picture-book Germany of high-pitched Gothic gables, cobbled streets, and horse-drawn ploughs tilling the good earth in the surrounding fields. '*Grüss Gott!*' said the charming vicar in the little town of Sackelhausen (now Săcălaz) and asked where I came from. 'Ah, Oxford!' he exclaimed, in his gentle, lilting German. 'Do you know Newman?' Since Cardinal John Henry Newman had died in 1890, this seemed a bit of a stretch.

These were superficial observations, but in time I discovered something deeper. With new acquaintances like the East Berlin pastor Werner Krätschell, who would become a lifelong friend, Eberhard Haufe, a gentle literary scholar in Goethe's Weimar, and the intellectuals I spent long hours talking to in the cafés of Warsaw, Prague and Budapest, I found qualities of cultural life that seemed absent, or at least much attenuated, in the West. Here was a realm where, as the poet Paul Celan said of his native Czernowitz before the Holocaust, 'people *and books* lived'. Ideas were taken as seriously as armies. Religion still mattered. Music was made around the piano in the sitting room, as in nineteenth-century novels. There was time and space for friendship. The West might be richer in money but the East seemed richer in time. Conversations had a special intensity. I came back to the West with the impression well captured by the American novelist Philip Roth: 'I work in a society where as a writer everything goes and nothing matters, while for the Czech writers I met in Prague, nothing goes and everything matters.'

None of which is to idealise what I found. I understood all along that these were Shakespeare's 'uses of adversity', a phrase that I would subsequently use as the title of a book of essays drawing on my experiences. How could I possibly ignore all the critical things people told me, once they had satisfied themselves I was not working for the secret police? I was acutely aware of likely secret police surveillance. Following a performance of Goethe's *Faust* in the East German town of Schwerin, someone whispered to me: 'Watch out, Faust works for the Stasi.' When the actor playing Faust asked me home for drinks afterwards, he tried to wheedle out of me what I was really doing in East Germany. Back in East Berlin, I was sitting up into the early hours drinking and gossiping with my friend Mark Wood, the Reuters correspondent, when the telephone rang and a voice said: 'I see you have an additional.' The Stasi listener obviously wanted us to go to bed, so he could catch up on his beauty sleep. (After East Germany collapsed, I was able to read the file the Stasi had compiled on me, then track down and talk to the informers and secret police officers who had followed me, and write a book about it called *The File*.)

Yet someone who gets their ideas from the film *The Lives of Others* could come away with the impression that life behind the Wall was all about secret police oppression and that people were somehow just waiting and yearning for the moment of liberation. It was not like that. Most people could not imagine how liberation could ever happen. The Soviet invasion of Czechoslovakia in 1968, which extinguished the hopes of the Prague Spring, was still fresh in everyone's mind. How on earth could you get rid of a nuclear-armed superpower that was ready to send in tanks to crush you? At Helsinki, in 1975, the West seemed to have accepted the permanence of the East–West divide. 'Normalisation' was the word used by communist propaganda for the way in which, after the Soviet invasion, Czechoslovakia was returned to Soviet-type norms. Most people accepted this abnormal normality as a long-term reality and tried to make the best of it.

Compared with what life had been like ten or fifteen years before, things were actually getting a little better. You might qualify for an apartment in a new high-rise block, acquire a hi-fi and a colour TV, and even, after several years of waiting, a small car, be it a Polski Fiat (a version of the Fiat 500, built under licence in Poland), puttering East German Trabant, box-like Soviet Lada or tinny Romanian Dacia. More Western consumer goods, music, films and television programmes were allowed in. The division of Europe was apparently sealed and settled, but the dividing line was becoming more porous, a process encouraged by the Helsinki agreement and West German Ostpolitik, which promoted human contacts between East and West.

Most East Germans were allowed to travel only inside the Soviet Bloc. My East German 'travel atlas' from that period shows nowhere else. But Poles, Hungarians, Czechs and Slovaks were increasingly allowed to travel to the West. In Prague, a man my diary identifies only as Jiří spent many hours helping me to get my car mended. He told me that it had taken him seven years to gather the necessary permits and funds to drive to Paris for a fortnight. Since the maximum amount of foreign currency an ordinary Czechoslovak citizen could legally obtain was $12 a day, he and his wife would take most of their food in cans and sleep in the car. But still, it would be a wonderful way to celebrate their tenth wedding anniversary. As we parted, Jiří said: 'When you are next in central Europe, telephone me.' That was the first time I heard anyone use the words 'central Europe' with reference to the present.

Things might be better than ten years ago, but they were worse than in 'the West', as people like Jiří could now see for themselves – and that gap was getting wider. Those I met spent a great deal of time telling me about the endless shortages, the poor quality of consumer goods, the petty regimentation of life, the time-wasting bureaucracy, the Marxist–Leninist indoctrination at school and university, the lies and censorship. I still have on my wall at home a poster done by Manfred Schütz, a graphic designer, for a performance of Heine's *Germany: A Winter's Tale* in the Deutsches Theater in East Berlin. Manfred wanted to reproduce around the edges, ironically of course, the pre-1914 German national colours of red, white and black, but humourless censors ordered him to remove the black. I have restored it by means of a black picture frame.

These discontents were captured in political jokes – the one commodity of which there was no shortage. 'What's the difference between capitalism and communism? In capitalism, you have the exploitation of man by man; under communism, it's the other way round.' 'What happened when the communists took over the Sahara? Within a week, there was a shortage of sand.' 'What's a string quartet? An East German orchestra after a trip to the West'.

The brilliant statisticians of the World Bank might conclude that per capita income in East Germany had overtaken that in Britain; living there, I knew this was nonsense. I certainly did not credit everything I was told. I echoed Herodotus: 'My business is to record what people say, but I am by no means bound to believe it.' So wherever possible, I checked it out. To be sure, I was not objective. I was on the lookout for discontent and in search of dissent. But at the end of the day, I sat down and described, as fairly and accurately as I could, the reality as I found it. For the most part, that reality did not include outright, let alone widespread, opposition to communist rule. The exception was Poland.

In July 1979, on my first visit to Poland, I stayed for three nights in a steelworker's apartment in Nowa Huta, the town built by the communist regime around a giant new steelworks on the outskirts of Kraków. Nowa Huta was intended to be a proletarian counterweight to the Catholic, conservative and achingly beautiful former royal capital of Kraków. At the door of the apartment, I was greeted by a jolly, rotund steelworker, naked from the waist up, who made me a cup of very hot, very sweet coffee and, with the aid of sign language, explained that his wife – hand gestures delineating enormous breasts – was still at work. Then he settled down, beer in hand, to watch a Western on television. 'The flat compares favourably with many I saw in Wandsworth,' I noted, recalling the run-down concrete blocks of council flats, reeking of garbage and urine, that I had visited while doing a holiday job in the housing department of that resolutely unglamorous South London borough. This warm little apartment, with running water and inside lavatory, was certainly a great improvement on the material conditions of my host's rural forebears. But, I wondered, what more had the system to offer him, apart from a bigger television on which to watch more Westerns, or perhaps a trip to the real West?

The most surprising sight in this model socialist development was a new church, shaped like a giant Noah's ark, with a large crucifix mounted on its prow. This had been built over the past decade with financial contributions from, and volunteer labour by, the inhabitants of the new town, against the resistance of the communist authorities. Some 50,000 people – roughly a quarter of Nowa Huta's then population – had attended its inaugural dedication to 'Mary, Queen of Poland' by the then Cardinal Archbishop of Kraków, Karol Wojtyła. Wojtyła was now Pope John Paul II, and when I got there, Poland had just been electrified by his first, unprecedented pilgrimage to his native land. On the Błonia, the large meadow that reaches into the centre of Kraków, nearly two million people had hung on his every word, prayed with him, sung with him, and spoken back to him with one voice. In Warsaw's Victory Square they had chanted: 'We want God in books, in schools, we want God in government orders . . .' For the nine days of the Pope's visit, it was as if the communist state had ceased to exist. There was only Polish society. Individual men, women and children discovered for the first time that millions felt as they did and experienced the strength that comes from solidarity.

I learned more about the spirit of the Polish Pope over dinner at a small, recently opened private restaurant in the woods outside Kraków. (Much shorter menu than in the cavernous grand hotels, much better food.) Róża Woźniakowska was the daughter of Jacek Woźniakowski, an art historian from a distinguished gentry family and a close friend of Wojtyła. A chubby, bubbly young woman with short-cut blonde hair and an infectious laugh, Róża told me her story over a dish the name of which she translated as 'Nelson's bowels' – that is, tripe Nelson-style. She had grown up in a sophisticated, patriotic oasis of family and friends, sedulously detached from and contemptuous of the communist regime. In 1976, as she set off for Paris, she learned about the brutal suppression of workers' protests in the industrial towns of Radom and Ursus, and she felt that she just could not go on living in this kind of inner emigration.

After some glorious months enjoying 'the West' in Paris and Vienna, and learning German (coincidentally at the same Goethe Institute I had attended in Prien am Chiemsee), she returned to university in Kraków. The mysterious death of a fellow student prompted her to get involved in founding a Student Solidarity Committee. They organised a lecture entitled 'George Orwell: how much of *1984* is true today?' It was broken up by the police. She went to her local priest, a family friend, and he arranged that the same lecture would be delivered in his church. That was not broken up. After one protest action, she was detained and locked up with local prostitutes for forty-eight hours. 'It was very good for me,' she said. 'Do you know how they live?'

Forty years later, Róża – now known by her married name of Thun – would be a member of the European Parliament, fighting with all her strength against creeping authoritarianism in her native land and for a united, free Europe. As with south Europeans such as Barroso and Solana, the memory of her youthful experiences of dictatorship drove her passionate commitment. The memory engine.

In my journal of that visit in 1979, the abbreviation I used for newfound friends like Róża was PLO – standing for Polish liberal opposition. Back in Warsaw, I met one of its most courageous figures, the writer and activist Władysław Bartoszewski. A tall, wiry, slightly stooped man with a nose like an eagle's beak – today, you can see a very lifelike statue of him in the Baltic city of Sopot – Bartoszewski walked, ate and talked faster than anyone I have ever met. He had survived more than six months in Auschwitz, where he was prisoner number 4427, and more than six years in Stalinist prisons for resisting the next dictatorship. Now, over lunch in a restaurant in the hideous Stalinist Palace of Culture, he explained to me, at the top of his voice and with the rapid-fire rhythm of a machine gun: 'We count on the collapse of the Russian empire in the twenty-first century!'

Rising
(1980–1989)

Freedom's battle

On Tuesday 19 August 1980, I walked through the blue-grey metal gates of the Lenin Shipyard in Gdańsk and into a new chapter of central European history. The huge, sprawling shipyard on the Baltic coast, once the pride of Poland's communist regime, was now occupied by workers on strike against what was supposed to be a 'workers' and peasants' state'. Gdańsk became the co-ordination centre for a nationwide wave of strikes which ended only when the regime accepted the formation of an independent trade union, something unprecedented in the entire communist world. The new union was christened Solidarność – Solidarity – and rapidly became a movement of national liberation. Counting some ten million members at its peak, Solidarity lasted for sixteen months before being suppressed, but not eliminated, by the imposition of martial law in December 1981.

We know now that the Gdańsk shipyard strike initiated a decade of political transformation that culminated in the end of communist rule across central Europe in 1989. At a pioneering Round Table in the spring of that year, the representatives of a revived Solidarity negotiated the end of communist rule in Poland. Hungary soon followed. Then it was the turn of East Germany, where the Berlin Wall was breached on 9 November 1989, and Czechoslovakia, where Václav Havel's Velvet Revolution began eight days later. These events would lead to the end of the Cold War division between East and West which so many Europeans had accepted almost as a fact of nature.

But I knew none of this future when, aged twenty-five, I excitedly stood before the blue-grey shipyard gates, now festooned with flowers, flags and a large photograph of the Polish Pope. Enormous cranes loomed silently above us, like giant grasshoppers. In the summer heat, a young worker standing guard outside the left-hand gate was naked to the waist, except for an armband in Poland's national colours of red and white. After checking my passport and those of the Austrian and Brazilian journalists who arrived with me, he announced our nationalities while the gate opened to admit us. As he led us down the works drive to a large redbrick building, a double line of workers in blue overalls and metal-tipped boots applauded us, as if we had personally brought our countries' support. 'Brazylia! Austria! Anglia!' they shouted. This is forty years ago as I write, but I will never forget the expressions on those lined, unshaven faces, the shipyard smells, the warmth of the sun, the tension and determination. It was one of those moments when hope and history rhyme.

Loudspeakers blared out strike communiqués, patriotic music and, yes, the Beatles' 'Yellow Submarine'. Strikers young and old sat around in the sunshine, smoking and joking, but drinking only water or tea. One of the strike committee's first actions had been to ban alcohol. Great baskets of food, brought to the gate by friendly farmers, were turned into sausage and ham rolls that lay between half-emptied glasses of tea on three narrow lines of conference tables running the length of a large hall. The men and women at these tables came from more than 200 factories up and down the Baltic coast, and soon from even farther afield, for the historic innovation of this moment was the formation of an Inter-Factory Strike Committee. Each factory's name was handwritten on a sheet of folded paper perched on the table at which its delegation sat.

Everywhere I saw home-made posters, flysheets and samizdat (underground self-published) periodicals, most of them printed on primitive hand-operated duplicators – a technology closer to Gutenberg's time than to today's. The most advanced communication devices in the room were small audio-cassette recorders. Delegates from other factories recorded key moments from the Lenin yard and then played them back to their mates, sometimes over the loudspeakers of the 'works radio'.

'Proletarians of all factories, Unite!' declared a large red banner strung above the gate, adapting Karl Marx's slogan 'Proletarians of all countries, Unite!' to turn it against a communist state. A statue of Lenin sat at the front of the hall throughout the strike, his plinth serving as a useful resting place for glasses of tea and half-eaten sandwiches. But above the top table for the strike committee there now hung a crucifix. A workers' revolution under the sign of the cross! Western leftists were confused. 'How can a workers' leader be religious?' exclaimed the Spanish filmmaker Luis Buñuel. 'This is a contradiction in terms.' In the late afternoon, mass was celebrated at a makeshift altar erected just inside those gates and broadcast through the loudspeaker system. At another gate, a handwritten sign said: 'The Madonna is on strike'.

Dashing, dancing, bubbling, bouncing through it all was the skinny figure of an unemployed thirty-eight-year-old electrician with the long moustaches of a seventeenth-century Polish nobleman. His facial expressions were as vivid and rapidly changing as Charlie Chaplin's. The only time this Lech Wałęsa seemed to sit still was when he was taking communion. There is a photograph of the local priest, Father Henryk Jankowski, putting a communion wafer into his mouth, while behind the priest's head, instead of a gilded baroque altarpiece with angels and archangels, we see a battery of cameras jostling to capture what press photographers call 'the money shot'. After mass, Lech – all the strikers referred to him by his first name – would deliver his 'vespers'. Standing on a van so he could be seen above the flower-garlanded gate, he would report to the crowd outside, in his fast-talking, joking, ungrammatical but irresistible colloquial style. Lech was a laugh a minute. No one then imagined that Wałęsa would go on to be the leader of an entire nationwide movement, receive the Nobel Peace Prize in 1983 and become the first president of a free Poland in 1990.

People often quote the novelist William Faulkner's epigram: 'The past is never dead. It's not even past.' But there is one important sense in which this is profoundly untrue. The irreversible pastness of the past consists in the fact that we never can recover what it felt like to be there – even if the moment was so pivotal, so formative, that you have always remembered it. The reason you cannot recover the feeling is that you now know, and cannot unknow, what happened afterwards. Yet much of the drama in our lives comes precisely from not knowing what will happen next. Try watching a football match on digital catch-up when someone has already told you the result. It's not the same, is it? So also with a revolution, a romance, a childhood, a life.

On the Sunday before I arrived, a simple wooden cross had been placed just outside the shipyard gates, at the spot where protesting workers had been shot and killed by security forces as they spilled out onto the streets in December 1970. (The erection of a permanent monument was now, in August 1980, one of the strikers' first demands; hence the soaring three-cross monument you see there today.) To this makeshift cross someone had pinned a small piece of paper on which were written lines from Byron's poem 'Giaour', in a translation by Adam Mickiewicz, the Polish Byron, widely taught in Polish schools:

> For Freedom's battle once begun,
> Bequeath'd by bleeding sire to son,
> Though baffled oft is ever won.

But whoever wrote this message had omitted the word 'bleeding'. Here there was to be no more bloodshed.

These lines were to become my personal leitmotif. Europe, my Europe, was – and still is – about the struggle for freedom. Where the cause of Europe has marched arm in arm with that of freedom, I have been happiest; where Europe has seemed to conflict with freedom, or at least be indifferent to it, I have been most dismayed. Freedom, never perfectly achieved, entails much more than the mere absence of dictatorship. But as a first step, you do have to get rid of your dictatorship, as the Spaniards, Portuguese and Greeks had recently done.

'Poland is my Spain,' I wrote in my notebook in December 1980. 'Like G.O. and his Italian militiaman.' I was referring to a passage in *Homage to Catalonia* where George Orwell describes a brief encounter with an Italian volunteer fighting, like him, on the Republican side during the Spanish Civil War – and more generally to the way Spain was Orwell's formative political experience. This was mine. To political romanticism was added personal romance. It was at this time that I got together with the beautiful young Polish woman, Danuta, who would become my wife. So my involvement with Poland was doubly romantic. And why not? That, too, is Europe.

Yet this kind of romantic political engagement carries dangers for a writer. One is that you idealise the people whose cause you support.

Although I tried hard to follow Orwell's injunction to be most critical of your own side, I definitely missed some warning signs. Father Jankowski, for example, the priest popping the communion wafer into Wałęsa's mouth, would later turn out to be a bombastic, anti-Semitic nationalist, also accused of paedophilia.

A related danger, visible in all memoirs, is overstating the historical significance of those events in which you happen to have been involved. *The Polish Revolution* was the title I gave to the witness-history of the Solidarity movement that I finished in 1983. But was it really a revolution? Certainly it felt like one and had many of the features we find in earlier revolutions. The whole experience was like riding a raft through white-water rapids for sixteen months. Nobody knew what would happen next. There was genuine, spontaneous, mass popular action. I spent many hours in crowds that chanted, a capella, in a four-beat rhythm: 'Sol-i-*dar*-ność! Lech-Wa-*łę*-sa! dem-o-*kra*-cja!'

The third of the Gdańsk strikers' 21 Demands was for free speech and independent media, and this was a festival of free speech. The entire country flowered with posters, flysheets, cartoons and graffiti, full of pathos and humour. A prime example of this revolutionary creativity is the logo of Solidarity, with the red letters of Solidarność jumping around like the young Lech and the second vertical of the n elongated upwards to make the flagpole for a Polish flag, red against the white background. Brilliant revolutionary iconography.

Above all, these events had the quality that the political philosopher Hannah Arendt most prized in revolution. She argued that, at its best, revolution demonstrates the human capacity for beginning genuinely new things through the creative action of individual human beings. It is thus the most salient political manifestation of human freedom, refuting the dehumanising view that history is determined by automatic processes and irresistible forces. Solidarity was something genuinely new, not only a workers' revolution under the sign of the cross against a so-called workers' state, but also a coming together of social classes (intelligentsia, workers and peasants) and political forces (such as the Catholic church and the secular left) that had never before combined in this way. Ideologically, it was an unprecedented melange of socialism, Christianity, nationalism and liberalism.

'But revolutions are violent!' the revolutionary traditionalist would object. 'Revolution', said Mao Zedong, 'is not a dinner party.' Just two years before Solidarity exploded on the scene, the historian A. J. P. Taylor began a series of lectures on revolutions by saying: 'There have been violent political upheavals as long as there have been political communities.' Clearly, he saw 'violent' as a defining feature: no violence, no revolution. Thus it had been in 1789, thus again in 1917, and thus it would be in the Iranian revolution in 1979.

Yet the Polish events of 1980–81 were part of a larger, transnational attempt to reinvent revolution as a non-violent process of regime change. Solidarity's programmatic non-violence was partly born of the failures of past revolts against communist rule in the Soviet bloc: the Hungarian revolution in 1956 and the Prague Spring of 1968, both crushed by Soviet invasions, as well as what happened to Polish shipyard workers in the winter of 1970/71. They had marched onto the streets of Gdańsk, Gdynia and Szczecin, set fire to communist party committee buildings, and been gunned down by soldiers and police. ('Don't burn down Party committees,' concluded the dissident Jacek Kuroń. 'Found your own.') But this was also a link in a much longer learning chain, stretching back at least to the pioneering civil resistance of Mahatma Gandhi in British-ruled India, through the globally reported US civil rights movement in the 1960s and the largely peaceful toppling of dictatorships in Portugal, Spain and Greece.

'Taught by history,' the dissident Adam Michnik would later explain, 'we suspect that by using force to storm the existing Bastilles we shall unwittingly build new ones.' When an angry crowd threatened to lynch a policeman in the town of Otwock, Michnik stepped in, recounted his own experience of police beatings, and persuaded his audience not to take the fateful step from peaceful crowd to lynch mob. Throughout the entire sixteen months from the start of the Gdańsk strike until the declaration of martial law on 13 December 1981, nobody was killed. Looking back a quarter-century later, Bronisław Geremek would proudly assert that 'Solidarność was European history's greatest movement for change that did not resort to violence'.

Solidarity thus contributed to the worldwide development of a vocabulary of peaceful protest that would subsequently be seen in the toppling of the Marcos dictatorship in the Philippines in 1986, which gave us the term 'people power', and the mass mobilisation to unseat General Pinochet through a plebiscite in Chile in 1988. With the velvet revolutions of 1989 in central Europe, this became established almost as a new default model of revolution, non-violent and negotiated, in stark contrast to the violent model of 1789. Many of the same elements could be observed in Slovakia in the late 1990s, in the largely peaceful toppling of Slobodan Milošević in Serbia in 2000, the Orange Revolution in Ukraine in 2004 and, outside Europe, in the green movement in Iran, the Arab Spring of 2011 and popular protests in Myanmar. Some of these movements succeeded, others failed. Some were violently crushed, others themselves turned to violence. All contributed to a growing repository of experience with non-violent people power.

In August 2020, forty years almost to the day after the strikes that gave birth to Solidarity, mass peaceful protests erupted against an outrageously stolen election in Belarus. Since Belarus was the most Soviet of post-Soviet states, the echoes of 1980 were especially strong. The country still had vast, Soviet-style state-owned factories, like the Lenin shipyard, employing thousands of workers. Some of these now went on strike. When I heard that in the city of Hrodna – part of Poland until the Second World War and now just twenty kilometres from the Polish border – the workers in twenty-two state enterprises were trying to found an Inter-Factory Strike Committee, it felt like being transported back four decades. Even the colours were the same as in Poland, for protesters revived the red-and-white flag of the short-lived 1918 Belarusian National Republic.

In Belarus, forty years on, we saw again the extraordinary creativity that can be generated by a peacefully protesting crowd. Here too was that Pentecostal experience of long-silenced men and women seizing the chance to speak freely for the first time. 'People are tired of lies, of not having freedom of speech,' said Aleksandr, a forty-one-year-old worker at a state-run electricity facility. 'We just want to live in a civilised society with the rule of law.' 'Everything has changed,' said Lesya, a twenty-four-year-old anaesthetist. 'A new collective spirit has woken and that spirit can never be put back in the bottle. They stole our votes, but not our spirit.'

In music, too, we can trace the transnational relay. In 1968, the Catalan singer Lluís Llach wrote a song called 'L'Estaca' (the stake), with a haunting refrain insisting that 'the stake to which we are all tied' would *tomba, tomba, tomba* (fall, fall, fall). It became an unofficial anthem of anti-fascist resistance in Spain during the last years of General Franco's rule. 'L'Estaca' made such an impression on the Polish singer Jacek Kaczmarski that in 1978 he wrote a Polish version of it called 'Mury' (walls), set to the same tune. This became an unofficial Polish opposition anthem in the Solidarity years. Now, in 2020, the baton was handed on to a Belarusian version of 'Mury', taken from the anti-communist Polish version, itself adapted from the anti-fascist Spanish one.

Yet each new movement adds something to the lexicon of peaceful protest. In Belarus, it was the leading role of women. Not only was the opposition candidate for president a woman, Sviatlana Tsikhanouskaya. Not only was she supported by two other women, Maria Kalesnikava and Veronica Tsepkalo, making a female trio for democracy. Sometimes entire protest marches consisted of women, many of them dressed in white. That did not stop President Alexander Lukashenko's masked security forces from arresting them. But then brave women started pulling off the goons' black balaclavas, whereupon the faces of baffled bullies were quickly photographed on a protester's smartphone. In the short term, the 'women in white' were defeated. So was Solidarity at the end of 1981. As Byron knew, freedom's battle is 'baffled oft'. That is especially true if you remain resolutely peaceful, while the power-holders are prepared to use force. But by remaining non-violent, you get to a better place in the end. As Gandhi taught, and Michnik understood, the means you use determine the end at which you will arrive.

This was the case with Poland in the 1980s. Poles like to say that Solidarity punched the first hole in the Berlin Wall. Yet it needed many other major changes, above all the arrival of a new leader in the Kremlin, before the Wall would fall. The emergence of Solidarity was a necessary but by no means a sufficient condition for the negotiated revolutions of 1989. At the end of 1981, Solidarity looked like just another in a long line of defeated movements, sharing the fate of East German protesters in 1953, Hungarians in 1956, and Czechs and Slovaks in 1968.

After General Wojciech Jaruzelski declared martial law on 13

December 1981, there were tanks in the snow-covered streets. Workers were killed as the army broke up an occupation strike in a coal mine. Many of my friends were behind barbed wire in internment camps. At one of those camps, Władysław Bartoszewski, the survivor of Auschwitz and Stalinist prisons, was informally declared the prisoners' honorary 'commandant', while Bronisław Geremek, the survivor of the Warsaw ghetto, worked on an essay about the concept of Europe in the writings of the fifteenth-century Polish theologian Jakub of Paradyż. Other friends were in hiding, active in 'underground' Solidarity, or in exile. Many Poles had lost hope. Opinion polls suggested that close to half the population initially supported the imposition of martial law. The eight-year-old daughter of one of my closest friends showed me her hand-coloured story about 'The Land of the Vampires'. In this fabulous country, the king beat up his subjects, there was an unbridgeable gulf between the people and 'the power', barter was the main form of trade and people sold their hearts for US dollars.

This defeat could be seen as a victory only in the spirit of a wonderful saying by the man who led Poland to independence at the end of the First World War, Marshal Józef Piłsudski: 'To be defeated and not give in, that is victory; to be victorious and rest on your laurels, that is defeat.' After sixteen months of freedom, Poland had become a different country. What one worker described to me as 'a revolution of the soul' had transformed popular consciousness. This society could not be 'normalised' the way Hungary had been after 1956 or Czechoslovakia after 1968. In June 1983, I followed the Polish Pope on another pilgrimage to his native land. In Warsaw, vast crowds greeted him, waving Solidarity banners and chanting: 'Free speech! Democracy! Lech Wałęsa!' I wrote the chants down in my notebook, along with a new one: 'Am-nes-ti-a!' (amnesty for political prisoners). 'Come with us,' the Solidarity marchers chanted at hesitant onlookers. 'Today they won't beat you.'

Before the soaring red-brick fortress walls of the Jasna Góra monastery in Częstochowa, John Paul II used all his dramatic skills – the actor John Gielgud called his theatrical delivery 'perfect' – to reach the tense and even desperate crowd. 'I'm coming closer to you,' he said, striding down the distant white steps towards them. 'Chair for the Pope, chair for the Pope!' they chanted back. Then, speaking directly to the Black

Madonna of Częstochowa, he asked her 'to help us persevere in hope'.
(What a world away from the West German pop song 'Black Madonna'.)

'Thank-you, thank-you, thank-you!' cried the people.

But after the Pope left for Rome, one protester told me: 'That was our last day of freedom.'

That autumn, I talked in Warsaw to one of John Paul II's most outspoken disciples, Father Jerzy Popiełuszko, who had become something like the Solidarity chaplain of the Huta Warszawa steelworks. 'The kingdom of Satan must fall,' he told me. 'I am doing right, I have committed no crime, so what have I to fear?' Less than twelve months later, he was dead, murdered by the secret police. The year was, after all, 1984.

1984

It was a bright, warm day in 1984 and a friend of mine had just been air-brushed out of a photograph on the front page of the Soviet Communist Party newspaper, *Pravda*. There we all were, in grainy black-and-white, a gaggle of British journalists, notebooks dutifully raised, peering down a long wooden table in the Kremlin at which the Soviet leader Konstantin Chernenko sat, stiff as a Madame Tussauds waxwork, opposite the British Foreign Secretary, Geoffrey Howe. But Mark Wood, my friend from East Berlin days and now the Reuters correspondent in Moscow, had simply disappeared. Where he had stood, there was just a painted-in piece of wall panelling.

I would love to record that this was because Mark had been air-brushed out for political reasons, like Leon Trotsky in early photographs of the Russian Revolution. Almost certainly it was just because he made the picture look untidy. Mark tells me this happened to him more than once. In this real-life 1984, people were airbrushed out of photographs in Soviet papers as routinely as Orwell's Winston Smith would consign unpersons to the memory hole during his day's work in the Records department of the Ministry of Truth – a satirical invention itself partly inspired by *Pravda*. (The word means 'truth'.)

Yet some important examples of the systematic falsification of history remained. While I was in Moscow, Stalin's foreign minister Vyacheslav Molotov was readmitted into the Communist Party. Molotov had signed, together with Hitler's foreign minister, Joachim von Ribbentrop, the Nazi–Soviet Non-Aggression Pact in 1939, with its secret protocol partitioning Poland between Nazi Germany and the Soviet Union. In 1984, Soviet historians were still not allowed to admit the existence of this protocol. That cynical partition did not happen. It had never happened. For 'who controls the past controls the future; who controls the present controls the past'.

This was not the only aspect of Orwell's *Nineteen Eighty-Four* that central and east Europeans continued to find prescient in 1984. There was also the greyness and shabbiness, the smell of boiled cabbage on the stairs of apartment blocks and the constant shortages of basic goods, forcing people to turn to the black market. Or as Orwell called it, the 'free' market:

> Sometimes it was buttons, sometimes it was darning wool, sometimes it was shoelaces; at present it was razor blades. You could only get hold of them, if at all, by scrounging more or less furtively on the 'free' market.

'How did he know?' the exiled Russian poet Natalya Gorbanevskaya asked me. How could an English author possibly anticipate what life would be like in Moscow, Bratislava or Sofia in the 1980s? The surprising answer is that much of this detail was drawn from the drab, impoverished, food-rationed reality of post-war London in 1948, the date Orwell flipped to make 1984.

Orwell's three superpower blocs, Oceania, Eurasia and Eastasia, were in a state of permanent war, although the alignments between them shifted from day to day, without any acknowledgement in the relentless propaganda from the Ministry of Truth. 'Officially the change of partners had never happened. Oceania was at war with Eurasia: therefore Oceania has always been at war with Eurasia.' Orwell was obviously thinking of the overnight change in both Soviet and Nazi propaganda after the Molotov–Ribbentrop pact, and the subsequent invasion and occupation of Poland from both sides in September 1939. On my study wall hangs the great David Low cartoon: Adolf Hitler and Joseph Stalin greet each other with raised hats and courtly bows, over the body of a dead Pole. Hitler: 'The scum of the earth, I believe?' Stalin: 'The bloody assassin of the workers, I presume?'

Now, in the calendar 1984, Eastasia featured only at the margins, but Oceania and Eurasia were going at it hammer and tongs. In what some called the Second Cold War, the risk of a nuclear conflagration again seemed almost as real as it had at the time of the Cuban Missile Crisis in 1962. Looking back through my journals some years later, I was shocked to see my entry on the last day of 1980. 'There will be a nuclear war in the next decade,' I wrote. And then, as if that were not emphatic enough, I reformulated the thought in capital letters: 'WE WILL SEE A NUCLEAR WAR IN THIS DECADE.'

The American writer Jonathan Schell would soon publish a book called *The Fate of the Earth*, arguing that we faced the total extinction of humankind. Informed by such fears, there was a vast mobilisation of peace movements across western Europe against NATO's deployment of medium-range cruise missiles to counter the Soviet deployment of SS-20s. Bicycle mudguard stickers declared: 'It is five minutes to midnight.' West German Chancellor Helmut Kohl fought a hard political battle to get the deployment through the Bundestag in November 1983, thus building a stock of credit in Washington that he could draw on when the unexpected opportunity for German unification presented itself just six years later.

The peace movement was the great political cause for many west Europeans of my generation. It was not mine. Yet reviewing all the evidence scholars have now unearthed, we can see that there was a real danger of nuclear war breaking out through miscalculation. Shortly after midnight on 26 September 1983, a Soviet nuclear missile response to a false alarm was avoided only when the duty commander, Lieutenant-Colonel Stanislav Petrov, followed his instinct and did not confirm to the Soviet high command that this was an American nuclear attack. The British intelligence official turned historian Gordon Barrass records the sequel:

> Months later, Soviet investigators determined that bursts of sunlight reflecting off clouds above Montana had caused a faulty satellite computer to report the missile launches. This incident remained secret for another 15 years.

NATO's so-called Able Archer exercise in November 1983, practising a deliberate escalation to the use of nuclear weapons to repel a conventional attack by the Red Army, was greeted with genuine alarm in Moscow. The chief of the Soviet general staff went to his command bunker deep under Moscow. A retrospective report by the US Foreign Intelligence Advisory Board concluded that 'we may inadvertently have placed our relations with the Soviet Union on a hair trigger'. The then head of KGB foreign intelligence, Vladimir Kryuchkov, whom I met in Moscow years later, would confirm that this was 'the most alarming time'.

With hindsight, we know that all this changed after Mikhail Gorbachev came to power in March 1985. With hindsight, it may even appear that the Soviet Union was already on its last legs. All my friend Mark Wood and I could see at the time, as we stood in that room in the Kremlin in July 1984, was that the Soviet leader sitting opposite Geoffrey Howe was on his last legs. According to a report by Howe's interpreter, Konstantin Chernenko constantly struggled for breath. 'An air of abstraction and bewilderment' clung to him. Chernenko's reading of his prepared text was 'disastrously bad' and in subsequent exchanges he showed an 'apparent lack of conviction and even, at times, of comprehension'.

No better future was yet apparent to most people in Russia or the rest of the Soviet bloc. Back in 1970, the Russian dissident Andrei Amalrik had published a book called *Will the Soviet Union Survive until 1984?* He was imprisoned for five years and then forced into exile, where he died in a car accident. Now, in 1984, the KGB officers interrogating another dissident, Anatoly (subsequently Natan) Sharansky, jeered at him: 'Amalrik is dead and the KGB is still here!' The Russian satirist Alexander Zinoviev proclaimed the emergence of a new kind of human being: Homo Sovieticus.

In Czechoslovakia, Orwell was compounded by a touch of Kafka. On a chilly Tuesday in January 1984, I visited the Olšany cemetery in Prague, just across the road from the Jewish graveyard where Franz Kafka lies. I was looking for the grave of a woman called Marie Jedličková. Quite often, people would light candles and leave flowers on this grave, with messages such as 'We remember'. These would rapidly be cleared away by 'persons unknown'. Who was Marie Jedličková? No one could tell me. All those mourners knew was that a man called Jan Palach had previously been buried in this place.

Palach was a Czech student who, in 1969, at the age of twenty, set fire to himself on Wenceslas Square in protest against the Soviet invasion and occupation of his country. He subsequently died of his wounds. His grave had become a site of pilgrimage. So one night the authorities removed his body, had it cremated and delivered his ashes in an urn to his mother in her country town. Then they buried an old woman from a care home, Marie Jedličková, in his place in the Prague cemetery. But those who wished to honour Jan Palach would not be cheated, so they placed their tokens of remembrance on the grave of Marie J. What was it the exiled Czech novelist Milan Kundera had recently written in his *Book of Laughter and Forgetting*? 'The struggle of man against power is the struggle of memory against forgetting.'

Having been banned from entering East Germany after publishing (in German) a critical book about that Orwellian state, I was allowed back in October 1984, to admire its thirty-fifth anniversary celebrations. A frontier guard at Checkpoint Charlie, clearly well briefed, told me: 'You were here for the thirtieth anniversary.' I asked if he saw any changes. Yes, he said, particularly in the economy. 'Our growth rate is certainly as good as that of most industrial nations.' At the anniversary ceremonies, the party leader Erich Honecker trumpeted the fact that the German Democratic Republic was now diplomatically recognised by 132 countries (most recently, the Ivory Coast) and declared that 'no one will be able to turn back the wheel of history on German soil'. Three cheers greeted Moscow's high representative, foreign minister Andrei Gromyko, identified in my notebook as Grim-Grom. When I visited my friend Werner Krätschell in his vicarage in Pankow, five plain-clothes men appeared outside in a green Lada car. The Stasi state seemed quite secure.

Still more Orwellian, and certainly more brutal, was the regime of Nicolae Ceaușescu in Romania. The author Herta Müller, who would subsequently win the Nobel Prize in Literature, was arrested just for buying nuts at an 'exorbitant' price at a 'private market' in Timișoara. During her incarceration, she met people locked up for stealing candles. (The electricity was routinely turned off for hours on end.) She is certain the Securitate, the secret police, arranged a bicycle accident for her. Starting in 1983, every typewriter in the country had to be registered. Subsequent research suggests that roughly one in every thirty adults was employed by the Securitate. Of half a million political prisoners in the history of communist-ruled Romania, some 100,000 died in prison.

Poland was different, but there too, it was a dark time. Danuta and I felt acutely the contrast between our life in a peaceful, prosperous Oxford and that of our Polish friends. Most of them were in exile, in prison, or working underground. In Warsaw, I paid a conspiratorial visit to Jan Lityński, a small, intense activist from the Polish class of 1968, who was hiding in an anonymous apartment, under another name and with forged identity papers, for all the world like a Polish resistance fighter in the Second World War. As we talked, a shortwave receiver crackled on the police wavelengths. 'It was a horrible time, really insufferable,' recalls Helena Łuczywo, who kept the underground weekly of the Mazowia region of Solidarity alive throughout the 1980s.

I carried in messages from exile groups, which I wrote in tiny pencil letters on the back of travellers' cheques, and smuggled bundles of low-denomination US dollar bills from foundations and NGOs to support underground publishing and Solidarity. When I met the underground activist Barbara Labuda on a designated park bench in Wrocław, she looked carefully all around us and then produced from her pocket a cig-arette paper on which she had written a few important requests. After I had noted them down, in suitably cryptic pencil minuscule, she popped the paper into her mouth, briefly chewed, and then swallowed it. This is the only time I have seen someone actually eat their words. Later, after freedom's battle seemed won, Barbara became a politician and power-ful advocate for women's rights.

Then there was the murder of that Solidarity priest, Jerzy Popiełuszko. In the autumn of 1984, he was kidnapped by three secret policemen, thrown into the boot of a car, repeatedly taken out and beaten, and then, weighed down by a bag of stones, hurled into a reservoir to drown. His funeral, at his own church, was a supremely Polish blending of the religious, patriotic and political, irresistibly recalling the country's nineteenth-century image of itself as the 'Christ among nations'. To the side of the altar, I noticed an oil painting showed Popiełuszko as St George (Jerzy in Polish) slaying a red dragon. Lech Wałęsa declared in his eulogy that 'Solidarity lives, because you gave your life for it.' An engineer from the Huta Warszawa steelworks gestured to the church bells ringing above his head and spoke directly to his martyred chaplain, using an intimate form of his first name: 'Jurek! Do you hear how the bells of freedom ring?'

Yet freedom still seemed a remote prospect. Even in Hungary, the 'merriest barracks in the block' with the most tolerant and reform-minded communist regime, the dissident author György Konrád wrote that 'the Soviet empire, despite all of its internal difficulties, is in good shape, not headed towards collapse'. The most hopeful scenario I could come up with was an 'Ottomanisation' of the Soviet empire. As in the last period of the decaying Ottoman Empire, the more peripheral territories might gradually, over decades, gain more autonomy, as the grip of the imperial centre weakened. Emancipation through decay. But many of my friends found this altogether too optimistic. They referred me instead to this quintessential Soviet bloc joke:

> Two acquaintances meet on the street.
> 'How are you?'
> 'Thanks. Better than tomorrow.'

68ers and post-68ers

Dark shirt unbuttoned, thinning hair still long over the neck, stubble accentuating an ample jowl, the old 68er lifts a glass of good red wine above the white tablecloth. '*Tu*', he says, or '*Du*', '*Ty*' or '*Te*' – always, whatever the language, the more informal second person form of 'you'. An ironic smile plays across his face when we talk about his revolutionary views back in the day. The day was, after all, more than fifty years ago, and his views are so very different now. Except perhaps, on sex, which he still embraces – at least in principle – as warmly as the good red wine. Lots of it.

I could be in Paris, Berlin, Milan, Lisbon, Prague, Sarajevo – or, for that matter, in Berkeley, Cape Town, Sydney or Rio de Janeiro. He might be a lawyer, an academic, a journalist, a publisher, a schoolteacher, a politician, an NGO activist or an artist. Before we even pull our dark wooden chairs up to the bistro table, I have noted the telltale signs.

The 68ers – Soixante-huitards, Achtundsechziger, Sesantottini – are the most distinctive and influential generation of Europeans after the 39ers. As with the 39ers, there is a core group of men and women defined by participation in life-shaping events, but they are located within a broader demographic cohort. The core group of 39ers consisted of people like my father and Bronisław Geremek who had direct personal experience of the Second World War, with its violent preludes and aftermath. For really we should talk of a long 1939, stretching from the early 1930s all the way to the late 1940s. But there was also a wider cohort, ranging from the elderly parents of those who died at the front to the young Helmut Kohl, who, although only fifteen in 1945 – he famously called this 'the mercy of a late birth' – nonetheless lost his older brother in that war and saw at first hand the physical and moral devastation of his homeland. Kohl talked often – very often – about how it had formed his commitment to building a better Europe.

The core group of 68ers comprises those who participated in the long 1968, lasting from the early 1960s to the late 1970s, with its hallucinogenic kaleidoscope of political, cultural, social and environmental radicalism. 'Be realistic, demand the impossible!' 'It is forbidden to forbid!' 'Beneath the pavement, the beach!' A rainbow spectrum ranged from the 'Provos' demonstrating at the marriage of Princess Beatrix of the Netherlands to the ideological contortions of Portuguese Maoists, from the student protests in Warsaw in March 1968 through *les événements* in Paris in May 1968 to the Prague Spring, from Commune 1 in West Berlin to the Yellow Submarine Commune in Leningrad (today St Petersburg), from the nude revelling of the Woodstock festival in New York State to Britain's Paedophile Information Exchange, from anti-war conscientious objectors to the bloody terrorism of the Baader–Meinhof gang in the 'German autumn' and the Red Brigades in Italy's *anni di piombo* (years of lead). A canvas of these years would resemble nothing so much as Breughel's painting of Dutch proverbs, every square centimetre crammed with strange actions: two naked arses stick out of a hole in a wooden wall ('they shit from the same hole'), two men pinch each other's noses ('to lead each other by the nose'), a man runs across the landscape with flames coming out of his backside ('he who eats fire, craps sparks').

The force behind it all was a new and numerous generation, the baby boomers, erupting on the public stage, making their voices, tastes, desires and ideals heard, in a sweeping, anti-authoritarian *prise de parole*. The young were seizing the microphone. 'We want the world and we want it now,' sang Jim Morrison of the rock band the Doors. Down with the old men in suits and ties! In the United States there was a group called the Youth International Party, and wherever in Europe those old men in suits turned, there seemed to be a youth international party.

The French journalist Bernard Guetta captures the moment. As a seventeen-year-old schoolboy he got caught up in a police round-up of students – many of them, he notes, still wearing ties – who were protesting in the courtyard of the Sorbonne on 3 May 1968. When the police van stopped at a red light at the corner of rue Gay-Lussac, one of the students suddenly cried *'On y va!'* ('Let's go!') and they all jumped out of the van and ran away, laughing out loud, leaving the startled Guetta sitting alone, exchanging embarrassed glances with two equally gobsmacked policemen. At that red light, he writes, you saw the gulf between two generations: the old, exhausted by war, occupation and post-war recovery, with nothing more to offer, and the new:

> the baby boomers, accustomed to never being resisted, raised as little redeeming gods, self-assured, joyous, insolent, iconoclastic and determined to take the world in hand, tear off those ties, defy anyone and replay the revolutions of yesteryear, 1789, 1848, the Resistance, to march towards new horizons with a devastating burst of laughter.

As usual, the demographers' statistical cohorts (baby boomers, generation X, millennials) do not map neatly onto the generations of historical experience. Several leading 68ers were actually born during the Second World War – Rudi Dutschke, for example, a key figure in West Germany's 1968 protests, was born in 1940. Guetta, born in 1951, belonged to one of the youngest year groups actively to participate in the calendar 1968. That leaves the rest of us boomers, the majority, born during a post-war birth bulge that lasted until about 1965. From the start, there were also millions of non-68ers and anti-68ers. The anti-68ers would become more numerous and vocal as the decades passed. Indeed, 'anti-68' is one way of summarising a good part of today's right-wing populist agenda in many western democracies. Yet that very fact is testimony to the 68ers' transformative impact.

Born in 1955, I was a post-68er. In the London of my teenage years, I caught only the spliff end of hippiedom. By the time I went to live in West Berlin in 1978, '68' was fading graffiti on the walls of the Free University and communard flatmates having long, jargon-clotted conversations about their sexuality and politics. I never got to meet Rudi Dutschke but I did attend his funeral in January 1980, standing in a large crowd outside St Anne's church in the leafy Dahlem suburb of West Berlin. 'The burial of the student left,' my diary records. 'Unexpectedly moving. Very, very cold.' (I cannot for the life of me remember why I was so moved but I can remember exactly how cold it was. Speak, memory – but don't give me such trivia.) That funeral was an ending but also a beginning. After the Breughelesque extravagances of the long 1968 had worked themselves out, those who had not irrevocably become terrorists or junkies turned to making the rest of their lives in more conventional ways.

I vividly remember a conversation with a fine journalist on the *Süddeutsche Zeitung* who told me that in the early 1970s he had been within a centimetre of becoming a terrorist. In 1973, members of a revolutionary group styling itself Putzgruppe (roughly Clean-up Group) were photographed assaulting a policeman in Frankfurt. One of the street fighters, Hans-Joachim Klein, would subsequently participate in a terrorist attack in Vienna which killed three people. Another was called Joschka Fischer. Just ten years later, in 1983, Fischer became a member of the West German parliament for a new political party, the Greens. By 1999, he was Germany's foreign minister, arguing that precisely because of its own heavy historical responsibility for the Holocaust – a great theme of German 68ers – Bundeswehr troops should join the NATO intervention to prevent another genocide in Serbian-controlled Kosovo. From kicking the policeman on the street to kicking the dictator out of Kosovo.

By 1988, the sociologist Jürgen Habermas, a post-39er who was himself a powerful intellectual influence on this generation, could announce that what Dutschke famously called the 'long march through the institutions' had even reached the Christian Democrats. Sixty-eight, he argued, had led to a deep liberalisation of West German society. In the 1990s and the 2000s, even into the 2010s, 68ers and post-68ers occupied the commanding heights of most European societies. They were heads of government (Lionel Jospin, Gerhard Schröder, Massimo D'Alema), interior ministers (Jack Straw, Otto Schily), judges, top civil servants, university presidents, chief editors, publishers and novelists.

This predominance was not merely a biological inevitability: the generation of the boomers moving through the decades like a goat passing down the digestive tract of a python. It was a distinct social and cultural phenomenon. Only in the late 2010s did a new generation, born after 1989 and, like Guetta's French boomers, the self-confident children of two decades of relative peace, prosperity and optimism, start knocking the old 68ers off their perches, berating them for sexism, offensive speech, environmentally heedless capitalism and other sins. The 68ers were the old men now.

Writing to the philosopher Karl Jaspers in June 1968, Hannah Arendt speculated that 'children in the next century will learn about the year 1968 the way we learned about 1848'. Arendt would probably be shocked to discover how little most European children now learn about anything that happened in the twentieth century, but her comparison with 1848 is illuminating. The historian Lewis Namier described what happened in 1848 as a 'revolution of the intellectuals'; so, to a significant degree, was 1968. As in 1848, popular protest erupted in many European countries in quick succession.

To the extent that something big happened simultaneously in 1968 in Paris and Prague, West Berlin and Warsaw, with a leading role being played by the boomer generation, this was the first major shared European moment since the Iron Curtain divided the continent after 1945. Yet politically, the pan-European quality of 1968 was superficial. Tony Judt, the author of *Postwar,* was himself a 68er, born in 1948 and in his formative years a francophone leftist who participated in protests in Paris and sleepy Cambridge. Near the tragically early end of his life, Tony reflected: 'What does it tell us of the delusions of May 1968 that I cannot recall a single allusion to the Prague Spring, much less the Polish student uprising, in all our earnest radical debates?' Students in Warsaw and Prague took only a little more notice of what was happening in Paris.

When Rudi Dutschke did go to seek comrades in Prague, he found himself in a political dialogue of the deaf. Adam Michnik had similar difficulties when he came to Paris a few years later. French and German 68ers spoke a language of revolutionary Marxism that for Poles, Czechs and Slovaks was the discredited newspeak of the regimes they were rebelling against. So the political goals of 68 were quite different, even conflicting, in east and west. One thing, however, both sides had in common: if the goal was to change their political system, they failed. From the perspective of a believer in liberal democracy, that failure was regrettable in Prague and Warsaw but a blessing in Paris, Rome and West Berlin.

Looking back forty years later, Daniel Cohn-Bendit, who as 'Dany the Red' had been a totemic figure of 1968 in both France and Germany, summed it up: 'We have won culturally and socially while, fortunately, losing politically.' Although the cultural and social transformation did not change the system on either side of the Iron Curtain, it would have profound political consequences. The norms and attitudes with which most young Europeans grew up in the late twentieth and early twenty-first centuries were those established by the 68ers and post-68ers.

Painting with a broad brush, one could say that these attitudes were anti-imperialist, anti-fascist, anti-war, internationalist, educationalist, environmentalist, agnostic if not atheist, sexually liberated and socially liberal. In the 1950s and 1960s, several west European countries still possessed centuries-old overseas empires and fought colonial wars to hang on to them. Some of those territories, such as French possessions in the Maghreb, were considered an integral part of the European homeland. But by the mid 1970s, overseas decolonisation was largely complete. In Portugal, the struggle to end its futile colonial wars in Angola and Mozambique kick-started the transition to democracy. After that, only a scattering of territories such as Britain's Hong Kong and France's Martinique remained. Europe could now, with only modest cognitive dissonance, embrace a pleasing image of itself as anti-imperialist.

Opposing and eventually casting off the late fascist or post-fascist dictatorships in Greece, Portugal and Spain, the Europe of the 68ers was not merely anti-fascist. In Germany especially, it made a major point of facing up to the fascist past that an older generation of Germans had swept under the carpet. ('How comforting it is, once or twice a year,/ To get together and forget the old times', James Fenton wrote in 'A German Requiem', a poem that grew out of our shared time in Berlin). Again, this was a major shift. The act of oblivion after war or revolution, a practice of deliberate forgetting, had been a European norm for centuries. Churchill had called for a 'blessed act of oblivion' after 1945. Now, in the 1960s and 70s, a new norm was established: never forget! The difficult past must be documented, examined, psychologically, morally and politically 'worked through', in a process of private and public acknowledgement.

This new Europe, in another sharp contrast to the old, was anti-war. The original historical impulse for this shift was given by the horrors of Europe's second Thirty Years' War, ending in the hell of 1945, yet west European countries went on fighting colonial wars for thirty years afterwards. The immediate catalyst for anti-war protest in the 1960s was Vietnam – which had been a French war before it became an American one. The anti-imperialist and anti-war impulses were thus closely connected. Opposition to the Vietnam War was a cause for 68ers all across western Europe. Several of my West Berlin acquaintances had originally moved there to avoid compulsory military service in the West German army. (West Berliners were exempt due to the city's special four-power status.) The 68ers thus both reflected and accelerated an existing trend. As the historian Michael Howard wrote: 'Death was no longer seen as part of the social contract.'

Anti-imperialist, anti-fascist and anti-war, the 68ers were also internationalist. The salience of the Vietnam War was itself a backhanded tribute to the soft power of the United States, whose anti-war and civil rights movements had huge influence across the continent. Martin Luther King had more hold on the imagination of young Germans than Martin Luther. Students in Frankfurt and Amsterdam looked to the American university protests at Columbia and Berkeley more than they did to those of Warsaw or Prague. But there were many other influences. While still at school, I acquired a copy of Chairman Mao's *Little Red Book*. Above the generous double bed in my West Berlin apartment hung a large poster saying, in blood red letters on black paper, 'Death to the Shah!' (The previous occupants had been refugees from Iran.) Many students sported posters of Che Guevara on their bedsit walls. Others took the hippie trail to India and Afghanistan. These sallies into a wider world, both as travellers and as fellow-travellers, may have been superficial and – in their fascination with revolutionary violence in places safely faraway – morally frivolous. Yet their legacy included a broader internationalism. An early interest in what was then called the Third World sometimes translated into a lifetime's work for humanitarian charities and international development aid. There, too, you find the old 68ers.

Often being the first in their families to go to university, following a major expansion of higher education in the 1950s and 60s, the 68ers were what one might call educationalist. Many of them went on to become schoolteachers or academics. They thought educational opportunity, up to and including higher education, should be extended to an even wider tranche of society. Education, insisted the liberal thinker Ralf

Dahrendorf, was a civil right. Only many years later, during the populist wave of the 2010s, did we realise that this liberal egalitarian project had unintentionally created a new social divide: between the half of society that had gone to university and the half that had not.

There was also a distinct, though not predominant, environmentalist tendency. One of the channels into which the long 1968 ultimately flowed was Green movements and parties. Environmental activism was virtually unknown at the beginning of the 1960s but by the 1980s was a feature of most European societies, East and West. Maria Damanaki, for example, the student radio announcer from the occupation of the Athens Polytechnic, subsequently devoted much of her time to the cause of conserving the oceans and marine life. In a notebook from October 1984, I record an internal discussion of the West German Greens' parliamentary group. Today should be a day of symbolic renunciation of meat, they said. Green MPs should in principle not fly inside Germany. They could take the train instead. 'Here we are protesting against the new western runway at Frankfurt airport and then we fly from it!' Through the scribbled lines, I can hear my younger self laughing at them. Yet we might not be facing a climate emergency today if we had done what the Greens suggested nearly forty years ago. When in 2016 a conservative nationalist Polish foreign minister denounced a world of 'cyclists and vegetarians, who only want renewable energy' it was probably a 68er German schoolteacher he had in mind.

Typically, the 68ers were not practising Christians. Many were atheist or agnostic, although there was also a new interest in other religions, such as Buddhism. One cannot overstate the change this marks for the West in general and Europe in particular. Many parts of Europe had been Christian since the late Roman empire and most of Europe for close to a millennium. (Lithuania was a pagan hold-out until the fourteenth century, much to the delight of the poet Czesław Miłosz.) As Geremek argued, the mediaeval idea of Europe was inseparable from that of Christendom. The founding fathers of the European Union did not hesitate to evoke the values of Christian civilisation. In his book *Dominion*, the author Tom Holland goes even further. He writes of Christianity as 'the most influential framework for making sense of human existence that has ever existed' and of 'the collapse of a 1,900-year-old world order'. After 1968, much of western Europe became post-Christian.

The loosening of the constraints of organised Christianity hastened both sexual liberation and social liberalism. In the very year of student revolt, the papal encyclical Humanae Vitae reasserted the Catholic church's traditional teaching that sex should take place only between married couples and with the divine purpose of procreation. The 68ers, by contrast, insisted that men and women should be free to seek sexual pleasure with whatever partners they chose. This freedom was made possible without the traditional consequences because the contraceptive pill was now widely available to women. So young Europeans could have more sex but fewer children – which is exactly what they did.

In 1972, the British author Alex Comfort published a book that would rapidly become a bestseller, *The Joy of Sex*. The title riffed off a popular American cookbook, *The Joy of Cooking*, and was similarly organised, with sections titled 'Ingredients', 'Appetisers', 'Main Courses' and 'Sauces and Pickles'. It is important to say that the joy was probably not equally distributed between the sexes. If a young European woman of today were time-machined back into a commune in West Berlin or Frankfurt in 1968, she would be shocked by male behaviour that she would regard as sexist or worse. One of the slogans from this time was: 'He who sleeps with the same woman twice already belongs to the Establishment.' Patrick Viveret, a student Trotskyist at Nanterre in 1968, recalls: 'I was struck by the number of men who used revolutionary ideology to persuade young women to have sex with them, saying that if they refused it was because of their petty bourgeois mentality.' The academic Jean Seaton, a student in the late 1960s, says women of her generation should have a T-shirt emblazoned with 'We Survived the Groping Years'. And when the #MeToo movement erupted in the late 2010s, it was also calling out the sexual mores of old 68er men who had not realised that, well, the times they were a-changin'.

Yet 1968 also led to what was called the Women's Liberation movement or 'second wave feminism'. The first wave had been focused on women's suffrage. Women's right to vote, which we now regard as an elementary component of equal political liberty and our shared European values, was, incredible as this now seems, only conceded for federal elections in Switzerland – that motherland of democracy – after a referendum in 1971. (Crypto-feudal Liechtenstein held out until 1984.) This second wave of feminism moved on to women's rights and opportunities in other areas, from the workplace to the home, from divorce – which Spain only legalised in 1981 – to a woman's right to choose whether, when and how to have children. No one could claim that its victory was complete, but the transformation in the position of women in most European societies from the 1950s to the 2010s was enormous – and enormously for the better. This was accompanied by other big steps of social liberalisation. Starting with the legalisation of homosexuality, it moved towards full recognition of the identities we know today by the acronym LGBTQ+. And if people could freely choose their sexual partners and orientation, so could they choose other aspects of their lifestyle.

There were still many families, communities and even whole countries that presented exceptions to these generalisations. It's hard to separate out the specific impact of the 68ers from broader forces of social and cultural change. By the early 2020s, these values and attitudes were being fiercely challenged in countries such as Poland and Hungary – not to mention the United States. Nonetheless, this much is clear: what was the European 'normal' for most European teenagers in 2015 would have been completely unrecognisable to a European teenager in 1955. This new normal was shaped by a set of intersecting norms that emerged across the long 1968 and was consolidated by the subsequent ascendancy of post-68er boomers like me. So it was a revolution after all; just not the kind of revolution that the students on the Paris barricades expected, and one that took half a lifetime to prevail.

Angelo Gotti

'Have you had any Gastarbeiter in Westen?'

'Oh yes, there's Angelo Gotti, at Hoffmann the baker's.'

Angelo Gotti was probably the first foreigner to come to live in the little north German village of Westen since my father and his fellow British soldiers left in 1946 and the last of the Nazis' forced labourers dispersed to rebuild their lives, as best they could, in old or new homelands. He started work at the bakery on 13 August 1961, the day the Berlin Wall went up. Like so many other 'guest workers', he ended up staying for life.

So now he sits with me in the tidy guest kitchen of the Sieling family farmstead, a sturdy, broad-faced, cheerful man in his seventies, and tells me his story in still slightly scattershot German. He was born near Lake Como in 1943. His father was an Italian soldier killed in 1944. Four years later his mother married again. The stepfather was not simpatico. So when a German baker called Herr Hoffmann came to stay in the Italian hotel where the seventeen-year-old Angelo was working and offered him a job in Westen, he was happy to accept.

'They needed me to liven the place up!'

The Westeners called him 'the Italian'. It was not so easy to settle in. Fortunately, he was good at football. He joined the local sports club and eventually became its vice chairman. That helped.

The most difficult thing was when he got serious with a local girl. 'Her parents were against it.' The difficulties lasted for years. (Two other Westeners had already told me about this, so it was clearly a cause célèbre in the village.) But finally he and his Hannelore were married in the local church in 1970.

Did he convert to Protestantism?

'Yes, my wife wanted that.' He grins. 'But Catholic *here*' – and taps his heart.

They sometimes go on holiday in the Lake Como area. But he doesn't like to stay in Italy for more than a few weeks. 'The mentality is so different.'

Angelo's tale is just one among millions – each a potential novel – from a mass migration that would transform the societies of north-western Europe by the time the Berlin Wall came down. In the 1947 British film *Frieda*, a British fighter pilot takes his beautiful young German wife, who has helped him to escape from a prisoner-of-war camp, back to a place called Denfield. 'It's quite an ordinary town,' he tells her, 'like any other town in England. Most of the families have lived there for donkey's years. Ours has.' By 1989, it would be hard to find any large town in north-western Europe of which that could still be said. Everywhere, now, there were families who had come from somewhere else: from the south and east of Europe, from the four corners of the world. These societies had become multicultural.

Behind this mass movement of people was one big push factor, decolonisation, and one big pull factor, an economic boom. What the French call the *trente glorieuses*, the thirty glorious years of economic growth between 1945 and a major downturn following the oil price shock of 1973, were also the thirty years in which west European countries lost their empires. The boom accentuated what was already a shortage of manpower due to the number of men killed and maimed in the war. The flow of men and women from the former colonies was not simply a response to the manpower demand of fast-growing economies; rather, the two phenomena overlapped and reinforced each other.

More than five centuries earlier, Europeans had started sailing out on the high seas to discover the globe and then colonise it. The first modern overseas European colonies were the Canary Islands and what is today the Spanish enclave of Ceuta, on the North African shore of the Mediterranean, which was originally conquered by Portugal in 1415. Europe had gone out to the world; now, as those colonies were dissolved in the second half of the twentieth century, the world came back to Europe. Old colonials settled disconsolately in Lisbon, Marseille or Tunbridge Wells, bringing with them the future contents of a thousand provincial auction rooms: pieces like the beautifully carved Burmese abbot's throne that now sits in our hall at home. I am always struck by how many people in Britain turn out to have some colonial background in the family, whether an early childhood in Africa or, like me, a grand-father in the Indian Civil Service. In Portugal, some 800,000 *retornados* from Angola, Mozambique and other colonies made up around fifteen per cent of the country's population. In Italy, the returnees came from Libya, Ethiopia, Eritrea and Somaliland; in the Netherlands, from the Dutch East Indies and Surinam. In France, there were around one million so-called *pieds-noirs*, descendants of colonial settlers, from Algeria alone.

Along with the former colonisers came the formerly colonised, often drawing on ambiguous citizenship rights granted when the imperial power wanted to see the overseas territory as part of its own larger self: la France d'Outre-Mer, Africa Orientale Italiana, the British Com-monwealth and Empire. Together with the *pieds-noirs* came 200,000 former Algerian Muslim soldiers in French service, known as *harkis*. Particular areas and groups in the Indian subcontinent – not just Pun-jabi, but specific communities in the Punjab, not just Kashmiri but spe-cifically Mirpuri – were translated into rows of terraced redbrick houses in Bolton or Leicester. This quarter of a Spanish city became Moroccan, that quarter of a Dutch city, Moluccan. Local councillors had to know the culture of origin as well as the society of arrival. The ethnography of distant territories was transmuted into a new ethnography of Euro-pean suburbs.

When my wife and I lived in east Oxford in the 1980s, our neighbours were both workers in the nearby Cowley car works: to our left, Len and his wife Mollie, English-born white working class; to our right, Laurie and his wife Jeanette, first-generation immigrants from the Caribbean. The old Britain and the new. 'A lot of foreigners down the Cowley Road,' our very English builder informed me and my Polish wife. 'Crooks and foreigners.'

In most European countries that had possessed overseas empires there was scant acknowledgement of any moral obligation towards those they had colonised and oppressed. Looking back, I find that the fact my maternal grandfather had spent his life serving the British Empire in India hardly featured in my own thinking at the time. All that seemed so much ancient history. Europe was the future. It took the generation of our children, the post-1989ers, to remind us that we still needed to face up to our colonial pasts.

In German-speaking Europe, the mix was rather different. The German and Austrian empires had mainly been contiguous land empires, grown slowly over centuries. The Austrian Empire was abruptly dissolved at the end of the First World War. Germany's continental territories were first brutally expanded and then punitively truncated in a single terrible convulsion between 1937 and 1945. Germany, West and East, took in at least twelve million Germans from the former eastern territories of the Reich after the end of Hitler's war. Between 1950 and 1989, West Germany then received another two million ethnic Germans – more precisely, people who qualified as German under its peculiar nationality law – from the Soviet bloc. In the case of those from the centuries-old German settlements in Ceaușescu's Romania, like that charming pastor who asked me if I knew Cardinal Newman, the Bonn government paid the Romanian regime directly to get them out to West Germany. The ransom for each Romanian German was DM 8,000 in 1984 (about €5,500 in current prices).

Diverse though they were, these ethnic Germans were not what made the societies of German-speaking Europe multicultural. Rather it was that, to address the shortage of labour, Germany, Austria and Switzerland went looking all round the Mediterranean for 'guest workers' like Angelo Gotti. As early as 1956, Chancellor Konrad Adenauer offered free train tickets for workers from Italy. West Germany went on to sign agreements with Greece, Spain, Turkey, Morocco, Portugal, Tunisia and Yugoslavia. Switzerland, Austria and the Netherlands did something similar, although on a smaller scale. The workforce-importing countries did not think of the newcomers as people who would become a permanent feature of their societies, let alone that they would go on to be equal citizens, compatriots and fellow Europeans. As the Swiss writer Max Frisch observed in 1965: 'Man hat Arbeitskräfte gerufen, und es kommen Menschen.' ('One called for a workforce and what arrives are human beings.')

When it came to immigrants being accepted in the host society, there was no simple line between newcomers who were compatriots, for whom everything was easy, and foreigners, for whom everything was difficult. The topography of native European prejudice was more convoluted than that. As young Helga Allerheiligen, the German Silesian refugee in Westen, discovered when she wanted to marry local farmer's boy Wilhelm, gaining acceptance was often difficult even for undoubted compatriots – fellow white Christian Germans, Dutch, French or British. In Westen, to this day, the 'German Russians' – ethnic Germans who emigrated from the former Soviet Union – keep themselves to themselves in a distinct neighbourhood of neat modern houses.

Nor was being a fellow European any safeguard against prejudice. In 1964, a guide for French households employing Spanish maids helpfully explained:

> In general they do not complain, and they accept their fate as a destiny inherited from the Arabic occupation of their country.

Two ethnic stereotypes in a single sentence! A dark-skinned Sicilian or Albanian was as likely to encounter casual racism on the street as a light-skinned Egyptian or Turk. In the early 1980s, the German journalist Günter Wallraff had only to don a wig, wear tinted contact lenses and pretend to speak bad German in order to pass himself off as a Turkish 'guest worker', and experience the abuse he recorded in his reportage *Lowest of the Low*.

Every kind of difference, from skin colour and dress to food, festivals, religion and manners, could be a trigger for prejudice and discrimination. A generation of British children of South Asian origin grew up with the threat of being beaten up and abused on their way home from school. An Indian Buddhist was as likely to catch it from the local thugs as a Pakistani Christian. There was also prejudice between different immigrant communities. Mr Patel, an enterprising newsagent and property owner in east Oxford, several times instructed me that I should never, but never, rent to Nigerians.

Yet there is no doubt that if a white Christian compatriot such as Helga Allerheiligen was at the easier end of the spectrum of acceptance, then a dark-skinned Muslim from a non-European country was close to the other end. Islam had been, for centuries, the defining Other of Europe. The first recorded mention of Europeans (*europenses*) comes in a chronicle of the Battle of Tours in 732, when King Charles Martel ('the Hammer') defeated the invading Arabs. When Pope Pius II popularised the use of the term Europe in the fifteenth century, it was to defend the cause of Christendom against the encroaching Ottoman Turks. From the plays of Shakespeare to a nineteenth-century Polish painting of the 1683 Battle of Vienna that still hangs prominently in the Vatican, 'the Turk' was a synonym for exotic threat. Talking to a close associate, Charles de Gaulle evoked, as a nightmare, the prospect that his beloved village of Colombey-les-deux-Églises (Colombey-of-the-two-churches) might one day become Colombey-les-deux-mosquées (Colombey-of-the-two-mosques). (By 2021, the administrative region in which Colombey is located, the Haute-Marne, had twelve mosques for fewer than 180,000 people, although there was still no mosque in the village itself.)

Integration was made doubly difficult where the immigrant was treated as a 'guest worker', not expected to stay long-term. In Germany, an official ceremony was organised in 1964 to welcome the one millionth 'guest worker', a Portuguese carpenter called Armando Rodrigues de Sá, who received carnations and a moped. In 1969, the head of the German employers' organisation presented the millionth Turkish 'guest worker', Ismail Babader, with a television set. In 1972 it was the turn of the two-millionth 'guest worker', a Yugoslav woman called Vera Rimski, who received a portable TV and thanks for the foreign workers' 'significant contribution to the Gross National Product'. In time, their wives and children were allowed to join them. Some of them had very positive experiences. This was the case for Ricardo and Julia Cuesta, the grand-parents of Sonia, my Spanish student researcher. 'I was received with open arms,' Ricardo recalled in conversation with his granddaughter. 'I worked hard and they respected me for it. There was a huge sense of solidarity too.' He will never forget how, without saying a word to him, dozens of his co-workers wrote to the immigration office in Wuppertal to attest to his good character.

But when the economy slowed down after the 1973 oil shock and the thirty glorious years of growth were over, the 'guest workers' were encouraged to go home. Many did in fact return to their homelands, especially in southern Europe. But millions remained. In 1977, an offi-cial commission declared that 'the Federal Republic of Germany is not an immigrant country', a formula repeated in the coalition agreement between Christian Democrats and Free Democrats when they formed a new government in 1982. What it meant was 'we don't *want* to be a country of immigrants like the US or Canada'. Yet even a brief skim through the Frankfurt telephone directory would have shown that Germany already was an immigrant country.

What is more, while birth rates in most native-born populations declined sharply from the 1970s onward, in what has been called Europe's second demographic transition, birth rates among immigrant populations generally remained higher. In 1974, one in every six children born in West Germany was the offspring of someone born abroad. Yet most of those children were still classed as 'foreigners', not eligible by birth for German citizenship. In 1989, these so-called foreigners – some of whom had been born and lived their entire lives in Germany – made up eight per cent of the West German population.

By the 1980s, west Europeans, especially those in cities with large immigrant populations, were waking up to the fact that this was a major, long-term change in Europe's kaleidotapestry. They started looking for new ways to include these minorities in the life of a tolerant, modern, urban European society. In 1989, the iconic old 68er Daniel Cohn-Bendit was appointed to head a new 'office for multicultural affairs' in Frankfurt, where more than twenty per cent of the city's population was now of foreign origin. 'Multiculturalism' would develop into a hopelessly fuzzy ideology. At best, it advanced the good idea that people should know something of the religion and culture of their immediate neighbours. At worst, it licensed the acceptance of very illiberal practices, such as the continued oppression of women in some minority communities, in the name of 'cultural difference'. Yet at least these initiatives recognised the reality that western Europe was becoming multicultural.

In this respect, there was an interesting contrast with the other half of Europe, a contrast that would become sharply apparent in the refugee crisis of 2015. Over the entire course of the 'short twentieth century', between 1914 and 1989, the two halves of Europe were, in this respect, like ships passing in the night, steaming in opposite directions. In 1914, central and eastern Europe was much the more multicultural part, with ethnicities, cultures and religions jumbled together inside the region's sprawling empires. The city we now call by its Slovak name, Bratislava, was Pressburg for German-speakers, Pozsony for Hungarians and all three to its large Jewish population. I have an old black-and-white photograph of the old centre of the city, with a Catholic church, Protestant chapel and Jewish synagogue sitting cheek by jowl. In today's Bratislava, I once met an aged musicologist called Jan, Hans or 'Hansi' Albrecht who really had spoken three languages before lunch in the pre-1914 city. To describe this everyday cosmopolitanism of central Europe, the Prague-born, German-Bohemian writer Johannes Urzidil coined a new word: hinternational.

Then, across the short twentieth century, there came wave after wave of separating-out: from the formation of a patchwork of more or less national states after 1918, to the population exchanges sanctioned by post-First World War international agreements, to the genocidal ethnic cleansing ordered by Hitler and Stalin, and on to the expulsions and pogroms of the immediate post-war period. To adapt a simile first used by the anthropologist Ernest Gellner: a painting by Oskar Kokoschka, with multiple shades and stiplings of colour, became a picture by Piet Mondrian, with sharply defined, solid blocks of a single colour. And the separating-out did not stop there. In the 1950s, Bulgaria expelled some 140,000 Turks and Roma. In Poland, an anti-Semitic campaign in 1968 resulted in the departure of many of the country's already tiny post-Holocaust community of Polish Jews. By 1989, it was estimated that ninety-eight per cent of the country's population was ethnically Polish.

Some very large minorities remained, such as the millions of Hungarians in neighbouring Romania and Slovakia, while Czechoslovakia and Yugoslavia were still multi-ethnic states. But these were established, legacy minorities, many of which had been there for centuries. They did not derive from recent immigration. A small number of migrants from countries like Vietnam and Angola found a precarious perch in Soviet bloc states. (When I studied in East Berlin in 1980, the other room in my apartment was occupied by an Angolan taxidermist.) They encountered widespread racism and struggled to gain acceptance in the wider society.

As Europe approached the moment when the physical barriers dividing it would come down, its two halves had thus evolved in different directions. Upwards of one in ten inhabitants of France and Belgium had been born abroad; in Czechoslovakia and Romania, the proportion was less than one in a hundred. The West was going from Mondrian to Kokoschka, the East from Kokoschka to Mondrian. And that process of ethnic separation would continue, brutally, in what would soon be known as former Yugoslavia.

Spectator Britain

Ten pink-cheeked men in suits sit around a well-polished dining table in a small room on the top floor of 56 Doughty Street. This elegant early nineteenth-century house, just a few doors down from No. 48, where Charles Dickens wrote *The Pickwick Papers*, is home to England's oldest weekly magazine, the *Spectator*. Although my watch tells me it is 3.30 in the afternoon, the lunch, served by a large, cheerful lady called Jennifer Paterson and washed down with generous quantities of claret, is still going on. Our principal guest, Kingman Brewster Jr, US ambassador to the Court of St James's, has just taken his leave and conversation now turns to vinous gossip.

Why is it, muses the *Spectator* writer Patrick Marnham, that so many establishment Americans have reversible names?

Kingman Brewster.

Winston Lord.

Clark Clifford.

'Oh yes, is he dead?' someone asks.

A pause. Audible sipping of claret.

Then the editor, Alexander Chancellor, says in his slightly spluttering upper-class tones: 'I don't think he is . . . *completely.*'

This was the summer of 1980. A week earlier I had been crouching in a shabby East Berlin back corridor while a friend nervously whispered to me about his interrogation by the Stasi. A week later I would stand in the courtyard of the former Wehrmacht headquarters in Berlin at a ceremony marking the anniversary of the 20 July 1944 bomb plot to assassinate Hitler, surrounded by survivors of the Prussian officer class – von Hammerstein, von Weizsäcker, von dem Bussche, and others both von and zu. In between the heaviness of two German dictatorships there was the lightness of England, this England.

It was my strange fate – the result, like so much in life, of pure fluke – to spend more than ten years writing about Europe for the most Euro-sceptic periodical in Britain. I was a pro-European fish in strange waters, as were two of my successors as foreign editor, Ian Buruma and Anne Applebaum. Ian recalls being startled over the same polished luncheon table by the then editor, Charles Moore, asking him: 'Ian, tell me, which Bible do you use?' Anne writes that at the *Spectator* she was 'a useful foil, an earnest foreigner, the person always trying to get my English colleagues to stop making jokes and write about difficult foreign places like Russia or China ("We need something serious in this issue: let's get Anne to write it")'.

How tempting, then, to see in the *Spectator* of those days just a car-icature of a certain kind of anachronistic, insular Englishness, and to draw a straight line from its Thatcherite Euroscepticism in the 1980s to Brexit in 2016. The truth is a little more complicated, and therefore more interesting.

To be sure, some of the dialogue I heard at lunches round that table could have come straight out of the 'Podsnappery' chapter of Dickens's *Our Mutual Friend*, which introduces the reader to that ruddy epitome of English insular pride, Mr Podsnap. While his business was sustained by trade with other countries, Mr Podsnap

> considered other countries, with that important reservation, a mis-
> take, and of their manners and customs would conclusively observe,
> "not English!" when PRESTO! with a flourish of the arm, and a flush
> of the face, they were swept away.

But Alexander Chancellor, even if he sounded a bit like Bertie Wooster, had been a Reuters correspondent on the continent, spoke fluent Ital-ian and had an excellent understanding of what made other Europeans tick. Charles Moore, although with less personal experience of the con-tinent, was a man of wide interests who went on to write a fine biogra-phy of Margaret Thatcher. They and their successors as editor not only displayed catholic taste in having Europhiles like me, Ian and Anne write regularly for the magazine; they also actively sought a battle of ideas about Europe. That was something you seldom found in the west European press at the time, when 'Europe' was often, especially in reporting from Brussels, simply assumed to be a good thing.

On my wall at home I have a set of humorous maps of imagined Europes, designed and printed as New Year's cards by *Střední Evropa* (central Europe), a samizdat journal in Prague, and given me by one of its editors. The map card for 1988 shows European countries as different rooms in what Mikhail Gorbachev, visiting Prague the year before, had described as 'our common European home'. East Germany is the television room, West Germany consists entirely of a serried rank of bathrooms (*Bad. Bad. Bad.*), Italy is 'Showroom Extravaganza' and France 'Le Grand Salon'. Britain is marked 'Great Observatory'.

Offshore Britain was – and remains – a great observatory, not just on account of its semi-detached position but also thanks to its tradition of sceptical, empirical enquiry and robust debate. This meant that tough, fundamental questions about the European project were posed in journals like the *Spectator* earlier and more clearly than elsewhere in Europe. Hard questions from the historian Noel Malcolm about democracy and sovereignty, and from a leading banker, Martin Jacomb, about the likely effect of having a European monetary union without major fiscal transfers between its member states. Richer regions would get richer, Jacomb argued in the *Spectator* in 1989, and poorer ones poorer. Twenty years later, exactly these concerns were being raised across the continent, as north Europeans suffered incomparably less than south Europeans from the eurozone crisis and there was not much solidarity from north to south.

Yet there were also lines that pointed directly towards Brexit. When preparing to write this chapter, I made my way to the Victorian Gothic halls of the Oxford Union, the student debating society where Boris Johnson, Michael Gove, Jacob Rees-Mogg and others started practising the rhetorical skills they would successfully deploy in the 2016 Brexit referendum debate. In the Union's Gladstone room, all nineteenth-century polished wood and sagging leather armchairs, I went through bound volumes of the *Spectator* for the 1980s. Almost at once, I found an April 1980 article by the Conservative commentator Ferdinand Mount observing that withdrawal from the European Community 'is now, for the first time, being seriously discussed by politicians of all sorts as a practical possibility'. In October that year, one J. Enoch Powell (he of the 'rivers of blood' speech about immigration) says the Labour party is 'speaking for England' in calling for Britain to withdraw from the European Community – a party line then supported by an ambitious young Labour politician called Tony Blair – and urges the Conservatives to follow suit. Otherwise, Powell suggests, the Tories would be seen as an 'anti-national' party and the UK might become 'a province in a European state'.

Unsurprisingly, the *Spectator* welcomes Margaret Thatcher's 1988 speech to the Collège d'Europe in Bruges. Thirty years later, one of her then acolytes, David Willetts, would argue that the Bruges speech 'put Britain on the road to Brexit'. There is some truth in this, but only some. When I discuss it now with Charles Moore, he says that from the time of the 1975 referendum – in which two out of every three people who turned out to vote, including my father and an eighteen-year-old Moore, opted to stay in the European Community – until the Bruges speech in 1988, being Eurosceptic in the Conservative party was something like being gay in the 1950s. Only between consenting adults in private. After Thatcher's broadside, they came out. The Bruges Group, named after her speech and founded just three months later, would become the vanguard of Conservative Euroscepticism in the next decade.

The Bruges speech expressed Mrs Thatcher's rising anger at how Jacques Delors, the forceful French president of the European Commission, was pushing forward in both a federalist and a socialist direction, the latter exemplified by his appearance before the Trades Union Congress. Crucially, the way her press secretary Bernard Ingham briefed her speech to the British press positively encouraged headlines like the *Sun*'s three-word and two-finger summary of it: 'Up Yours Delors'. Ingham initiated a long line of press secretaries to Conservative prime ministers, from Thatcher to David Cameron, who described each European summit to British journalists as a replay of the Battle of Waterloo.

Yet the real turning point came more than a year later, with German unification and a firm Franco-German commitment to European monetary union, the two being causally connected and both abhorred by Thatcher. That project of monetary union was at the heart of the 1992

Maastricht treaty, which created what only then became the European Union. It was the parliamentary civil war inside the Conservative party over ratifying Maastricht that really launched Conservative Euroscepticism on the path that would end in Brexit.

Back in 1988, it was still possible to read the Bruges speech as an alternative vision for the European Community. Yes, Thatcher railed against 'a European super-state exercising a new dominance from Brussels' (up yours, Delors). But she also said that

> Britain does not dream of some cosy, isolated existence on the fringes of the European Community. Our destiny is in Europe, as part of the Community.

Her vision was Gaullist at home and Atlanticist abroad. She wanted what Charles de Gaulle had called a 'Europe of states', intergovernmental rather than federalist. She emphasised that people stuck behind the Iron Curtain, in 'great European cities' such as Warsaw, Prague and Budapest, were Europeans too. Soon afterwards, she visited Warsaw and Gdańsk, where she met with Lech Wałęsa and other Solidarity leaders. (I witnessed her visit and remember just how electrifyingly popular she was; one handwritten poster said: 'Mrs Thatcher – buy Poland!') Her support for the democratic opposition in central Europe would be followed in the 1990s by strong British support for an eastward enlargement of the EU.

'On many great issues,' she continued in Bruges, 'the countries of Europe should try to speak with a single voice.' They should work more closely together on trade, defence and relations with the rest of the world. Even if these lines were originally drafted by someone in the Foreign Office, Mrs Thatcher was not one to say anything she did not mean. Her advocacy of achieving a Single European Market by 1992 was full-throated and all her own.

Tony Blair's European adviser, Stephen Wall, recalls that some time in the early 2000s Blair asked for a copy of the Bruges speech so he could read it. 'When he had done so, he spoke out loud the thought that had come to my mind on re-reading it: that it was a good, and far from extreme, speech.' And then Wall, looking back from 2020, reflects that 'today, it represents a view of the European Union to which probably all its member states could subscribe'. That's an overstatement, but certainly in the early 2020s a large number of Europeans, including many French and Germans, would feel more comfortable with Thatcher's Bruges vision of Europe than with the federalist vision that Delors outlined in his own Bruges speech in 1989.

This might even be true of another iron lady, Angela Merkel. In her lecture to the Collège d'Europe in Bruges, in 2010, Merkel's tone was far more emollient and pro-European than Thatcher's. But the thrust of her argument was to promote the intergovernmental component of the Union, represented by the European Council of national leaders, as at least co-equal with the 'community method' represented by the European Commission and European Parliament. The combination of the two, she argued, should be described as the 'Union method'. Centrist in this as in everything else, Merkel presented an idea of Europe somewhere between those of Thatcher and Delors.

Nor was Thatcher's Bruges speech the articulation of an alternative view by a mere spectator on the European scene. For several years after the British prime minister finally secured a rebate on Britain's contributions to the European Community budget at the Fontainebleau summit in 1984 – 'I want my money back,' she had famously remarked – the UK was one of the main drivers of European integration. When I visited Brussels in 1986, David Hannay, the British permanent representative (i.e. ambassador) to the Community, told me that Fontainebleau had been the 'end of the beginning' and that Britain was becoming steadily more European. A French official murmured to me, with more than a hint of regret, that Europe was becoming more British. At the heart of this integrationist drive was the project of creating a single market by 1992, bringing down all sorts of protectionist barriers between states to produce a level playing field. That undertaking was led with bulldog determination by the British European Commissioner, Lord Cockfield, working closely with Delors. It required, and Thatcher fully accepted, a significant extension of majority voting inside the Community, so that recalcitrant protectionist governments could be overruled. The resulting single market remains at the core of the European Union to this day.

Like a good comedian, history takes her time delivering her best jokes. One of them, packed with irony, is that three decades later one of the biggest obstacles to post-Brexit Britain securing a trade deal with the EU was to be the level playing field for access to the single market. Britain was hoist with its own petard. Nonetheless, the fact remains that Britain did make a significant contribution to the most consequential upward turn in recent European history.

The upward turn

If ever the stars aligned for freedom in Europe, it was in the second half of the 1980s. A cast of extraordinary individuals, a set of historical processes and a sprinkling of happy accidents combined to produce a peaceful transformation of our continent. The combination was so exceptional that it could be described as a miracle. Yet Europeans soon started to make the mistake of regarding this as somehow the normal path of development. Not for the first or last time, the way history had gone was projected forward as the way history must go.

Were one to assign a single starting date for this upward turn, it would have to be Monday 11 March 1985. On the previous evening, Soviet leader Konstantin Chernenko, who already looked half-dead when I saw him in the Kremlin in 1984, had become, to recall Alexander Chancellor's formulation, *completely* dead. Now the Politburo gathered in the Walnut Room of the old Tsarist Senate building and chose the fifty-four-year-old Mikhail Gorbachev to be their new leader. If they had gone for another politburo member, such as the sixty-two-year-old Grigory Romanov, who definitely wanted the job and had a good surname for a tsar, the history of the world would have been different. The decisive role played by the individual in history was demonstrated by a system whose ideology insisted history was made by large impersonal forces.

And what an individual he was. Just ask Margaret Thatcher. A few months earlier, in December 1984, she received him for lunch at Chequers, the prime minister's country residence. Gorbachev came through the front door 'bouncing on the balls of his feet', as one eyewitness put it, radiating energy and purpose. Throughout lunch, he and Mrs Thatcher argued – undiplomatically, heatedly, sincerely – about the relative merits of communism and Western democracy. After lunch, they got down to discussing arms control. The British interpreter noticed the 'palpable human chemistry at work between them' and concluded that he had witnessed something akin to a flirtation. One of Thatcher's close advisers then came up with a phrase that would become famous. In Gorbachev we had a man we could 'do business with'.

Twelve years later, when I chaired an event for Gorbachev to present his memoirs to more than 2,400 people in Westminster Central Hall, all that personal warmth, energy and directness were still apparent, but now enhanced by the nimbus of a world-historical figure. Glasnost and perestroika had, in the meantime, entered the political vocabulary of many languages.

I asked Gorbachev what he saw as his three greatest achievements.

'Freedom, openness among nations and an end to the arms race.'

Wave after wave of rapturous applause engulfed this superhero of the West (although no longer a hero to his own people).

Afterwards, over dinner, his wife Raisa seemed to feel we were getting too familiar with the great man. She instructed us, in her slightly schoolmarmish way, that no previous Soviet leader would have sat talking with us so informally.

'No, Lenin would not have,' she said.

'Stalin would not have'. A nervous titter went round the table.

'Not Khrushchev. Or Andropov. Or Chernenko.'

'Well, Andropov might have, you know,' Gorbachev twinkled back, singling out his former mentor.

Gorbachev's story is rich in unintended consequences. The Soviet patriot whose policies ended up destroying the Soviet Union. The reformer who unleashed revolution. The communist who opened the door to democracy. Without him, freedom would certainly not have come so quickly and peacefully to half of Europe, nor such a rapid, decisive end to the Cold War across the world.

Four other countries or groups of countries, each with its own exceptional individuals and distinct historical processes, combined with Gorbachev's reforms and the subsequent dissolution of the Soviet Union to create this great change: the United States, western Europe, eastern Europe and Germany. One way to understand what happened is to follow in turn their interactions with the pivotal man.

The other superpower came first. As luck would have it, Gorbachev ascended to power when the United States was itself on an upward curve. Ten years before, in the wake of Vietnam and Watergate, the international reputation and influence of the United States had been at a low point. Many still saw the Soviet Union as a serious economic and technological competitor to the United States. Now, after climbing out of a sharp recession, the US economy was booming. Its technology sector, turbocharged by Cold War federal funding of defence research, was on the way to creating the internet. President Ronald Reagan convinced many Americans that, in the words of his 1984 presidential election advertisement, it was 'morning again in America'. The old movie actor well understood that the soft power of a narrative can be every bit as important as economic and military power. Hollywood complemented the Pentagon and Wall Street, making three-dimensional American power.

Reagan was jeered at by many west Europeans, who dismissed him as a 'cowboy' and 'B-movie actor'. (I may even have done a little jeering myself.) Yet his personal role was almost as important as Gorbachev's when it came to ending the Cold War. Unlike most Washington professionals, Reagan was convinced that the United States could win the Cold War with the Soviet Union by revving up the arms race and mounting an open political, technological and ideological challenge to what he called, in 1983, the 'evil empire'. So he increased military spending, especially on the Strategic Defence Initiative, known colloquially as Star Wars.

In Reagan's first term, the world came closer to nuclear war than it had been since the early 1960s, but with historical luck, Reagan's gamble paid off. When Gorbachev set out to transform the Soviet Union by a 'revolution from above', he soon realised he could not modernise his country and keep pace with the United States in the arms race at the same time. He needed co-operation rather than confrontation with the West. The Chernobyl nuclear power plant disaster in 1986 brought home to him both how ramshackle the Soviet system was and how terrible would be the human cost of any nuclear exchange.

When the dynamic fifty-four-year-old Soviet leader first met the seventy-four-year-old US president – born in 1911, the same year as Chernenko – he found him a political 'dinosaur'. But, unlike most people in their mid-seventies, this 'dinosaur' could learn and adapt. Through several years of successive summits and exchanges, assisted by skilful colleagues such as George Shultz, Reagan made a dramatic turnaround from arms race and confrontation with the 'evil empire' in his first term to nuclear disarmament and seeking to end the Cold War in his second. By the time of their 1988 summit in Moscow, the two leaders were calling each other 'Mikhail' and 'Ronnie'. Needless to say, the American-style informality was proposed by Ronnie. Now, asked by a journalist in Moscow whether he still considered the Soviet Union an evil empire, Reagan replied: 'No, that was another time, another era.'

I reported for the *Spectator* on the superpower leaders' first meeting in Geneva in 1985 and the Washington summit in 1987 at which they signed their first major arms control agreement, the INF (Intermediate-range Nuclear Forces) treaty. The drama of these encounters is hard to recapture and unlikely ever to be repeated. Perhaps some time in the 2020s a summit between the US and Chinese presidents may come close. But even if the two twenty-first-century superpowers, China and the United States, lock horns in something resembling a new Cold War, there will be other giants around them: the European Union, India, Russia. This will be a multipolar or no-polar world, whereas in the 1980s the world was still bipolar: American-led West, Soviet-led East. These Soviet–American summits felt like mythical epic encounters between, say, Zeus and Cronus, clashing on high while we mortals trembled below.

My notebooks are filled with a mixture of the trivia that always accompanies such summits, as journalists scramble to fill the empty hours of air time, and the genuinely historic. 'I think the president was in his customary underwear,' I note Reagan's spokesman informing us in reply to a journalist's question – it was cold in Geneva that November of 1985 – before proceeding to record every tiny detail of the two men's chat in front of a blazing fire in a luxurious poolhouse at the Château Fleur d'Eau. But then, a few pages on, I have Gorbachev saying 'at such a watershed in history you need truth like you need air to breathe' – a sentence more reminiscent of Aleksandr Solzhenitsyn than of Leonid

Brezhnev, let alone Joseph Stalin. In the middle of my hastily scrawled notes from the Soviet leader's final press conference at the Washington summit, in December 1987, I find four heavily underlined words: 'end of Cold War'. There is no record in the official transcript of Gorbachev using those exact words, but I was not alone in sensing that prospect.

With the habitual self-importance of great powers, Americans sometimes ascribe the end of the Cold War almost entirely to America. To listen to some, you might think that Reagan did it all single-handedly with his 1987 speech in front of the Brandenburg Gate in Berlin, calling on Gorbachev to 'tear down this Wall'. Certainly, the improvement of relations with the United States through the Geneva, Reykjavik, Washington and Moscow summits was indispensable, and made possible only by Reagan's remarkable personal turn from confrontation to detente. The final summit of Reagan's presidency, in New York in December 1988, was a threesome between Gorbachev, Reagan and his vice president, now President-elect George H. W. Bush. The transition between these two very different Americans was fortuitous. Bush's more low-key, professional style appealed to Gorbachev and would prove a great advantage when it came to negotiating the unification of Germany in 1989–90. 'Don't dance on the Wall!' Bush would advise his team after the Berlin Wall came down, whereas Reagan might have been unable to resist the triumphalist temptation.

Yet Gorbachev himself insisted that this great thaw was also due to 'Europe', by which he meant western Europe. 'As I said to Mrs Thatcher,' he explained during his final press conference at the Washington summit, the role of the UK, the Federal Republic of Germany and other European countries had been and would be essential. 'One could even say that this was what stimulated the Soviet Union to act more constructively.' Anatoly Chernyaev, one of his closest aides, records him reflecting after another invigorating exchange with Thatcher, 'I believe we haven't studied Europe enough and don't know it very well. We have to get up to speed on it ourselves and educate our people . . .' And:

> This, comrades, is very complicated. It is obvious that not a single issue can be decided without Europe . . . We even need it for our domestic affairs, for perestroika. And in foreign policy Europe is

simply irreplaceable. Theirs is the strongest bourgeoisie, not only economically but politically too. It seemed that Japan had surpassed everyone else in the world, and suddenly the FRG [Federal Republic of Germany] made an incredible leap in science and technology.

The European Community, he observed, 'is a giant rising in our neighbourhood'.

Western Europe contributed to the upward turn in several ways. Gorbachev's conversations with west European leaders such as Willy Brandt, the architect of West Germany's Ostpolitik, and President François Mitterrand of France, helped convince him that there was an acceptable alternative to the arms race. In effect, there was something like an unplanned division of labour between the United States and western Europe: hard cop, soft cop. Gorbachev's first foreign visit as Soviet leader was to France and it was there he first said: 'Europe is our common home.' The dynamism of the European Community, with its grand project of creating a single market by 1992, convinced him that he could not hope to modernise the Soviet Union without close co-operation with west European states and their 'strongest bourgeoisie'. Hence, his originally spontaneous image of the 'common European home' became a settled ideological formula for a dynamic capitalist western Europe and a reformed socialist eastern Europe living happily together in two halves of a modern semi-detached house. Western Europe also had a large direct impact on the societies of eastern Europe, preparing the mental ground for the velvet revolutions of 1989. In apparent defiance of historical logic, we might even say that '1992' was one of the causes of 1989.

Here I must pay tribute to another exceptional individual: Jacques Delors, president of the European Commission from 1985 to 1995 and the architect of '1992'. Seeking a 'big idea' to relaunch the European project as he prepared for the Commission presidency in 1984, he was advised by the Dutchman Max Kohnstamm, who had been chief assistant to Jean Monnet, to concentrate on the single market. Making a tour of the ten national capitals of the Community, Delors discovered that the single market was the one big idea that could command support in all of them – not least, from No. 10 Downing Street. It was then the unusual partnership of the French Socialist Delors and the British Tory

European Commissioner Lord Cockfield, under licence from the Iron Lady, that drove this project to fruition.

Yet Delors and Thatcher had different ends in mind. For Thatcher, the single market was an end in itself. For Delors, it was a means to a larger end: a federal European Union. By the last year of the millennium, he told French television viewers in 1990, Europe should have 'a true federation'. The next step down the path already envisaged by Monnet forty years earlier would be a monetary union. With support from Helmut Kohl, Delors chaired a committee of central bank governors which prepared a blueprint for monetary union. This was approved in principle by Community leaders in mid-1989.

Delors also paid attention to soft power. He encouraged the playing of the 'Joy, spark of the Gods' passage from Beethoven's Ninth Symphony, the music (but not the words) officially adopted as the European anthem in 1985. He almost single-handedly decided that the flag of the Council of Europe – those twelve yellow stars on a blue background – should become the flag of the European Community. Today, that European flag, usually flown next to the national flag of member states, is the most widespread, emotionally affecting symbol of the European project. I felt a pang when the European flags came down on official buildings in Britain after Brexit and we were faced instead with the spectacle of Churchill-parody Boris Johnson blustering away flanked only by two Union Jacks. Something larger was lost, as important as freedom of movement or membership of the single market: an aspiration to be at once our national selves and something more than just our national selves.

All this dynamism produced, in the decade of Delors' presidency, what the historian Andreas Rödder calls a transition from Europe I to Europe II. There was no Reaganesque, soft-focus television advertisement proclaiming 'it's morning again in Europe', but that was very much the feeling by the end of the 1980s. Western Europe, like the United States, radiated historical optimism. Although Delors himself took relatively little interest in the East, this radiance had an enormous impact on the countries to the east of the Iron Curtain that people were just beginning to refer to, once again, as central Europe. One symptom of this metamorphosis, subtle but very telling, was the change in what Hungarians, Poles and Czechs meant by 'normal'.

In 1984, one of my Prague friends told me: 'If someone stands up to speak his mind in public, his colleagues will say "he's not normal"'. The Soviet attempt at 'normalisation' – returning a European society to Soviet norms – could still chalk up these little successes. But by the late 1980s, when people all over central Europe told me 'we just want to be a normal country', they meant somewhere like France, Britain or West Germany. Heavy industrialisation had produced substantial economic progress in eastern Europe until the 1970s, but the region failed to keep up when Western economies turned to services and tech. Instead, several of the east European regimes, including Poland, Hungary and East Germany, became ever more heavily indebted to the West, in hard-to-find hard currency. Communism, a Polish taxi driver told me in 1985, is a 'system for angels'. For human beings, it was better to have democratic capitalism. 'Socialism', went the joke in Budapest, 'is the longest and most painful road from capitalism to capitalism.' In one of my notebooks I concluded that the West had won 'the battle of norms'. What the founding chancellor of West Germany, Konrad Adenauer, had called Magnet Europa (the magnet of Europe) was exercising a powerful attraction.

Gorbachev's role in this changing eastern Europe was pivotal, but also complicated. His perestroika and glasnost were an inspiration to many. Wherever he went, in Prague, Warsaw or East Berlin, they chanted 'Gorbi!' But while he still cherished the core belief of the 1968 Prague Spring, that one could create 'socialism with a human face' by reforming the existing communist system from above, few in eastern Europe shared that hope any more. Gorbachev gave an influential example of reform at home but he did not forcefully promote reformers at the top of east European communist parties. His biographer William Taubman observes that he paid relatively little attention to the Soviet Union's European satellites. They were a problem, a distraction from his project of modernising the Soviet Union. Stiff, boring, arrogant old comrades like Erich Honecker in East Berlin, Gustav Husák in Prague and, worst of all, Nicolae Ceaușescu in neo-totalitarian Romania were insufferable. How much more interesting to talk to Willy Brandt and the Spanish socialist

Felipe González (two of his favourite foreign leaders), argue vigorously with Margaret Thatcher and hobnob with Ronnie.

One of his key aides, Andrei Grachev, says Gorbachev articulated the general principle of 'freedom of choice' without thinking through where this might lead in eastern Europe. Being himself a true Soviet patriot, the Soviet leader did not sufficiently appreciate that for most Lithuanians, Estonians and Latvians, the Soviet Union was not a single country, a *patria* towards which one might feel patriotism. For them, it was Russia's oppressive internal empire. By the time the movement towards freedom accelerated in the outer empire, in eastern Europe, Gorbachev was already preoccupied with discontent amongst the non-Russian nationalities inside the Soviet Union. In the end, his greatness lay in allowing to happen what he had neither anticipated nor originally desired. As the poet and essayist Hans Magnus Enzensberger memorably put it, he was 'a hero of retreat'.

In the meantime, he gave eastern Europe an amber light, which might or might not eventually turn green. At this point, key figures in Poland's Solidarity movement came decisively back into the picture. In the political equivalent of a judo throw, they took the thrust of a proposal from General Wojciech Jaruzelski for 'round table' talks with all forces in Polish society and turned it into a negotiation between Jaruzelski's regime and Solidarity about the terms of a political transition. One of the masterminds of that judo throw was Bronisław Geremek.

In Poland's first semi-free election for more than forty years, on 4 June 1989 – the same day as the Tiananmen massacre in Beijing – Solidarity swept the board, robbing the regime of its last vestiges of legitimacy. At one polling station in Warsaw, I shared the quiet satisfaction of my underground publisher Andrzej Rosner and his wife Ania, as they crossed out name after name on the long list of official regime candidates. Less than three months later, Tadeusz Mazowiecki, a liberal Catholic intellectual and, like Geremek, a Solidarity adviser since the Lenin Shipyard strike in August 1980, became the first non-communist prime minister in the Soviet bloc. It is futile to argue over whether Gorbachev or the Polish democratic opposition deserves the credit for this negotiated revolution. It needed both. Without the Soviet leader opening the door, none of this could have happened; but it still required someone to walk through the door and keep heading west, towards being a 'normal' country.

In Hungary, the great symbolic event was the ceremonial reburial of Imre Nagy, the reform communist leader of the 1956 Hungarian revolution, on 16 June 1989. My notebook records the extraordinary scene of black-draped grandeur on Heroes Square in Budapest and an electrifying speech by a then unknown young man called Viktor Orbán, who, violating an informal agreement among the opposition speakers not to be so provocative, called for the withdrawal of Russian troops. In Hungary, as in Poland, there followed a kind of negotiated transition that I christened 'refolution', meaning a combination of reform and revolution. For Europe as a whole, however, the most consequential thing that the still notionally communist Hungarian leadership did was to start opening the Iron Curtain to Austria, Hungary's constitutional twin in the Austro-Hungarian Empire until the end of the First World War. The Hungarian and Austrian foreign ministers were photographed symbolically cutting a stretch of barbed wire fence with giant wire-cutters. It looked wonderful on the front pages of western newspapers, but Hungarian border guards were still under orders to stop East Germans crossing the border.

So there was one more star that needed to move into alignment. After the Soviet Union, the United States, Poland, Hungary, France, Britain and the European Community, this was Germany – the divided centre of the divided continent. The West German government of Helmut Kohl had made a rocky start with the Soviet leader, not least because, in an incautious interview, Kohl had compared him to Joseph Goebbels, Hitler's propaganda chief. But when Kohl visited Moscow in the autumn of 1988, the two men, who were almost exactly the same age, established a good rapport, helped by a large delegation of leading German businessmen and a three billion Deutschmark loan.

Everything came right between them on Gorbachev's return visit to West Germany, in June 1989. After the breakthrough election in Poland and before the funeral in Hungary, I dashed back to the West German capital, Bonn, to witness what was accurately described as a 'Gorbasm'. The outpouring of public emotion on Town Hall Square in Bonn matched anything I had experienced in Warsaw or Budapest. Wherever he went, the Soviet leader was greeted as a rock star, conquering hero and saint: 'Gorbi! Gorbi! Gorbi!' My notebook reminds me that, asked in an opinion poll to identify their 'most trusted' leaders, ninety per cent of West German respondents said Gorbachev, against fifty-eight per cent for President Bush and just fifty per cent for Chancellor Kohl.

As remarkable was what happened behind the scenes. Two years later, Kohl would tell me about his late-night conversation with Gorbachev. After an intimate dinner in the so-called Chancellor-bungalow (yes, the official residence of West Germany's Chancellor was a bungalow), the two men strolled down the garden to sit on a wall overlooking the Rhine. As the German and the Russian mused ponderously together, Kohl told Gorbachev that history would surely flow on, like the river below them, towards German unity. When they parted in the early hours, they embraced for the first time. This, Kohl told me, was 'the decisive moment', and he repeats the story at length in his memoirs. One can imagine that this heavy philosophising about History would have appealed to Gorbachev, but the Soviet leader does not mention the 'decisive' conversation in his memoirs. Rather, he singles out the enthusiastic reception from the crowd on Bonn's Town Hall Square and particularly that from workers at the Hoesch steelworks in Dortmund.

There is no doubt that the establishment of a trusting relationship between the two leaders was significant, as was the public love-bombing. But most important of all was the commitment, contained in a joint document informally called the Bonn Declaration, to a comprehensive partnership between the two countries. For Gorbachev, this meant the promise of West German economic, technological and political help in his embattled project to modernise the Soviet Union. In effect, Moscow was prioritising its relations with West Germany over those with its East German satellite.

Looking back, Gorbachev's aide Chernyaev says the Bonn visit was 'in fact the beginning of the process of German unification'. So indeed it might appear to posterity. A month earlier, it had been President George H. W. Bush who visited West Germany. He told the West Germans they should be 'partners in leadership' and he looked forward to a 'Europe whole and free'. That resonant phrase was written into Bush's keynote speech in Mainz by a long-forgotten State Department official called

Harvey Sicherman. For me, it remains the simplest, most eloquent summary of what my generation worked to achieve on our continent. There were now excellent relations among the three key statesmen, Gorbachev, Bush and Kohl, and by the end of June 1989 all the big pieces were in place to explain what followed. Surely we must acknowledge that German unification was by then inevitable?

Yet nothing in life is inevitable except death. At the time, we did not know that this was the path history would take, and in our cloud of unknowing we probably made a better assessment than does all-knowing posterity. In early July 1989, continuing my exhilarating round of European capitals, I went to East Berlin, where I had some ludicrous conversations with apparatchiks and official think-tankers. One of them refused even to speak of 'Germans'. He talked instead of 'FRG-people' and 'GDR-people', although he did daringly add that when a GDR-person met an FRG-person 'we somehow get on well'. Yet even the small group of dissidents whom I met in the back courtyard apartment of Gerd and Ulrike Poppe had no idea what was coming. It was great to hear about all the wonderful things that were going on in Poland and Hungary, they told me, but it couldn't happen here.

Joachim

On Thursday 6 July 1989, I sat in bright summer sunshine on the veranda of the old vicarage in Pankow, talking to Joachim, the twenty-one-year-old son of my dearest East German friends, Werner and Annegret Krätschell. The little boy I remembered had grown into a tall, strong and angry young man, who now poured out his heart to me. He and some mates from theological college had mounted a protest demonstration against the falsification of local elections a month before. They had been arrested and dragged by their hair across the street while – this was what most angered Joachim – nearby residents audibly supported the police action from their balconies. A night in a Stasi cell and a nasty interrogation followed. East Germany wouldn't change, young Joachim fumed. In the end, there would be no one left behind the Wall but 'the stupid philistines and a handful of idealists'. He'd had enough. He wanted to live. Perhaps there was a way to breathe free air.

More than thirty years on, Joachim, now a pastor in West Berlin, tells me what happened next. A few weeks after our conversation on the veranda, he and his girlfriend, Sirka, went on a long-planned holiday to Hungary. There, they decided to attempt an escape across the half-open Iron Curtain, to Austria. West German friends – honour to them – had checked out an escape route near the pretty Hungarian town of Sopron. They would wait for the escapees just across the border, next to the church in the Austrian village of Deutschkreutz. So one hot August night, by the light of a full moon, Joachim and Sirka set out, stealing past the Hungarian guardpost tower, over some train tracks and under the barbed wire, until freedom was in sight across a moonlit meadow.

At that moment, alarm sirens sounded, guard dogs barked furiously and a frontier police jeep roared up. 'Hands up! Lie on the ground!' Early the next morning the young couple were released, somewhere in a forest. Fearing arrest if they returned to East Germany, they resolved to try again that very evening, taking an alternative route reconnoitred by their West German friends. This time they were even more frightened.

Through the barbed wire again. Across a maize field. Onto the train tracks. Suddenly, in the distance, two men appear, waving torches. Joachim and Sirka press themselves down flat between the rails, praying no train will come. When the men have disappeared they press on to find a small wood, exactly as their friends have told them. But because this wood has been in the frontier zone for decades, the undergrowth has grown thick with brambles. The night is dark as death and they have no tools to cut through the thorny thickets. Eventually they emerge, exhausted and bleeding, only to find that what should have been a field of shoulder-high maize has just been harvested. Now it is a bare field, brightly lit by the floodlights from the nearby frontier post. 'I felt like Frodo,' Joachim tells me. Frodo Baggins in *The Lord of the Rings*, crossing Mordor while the roving searchlight eye of Sauron seeks him out.

Turn back or press on? Desperate indecision. Hellish fear. No, we've come this far, through all those bloody brambles. Let's risk it! They set off, running as fast as they can across the brightly lit field. Out of the corner of his eye, Joachim sees a jeep driving towards them from the frontier guardhouse. 'They could easily have caught us.' But it stops. Run, rabbit, run; run for your life. Suddenly they see a frontier sign: Republic of Austria. Freedom. What a feeling. 'I can't describe it'.

O welche Lust, in freier Luft
Den Atem leicht zu heben!

(O what joy, to breathe freely in the open air!) The prisoners' chorus from Beethoven's *Fidelio*.

Less than a week later, East Germans attending a 'pan-European picnic' in the same Sopron neighbourhood were able to flee en masse without being stopped. A few days after that, Hungarian leaders met discreetly with Helmut Kohl and Hans-Dietrich Genscher, his wily foreign minister, in Schloss Gymnich, a castle near Bonn. In the course of a dramatic conversation, the Hungarians said they would abrogate their agreement with the comrades in East Berlin and let East Germans like Joachim cross freely to the West. In return, the heavily indebted Hungarian state got a loan of 500 million Deutschmarks and a promise to support its wish to join the European Community. With adroit timing, Hungary had changed sides, putting West Germany before East Germany and western Europe before eastern Europe.

By September, Joachim was in West Berlin, where his West German relatives gave him a cool and ungenerous welcome. The poor cousins in the East were meant to stay where they were, not turn up on your doorstep expecting family solidarity. Joachim was quite certain the Berlin Wall would be there for many years to come and he would never be allowed back to visit his siblings. But he could talk to them on the phone – at the cost of a local call from West Berlin to East Berlin, whereas from East to West it was charged as an expensive international call.

'I wish we could see you,' said his fourteen-year-old younger brother, Johannes. Or at least, *see* you. And so they hatched a plan. In one of those crazy details of divided Berlin that always fascinated me, there was a place at which a section of the overground city railway used only by West Berliners not merely passed through East Berlin but came so close that East Germans on the other side of Schulzestrasse, a street running parallel to the line, could look up, past a frontier watchtower, and see those fortunate Westerners standing on the elevated platform of the Wollankstrasse S-Bahn station. Just a few metres away, but in another world. Joachim had often passed what he calls 'the railway station of desire', staring up at 'those people in paradise, while we were down there in the darkness'.

So he arranged for Johannes and their little sister Karoline, just seven years old, to go to exactly the right spot on Schulzestrasse and clamber onto a concrete flower box. At the appointed time, their older brother was standing on the railway platform, in the Western heaven above.

They waved and shouted at each other, emotion choking their voices.

'How are you? How's it going?'

'Achim! Achim!' cried the seven-year-old Karoline, as loud as she possibly could. Joachim will never forget the distant sound of her little girl's voice.

'Achim! Achim!'

That night, she was in tears and could not sleep. Why can't my brother come to see me?

A good question, to which there was no good answer.

Wall's fall

In *War and Peace*, Tolstoy devotes a whole chapter to the innumerable causes, great and small, that led Napoleon's army to cross the Russian frontier in June 1812. 'So all those causes – myriads of causes – coincided to bring about what happened,' Tolstoy writes. 'And consequently nothing was exclusively the cause of the war, and the war was bound to happen, simply because it was bound to happen.' In fact, 'it was predestined from all eternity'. In trying to explain the opening of the Berlin Wall on the night of Thursday 9 November 1989, one has the same sense of a multiplicity of causes all converging on one great turning point. Yet the right conclusion to draw is the opposite of Tolstoy's: not that it was predestined but that it was an exceptional, one-in-a-million piece of historical luck.

The significance of what happened on that November night is inseparable from *how* it happened. If this had been a planned, controlled opening of the frontier, as the East German authorities intended, with everyone dutifully queueing up to get permission the next day, it would still have been an important milestone, but it would not have been 'the fall of the Wall' – that spontaneous, joyful epitome of people power.

All the developments in the upward turn of the late 1980s – those long-term processes and examples of individual leadership in the Soviet Union, the United States, western Europe, eastern Europe and Germany – were needed to get to this point. So was the peaceful protest of the East German people. Before 9 November in Berlin there was 9 October in Leipzig. That evening, it nearly came to what my East German friends called 'the Chinese solution' – violent repression, as in the Tiananmen massacre just four months earlier, on 4 June, the day of the Polish election. But in Leipzig the impressive non-violent discipline of the protesters, mediation by civic leaders and a mix of indecision and restraint on the part of the communist authorities all combined to enable that Monday's demonstration to go ahead peacefully, with an unprecedented 70,000 people processing around the city's ring road. Domestically, this was the turning point. The barrier of fear was broken. After an even larger demonstration in East Berlin on 4 November, East Germans would at last have the insubordinate self-confidence to come knocking at the frontier.

Yet on the day itself, incompetence, confusion and miscommunication were the handmaidens of liberation. Under acute pressure from Czechoslovakia, which was fed up with thousands of East Germans trying to escape through its territory, East German officials hastily drew up a new regulation allowing people to leave directly from East to West Germany. Crucially, it mentioned West Berlin and applied 'with immediate effect'. It was meant to be implemented in an orderly fashion the next morning, but a bungling Politburo member called Günter Schabowski read it out at an early evening press conference and, in response to a journalist's question, said it came into force 'at once, immediately'. My former West Berlin flatmate Daniel Johnson, then a correspondent for the *Daily Telegraph*, took his place in world history with the last question, at 6.58 p.m.: 'Herr Schabowski, what will now happen with the Berlin Wall?'

Journalists then turned what was already a remarkable piece of breaking news into a sensation. The lead item on the 8 p.m. West German television news had a strapline proclaiming 'GDR opens frontier'. A reporter explained that 'the Wall, too, should become permeable overnight'. The pinnacle of journalistic hype was reached when, shortly after 10.40 p.m., a silver-haired, widely respected West German television anchor called Hanns Joachim Friedrichs declared: 'The gates in the Wall stand wide open.' This was not true. One might even say, in the vocabulary of the 2020s, that it was 'fake news'. But because West German television was so widely watched and believed in East Berlin, the inaccurate report became a self-fulfilling prophecy. Thousands of East Berliners hurried down to the frontier crossings.

Among them was my old friend Werner Krätschell, Joachim's

father. At a church service earlier in the evening he had heard from a French journalist about a new travel regulation, so when he got home to the Pankow vicarage at about 9 p.m. he asked his daughter Tanja and her friend Astrid whether the West German television news had said anything about opening the frontier. Yes, there was something like that. The three of them jumped into Werner's yellow Wartburg car and drove down to the Bornholmer Strasse frontier crossing to see what was going on.

'Am I dreaming?' Werner asked the frontier guard who lifted the first barrier for them.

'Yes,' said the guard, 'you're dreaming.'

'But I can come back?'

'No, you have emigrated and are not allowed to re-enter.'

Horrified, because Johannes and little Karoline were asleep on their own in the vicarage, Werner did a U-turn inside the frontier crossing and prepared to head home. Then he heard another frontier guard tell a colleague that the orders had changed: 'They're allowed back.' So he did another U-turn, to point his yellow Wartburg again towards the West.

Soon they were being greeted by jubilant West Berliners, cheering and clapping. When Werner eventually decided he must return to East Berlin, Astrid spoke up from the back seat. 'Please stop the car for a moment,' she said. So he stopped and then this young woman, who had never in her life been in the West, did something extraordinary. She opened the car door and just put one foot on the ground. The West! It was, Werner would later write, like Neil Armstrong taking his first step on the moon. One small step for Astrid, one giant step for humankind.

Werner's story illustrates the confusion at the heart of great events. As we now know, he had only been let out to the West because the local commander at Bornholmer Strasse, a Stasi officer called Harald Jäger, had implemented what he called a 'safety valve solution' – letting particularly insistent individuals out with an 'invalid' stamp on their identity cards, intended to expel them for good. But the frontier officers later allowed some returning citizens, including Werner, Tanja and Astrid, back in. So when Werner heard that frontier guard say 'They're allowed back', he may have caught the exact moment the orders changed. Or it may have been a misunderstanding that subsequently became a reality.

The world-historical turning point came slightly later. At around 11.30 p.m., as the crowd on the eastern side of the Bornholmer Strasse crossing point grew huge and raucous, chanting 'Open the gate! Open the gate!', Jäger gave an unprecedented order: Let everyone through! Other frontier crossings followed suit. By the early hours of Friday 10 November, tens of thousands of East Germans had put their feet on the moon.

When I got to Berlin the next day, it felt like Pentecost. The whole city was on the move. Ordinary people spoke in tongues. 'I think the sick will get up from their hospital beds,' one East Berliner told me. As if in a dream, I walked to and fro across what had been the death strip at Potsdamer Platz, stopping to pick up a small, irregular, red spray-painted chunk of the Wall, which is before me as I write. Later, I sat with Werner in a hotel room overlooking the Friedrichstrasse frontier crossing, with its glass-walled entry hall popularly known as 'the palace of tears'. We watched the crowds of excited people walking to and fro, East to West, West to East, and it seemed in that moment that all would be well, and all manner of things would be well.

On the tenth anniversary of the fall of the Wall, in November 1999, I chaired a retrospective 'summit meeting' in Berlin between Mikhail Gorbachev, Helmut Kohl and George H. W. Bush, high up in the tower block headquarters of the Axel Springer publishing house, overlooking the line of the former Wall. I started by asking Gorbachev what he did and thought on the historic night. His response was characteristically long and distinctly Tolstoyan in its view of history, but about twenty minutes into our subsequent discussion I finally got my answer: he slept soundly through the night. As we know from other sources, his advisers did not think it worth waking him. When he received a telephone report from the Soviet ambassador in East Berlin on the morning of 10 November, his reaction was 'they did the right thing'. He did not even call a special session of the Politburo.

Yet looking back, all three elder statesmen emphasised just how fragile, uncertain and even dangerous the situation was in the days and weeks that followed. There were still hardliners in Moscow who wanted to use force, as they had so often before, to reimpose the Soviet version of normality. Fortunately, Gorbachev was just then at the height of his powers, having become head of state as well as party general secretary. There was a relationship of trust between these world leaders and they felt their historic responsibility.

'All three still knew what war was,' Kohl said. 'His father badly wounded' – he pointed to Gorbachev – 'an uncle killed; my brother was killed . . . George Bush was a naval pilot in the Pacific.' The memory engine, again.

The former US president explained why he had resisted calls from some in Washington to fly to Berlin the next day (as Reagan might have done) and celebrate this Western triumph. Everyone had to show prudence and restraint. He was always worried about Gorbachev's domestic position. 'I thought it would be obscene for the president of the United States to appear to be putting my fingers in his eyes, sticking them arrogantly in his eyes' – and the usually undemonstrative, patrician Bush made a vivid gesture of stabbing with two forefingers of his left hand. Yes, Gorbachev responded, and when he and Bush met in Malta at the beginning of December: 'George told me "I have no intention of dancing on the Berlin Wall."'

Meanwhile, the photographs that everyone remembers, that media will reproduce until the end of time, are precisely those of people dancing on brightly painted stretches of the Wall. But that is the Western side, the graffiti-covered outer wall of the East German frontier complex, and most of the people standing on it were probably Westerners. Joachim was there that night, on the western side of the Brandenburg Gate, but he didn't dare clamber up. The Easterner's fear of the frontier was still deep in his bones.

The unplanned, spontaneous character of the opening, in which an essential part was played by East Berliners demanding to be let through the border crossings, means that it can be seen as a continuation of people power, from 9 October in Leipzig to 9 November in Berlin, and therefore of the East Germans' 'peaceful revolution'. Yet it was also the moment when that turned into something else. Just ten days later, I would watch a large crowd in a cold, foggy Leipzig chanting 'Germany, United Fatherland'. One banner summed up the new direction. It read: 'We are the people and demand reunification.'

'The Wall' was a Western term. Most East Germans spoke of 'the frontier'. But 'the opening of the frontier' rapidly became 'the opening of the Wall', and then someone, somewhere – a media archaeologist should try to pin down exactly who and when – turned this into 'the fall of the Wall'. With its internal rhyme in English and its Biblical echo of trumpeters bringing down the walls of Jericho, this phrase would establish itself as the received standard description of the event. It went back into German as a single word: *Mauerfall*.

The fall of the Berlin Wall was a turning point in European history that would soon be a reference point well beyond Europe. On the evening of 4 November 2008, in Washington, I witnessed another moment of great hope: joyous crowds dancing in front of the White House to celebrate the election of Barack Obama, the first Black president of the United States. Car horns honked. A young man drummed on a saucepan with a metal spoon. A saxophone blared from the passenger window of a bright red pickup truck. When I got back to my hotel room late that night, I could still hear ecstatic chants of 'Yes we can! Yes we can!' sounding through the heavily curtained windows. I turned on the television to watch Obama give his victory speech in Chicago.

Obama was describing the experience of a 106-year-old woman in Atlanta called Ann Nixon Cooper. He evoked the long arc of her life, starting in a time when 'someone like her couldn't vote, for two reasons – because she was a woman and because of the colour of her skin'. 'She was there for the buses in Montgomery,' he continued, 'the hoses in Birmingham, a bridge in Selma, and a preacher from Atlanta who told a people that "We Shall Overcome". Yes we can.' And then Obama said: 'A man touched down on the moon, a wall came down in Berlin, a world was connected by our own science and imagination.'

Like the moon landing, the fall of the Wall had become part of the shared historical mythology of humankind.

Triumphing
(1990–2007)

Post-Wall world

'Do you realise', Helmut Kohl asked me, 'that you are sitting opposite the direct successor to Adolf Hitler?' The chancellor who had just succeeded in peacefully uniting Germany was a giant of a man, both in height and girth. Even seated in a low easy chair, he towered over me. 'I don't like it,' he went on, 'but that's the fact.' His predecessors had only been chancellors of West Germany. He, Kohl, was the first chancellor of a united Germany since Hitler.

He mentioned this disagreeable fact only to emphasise his heavy sense of historical responsibility. Had not the treaty he signed with Gorbachev on the first anniversary of the fall of the Wall declared that Germany and the Soviet Union wished 'to finally finish with the past'? Hitler had sought a German-dominated Europe. He, by contrast, wanted to put a European roof over Germany. That is why he welcomed the plan for European economic and monetary union, agreed in principle by a summit of European leaders in Strasbourg as early as December 1989 and now – we were talking in his office in Bonn in autumn 1991 – to be enshrined in the Maastricht treaty. That economic union should soon be followed, he insisted, by a European political union.

Everyone felt the hand of history on their shoulders in those heady months after the fall of the Berlin Wall. Margaret Thatcher said as much when she summoned me and five other historians to Chequers, the country house where she had done lunchtime battle with Gorbachev, for a seminar about German unification in March 1990. Had Germany changed? she wanted to know. Or, as our advance briefing note ripely put it: 'Are we really dealing with the same old Huns?' At that time, Mrs Thatcher kept producing from her handbag, at meetings with fellow leaders such as François Mitterrand, a map of central Europe on which were marked, with a heavy felt tip, Germany's pre-1939 frontiers and the former German territories in the East which had provisionally been given to Poland and the Soviet Union at the Potsdam conference in 1945, pending a final peace settlement. 'That damned map', her private secretary called it.

For close to five hours at Chequers that day, we all – among us such notable historians of Germany as Fritz Stern and Gordon Craig – tried to persuade her that this was a very different Germany which intended to play a very different role in Europe. This was, of course, exactly what Kohl wanted me to understand with his reference to Adolf Hitler. Yet oddly enough, Helmut Kohl himself was almost as much the problem for Mrs Thatcher as the Nazi past. 'You didn't see how Helmut browbeat us all in Strasbourg!' she exclaimed, referring to the December 1989 summit which opened the door to both German unification and European monetary union. The Iron Lady had been handbagged by the gargantuan chancellor. That she found hard to forgive. But the venerable historian Hugh Trevor-Roper visibly struck a chord with her when he said that he had been in Germany in 1945, interviewing the surviving Nazi leaders, 'and if you had told us then that we could have a united Germany as part of the West, we would not have believed our luck'. In the end, she seemed to take our message on board. 'All right,' she concluded unforgettably, 'I'll be very nice to the Germans.'

The former East German leader Erich Honecker felt the hand of history on his shoulder in an even more direct way. In 1992, I visited him in Moabit prison in West Berlin, where he was awaiting trial on charges of being responsible for the deaths of East Germans shot while trying to escape across the Berlin Wall. A diminutive, defiant, pasty-faced old man greeted me with a stiff, ceremonial manner, almost as if I were a visiting head of state, despite the fact that he was now in jail and wearing khaki prison pyjamas. He conceded that allowing a few more people to travel to the West had not made them any more satisfied with their lot in the East ('nope, obviously not') but insisted that he now received hundreds of letters from citizens of the former German Democratic Republic, saying the old times had been better: 'They lived more tranquilly.'

Honecker talked at length about his excellent relations with many

West German politicians and 'comradely' ties with West German Social Democrats. But things were good with Helmut Kohl too. Why, he used personally to dial through to the chancellor in Bonn. Then, to my astonishment, he pulled out of the pocket of his prison pyjamas a slightly dog-eared card on which his secretary had typed the telephone number. He placed it in front of me and urged me to write it down: 0649 (for West Germany) 228 (Bonn) 562001. When I tried it afterwards, it went straight through to the chancellor's office.

These years saw the post-war era segue into the post-Wall era. After the Second World War, Europe had not reached the final peace settlement envisaged at the 1945 Potsdam conference because the Cold War intervened. Nor was there now a single grand peace conference to seal the end of the Cold War, as there had been at the end of the First World War, when the victorious Western allies dictated punitive terms to a defeated Germany in the Versailles treaty of 1919, as well as to other defeated powers such as the Ottoman Empire, in the Sèvres treaty of 1920, and Hungary, deprived of two-thirds of its territory in the Trianon treaty the same year. Yet what happened in 1990–91 was, in all but name, the final peace settlement left unfinished in 1945. As that unknown Berliner had scribbled on a handmade poster when the Wall came down: 'Only today is the war really over.' In effect, the Cold War and the Second World War ended together.

The '2+4' treaty on German unification, signed in Moscow in September 1990, was negotiated between representatives of the two German states and the four occupying powers of 1945 (the Soviet Union, the United States, France and Britain), which had never ceased to exercise their residual occupation rights, especially in Berlin. It explicitly referred back to 'wartime and post-war agreements and decisions of the Four Powers'. In November 1990, soon after the unification of Germany on 3 October 1990, the 'provisional' Polish-German frontier on Mrs Thatcher's handbag map was formally accepted by united Germany as permanent and inviolable.

When George H. W. Bush and his national security adviser Brent Scowcroft dreamed up the term 'New World Order' on a fishing trip off the coast of Maine one August day in 1990, they were thinking of the kind of Soviet–American co-operation that Franklin D. Roosevelt had hoped for in 1945. Bush later wrote to Gorbachev proposing 'a new world order of Soviet–American co-operation against aggression'. The aggression, in this case, was real and immediate: Saddam Hussein's invasion of Kuwait, which was reversed in the Gulf War. The United States and the Soviet Union also agreed two major arms reduction treaties, one on conventional forces in Europe and the other on strategic nuclear weapons, the latter signed just five months before the Soviet Union ceased to exist.

And what of the 'Declaration on Liberated Europe' which, at the Yalta conference in February 1945, had promised free elections across Soviet-occupied Europe? Well, starting with the Helsinki Conference on Security and Co-operation in Europe in 1975, through a long series of subsequent review conferences, the 'Helsinki process' culminated in a Charter of Paris for a New Europe, promulgated in November 1990. Unlike the vague commitments in the Yalta declaration, which Churchill would soon describe as 'a fraudulent prospectus', this Paris Charter was a detailed, specific prescription for a reordering of the entire continent, including the Soviet Union, on Western liberal democratic terms. Gorbachev signed on the dotted line and, unlike Stalin, he meant what he said. Unfortunately he had failed to notice that since the Soviet Union was composed of different peoples, some of whom did not wish to stick with Russia, a democratic Soviet Union was a contradiction in terms, like fried snowballs.

'We undertake to build, consolidate and strengthen democracy as the only system of government of our nations,' declared this remarkable document. The Charter of Paris went on to give a clear liberal definition of democracy, including not just 'free and fair elections', but also 'respect for the human person and the rule of law', freedom of expression, association and movement, and political pluralism. Besides a new Conflict Prevention Centre, based in Vienna, it established an Office for Free Elections, based in Warsaw. This was subsequently renamed the Office for Democratic Institutions and Human Rights, while in 1995 the world's longest running conference finally became a permanent Organisation for Security and Co-operation in Europe, the OSCE. Its election monitors had – and still have – a minutely detailed description of what is needed for a free and fair election. All this was subscribed to by Gorbachev for the Soviet Union, along with the leaders of the United States, Canada and most European countries.

A more comprehensive Western victory declaration it would be hard to imagine, and one covering the largest possible 'Europe' – from Vancouver to Vladivostok. 'We moulded it so there were no losers, only winners,' Bush would reflect a few years later. Recalling the punitive settlement imposed on Germany at the end of the First World War, he added: 'We eluded the shadow of another Versailles.' But some years later many Russians would come to view the post-Cold War settlement as, precisely, another Versailles. In private, Bush could be less Olympian. During a vigorous discussion with Kohl in summer 1990, he explained that the 'Soviets' could not have a veto on united Germany's membership in NATO. 'To hell with that!' the US president exclaimed. 'We prevailed, they didn't.'

By 1991, the Soviet Union – which Gorbachev had thought of as a single country, a Soviet motherland – was already reeling from the impact of the independence struggles of the Baltic nations, which were quite as dramatic and inspiring as the velvet revolutions I witnessed in Warsaw, Prague and Budapest. When the republics of Ukraine, Belarus and, decisively, Russia itself under Gorbachev's power-hungry rival Boris Yeltsin, decided to create a Commonwealth of Independent States, the Soviet Union ceased to exist at the end of that year. This was the final scene of the last act of the Cold War.

The enlargement of the West

What followed, across the first two post-Wall decades, was a spectacular enlargement of the West. From tentative beginnings in the wartime alliance of Western democracies against the 'Axis' of Nazi Germany, Fascist Italy and Japan, the geopolitical 'West' had grown through the Cold War into a close partnership linking most of the democracies of western, northern and southern Europe with those in North America. Its core institutions were NATO and the European Community, which was soon to become the European Union.

A politically interested Snow White who went to sleep on New Year's Day 1989 and woke up on New Year's Day 2007 would have rubbed her eyes in disbelief. Countries such as Estonia, Latvia and Lithuania that did not even exist as sovereign states on most political maps of Europe in 1989, although they had always continued to exist in the hearts of their peoples, were now members both of the European Union and, even more incredibly to a Cold War eye, of NATO. So were two other new states, the Czech Republic and Slovakia (the divorced halves of former Czechoslovakia), as well as Hungary, Poland, Romania, Bulgaria and – first among the states of former Yugoslavia – Slovenia. Looking west or south-west from a window in the Kremlin and peering across the territory of the new post-Soviet states of Ukraine, Belarus and Moldova, a Russian leader would see an arc of Western allies from the northernmost tip of Estonia to the southern extremity of Bulgaria, where the arc joined up, on Russia's southern flank, with existing NATO members Greece and Turkey. All but Turkey were also members of the EU.

This eastward enlargement of both the key security alliance of the West and the core political organisation of Europe was far from universally supported in the West. When I argued at a Franco-German-British conference in January 1990 that the newly free Poland, Hungary and Czechoslovakia should be admitted to the European Community and NATO, most of the assembled politicians, officials and diplomats treated me as a dangerous extremist. In 1991, I participated in a meeting in Prague Castle, supposedly to launch a European Confederation, a project proposed by François Mitterrand and initially supported by Václav Havel. Havel realised too late that he had been played by the wily French president, whose underlying idea was to keep the new democracies of central and eastern Europe in a velvet-wallpapered waiting room for as long as possible, while France remained as the leading power in what would soon formally become the European Union. Fortunately, we managed to foil this diversionary manoeuvre, so that by the end of the meeting Mitterrand's emissary Robert Badinter was left pleading for *une structure légère, très légère* (a light structure, very light). The EU went on to make its big eastward enlargement in May 2004, with Romania and Bulgaria following at the beginning of 2007.

NATO enlargement was even more controversial. Many policymakers in the West opposed it. Russians would repeatedly claim that the West had promised not to do it. Vladimir Putin, who became Russian president in 2000, furiously declared at a press conference in December 2021 – just two months before ordering his armies to invade Ukraine – that NATO had 'blatantly tricked' Russia by promising to expand 'not one inch eastward' in the 1990s. The phrase comes from a conversation between US Secretary of State James Baker and Gorbachev on 9 February 1990. Straining every sinew to get the Soviet leader's consent to German unification, with the whole country being in NATO, Baker asked:

> Would you prefer to see a unified Germany outside of NATO, independent and with no US forces, or would you prefer a unified Germany to be tied to NATO, with assurances that NATO's jurisdiction would not shift one inch eastward from its present position?

In a conversation with the Soviet leader the next day, Helmut Kohl, who had been briefed by Baker, declared that 'naturally NATO could not expand its territory to the current territory of the GDR'. Kohl's foreign minister, Hans-Dietrich Genscher, was even more expansive. He told his

Soviet counterpart, Eduard Shevardnadze, that 'for us, it is clear: NATO will not extend itself to the east'.

Yet these conversations were specifically about East Germany, not about the rest of central and eastern Europe. The United States soon rowed back from Baker's suggestion that NATO's 'jurisdiction' should not apply to East German territory. Gorbachev secured no formal, written commitment to preclude NATO's eastward expansion in exchange for his eventual, reluctant agreement to the whole of united Germany being inside NATO. Article 5(3) of the September 1990 '2+4' treaty on German unification stated that 'foreign armed forces and nuclear weapons or their carriers will not be stationed in that [i.e. the eastern] part of Germany or deployed there'. By this time, the Americans were waking up to the fact that the new democracies in Czechoslovakia and Poland might one day want to join NATO. So in a dramatic piece of late-night diplomacy in Moscow, just hours before the treaty was signed, the United States insisted on attaching to the treaty an 'agreed minute' which provided that the meaning of the word 'deployed' in that article would

> be decided by the Government of the united Germany in a reason-
> able and responsible way taking into account the security interests
> of each Contracting Party as set forth in the preamble.

Robert Zoellick, the author of this piece of diplomatic finesse, recalls that the wording was intended to allow for the possibility that the United States might at some future date want to move forces across eastern Germany to Poland. Gorbachev and Shevardnadze, negotiating from a position of weakness and seeking economic support from the West for the modernisation of their deeply troubled Soviet Union, agreed to this too.

In any case, an entirely new situation was created by the disintegration of the Soviet Union at the end of 1991. In the 1994 Budapest Memorandum, which provided for Ukraine to give up its large arsenal of nuclear weapons, the Russian Federation committed itself to respecting the country's territorial integrity. That promise was repeated in a bilateral friendship treaty with Ukraine in 1997. In the same year, NATO and the Russian Federation signed what was called a Founding Act on their mutual relations, in the full knowledge that NATO would enlarge eastward, to include some of the countries between Germany and Russia.

'NATO and Russia do not consider each other as adversaries,' it declared. Among the principles both sides agreed to was 'respect for [the] sovereignty, independence and territorial integrity of all states and their inherent right to choose the means to ensure their own security'. For their part, NATO's existing members affirmed that they had 'no intention, no plan and no reason to deploy nuclear weapons on the territory of new members', thus clearly indicating that there would be new members.

In his first years as Russian president, Vladimir Putin himself stuck to this line. Interviewed by the British journalist David Frost in March 2000, Putin said: 'It is hard for me to visualise NATO as an enemy.' When Frost followed up, asking: 'Is it possible Russia could join NATO?', Putin replied:

> I don't see why not. I would not rule out such a possibility – but I repeat – if and when Russia's views are taken into account as those of an equal partner.

Standing beside the NATO general-secretary George Robertson at a press conference in Rome in May 2002, following the inaugural meeting of a new NATO–Russia council, Putin said: 'Ukraine is an independent, sovereign nation state and it will choose its own path to peace and security.' Robertson recalls that in his nine meetings with the Russian president, Putin at no point raised any objections to the impending seven-country NATO enlargement. Condoleezza Rice, President George W. Bush's national security adviser and subsequently Secretary of State, says the Russian leader did not signal any concern to them either – until 2007, when he challenged both the proposed deployment of a missile defence system in Poland and the suggestion that Ukraine should be offered NATO membership.

Thus, while Western leaders did make some expansive verbal promises to Soviet leaders in negotiations in early 1990, those promises were not repeated in the treaty on German unification – and the Soviet Union subsequently ceased to exist. The state that Putin actually led, the Russian Federation, accepted NATO enlargement and formally guaranteed the territorial integrity of Ukraine.

In May 2001, I was summoned to the White House with four other experts to brief President George W. Bush before his first official visit to Europe and first meeting with Putin. I urged him to support NATO membership for all qualifying central and east European countries.

'Including the Baltic states?' Bush asked, in his abrupt, clipped manner.

'Yes, definitely.'

Michael McFaul, who subsequently became Barack Obama's ambassador to Moscow, took the same view, as did Lionel Barber, who would go on to become editor of the *Financial Times*.

'Well,' concluded Bush, 'very interesting . . . I'll take that under advisement.'

I have no illusion that ours were anything but three small voices among many far more important ones pushing in the same direction. But given the revanchist turn that Putin's Russia took a few years later, culminating in its full-scale invasion of Ukraine in February 2022, I sing hallelujahs that we urged this course. Imagine how mortally threatened, if not utterly strangled, would be the peace and freedom of Estonia, Latvia and Lithuania today, were those countries not in NATO.

Many Russians would, like Putin, come to view this double enlargement of the West, and especially that of NATO, as an anti-Russian move. Without question, most central and east European countries still valued NATO primarily for defending them from Russia. Some central Europeans even saw the European Union in that way. Visiting a Lithuanian member of parliament in 1994, in a parliament building that had been barricaded against an anticipated Soviet assault only three years before, I noticed on his cupboard door a blue and yellow sticker proclaiming 'My country Europe'.

What is Europe? I asked him.

'*Europa ist nicht-Russland*,' he replied. Europe is not-Russia.

I have always rejected this view of Europe – and of the West. Properly understood, the enlargement of the West does not entail the diminishment of Russia. Quite the contrary. When the conversation in the White House turned directly to Russia, Michael McFaul and I both urged George W. Bush to keep open the possibility that a democratic Russia might itself one day become a member of NATO. Russia, McFaul argued, was at that very moment agonising over whether to keep orientating itself towards the West and Europe, as it had done for most of the 1990s, or turn away from them.

Western help in modernising Russia was what Helmut Kohl and President Bush Sr had promised Gorbachev. To a significant degree, this is also what united Germany and the Clinton administration in the United States tried to deliver for Russia under President Boris Yeltsin in the 1990s. The West went a long way to accommodate – or, according to your point of view, incorporate – this new Russia in the Western-built structures of liberal international order. Not only did the 1997 NATO–Russia Founding Act envisage a future of far-reaching co-operation, subsequently given substance in a NATO–Russia council inaugurated by Putin himself. In 1998, Russia was invited to sit at what was in effect the top table of the West, the G7 group, which became the G8. It was only several years into Putin's presidency, in the second half of the 2000s, that Russia's relationship with the West turned decisively towards confrontation.

Integration and disintegration

The 'common European home' thus underwent its most fundamental reconstruction since 1945. The plumbing, wiring, furniture and decoration were re-done across most of the house in a fashion meant to resemble that of the west wing. Most residents now paid rent to the western landlords (EU, NATO & Co.) rather than to the old one in the east wing. In return, the new landlords arranged repairs, window locks and a security alarm. The very clothes that people in the east wing wore, the products they used, the ways they worked, communicated and lived, changed to resemble those in the west wing. Beyond that, all the rooms in the western quarters of the house had their connecting walls knocked down, providing pooled utilities, common dining spaces and even shared cutlery, so that everyone found themselves living in a new kind of home.

A novel pair of terms came into use to describe this reconstruction: 'widening and deepening'. The basic direction was already set in the early 1990s, although the building work took almost as long as that on a new Berlin airport. I take from a dusty old folder the text of a speech delivered by Chancellor Kohl at Oxford on 11 November 1992 – he had committed to come when we spoke in Bonn a year earlier – and I find the whole building plan laid out there.

In order not to go back to the politics of ever-changing coalitions and European fraternal wars, Kohl argues, of which we think particularly on 11 November (Armistice Day, marking the end of the First World War), we must move as decisively to achieve European unity as he had just done to achieve German unity. The Maastricht treaty must be ratified. The common currency must have an independent European central bank, ensuring monetary stability, and it must be embedded in an economic union. But an economic and monetary union would only be sustainable if founded firmly on a political union. The European Union, as it would become once the Maastricht treaty had been ratified, would also require more internal security. As essential would be stronger democratic control, therefore the powers of the European Parliament should be enhanced. The war that was already raging in former Yugoslavia should bring home to us how urgently we need a common foreign and security policy, to complement the still indispensable Atlantic Alliance.

So much for 'deepening'. As for 'widening': accession negotiations should soon begin with Austria, Sweden, Finland, Switzerland 'and probably also Norway'. But the eastern dividing wall must also be knocked through. 'For me as a German it is completely unacceptable that the eastern frontier of Germany could permanently be the eastern frontier of the European Union.' After all, Poland is not – 'as some thoughtlessly put it' – in eastern Europe but in central Europe. The one thing the chancellor of German unity did not envisage in 1992 was the inclusion of the Baltic republics. The membership of former Soviet states in the future EU was, he roundly declared, 'ruled out'. He concluded with a lyrical passage about how, on New Year's Day 1993, all border controls between France and Germany would be removed, and how a few months earlier he had sat in the summer sunshine on the Charles Bridge in Prague, surrounded by young Italians, Germans, Brits and Russians who were already enjoying the Europe of which his generation had dreamed.

At the time, I thought his speech was quite boring. I had heard it all before and Kohl's rhetorical style was like his taste in food – ample and heavy. But reading it again at the beginning of the 2020s, I found myself thinking: 'If only we had any leaders now who could lay out such a clear and large vision of where they wanted Europe to be in ten years' time!' Thirty years on, two big things on Kohl's agenda had not been achieved: a genuinely common foreign policy and the political union that he regarded as an indispensable complement to the monetary one. Otherwise, the building plan had essentially been implemented.

Yet to stop there is to tell only half the story, the half most Europeans would regard as positive. If you go carefully through the chronology of these years you find a constant to and fro, a push and pull, between integration and disintegration, freedom and oppression, peace and war.

In January 1993, the single European market comes into effect, but there is also the velvet divorce between the Czech Republic and Slovakia. In 1994, we enter the second stage of preparations for European monetary union, Hungary applies to join the EU and the Channel Tunnel is opened, but a terrible bombing of the marketplace in Sarajevo marks a further deterioration in what is already the third war of the Yugoslav succession (after those in Slovenia and Croatia, Bosnia). Fifty-two per cent of Swedes vote to join the EU but fifty-two per cent of Norwegians vote to stay out. In 1995, an 'irreversible' timetable is agreed for introducing what is now called 'the euro' by the end of the century, but there are riots in Northern Ireland, ethnic cleansing in the Krajina area of Croatia and genocide in Srebrenica. Here the Europe of Maastricht, there the Europe of Sarajevo.

In 1998, the Good Friday agreement in Northern Ireland ends three decades of sectarian violence, but simultaneously we see an insurrection in Kosovo. As the Irish Republican Army lays down arms, the Kosovo Liberation Army takes them up. In 1999, the euro is introduced (although not yet the coins and notes) in eleven of the EU's fifteen member states, but there is war and an attempted genocide in Kosovo. NATO bombs targets in Serbia and brings in land forces to occupy the disputed province. One day in May that year, I am standing in a British army field headquarters in Macedonia, near the frontier to Kosovo, while the gravel-voiced General Michael Jackson is showing me the invasion geography on a Second World War Wehrmacht map of Yugoslavia. (The Germans, he says, with a leathery smile, knew exactly the best way to go in.) The next day I am in Aachen, to witness Tony Blair receiving the Charlemagne prize. He tells me afterwards that during the High Mass in Charlemagne's cathedral he was thinking how lucky his children are to grow up in a European Union like this.

And so it goes on. More of the violence and disintegration is in the eastern half of the continent, more of the peace and integration in the western, but by no means always. Besides the horrifying bloodshed in Northern Ireland there are the ETA Basque extremist bombings in Spain, Mafia killings in Italy and, soon enough, Islamist terrorism across western Europe. I have rarely seen so many European flags so enthusiastically waved as I did on the Maidan, the great square of Kyiv, during the

Orange Revolution in the winter of 2004. Meanwhile, it was the French and Dutch who would soon vote in referendums to reject the EU's proposed constitutional treaty.

Across the continent, the forces of order and disorder, co-operation and confrontation, integration and disintegration, were engaged in a constant struggle.

Good King Wenceslas

We are sitting at a large, circular dining table in Brussels in early 2020, a group of Europeans discussing the future of Europe. Pierre Vimont, a wise, soft-spoken French diplomat tells us how a top EU figure was floored by a television interviewer asking the simple question: 'Who is your European hero?'

We decide to go round the table and offer our own answers. The clear winner, with six votes out of seventeen, is Václav Havel. The only other 'European hero' to receive more than one vote is Winston Churchill. King Juan Carlos of Spain, the Estonian Lennart Meri, the French politician Simone Veil, Willy Brandt, Erasmus and Pericles must all settle for a solitary advocate. Coming at the end of this tour de table, I cast the sixth vote for Havel.

The life stories of figures like Churchill, Konrad Adenauer, Jean Monnet, Charles de Gaulle and Alcide de Gasperi show how the tragic experience of the 'European civil war' from 1914 to 1945 found positive expression in the building of post-war Europe. Havel is the great example, along with Bronisław Geremek, Lennart Meri and a few others, of the tragic experience of central Europe from 1945 to 1989 finding positive expression in the building of post-Wall Europe.

The tale of how he went from dissident playwright to president, from prison to Prague Castle, has often been retold as simplistic celebrity myth. It's easy to turn him into some latter-day version of Good King Wenceslas, the tenth-century Bohemian ruler who, in the story retold in a much-loved English carol, goes out into the snow with his servant at Christmas time to bring food and wine to a poor peasant: 'Mark my footsteps good my page/ Tread thou in them boldly.' Wenceslas is Václav in Czech, as in Václavské náměstí (Wenceslas Square) in Prague, named after the mediaeval ruler who was subsequently beatified, becoming St Václav. Havel not only shared his first name and was, as first president of the Czech Republic, his remote successor as titular ruler in Bohemia; as a historical figure, he has experienced the political equivalent of post-humous beatification, becoming a second St Václav.

The word 'hero' is used loosely in our time. When I was young, I believed in heroes, meaning flawless, superior kinds of human being. Today I know better, not least from watching how some of my former idols among the central European dissidents changed after 1989. Some-one who is a hero in one situation can behave quite badly in another. Yet although there are no perfect heroes, there is heroism.

In his dissident years, Václav Havel showed true heroism. Born into a wealthy bourgeois family in 1936, he was denied higher education during the early years of communist rule simply on account of his 'wrong' social origins. But he educated himself. One of his most important early influences was a family friend, the philosopher Josef Šafařík. Šafařík taught that one must follow the voice of conscience 'of one's own accord, at one's own risk, on one's own responsibility'. Each person had to find the truth to the best of their ability, the truth as they understood it, and then stand up and be counted for it, even unto death. What mattered above all was this personally avowed truth.

Havel worked his way up, via workaday theatre jobs as stagehand and lighting gaffer, to being an internationally celebrated dramatist – a Czech Samuel Beckett or Harold Pinter, with a distinct Kafkaesque twist. His play *The Memorandum*, for example, revolves around the director of a nondescript office struggling with communications received in an inde-cipherable bureaucratic language called Ptydepe. The young playwright participated in the Prague Spring of 1968 and offered instructions to his compatriots for opposing the Soviet invasion of Czechoslovakia in August of that year, and subsequent occupation:

> Use against the enemy every method that he does not expect: do not show him any understanding, ridicule him and reveal to him the absurdity of his situation . . .

After that, however, came a time of hopelessness, given over to partying, drinking and womanising, as well as some creative work. He would later describe his memories of the first half of the 1970s as 'a single shapeless fog'. But then, starting with a superb open letter to the communist party leader, Gustáv Husák, in 1975, he became a 'dissident'. The time had come for what, echoing his early teacher, he called 'living in truth'. He was instrumental in pulling together a coalition of diverse individuals, from ex-communists to Catholic conservatives, to launch, in January 1977, the manifesto known as Charter 77. It demanded respect for the human and civil rights codified in UN international covenants and the Helsinki Final Act, all signed by the Czechoslovak regime. Those who signed the manifesto would be known as Chartists, and 'Charter 77' became an organised dissident movement.

There followed a moment of doubt and shame. Detained, repeatedly interrogated and threatened with a long imprisonment, he signed a petition requesting his release, pledging to 'refrain from public political activities' and to concentrate solely on his artistic ones. This pledge was stitched together with other statements he had made under interrogation and published as a full-scale recantation in the communist party daily *Rudé právo*. Havel was haunted by this 'failure'. He agonised over it, wrote about it in letters and plays. Most importantly, he learned from it. Faced in 1979 with the prospect of a long jail term for his dissident activity, he marched eyes open into the ordeal. As Šafařík had taught, living in truth meant being ready to pay that price. He was in prison for 1,351 days. Initially, he had to undertake hard manual labour as a welder. The first prison commandant was a sadist who told him that Hitler had handled things better: 'He gassed vermin like you right away'. Finally, he was released into hospital, seriously ill. His health would never entirely recover. His fellow political prisoner Jiří Dienstbier once told me that the jailers gave Václav an especially hard time because he seemed so diffident, even apologetic, and was constantly trying to explain things. They were very surprised – Jiří chuckled into his beer – to discover that prisoner Havel was actually the toughest of the lot.

When I first met the dissident playwright, in his apartment in Prague, he was not long out of prison. My notes describe him as 'walrus-like', with a drooping moustache, curly blond hair, tubby barrel body on short legs and an 'unexpectedly deep voice'. He told me there were two vital questions: Does Charter 77 speak the truth? If yes, is that truth gradually reaching the wider society? He answered the first with a definite yes, the second more tentatively. In 1986, I drove out to visit him unannounced in his farmhouse in northern Bohemia. As I approached, I saw a police car blocking the entrance. Quickly readjusting, I drove on up a country lane, hid my car in the woods and worked my way down the hillside on foot, through the long grass, to the back of the farmhouse, cursing my light-coloured Burberry raincoat for making me so visible. If the police had filmed me, it would have made a perfect propaganda clip: 'visit from an agent of Western imperialism'. I tapped on the kitchen window and Havel emerged to greet me, wearing slippers, dark red cord trousers and a T-shirt saying 'Temptation is Great'. (*Temptation* was his latest play, just premiered in Vienna.)

'I wondered who the police were waiting for.'

What followed, over beer and soup, while the police waited outside in perfect ignorance, was one of the most memorable conversations of my life. We talked for hours about the tension of writing when at any moment his typescript could be confiscated by the police, about the mission of the political writer, the moral ambiguities of Western détente policies and the cowardice of Western embassies. (The French ambassador refused to allow Havel's honorary doctorate from Toulouse University to be presented in the embassy.) What he said revealed, beside his intensity and humour, a shrewd political instinct.

By this time, Havel had already distilled his hard experience into some of the finest political essays of the twentieth century. In 'The Power of the Powerless', he gives the example of the greengrocer who puts in his shop window, among the onions and carrots, a sign saying 'Workers of the World, Unite!' Why is the greengrocer doing it? Is he overflowing with enthusiasm for unity among the workers of the world? No, he is signalling to those in power his readiness to conform and obey. Were he asked to display the words 'I'm afraid and therefore unquestioningly obedient', this would be the truth, but he would not be half so willing to display the sign. Thus the system of power depends on the self-deceiving complicity of the many. Let people only see and acknowledge the truth, tear away the Lilliputian threads of self-deception and lies, and they will discover the power of the powerless.

This analysis was local but also universal. Fourteen years later, I was sitting with the Burmese opposition leader Aung San Suu Kyi in Yangon, during one of her brief periods of release from house arrest, and discussing it with her. She said Havel's writings had been an inspiration. (Tragically, she lacked his shrewd political instinct.) I have been asked about 'The Power of the Powerless' by students in Tehran, Delhi, Kyiv and Beijing. They had read it in their own samizdat translations or located versions of it on the internet. During the pro-democracy demonstrations in Hong Kong in 2019, a new edition of 'The Power of the Powerless' was to be found in bookshops and quoted on social media. Even if Havel had died in hospital at the end of his long prison term, in 1983, these essays would have endured as a distinctively European contribution to humanity's shared learning process.

Fortunately he survived, and we met often until his death in 2011. Our next meeting was also our shortest. In 1988, I and others had come to Prague to participate in an unofficial symposium he had organised to mark the twentieth anniversary of 1968. We gathered, as instructed, in the rundown but still gorgeous Jugendstil restaurant of the Hotel Paříž. Havel only had time to say 'I declare this meeting open' before he was arrested and carried off by the secret police.

Dissidents the world over are often forceful, loudspoken characters, admirable but not always lovable. Speaking quietly, in a deep rumbling voice, Havel was courteous, diffident, even apologetic, with a kind of vulnerability that was immensely attractive, not least to women. Václav was lovable and I, too, loved him. Inspired by his example, I spent much thankless administrative time over the next few years working, together with the German-British liberal thinker Ralf Dahrendorf, the French historian François Furet, the Swedish writer Per Wästberg and others, on a project to support independent and samizdat publications in central and eastern Europe, including many in Czechoslovakia. Havel appreciated this. It was one of the reasons that, when change finally came to Prague in November 1989, he gave me a ringside seat in the headquarters of what was soon labelled the Velvet Revolution. Suitably enough for a playwright, the headquarters was in the Magic Lantern theatre.

*

Then, almost in the blink of an eye, there he was up in Prague Castle, being installed as president at the end of December 1989, in a suit hastily made for him, with the trousers appearing much too short. Throughout his presidency, whether we met in London or Washington on his official visits, at a NATO summit in Prague, more quietly at the president's country residence at Lány or on a road trip through the north Bohemian countryside, each encounter brought some new insight or humorous anecdote. He gave a fine description of a large black box in Bill Clinton's presidential car, which he assumed must contain the nuclear codes. But then it was opened to reveal only numerous cans of Coca-Cola. 'All sorts of different Coke!', Havel rumbled, with his characteristic short chuckle.

He no longer had time to write essays or plays, he told me, so he treated his speeches as his 'great work', a term with alchemical overtones that he borrowed from one of his predecessors in Prague Castle, the eccentric seventeenth-century Habsburg emperor Rudolf II. He prepared for these speeches carefully, often with books piled high on his desk, and he wrote all the best ones himself.

In several of these speeches he carried on a friendly argument with me about intellectuals in politics. I argued, far from originally, that the roles of the politician and the intellectual are not only distinct but stand in a creative tension with each other. The intellectual's job is to seek the truth, and to speak truth to power. Politicians must use words in a different, more instrumental way, to advance their party and their programme by putting one side of the case as strongly as possible. Rather than seek intellectual nuance or perfect honesty, they must repeat themselves constantly for effect. In short, the intellectual should always try to live in truth while the politician has to work in half-truth. Both roles are legitimate and necessary for a flourishing liberal democracy, but they are different and should not be confused. I quoted, as my crowning witness, Immanuel Kant: 'That kings should philosophise, or that philosophers should become kings, is not to be expected but also not to be desired, for the possession of power unavoidably spoils the free use of reason.'

Havel disagreed and he used his speeches, sometimes in the most unlikely places, to explain why. A Japanese audience in the Asahi Hall in Tokyo in April 1992 must have been slightly bemused to find him continuing in front of them this long-distance argument with 'a British friend'. 'A new wind, new spirit, a new spirituality', he told them, should be injected into the established stereotypes of present-day politics. Politics should be 'humanised and its intellectual and spiritual dimension cultivated'. 'Philosophers and poets in ministerial chairs will not, of course, single-handedly save the world. But they could – under certain circumstances – contribute to its salvation.' And he concluded: 'It is up to those of us who fate has put in this position to demonstrate whether my British friend has shown foresight, or has simply been too influenced by the banal idea that everyone should stick to his own trade.'

His long period in high office, as president first of Czechoslovakia and then of the Czech Republic, retiring only in 2003, gives evidence for both points of view. None of his speeches, except perhaps for his first, on New Year's Day 1990, quite measures up to his finest essays. As a politician who had to seek re-election, he could not entirely 'live in truth'. He made compromises. He signed a law on 'lustration' that he profoundly disagreed with since it blacklisted from a wide range of public sector jobs entire categories of former employees and collaborators of the secret police. (He subsequently took the law to the Constitutional Court, securing some modifications.) He was sometimes humiliated by the Thatcherite Václav Klaus – the other Wenceslas, but one who would certainly never have walked out into the snow to feed a starving peasant.

Havel clung to office too long, as politicians often do. He should not have stood again for a second term as president of the Czech Republic in 1998. By the end, many Czechs were tired of his theatrical gestures and moralistic preaching. Often he seemed awkwardly suspended between the politician's 'ethics of responsibility' and the intellectual's 'ethics of conscience', to use Max Weber's terms. He himself spoke of having discovered, in high-level politics, the powerlessness of the powerful. If he had stuck to his original promise at the end of the Velvet Revolution, and served as president only until the first democratic elections in mid-1990, might we have had more great essays from an undisputed moral authority?

And yet, and yet. What would the Czech Republic, this new-founded state, have looked like had he not been there to set the tone? When, after his death, we saw the Dalai Lama welcomed in Prague and a Czech senator defying the power of communist China to pay homage to democratic

Taiwan, we witnessed his legacy. In 2020, I heard the Czech European Commissioner, Věra Jourová, talk passionately about the need for the EU to stand up for the rule of law in Poland and Hungary. 'Democracy has to be written in our hearts,' she said. Pure Havel. Sure enough, she had a large portrait photo of him on her office wall in Brussels.

He also had a broader message to Europe, a message that was probably heard more widely because he was a head of state and not just a writer. He was a lifelong enthusiast for European unity. At the age of sixteen he commented on the birth of the European coal and steel community in a letter to a friend: 'Look, the united Europe is already being born . . .' Yet in speeches through the 1990s, he added an important warning. He told the European Parliament in 1994 that reading the Maastricht Treaty he felt he was 'looking into the workings of an absolutely perfect and immensely ingenious modern machine'. Maastricht 'addressed my reason, but not my heart'. What the EU needed was 'a charter of its own that would clearly define the ideas on which it is founded . . . and the values it intends to embody'. Addressing the French senate in 1999, he praised the progress of European unification but added

> I cannot rid myself of the sensation that all this may have been a train ride which began earlier, in another time and under different circumstances, and which just keeps going on, without receiving new energy, new spiritual impulses, a renewed sense of direction and of the purpose of the journey.

And he returned to his idea of the charter. This he now called a European constitution, but it should be 'a constitution which every child in Europe can simply learn at school'.

So concerned was he about the lack of emotional appeal and a sense of direction that he and I worked together with the pianist and conductor Vladimir Ashkenazy on a project to launch a new text for the European anthem, to be premiered in Prague. The lines that I drafted for this began 'Europe in the hearts of nations/ Reaching for a higher law'. That still seems to me not bad. But the verse got worse thereafter and some of my friends tease me about it to this day. In the end, the project was abandoned, yet Havel's warning remains compelling for the European Union in our time. This Union speaks more to the head than to the heart.

One other thing that stands out in these speeches is his demand that Europe should be a defender of 'planetary civilisation'. Like his endorsement of James Lovelock's Gaia hypothesis, which describes earth as a single giant self-regulating system, this was generally regarded at the time as the mild eccentricity of a philosopher king. But today, as we see how climate change has become an existential threat and human activity is reducing biodiversity, it seems prescient. In his way, Havel anticipated Greta Thunberg.

More immediately, he was horrified by what was happening in another rapidly dissolving communist federation which, unlike former Czechoslovakia, was not divorcing peacefully. His was one of the most eloquent voices urging the United States and EU to intervene to end the bloodshed and prevent genocide there. If Václav Havel represents the best of the early post-Wall period, former Yugoslavia represents the worst.

Genocide again

One day in October 1995 I drove through the 'ethnically cleansed' waste-land of Krajina, in Croatia. 'Hard to describe the cumulative effect of mile upon mile, hour upon hour, of devastated, burned houses, plun-dered of everything of value,' I noted.

> The windows smashed. Bottles, bedclothes, broken furniture, papers strewn across the floor . . . No tractors or agricultural equipment. No cattle. No dogs. A few *cats* – hardiest of creatures. But above all, no people. Houses. Roads. The remains of shops. Farmsteads. Orchards. Vineyards carefully tended. But nobody, nobody, nobody – except the Croatian police patrols [and] a few UN vehicles.

'An amazing amount of hard work,' I added, 'went into this "cleaning".' Later, we met a few frightened old Serbian peasant women, dressed tra-ditionally, all in black. In the now largely abandoned town of Kistanje, we found family photo albums laid out on a table in the empty market-place: the wedding, the christening, a family party. An entire life that would never return.

Serbs had started it back in 1991, in the first months of the bloody dissolution of Yugoslavia, turning this beautiful, mountainous border region – the former 'military frontier' of the Austro-Hungarian empire – into a brutal, gangsterish para-state that called itself the Republic of Ser-bian Krajina. They drove out most of their Croat neighbours, killed some of them, plundered their houses, burnt Roman Catholic churches. But four years on, in August 1995, it was Croats who finished the job. Close to 200,000 Serbs fled in the face of Operation Storm, a Croatian mili-tary operation to liberate Krajina. Now again we saw Auden's 'Those to whom evil is done/ Do evil in return'. Now the plunderers were plundered, robbers robbed, and it was the turn of Orthodox churches to be trashed by good Christians from another denomination. Years later, men on both sides, Serb and Croat, would be convicted of war crimes.

Innocent Serbs who remained behind were assisted into the next life under cover of night. In the local capital of Knin, just two months after the end of Operation Storm, the UN 'protection force' gave me their tally of some one hundred murders so far. Barely a rounding error in the statistics of those killed, raped, maimed and displaced across the ten years it took to tear a European country apart. In the driveway of a plundered house, I picked up a large black-and-white photograph of Marshal Tito, the man who had forged and held together the socialist federal republic of Yugoslavia until his death in 1980. Across Tito's face there was the distinct muddy footprint of a large boot.

As the afternoon light faded we found, in the garden of yet another torched farmstead, a book of children's verse: *Bandit Katja and Princess Nadja*, published in Sarajevo in 1989. 'Oh yes,' said Ana Uzelac, a journalist who grew up in Yugoslavia, 'I loved that when I was a kid.' She opened it and recited into the gathering gloom:

> The actor
> acts,
> The singer
> sings,
> The judge
> judges,
> The student
> studies,
> The cook
> cooks,
> The watchman
> watches.
> This is how
> our Yugoslavia grows.

(I have the book in front of me now, still with the dirt on its cover.)

By dusk, we were back down from the mountain wasteland, mingling with German tourists in the lovely Dalmatian coastal resort town of Šibenik. Here there was electric light, running water, a young couple kissing on a scooter – and a good espresso awaiting us in the Café Europa. Ach, Europa.

A week later, I was in the Bosnian town of Tuzla, talking to a thirty-nine-year-old locksmith turned soldier who had survived the massacre of Srebrenica just three months earlier. His wounded foot had been operated on by Dutch surgeons in the supposedly UN-protected 'safe area'. They had assured him he was safe. But then he had been transported off by the Bosnian Serb forces who had overrun the small Dutch UN protection force. He told me he had seen his Dutch 'protectors' sitting drinking with the Serbs. By some miracle he had survived, but his wound was left to fester – crawling with worms, he said – and the Serbian camp commander deliberately kicked it. He still did not know the fate of his father and two brothers.

The massacre at Srebrenica in July 1995 was the single worst war crime committed in Europe since 1945. The international tribunal set up in The Hague to try crimes in the former Yugoslavia deemed it an act of genocide. The murder of some 8,000 Bosnian men and boys was hard work. The Bosnian Serb forces commanded by General Ratko Mladić had no gas chambers. Instead, the 'Muslims', as the killers usually called them, were transported in trucks to the killing fields and individually shot through the head. When the next truckload of captives arrived, they could see fresh corpses lying in rows.

One of the killers, Dražen Erdemović, recalled that the smell reminded him of a butcher's shop he used to frequent as a boy. Each victim reacted differently, some pleading ('Please let me live, I saved Serbs from Srebrenica, I have their telephone numbers'), some cursing, others offering money, others again just going silently to their deaths. Some did not die from the first bullet and needed to be finished off. Erdemović tried to avoid looking at their faces. But he could never forget the face of one boy, only fifteen years old or perhaps even younger, shirtless and pale-skinned in the bright sunlight. The boy's eyes opened wide when he saw the rows of dead bodies. As he knelt down, ready to be shot in the back of the head, he whispered 'Mother! Mother!'

'Never again!' Europeans had resolved after 1945. Now it happened again. A part of Europe once more descended into a man-made hell of fratricidal war, rape, ethnic cleansing and genocide. 'I have just come back from 1945,' I wrote in one of my fourteen surviving notebooks from former Yugoslavia. This tragedy unfolded while just a few miles away other Europeans went about their lives, drank coffee in the cafés, and praised the triumphant Europe of freedom, peace and prosperity. Me too. How could I have sat happily with friends in our garden in Oxford, celebrating my fortieth birthday, while on that very day – 12 July 1995 – Bosnians like the boy who cried 'Mother!' were being executed in cold blood? Worst of all, this happened under the very noses of Dutch, French and other European soldiers who were there to protect them in the name of the United Nations. Back in January 1993, Dr Hakija Turajlić, the vice president of the Republic of Bosnia and Herzegovina, was shot and killed by a Serb fighter while he sat in the back of a UN-flagged French armoured personnel carrier.

From Tuzla I went on to Sarajevo, there to face the bitterness and anger of people who had survived more than three years under siege by Bosnian Serb forces, while the rest of Europe looked away. These Sarajevans spat out the word 'Europe' with acid contempt. For them, Europe had become a dirty word. When they said 'before the war', they meant before 1992, not before 1939. Year Zero was about to recur.

Shortly before I got to Bosnia, Pope John Paul II was talking to President Bill Clinton in the city of Newark. The twentieth century had begun with a war in Sarajevo, the Pope told Clinton, and he must not allow the century to end with a war in Sarajevo. It was thanks to the United States that the war in Bosnia was finally ended, albeit with a peace settlement negotiated in Dayton, Ohio, that was based on far-reaching ethnic partition and stored up problems for the future.

Instead of a war in Sarajevo, the twentieth century would end with a war in Kosovo. This fourth war of the Yugoslav succession, following those in Slovenia, Croatia and Bosnia, culminated in a NATO-led occupation and the establishment of an international protectorate in summer 1999. For many of my contemporaries, the defining experience was Bosnia; my own most intense engagement was with Kosovo. I had discovered this little-known corner of Europe already in the 1970s, in my culture-vulture youth, when I visited and fell in love with the exquisite mediaeval Serbian Orthodox monasteries of Peć, Gračanica and Visoki Dečani. In 1983, I revisited Kosovo to write about the already burgeoning conflict between the majority Albanian population, who were mainly Muslim, and the Serb/Yugoslav authorities. My article in the *Spectator* was headlined 'Belfast in Yugoslavia'. It picked up on a joke I had heard in the provincial capital, Pristina. 'Did you hear they've decided to rename Pristina? From now on it will be called Belfast.'

In the late 1990s, I spent several weeks travelling around former Yugoslavia, talking to Albanians and Serbs in Kosovo and to all sides in Belgrade. Serbian repression in the province was intense. As the armed insurrection by the Kosovar Albanians' self-styled Kosovo Liberation Army (KLA) gathered force in 1998, I saw for the first time in my life the rigid corpses of murdered men sticking out of improvised plastic bodybags. And I contemplated the fresh blood of two murdered Serb policemen reddening the snow in a hamlet called Prilep, just south of the Dečani monastery. Weeping mothers sat beside their ruined houses. Children stood around with large, bewildered eyes. The forces of Slobodan Milošević, the post-communist leader of Serbia and rump Yugoslavia, responded with even more brutality than before.

'But surely even Milošević can't try to ethnically cleanse 1.8 million Albanians!' I exclaimed to the Slovene President Milan Kučan, when we talked in his office in Ljubljana in the autumn of 1998.

'You don't know Milošević.'

Hundreds of thousands of Kosovar Albanians fled for their lives, fearing a genocide on an even larger scale than Bosnia. They knew Milošević. The United States and Europe were finally stung into action by warnings of 'another Bosnia' from tenacious and principled journalists, politicians, and moral authorities such as Havel and the Pope. In March 1999, NATO started bombing Serbia. After seventy-eight days of bombing and facing growing external pressure, the Serbian leader finally conceded an international presence in Kosovo. In practice, that meant NATO forces under General Michael Jackson – with his excellent Wehrmacht maps – moving in, to be hailed as liberators by the Albanian population. I followed them a few days later, driving a battered old Lada jeep. (If Marlene Dietrich 'still has a suitcase in Berlin', I still have four large petrol cans in Skopje. I had to buy them – paying in cash, Deutschmarks of course – because the petrol supply could not be relied on around liberated and occupied Kosovo.)

In Pristina, I saw graffiti thanking the British prime minister 'Tony Bler' and proclaiming 'God Save the Quin'. Up in the hills, I tracked down a well-known KLA commander, Ramush Haradinaj. He came from the famously tough Drenica area of the province. Two of his brothers had been killed by Serb forces and he himself had been wounded in a firefight the previous year. But now his Kosovo Liberation Army unit had itself been credibly accused of committing war crimes, including the murders of those two Serb policemen whose fresh blood I had seen the winter before, bright red on the white snow. So I charged him with that crime.

'I hope it was more than two,' he replied. 'I was so happy to see more dead military police.' The country would respect his fighting record.

'Me, I couldn't be no Mother Teresa. I'm KLA.'

Over the next twenty years, Haradinaj would twice be tried in The Hague for war crimes, and twice acquitted. The court complained of strong indications of witness intimidation. He would also twice be prime minister of Kosovo, treated in many capitals of Europe with all the respect due to a holder of high office. But I will never forget our conversation in the hills.

In the nearby monastery of Dečani, stately, bearded Father Sava did not waste his breath blaming Albanians like Haradinaj. It was Milošević, he said, who 'not only lost Kosovo but completely destroyed his own people physically and spiritually'. The monks of Dečani had survived 500 years under the Turks and fifty years under the communists, but what the Serbian leader had done to them was the worst of all. 'In this sanctuary,' he concluded, 'it is not meet to mention his name' (using an old-fashioned religious sense of the word 'meet', meaning right and proper). Milošević as He-who-must-not-be-named, the Voldemort of Belgrade.

Then it was December 1999 and, back in what was now a strange kind of international protectorate, I met Detective Constable Colin Campbell of the Royal Ulster Constabulary (the police force in Northern Ireland), patrolling the battered streets of Pristina in a UN blue beret. Things here, he told me, were just like 'in our country'. There were two communities who hated each other and the police had the devil of a job keeping the peace between them. But things had got quieter in Northern Ireland since the Good Friday peace agreement the year before, so he had decided to take a job here. Belfast really had come to Pristina.

This was the end of the century, but not of the bloody dissolution of former Yugoslavia. In neighbouring Macedonia, Europe's twenty-first century kicked off with a fifth war of the Yugoslav succession. This was between more or less Christian, Slav Macedonians and more or less Muslim, ethnic Albanian Macedonians, who made up roughly one-quarter of the population. One of them, Ali Ahmeti, had fought in Kosovo as a senior officer of the Kosovo Liberation Army and now commanded a grandly named National Liberation Army in Macedonia. The United States included Ahmeti in a June 2001 executive order, signed by George W. Bush, listing people engaged in 'extremist violence' and describing them as 'an unusual and extraordinary threat to the national security and foreign policy of the United States'. George Robertson, the secretary general of NATO, had called the National Liberation Army a 'bunch of murderous thugs'.

So in October 2001, with the 9/11 attacks on the United States by Islamist terrorists fresh in every mind, I ventured up into the soaring mountains that connect Macedonia to Albania, to visit this Muslim terrorist in his lair. I found a quiet-spoken, educated man of roughly my age who had been a student protester at Pristina University in 1981 and subsequently spent years in far-left, nationalist revolutionary politics in Switzerland and Albania. Ahmeti's first action was to offer me a glass of what he described as 'very good' whisky – a fifteen-year-old Bowmore from the Scottish island of Islay. He downed a dram himself. Not the strictest of Muslims, then.

I asked Ahmeti how he would respond to someone who said: 'You are a terrorist.' His bodyguards shifted uneasily as my question was translated. But he replied quite calmly:

> That person cannot be a terrorist who wears an army badge, who has an objective for which he is fighting, who respects the Geneva conventions and The Hague tribunal, who acts in public with name and surname, and answers for everything he does . . . Someone who is aiming for good reforms and democracy in the country – and that people should be equal before the law.

Soon, following a peace agreement brokered by George Robertson for NATO and Javier Solana for the EU, Ahmeti would swap his uniform for a politician's suit. He became a leading ethnic Albanian politician in the country we now know as North Macedonia, serving in coalition governments alongside former enemies – as did the former IRA leaders Gerry Adams and Martin McGuinness in Northern Ireland.

After this extraordinary conversation, my interpreter and I were hurtling down from the mountains when the driver suddenly slammed on the brakes. A police officer and a Macedonian paramilitary had jumped out from the side of the road to stop us at an improvised roadblock. They verbally abused my Albanian companions, who were visibly petrified, and shouted at me too. What I most remember from this, one of my last glimpses of the tragedy of former Yugoslavia, was the moment just after our shuddering emergency stop when I looked out of my car window and saw, at eye level, only a gun and a wooden cross pendant hanging before the burly, camouflage-jacketed chest of the paramilitary. I remember it because, knowing how vicious these paramilitaries could be, I thought 'the cross – that's a bad sign'.

One reason for the West's long culpable inaction over the wars of the Yugoslav succession was a widespread notion that these were 'ancient tribal hatreds' – a view popularised by Robert Kaplan's book *Balkan Ghosts*. Apparently people over there had been killing each other for centuries. I actually heard a senior EU official say: 'We can't stop people who *want* to kill each other.'

It would be silly to pretend that there were not historical legacies that made inter-ethnic conflict somewhat more likely in Krajina or Kosovo than it would be in, say, Surrey or Provence. The Krajina had seen fierce fighting during the Second World War between fascist Croatian Ustashe guerrillas and royalist Serb nationalist Chetniks. When telling me how he barely escaped with his life from the Republic of Serbian Krajina, in the early 1990s, an old Croatian farmer used the word 'Chetnik' without a moment's hesitation to describe the marauding Serbs. The Bosnian Serb forces called the Bosniaks not just 'Muslims' but also 'Turks'. The day before his troops began their genocidal action at Srebrenica on 12 July 1995, General Mladić said: 'Finally, after the rebellion against the Dahis, the time has come to take revenge on the Turks in this region.'

He was referring to a Serb uprising against Ottoman Turk rule in 1804. When I asked a senior Serb official in Kosovo in 1997 to tell me the current ethnic composition of the province, knowing full well that the Albanians were now an overwhelming majority, he replied, 'In the twelfth century, ninety-eight per cent of the population of Kosovo were Serbs.' (This was presumably according to the UN Census of 1192.)

Yet as Detective Constable Campbell observed, such historic enmities were entirely comparable with those in Northern Ireland, where the 1690 Battle of the Boyne is celebrated every year on 12 July by Protestant Ulstermen as if it happened only yesterday. A nice joke has it that as your plane comes in to land in Belfast, the pilot's voice over the PA system says: 'Please fasten your seat belts; the weather in Belfast is fine today and the time in Belfast is 1690.'

The truth is that to visit Belgrade in 1988 was to find oneself in a place more free, and in some respects more modern and Western, than Prague at that time. Bosnia was a bit of a backwater, but a peaceful, easy-going Yugoslav one, where mixed marriages between Orthodox, Catholic and Muslim were quite usual. In Kosovo, Albanian–Serb tensions became acute after the student-led rising in 1981, but even there I met a young woman called Violeta who had been born to an Albanian father and Serb mother in the early 1980s. What was she to do now? Cut herself in half? (The likely answer was: emigrate.)

In every corner of former Yugoslavia, it required a lot of bad politics, propaganda, incitement and lies to take people down the road to violence. In 1997, I sat on a sofa in Belgrade with a retired army major called Dule who got his news from Radio Television Belgrade and the nationalist press. He informed me that at Srebrenica 'Muslims killed Muslims'.

Why? I asked.

'They were frightened, so they killed each other.'

West Europeans and North Americans would often say 'it couldn't happen here'. But after the storming of the Capitol in Washington on 6 January 2021 by Americans who were convinced that Donald Trump had won the presidential election, are we so absolutely sure? At the end of his history of Bosnia, Noel Malcolm quotes the Serbian journalist Miloš Vasić telling an American audience that if all the TV channels in the United States had been taken over by the Ku Klux Klan, 'you too would have a war in five years'.

The sad but universal truth is that, once bad politics, dangerous speech and brutalisation do their work, men can always be found to commit atrocities. Not just psychopaths and ideological extremists but 'ordinary men', to quote the title of Christopher Browning's remarkable book analysing how German reserve policemen came to be mass murderers of Jews in Poland in 1942. Ordinary men like Dražen Erdemović, who was not a Serb extremist but a half-Croat wheeler-dealer from a small village near Tuzla. You go along, out of some mix of ambition, conformism, fear and weakness – elements present in all of us – and down that path to hell you tread, step by step, until one day you find yourself in a field full of the stench of corpses, shooting a fifteen-year-old boy in the back of the head as he whispers 'Mother! Mother!'

The principal author of the bad politics that tore the fragile post-socialist federation of Yugoslavia apart was Slobodan Milošević. As the mournful monk of Dečani implied, he did for the Serbs what Hitler did for the Germans, besmirching their name for generations to come. It feels all the more vital to point out that it was not only the Serbian leader who was to blame and that many Serbs did what they could to resist him.

The Croatian nationalist leader Franjo Tudjman was directly complicit with Milošević in the violent partition of Bosnia. After drinking a lot of wine at a dinner in London in May 1995, Tudjman drew a map on the back of a menu card for Paddy Ashdown, a liberal politician deeply engaged in the affairs of former Yugoslavia. It showed the lines on which Bosnia should be partitioned between Serbia and Croatia. In his memoirs, Ashdown recalls that when he asked 'Where is Bosnia?' the Croatian leader replied 'No Bosnia'. When I see Croatia being celebrated today as a fine, upstanding Western Christian member of the European Union, I cannot help remembering the eerily 'cleansed' Krajina and thinking that, in the English colloquial phrase, Croatia got away with murder. The Bosnians were much more victims than victimisers, yet even they had some thugs and killers. In Kosovo, as I saw myself, there were also instances of brutality from the KLA side.

Meanwhile, there was another Serbia. It is true that throughout the

1990s a majority of Serbs re-elected Milošević in elections that were relatively free, although certainly not fair. It is also true that, throughout the decade, there were Serbs who opposed the Milošević regime and its many crimes. In 1997, I marched through the streets of Belgrade with students who had for months been demonstrating daily in order to get the true result of local government elections recognised. One placard read 'Euro police, Euro democracy, Euro standards, Euro law, Euro authority'. I am in touch with some of them to this day. They are still working to build a democratic, European Serbia.

What is more, in the end it was not outside powers, not all the might of NATO and the EU, but Serbs themselves who toppled Milošević, in a largely non-violent act of civil resistance in October 2000. I got to Belgrade the day after the parliament in Belgrade had been stormed, in time to hear Voldemort amazingly concede electoral defeat on television. This was, to be sure, nothing like as innocently joyful as Prague during Havel's Velvet Revolution of 1989. Some of those involved had very dubious pasts. I talked to one 'Captain Dragan', who had just taken over the customs administration at gunpoint, on behalf of the opposition. In 1991, this Dragan Vasiljković had been a commander of Serb paramilitaries in Krajina, glorified by nationalist propaganda when, as he now put it to me, 'I liberated or, if you like, occupied Glina'. But the overthrow of Milošević was nonetheless a genuine triumph of people power.

All the rest of Europe, all the enlarging West, permitted this ten-year-long return to hell. It is a terrible stain on what was otherwise one of the most hopeful periods of European history. The worst failures came in the first half of the decade. In May 1990, speaking on behalf of the European Community, the foreign minister of Luxembourg, one Jacques Poos, said: 'This is the hour of Europe . . . if one problem can be solved by the Europeans, it is the Yugoslav problem'. Cue hollow laughter. With their ludicrous uniform of white shirts, white sweaters, white trousers and white gym shoes, the EU monitors in former Yugoslavia were known as 'the ice cream men'.

The European and Western response did improve after Srebrenica. The West acted to prevent genocide in Kosovo, as it had failed to do in Bosnia. Bernard Kouchner, the first UN special representative for Kosovo, told me that his first concern was 'to prevent Auschwitz'.

Western leaders devoted months to finding a negotiated solution in Macedonia. And, because the EU and other institutions of the enlarged West insisted upon it, Milošević, Mladić and the Bosnian Serb leader Radovan Karadžić did finally end up before the international tribunal in The Hague, where they were held responsible for their crimes. (Karadžić is now serving his life sentence in a British prison.)

Nonetheless, we let it happen. Worse, most of us went on living quite happily while murder and rape was committed in the next room. Perhaps this, too, is just human nature. As an old Polish peasant explains in *Shoah*, Claude Lanzmann's documentary film about the mass murder of the European Jews: 'If you cut your finger, it doesn't hurt me.' While Kosovo descended into war in 1998, I stopped off in Bosnia and spoke to Ozren Kebo, who had lived through the siege of Sarajevo and chronicled it in a book called *Welcome to Hell*. 'To be honest,' he said, 'when I see pictures from Kosovo on television, I turn to something else. Our attitude is much as western Europe's was to us.' But that does not mean this attitude is right. At the very least, whenever we heard some smooth European dignitary mouth the easy platitude that Europe had lived 'at peace' for so many decades, we should have stood up and said, 'Not true!'

Fish soup

While Yugoslavia descended into war and genocide, the rest of post-communist Europe embarked on an unprecedented experiment. It was called 'transition', using the term popularised in the transitions from authoritarian dictatorship to democracy in southern Europe and Latin America, or 'transformation'. Neither word quite captured the scale of the challenge. Under communism, all the key ingredients of capitalism and liberal democracy had been destroyed: private property, the rule of law, multi-party politics, free and fair elections, uncensored and diverse media, academic independence, pluralism, constitutional checks and balances, a strong civil society built on private economic resources independent of the state. All had been liquidised. There were libraries full of books about the journey from capitalism to communism and from what Marx called 'bourgeois' democracy to a one-party state. There was no guidebook for travelling in the other direction. No one had ever done this before. No one knew if it could be done.

As so often, a joke best captured the truth: 'We know that you can turn an aquarium into fish soup; but can you turn fish soup back into an aquarium?' Over the next two decades, an answer emerged. 'Yes, but it's going to be a fairly odd sort of aquarium.' In fact, there was an entire gallery of peculiar aquariums. Whereas in January 1990 there had been just nine states in the eastern half of Europe, including the Soviet Union and Yugoslavia, by 2010 there were twenty-four, including Georgia, Armenia and Azerbaijan as well as Montenegro and Kosovo, which both declared their independence from Serbia. A monolithic eastern Europe had never existed, except in the minds of people in the West, but now the 'other half' of Europe was more than ever a kaleidotapestry. Every one of these new countries went through its own unique variety of transformation.

Unlike the French and Russian revolutions, which had staked out new, utopian political ideas, the velvet revolutions of 1989 were what the German social thinker Jürgen Habermas called 'revolutions of catching up'. The ideas whose time had come were old, well-tried ones. The former Polish dissident Adam Michnik revised the 1789 French Revolution motto to read 'Liberty, Fraternity, *Normality*'. With the exception of the Russians, who still had their own distinct dreams of imperial greatness, most of the peoples who had lived behind the Iron Curtain simply wanted the freedom, prosperity, civilised life and normality of countries like West Germany, France and Britain – or, indeed, Canada and the United States. This they had seen on rare, memorable trips to the fabled West (remember the Jiří I met in Prague in 1979, who had saved up for seven years to make one short wedding anniversary trip to Paris); in films (my steelworker host in Kraków, settling down with a beer to enjoy a Western on Polish TV); or, in the case of most East Germans, every day on West German television. And the West looked particularly appealing at this moment. Like the middle-aged woman in an American diner watching Meg Ryan spectacularly fake an orgasm in the 1989 film *When Harry Met Sally*, the East eyed the West and said: 'I'll have what she's having.'

In rather more elevated terms, central European leaders called their goal 'the return to Europe'. But this 'Europe' was to encompass all the good things achieved in forty-five years of development in western Europe, and those were seen through rose-tinted spectacles. Programmatically, the agenda of 'catching up' could be summarised in one of the West German Christian Democrats' election slogans from the 1950s: 'No experiments!' Yet getting to that non-experimental normality would require a huge experiment.

Looking back, people describe the early 1990s as a moment of liberal triumphalism, and there certainly was some of that. After all, this was a liberal triumph. But among those who suddenly had to assume governmental responsibility for an unprecedented transformation of their countries, joy and hope alternated with uncertainty and worry. Newly installed in Prague Castle, President Václav Havel told his team: 'We are coming in as heroes, but in the end, when they realise what a mess we're in and how little we can do about it, they will railroad us, tarred and feathered, out of town.' The writer and former political prisoner Árpád Göncz, who became president of Hungary in May 1990, wryly confided to me: 'I have survived forty years of communism, but I'm not sure that I'll survive one year of capitalism.' For as long as I had known him, Tadeusz Mazowiecki, the Catholic intellectual who became Poland's prime minister in August 1989, had always had a slightly worried expression on his face – but now he looked more worried than ever. After all, what did he know of capitalism?

Since they wanted to catch up with and become part of the West, they looked in every area – constitutions, media, education, the economy – to emulate how things were done there. As a result, they felt the full, frontal impact of developments that had been gathering force in the West since the 1970s. Thirty years on, these are often summarised in one word: neoliberalism. The historian Philipp Ther expresses the argument succinctly: 'a neoliberal train was being put on track in the United Kingdom and the United States that was set to cross Europe in 1989'. But neoliberalism has become a catch-all term which needs to be unpacked if we are to understand the complex processes that produced today's post-communist societies.

Certainly a few leading figures in the transition were intellectually fascinated by the work of thinkers such as Friedrich Hayek and Milton Friedman, who influenced the economic policies of Margaret Thatcher and Ronald Reagan. Václav Klaus, the architect of economic transformation in the Czech Republic, is a prime example. Even during the Velvet Revolution, in the frenetic corridors of the Magic Lantern theatre in Prague, he took time out to lecture me about free markets.

Yet most of the new political leaders in post-communist Europe were not true believers like Klaus. I recall few people at the time seriously debating 'neoliberalism' as an ideology in the way people had constantly debated communism and fascism earlier in the twentieth century, and justified their political actions by reference to theoretical texts. As an end-state, politicians such as Mazowiecki, Havel and Geremek would definitely have preferred something like West Germany's 'social market economy' or Scandinavian social democracy. But first they had to dismantle the centrally planned economy to create a market one – and the economists told them this was the best way to do it. Geremek explained his thinking to me with a vivid but far from scientific simile: the centrally planned command economy was like a giant concrete bunker, he said, and it probably needed a giant bulldozer to knock it down.

More important than the academic ideology of Hayek or Friedman was the 'Washington consensus', a term coined by a British economist in 1989 to describe the key components of the reform packages typically prescribed by the Washington-based World Bank and International Monetary Fund for developing economies in crisis. Since states like Poland and Hungary carried heavy burdens of hard currency debt run up by their former communist governments, and needed foreign capital to build capitalism, they had a strong incentive to take this medicine. The phrase 'Washington consensus' subsequently acquired a wider meaning, being equated with dogmatic market fundamentalism.

Moreover, the structure of capitalism was itself changing in the 1980s. It was becoming more globalised, as barriers to trade, investment and capital flows were removed, but also more financialised. Capitalism was becoming less about the industrial production of goods and more about services – especially financial services. Mind-boggling gazillions of financial capital were whizzed around the world on computer screens, by bankers, traders and investors who creamed off delicious profits for themselves along the way. The economist Angus Deaton characterised them as people who got rich not by making things but by taking things. The end of the Cold War opened up large new regions to economic liberalisation and globalisation.

In the financial crisis of 2008 this globalised, financialised capitalism would cause a major heart attack of the West, but in the 1990s and early 2000s it seemed triumphant, inevitable and invincible. Post-communist Europe, starting with few of the social, legal and institutional checks and balances that at least partly constrained the beast in western Europe, reproduced it in a particularly crude and raw form. Money seemed to be the source and measure of everything – social status, educational opportunity, celebrity, political power, effective freedom and even, if you believed the slick new TV ads, personal happiness and sexual satisfaction. Many people felt they were getting not just a market economy but a market society.

At the heart of this process was the largest privatisation the world has ever seen. It's sometimes forgotten that for Karl Marx the opposite of communism was not democracy but capitalism. He defined the essence of communism as the abolition of private property and the communist regimes of the Soviet bloc had largely achieved this goal. A few areas of private property remained, such as much of Polish agriculture and small to medium-sized businesses in Hungary, but all the rest was state, collective or co-operative property – often with very unclear ownership rights. In an entire decade, Margaret Thatcher's radical pro-market government had privatised some fifty state enterprises. At the start of the transformation, Poland had about 7,000 state enterprises.

In February 1990, I heard Václav Havel remind a crowd from a balcony on the old town square in Prague of the noble motto of the founding president and original philosopher king of Czechoslovakia, Tomáš Garrigue Masaryk: 'Don't Lie, Don't Steal'. But what followed, throughout the entire post-Soviet world, was an orgy of lying and stealing. The motto of the other Wenceslas, Václav Klaus, the Thatcherite architect of Czech privatisation, would be 'Speed is more important than accuracy'. There was, to be sure, a very wide spectrum of experience across the post-communist states. At one extreme, privatisation in the former East Germany, although marred by cronyism and often traumatic in its effects, was far from a lawless free-for-all. At the other extreme, privatisation in Russia was the robbery of the century. Vast fortunes were made from the appropriation of former state property, mainly by people belonging to or having close connections with the former communist ruling class, the nomenklatura, including Vladimir Putin and his associates. The result was accurately called kleptocracy – rule by robbers. In 2013, it was estimated that 110 billionaires controlled some thirty-five per cent of Russia's wealth.

These men were more politely described as 'oligarchs' – a word that, before 1989, I had encountered only in history books. Across post-communist Europe, I would now have conversations punctuated by phrases like 'he's one of our local oligarchs'. Because the structures of law, public administration, media and politics were weak, it was easy for the new rich to buy influence within them. In Ukraine, oligarchs had their own political parties and media, as well as corrupt officials and judges eating out of their pockets. Powerful oligarchs were to be found even in the westernmost parts of central Europe. Thirty years after 1989, the prime minister of the Czech Republic would be Andrej Babiš, an erstwhile informer for the communist security services who had got rich in agribusiness and bought his way into politics by purchasing media and creating his own political party.

Yet this model of the multimillionaire businessman turned political entrepreneur and prime minister had been pioneered by Silvio Berlusconi in Italy. In western Europe and the United States, too, there were strong tendencies towards the particular form of oligarchy (rule by a few) known as plutocracy (rule by the rich). Even in the most established liberal democracies, monied interests, those most direct beneficiaries of globalised, financialised capitalism, had a growing and disproportionate influence on politics. Post-communist Europe was like one of those fairground halls of distorting mirrors: look in this mirror, and you seem outrageously fat, in the next, ludicrously thin and tall. But the complacent Western man laughing into these distorting mirrors was himself dangerously overweight, with high blood pressure and a dodgy heart.

Freedom and its discontents

'Joy, spark of the gods', trills a choir of pale schoolgirls in front of Warsaw's Royal Castle, 'Daughter of Elysium!' They are singing Friedrich Schiller's 'Ode to Joy' words to Beethoven's music, singing them as the European anthem in a Polish translation they have learned by heart. 'With fiery hearts we enter/ Heavenly one, thy sanctuary!' The sanctuary is the European Union, promising freedom, peace, prosperity and all good things. For this 'Schuman parade' on Saturday 10 May 2003 is intended to persuade Poles to vote 'yes' in a referendum on joining the EU. It has been organised by the indomitable Róża Thun. The young woman I first met over a dish of 'Nelson's bowels' in Kraków a quarter-century ago is now middle-aged, like me, but she still has the same broad, infectious smile. Her bright blue cloak and blonde hair combine to present the European colours.

Balloons float into the sky above, blue and yellow for Europe, red and white for Poland. 'Poland yes, the Union no!' chants a small group of Eurosceptic hecklers, but our crowd chants back 'Poland yes, the Union *yes*!' The president of the republic admonishes us: vote yes. A message is conveyed from the ski jumper Adam Małysz, probably the country's most popular sportsman. Vote yes. Leszek Balcerowicz, architect of Poland's economic 'shock therapy', explains how Poland can join the common European currency. The first euro coins and notes have recently been introduced in neighbouring Germany and other founding eurozone countries. A handmade placard held up by another group of schoolchildren from a provincial town proclaims simply 'Eurolandia'. The mayor of Warsaw, Lech Kaczyński, concludes the list of speakers in favour of EU membership.

As the sun comes out, we set off down Krakowskie Przedmieście, Warsaw's Pall Mall. Tadeusz Mazowiecki is here, of course, his face still creased with worry, and so is Bronisław Geremek. Six decades ago, little more than a mile from here, an emaciated, shivering ten-year-old Bronek had been smuggled out of the Warsaw ghetto. Europe had descended into a hell of its own making and most of his family had been murdered in the Holocaust. Long years of dictatorship and struggle followed. Now, incredibly, Poland is a free country, increasingly prosperous and Western, secure in NATO and soon to be a member of the European Union. Joy indeed, spark of the gods.

Yet Mazowiecki had some reason still to look worried. This referendum would require a simple majority to pass, but also a turnout of at least fifty per cent. Abstention had been the dark shadow of Polish democracy ever since the first semi-free election on 4 June 1989, in which more than a third of Polish voters did not go to the polls even when given a once-in-a-lifetime chance to vote away communism. In the most recent Polish election, in 2001, turnout had been just forty-six per cent. So now they had to get out the vote. Tony Blair was about to do his bit, with a speech in Warsaw later that month. But my notebook records that the endorsements most wanted were from the US president, George W. Bush, and the Polish pope, John Paul II. If God could put in a personal word, that would be helpful too.

Much of the countryside, the Catholic hierarchy and other more conservative sections of society were far from enthusiastic about joining this secular, multicultural and perhaps German-dominated Union. (One of the hecklers' placards showed Hitler saying 'I'm a European'. Another complained that the Union had 'no place for God'.) In the event, three-quarters of those who turned out in the June 2003 referendum voted yes – but turnout was still only fifty-nine per cent. Elementary maths shows that three-quarters of fifty-nine per cent is less than a majority of the electorate. That was a warning from the future. But for now, it was the result that counted.

Like Róża Thun, like Bronisław Geremek, like all my university-educated, city-dwelling, pro-European, pro-Western Polish friends, I delighted in the successes of a free Poland, celebrated and publicised them. Even on the most critical reckoning, these were large. Poland's 'Third Republic' was not merely an independent, free country. Unlike the 'Second Republic' in the years before the Second World War, it was now safely anchored in the same economic, political and security communities as Germany and other west European countries. Poland was a significant middle-sized power in a Europe that seemed to be becoming ever more 'whole and free' and part of an enlarged West. In 2003, the talk was of a Polish zone of occupation in Iraq. 'We have to teach those Iraqis democracy!', explained foreign minister Włodzimierz Cimoszewicz, a former member of the Polish communist party, well aware of the irony.

Historians said you had to go back 300 years to find a better period in Polish history. After emerging from the valley of tears that followed Leszek Balcerowicz's free-market shock therapy in the early 1990s, Poland's GDP has grown at an impressive rate. Between 1989 and 2019, it increased by more than 800 per cent. According to a careful calculation of real purchasing power, in 1955, Poland's GDP per capita had been roughly the same as that of Spain, but by 1990 it was down to less than half of Spain's. In 2019, it was back up to nearly 90 per cent of the Spanish level.

Arriving in Warsaw now felt much like arriving in Lisbon or Madrid. The city centre looked increasingly Western, with nice cafés, restaurants and smartly restored squares. As EU funds began to flow in large quantities, those visible improvements spread to smaller towns. I started to hear the phrase 'civilisational leap'. There was a new middle class, with detached houses, a Volkswagen or Audi in the garage, foreign holidays and even fee-paying schools for the kids. In the 1980s, when my sons were born in England, their life chances were incomparably better than those of my Polish friends' children. By the 2010s, especially with the freedom of movement offered by the EU, they had similar prospects. The same is true for a whole generation of central and east European students who have come through my door. Chances for Márton and Marta, Hubert, Michal, Anna and Joasia.

But freedom also has its discontents and the travails of post-communist transformation made these especially acute. Some were avoidable, some not. For a start, reality never lives up to the dream. In the French Third Republic, which followed France's Second Empire in 1870, there was a saying: '*La république, comme elle était belle sous l'empire*' ('The republic, how beautiful it was under the empire'). So it was with Poland's Third Republic. People came to it with an idealised picture of life in a western, European, free Poland. Some disappointment was inevitable.

Freedom turned out to be challenging, risky, insecure. 'Freedom is *demanding*,' the former East German dissident Ulrike Poppe once laughingly told me. During the last decades of communism, most people had lived in a kind of relatively unchallenging security. They had less money than in the West but more time. As the saying went: 'We pretend to work and they pretend to pay us.' Now, in order to keep your job you had to work in stressful, unfamiliar new ways, for employers who often didn't treat you well either. The locus of unfreedom moved from the state to the workplace. In a revealing study of a Polish baby food factory taken over by a company from Michigan, one employee, Monika, complained about being treated at work like a 'grey object'. Only at home and with her friends did she feel like a proper human being. In 2005, Lech Wałęsa summed it up to me thus: before 1989, people had security and longed for freedom; now they had freedom and longed for security.

The initial transition under shock therapy was traumatic. If prices had gone up for a whole year as fast as they did in the month of March 1990, the annual inflation rate would have been 1,395 per cent. But the change did not stop there. Work practices, goods in the shops, regulations, school classes, clothes, cars, medicines, job titles, television programmes – everything changed. In the enthusiasm of success, my friends and I neglected the nineteenth-century writer Mary Shelley's warning: 'Nothing is so painful to the human mind as a great and sudden change.'

In everyday life, capitalism proved more profoundly revolutionary than communism ever was. It started by offering people what they wanted and then made them want more of it. 'You too can have a villa!' promised a TV advertisement I noted down in 2003. Another showed two slim and attractive women in a fitness club gushing: 'so great, so sporty, so considerate, so strong!' It turned out they were discussing not some perfect man but a new car. Václav Malý, the Catholic priest who had been the voice of the Velvet Revolution in Prague, explained to me that this constant commercial propaganda of success made many people feel like failures, because they didn't have the villa, car, great career, happy children and perfect sex life.

The Catholic Church had never been that keen on capitalism anyway. Pope John Paul II could often wrap his thoughts in impenetrable philosophical vocabulary, but in an unforgettable conversation (in Polish) round a dinner table at his summer residence at Castel Gandolfo in 1987, I heard him say, with stunning clarity: 'The trouble with capitalism and communism is that I dislike the one almost as much as the other.' Now, on his return visits to his homeland, he raged against the pursuit of 'having' at the expense of 'being' and a consumer society's 'web of false and superficial gratifications'.

It has become commonplace to talk about 'winners' and 'losers' from the transition, but one needs more than a few bald economic statistics to understand who exactly felt themselves to be 'losers' and why. If you think it's a good thing to have political freedom, freedom of speech, freedom of association, freedom to travel, then everyone had gained. Even in purely material terms, most people got richer. In a 2019 survey, four out of every five Polish respondents said their standard of living had improved. Visible economic inequality increased, but not to US or British levels.

Yet here the unhappiness about inequality had a special edge because of who got rich and who stayed poor or got poorer. In Poland, as elsewhere in post-communist Europe, it was members of the former communist ruling class who most often seized the opportunities of privatisation. To some extent, this 'privatisation of the nomenklatura' was part of an implicit deal in the velvet revolutions of 1989. The old ruling class would give up political power but retain or gain economic advantages. The social anthropologist Ernest Gellner called it 'the price of velvet'. In 1993, a study found that fifty-seven per cent of the elites in Poland's private economic sector came from the former nomenklatura.

This added a particular sense of historical injustice to the general concern about inequality found in most capitalist countries. Up there in Warsaw was Jerzy Urban, the much-disliked former spokesman of General Wojciech Jaruzelski's martial law regime, reportedly throwing extravagant parties in his luxurious villa. Back in Gdańsk, a shipyard worker who had suffered reprisals for his commitment to Solidarity was now unemployed, with barely enough to live on, stuck in a two-bedroom apartment in a crumbling tower block.

The grievance about historical injustice was exacerbated by the lack of an adequate public reckoning with the communist past. I argued at the time with ex-dissident friends like Adam Michnik about the need for a more systematic, symbolic confrontation with the difficult past, as happened in East Germany and in South Africa after the end of apartheid. But Michnik and others were inspired by the example of the 1970s transition from dictatorship in Spain, which had deliberately been accompanied by 'amnesty and amnesia'. (Yet in the 2010s, the past came back to haunt Spain too.) This omission opened the door for populist political entrepreneurs to garner votes with a 'politics of history', arguing that 1989 had not been a proper revolution, just a murky deal between communists and ex-communists, and the true anti-communist revolution was still needed.

Intermingled with these economic and historical discontents were social and cultural ones. From the start, everyone knew that the traumatic transition to a market economy would call for a strengthened social security net. In the dramatic first phase of shock therapy, a compassionate concern for those who were paying the highest price for the transition was articulated by Jacek Kuroń, a charismatic former dissident who became the minister responsible for social policy. If Leszek Balcerowicz was the right hand of the transition to democratic capitalism, Kuroń was the left. He wanted to be a man of the left in capitalism, he said, but first they had to build that capitalism. And he sold the necessity of rapid, radical marketisation to the Polish public in warm, caring 'conversations' on television. Later, as he saw just how many Poles now felt rejected, ignored and degraded, he came to regret his role as capitalism's social democratic salesman. Although social welfare spending in fact remained substantial, no one after Kuroń quite communicated that concern for the poorer, weaker, marginalised members of society – what Franklin D. Roosevelt once called 'the forgotten man'.

Here the social shades into the cultural. In the post-Wall decades, a gulf opened up in all European societies between those who had higher education, lived in cities, embraced secular, liberal values and enjoyed all the opportunities Europe offered, and those who did not. The divide had unique contours in each country. In Poland it was the east and south-east of the country, less economically developed, more rural and small-town, more given to traditional, conservative Polish Catholicism, where people felt themselves most ignored and disrespected by the snooty intelligentsia in what they called the 'Warsaw salon'. The intelligentsia, workers and peasants had been wonderfully united in Solidarity but now social rifts opened up again, albeit along slightly different lines. Under martial law, protesters had chanted 'There's no freedom without Solidar-ity'. In the early 2000s, they stood outside the government headquarters in Warsaw and chanted 'There's no solidarity in freedom'.

All these discontents were visible, in perfect miniature, at the birth-place of Solidarity, now called simply the Gdańsk shipyard. (Lenin's statue, and his name over the historic gate, had been removed in a joyful ceremony soon after 1989.) Despite efforts to save it, the yard had gone bankrupt in 1996, and the number of employees had sunk from more than 16,000, at the time Wałęsa worked there, to fewer than 3,000 when I went back with a BBC film crew in 1998. I talked to a gentle, knobbly-faced old shipyard electrician, Piotr Przybysz, who told me he had imag-ined freedom differently. He had thought 'there'd be a reckoning with those who oppressed us'. Now life was really tough, he sighed, and he kept having to take loans. His twenty-nine-year-old son Roland, who worked in a private printing firm for the equivalent of £35 a month, was even gloomier: 'I feel like a loser.'

We filmed a stormy confrontation between Wałęsa, who had been president of the country between 1990 and 1995, and his former work-mates in the yard. They were furious, and did not hesitate to show it. One of them summed up the mix of economic, historical and social dissatis-faction in a vivid sally: 'You said you'd leave the communists in nothing but their socks, but instead you left us without socks.'

In August 2005, I was back there again to speak at the twenty-fifth anniversary of the birth of Solidarity. It was a great party. But during an endless triumphal mass celebrated near the shipyard, I wandered away to the historic gate of the yard, which was now partly owned by a company called EVIP. Next to the entrance there was a cash machine. Through the vertical metal bars of the gate, I contemplated a wasteland of crumbling buildings, rubble and weeds. In front of the gate was a large wooden stocks, like those used in the Middle Ages to pillory criminals. The three head-holes contained straw men, dressed in dark suits and white shirts, with photos as faces. Underneath was written 'Marek Roman, chairman of the EVIP firm – thief', 'Janusz Szlanta, former chairman – thief', 'Jerzy Lewandowski, current chairman – swindler'.

A few weeks later, on a turnout barely exceeding forty per cent, Polish voters elected a party called Law and Justice (PiS) – the reference being to a deficit of legality and historical justice after 1989. Jarosław Kaczyński, a skilful right-wing political entrepreneur, had managed to pull together and exploit all the manifold discontents that had accumulated over the fifteen years of freedom. A month later his almost identical twin brother, Lech, the former mayor of Warsaw, was elected president. Lech Kaczyński's posters proclaimed that he would be 'President of the Fourth Republic'. In 2006, Jarosław himself became prime minister, so the country was effectively ruled by the twins. Their double act only lasted until 2007, but it was a warning of things to come in the next decade.

One coin to bind them all

In a drawer at home, I have an assortment of tattered envelopes containing spare notes and coins in foreign currencies. Started for purely practical reasons, as a store of cash for future trips, this has become a museum of Europe's dead currencies. Their deaths were the result of European disintegration, or integration, or sometimes both.

First come the tiny paper notes of the East German mark, with images of a combine harvester and of a young woman sitting at a very 1970s industrial control panel, all knobs, levers and dials. The 1-mark coin is so light that an undergraduate friend, visiting me in East Berlin, threw one into the River Spree exclaiming: 'I'm sure it will float!' (It didn't.) Then there is a particularly grubby brown envelope originally marked SU (Soviet Union) rubles, but with the SU crossed out. Next to what are now Russian Federation rubles nestle other post-Soviet currencies, such as the Belarusian ruble, with grandiose architectural themes, and the Ukrainian hryvnia, all bearded and moustachioed national heroes.

My collection of dinars fills several envelopes: socialist Yugoslav dinars, with heroic, grinning workers and jolly, grape-bearing peasant maidens; Milošević-era Yugoslav dinars, with Orthodox monasteries on the reverse; sadder but wiser Serbian dinars, still bearing the forlorn legend 'National Bank of Yugoslavia'. This former Yugoslav corner of my museum also contains proud Croatian kuna, eccentrically decorated Macedonian dinars and flimsy Bosnia-Herzegovinian dinars, the last bearing an image of the beautiful sixteenth-century Ottoman stone bridge at Mostar, destroyed in the Bosnian war but defiantly rebuilt. Finally, there is a note issued by the Central Bank of Bosnia and Herzegovina for '1 Konvertibilna Marka' (convertible mark) – convertible, that is, to the Deutschmark, the effective common currency of former Yugoslavia in the 1990s.

The next family of dead currencies comprises those that have passed away through integration rather than disintegration. Pride of place goes to the once dominant Deutschmark, its elegant DM 100 note displaying a grand piano, the composer Clara Schumann and the signature of Bundesbank president Hans Tietmeyer. Beside it are French francs (Gustave Eiffel and his tower), Italian lire with their multiple zeroes (always good for your mental arithmetic), Belgian francs, Austrian schillings and then, poignantly, Greek drachmas, the 1,000-drachma note showing an inscrutable Apollo. All have been superseded by the euro.

Most intriguing are the notes and coins that appeared due to the disintegration of larger states but then quickly disappeared through integration into the eurozone. Here are my Slovenian tolars (its name, like that of the dollar, derived from the Thaler of the Holy Roman Empire and Habsburg monarchy); a solitary Slovak crown, its reverse showing Christ on the cross; and some Estonian krooni, with a magnificently bouffant-haired lady, the nineteenth-century poet Lydia Koidula, adorning the 100-kroon bill. Slovenia adopted the euro in 2007, Slovakia in 2009 and Estonia in 2011, even as the eurozone was plunging into crisis.

And there it is at last, in a much-used envelope, the triumphant euro. No historical figures here, sacred or profane, bearded or unbearded, just a rather bland set of bridges, arches and windows. On the reverse is a geographical outline of Europe, artfully fudging the contested eastern frontier, which, roughly at the line of the Urals, mysteriously becomes a lettered wall. To the south, Turkey and the Maghreb suffer the indignity of being depicted in a paler shade than the continent to the north. An identity statement, to be sure.

Creating a European currency was the biggest single step in the process of European integration. It was also one of the most difficult: the eurozone was still causing major problems more than twenty years after its life began on 1 January 1999. The idea of monetary union goes back to the very beginnings of what would eventually become the European Union. Near the end of his life, Jean Monnet's Dutch assistant Max Kohnstamm told the journalist Geert Mak:

I still remember how Monnet came looking for me in summer 1957, out of the blue, because we had to get the monetary union rolling right then. The final decision to introduce the euro came forty years later. It was a long road indeed!

The project was first concretely proposed in a report by a committee chaired by the Luxembourger Pierre Werner in 1970. It was revived when, as part of the upward turn in the late 1980s, Jacques Delors chaired the committee of central bank governors which laid out a three-stage plan for complementing the single market with a single currency.

This was approved in principle by European leaders at a summit in Madrid in early summer 1989, but there was still no firm timetable for the inter-governmental conference to negotiate the indispensable new European treaty. In Germany, there was great reluctance to give up the cherished Deutschmark. Kohl, citing historical precedent, was still insisting that a European political union was the precondition for a successful monetary union. This was sometimes known as the 'coronation theory', in which a single currency would be the last, crowning step of an economic and political union, as had generally happened in cases of national unification.

Then the Berlin Wall came down. Kohl responded by proclaiming a Ten Point Programme for German unity without consulting 'dear François' Mitterrand. The French president was incandescent. This, he told his closest aides, was 'treason'. Mitterrand went on to instruct the German foreign minister that Europe was in danger of returning to the world of 1913 and to stoke up Thatcher's opposition to German unification with incendiary references to Germany in the 1930s. Germany must prove its commitment to European unity before he would give his consent to German unity.

The specific manifestation of European commitment required by France was monetary union. This was already an objective of the French president, bruised by repeated devaluations of the French franc against the Deutschmark. It also happened to be the one major project of deeper west European integration sitting ready on the table at that moment. If 'something must be done' to bind Germany more firmly into Europe, at a moment when German strength was to be enhanced by unification, then this was something.

There's a crude but influential version of this story which says 'the euro was the price for German unity'. It was already around at the time in a quip: 'Half the Deutschmark for Mitterrand, the whole of Deutschland for Kohl!' The historical record tells a more nuanced but still fascinating story. Reading through the original documents, published diaries and memoirs one sees how the essential deal that led to today's euro was done in just one month, between 9 November 1989, the fall of the Wall, and 9 December 1989, the second day of the European Community summit in Strasbourg that so upset Margaret Thatcher. The key German concessions were Kohl's endorsement of a specific timetable for the intergovernmental conference that would prepare the monetary union and his acceptance that a political union need not precede the monetary one but would, so it was fondly hoped, follow it. Thus the prospect of German unity that suddenly arose after the fall of the Wall was not the original cause of European monetary union but was a significant catalyst of it.

Monetary union now became the central *political* project of European integration in post-Wall Europe. For Carolingian Europe, in particular, this was by far the biggest game in town, with eastward enlargement in second place and bloody mayhem in the Balkans a troublesome or, for more sensitive souls, a conscience-troubling distraction. The intergovernmental conference agreed to by Kohl after the fall of the Wall led, through tortuous and intense negotiations, to the Maastricht treaty in 1992. This had many novel features, creating for the first time the European Union and something called European citizenship, as well as new 'pillars' for foreign and security policy and for justice and home affairs. But at its heart was a Franco-German compromise on monetary union. This would happen, as the French desired, but, as the Germans insisted, the currency would be managed by an independent central bank with a binding legal obligation to uphold monetary stability – in effect, a Euro-Bundesbank. Economic and fiscal convergence was to be achieved by a set of rules, but there was to be no fiscal union. Flanking political measures, such as increasing the powers of the European Parliament, did not come close to justifying the label 'political union'.

This treaty was sent for ratification to the parliaments and peoples of the twelve member states of the European Community. In the British parliament, the Maastricht debates became a battle royal between prime minister John Major and his own Eurosceptic backbenchers, whom he famously described as 'the bastards'. In a referendum, the Danes voted narrowly against ratifying the treaty, by fifty-one per cent to forty-nine per cent. Only after securing a number of 'opt-outs', including one from the single currency, did they endorse it in a second referendum. More remarkably, although monetary union had been above all a project of French elites, the French voted for Maastricht by the narrowest of margins: fifty-one per cent to forty-nine per cent the other way.

Most significant of all was the referendum that wasn't. Remembering the abuse of plebiscites in Nazi Germany, the Federal Republic's founding fathers had excluded referendums from the federal constitution. This was fortunate for Helmut Kohl. If the Germans had been asked, they might well have said no. In polling by the Allensbach Institute, a clear majority opposed replacing the Deutschmark with a single European currency throughout the first half of the 1990s. The Deutschmark was seen as the symbol and anchor of Germany's post-war success and the Bundesbank was, next to the Constitutional Court, the country's most trusted institution. When the Belgian banker Alexandre Lamfalussy confided to Kohl: 'I don't know how you will get the German people to give up the Deutschmark', the Chancellor replied: 'It will happen. The Germans accept strong leadership.' Perhaps – but they would remember they had not been asked.

Taken together, these national debates about Maastricht should have sent a powerful warning to European elites. Delors himself drew that conclusion in radical words: 'Europe began as an elitist project in which it was believed that all that was required was to convince the decision-makers. That phase of benign despotism is over.' But was it?

Preparations for introducing the euro – as the new currency was christened in 1995 – went ahead through the 1990s, with the Maastricht criteria being formalised into the rules of a Stability and Growth Pact. As the monetary union came nearer, the chorus of warning voices grew louder. I was among them. In 1998, the year a group of 155 economists declared 'the euro is coming too soon', I published an essay in the journal *Foreign Affairs* which started by summarising the economists' concerns. What if the single interest rate was right for some countries but wrong for others? Where were the compensatory budgetary transfers, such as were made between prosperous Massachusetts and struggling Alabama? Would there be sufficient solidarity among the nations of Europe? Europe, I went on to argue, had put the cart before the horse. Pointing to everything the European Union had failed to do because so much of its political and bureaucratic energy had been devoured by making the euro, I observed that 'we fiddled in Maastricht while Sarajevo began to burn'. A project designed to unite Europe could end up painfully dividing it.

All these warnings came too late. This project was already 'too big to fail'. The high-speed euro-train was nearly at its destination. On 1 January 1999, the monetary union was triumphantly introduced, bearing all the design flaws that critics had identified. Europe had moved from one unsustainable halfway house, the European Monetary System, to a more closely integrated halfway house: a monetary union without a fiscal union or a banking union, let alone a political union. From the outset, it contained a rainbow group of northern and southern European economies far more diverse than could easily be sustained in a single currency area. The extreme case was Greece, which just scraped into the euro in 2001, assisted by statistics doctored with the help of Goldman Sachs. A nordo-zone of more compatible, mainly north European economies would have made more economic sense. But since the project was supremely political, it was unthinkable to exclude Italy, let alone France.

Economic convergence was supposedly secured by the rules of a Stability and Growth Pact. Every member state's public debt should be less than sixty per cent of GDP and its current account deficit under three per cent. But one of those rules had been broken even before the euro was launched: Italy's debt was around 120 per cent of GDP and Belgium's a staggering 130 per cent. The other was soon to be violated by the union's central powers, when both France and Germany exceeded the three per cent limit in 2003. A 'rules-based system', to use a totemic phrase of the 2000s, only works if there is an effective arbiter and enforcer. Here there was none.

Ultimately, the project was based on a huge gamble: that economic integration would catalyse political integration. 'Europe will be forged in crises,' Jean Monnet had famously observed, 'and will be the sum of the solutions adopted for those crises.' My 1998 essay reported 'received wisdom in EU capitals' that the monetary union might face a crisis as early as 2001 or 2002. A notebook reminds me that Romano Prodi, then president of the European Commission, told me in 2001 that the euro would succeed 'through *crisis*'.

If this was wisdom, it was wisdom that most Europeans proceeded to forget. After all our prophecies of doom, the monetary union encountered no major outward crisis in its first decade. Yet we now know that explosive forces were building up under the surface, like magma under Mount Vesuvius. As elsewhere in the capitalist world, a bloated banking and financial services sector was a large part of the problem. By 2005, euro area banking assets had soared to nearly three times the combined GDP of eurozone member states. Germany had a mushrooming current account surplus, both because it had impressively massaged down unit labour costs in reforms introduced by Chancellor Gerhard Schröder and because its exports benefited from a lower exchange rate externally and a fixed exchange rate inside the eurozone. Its massive savings were recycled by imprudent north European banks to imprudent south European economies where unit labour costs and prices continued to rise.

This flood of mobile easy money fuelled private sector property booms in Spain and Ireland and public spending bonanzas in Greece and Portugal. The Greek government could borrow at almost exactly the same low rate as the German government. The 'spread' between the rates on their government bonds was minimal – 'a case of financial market mispricing on a colossal scale', as one leading chronicler of the euro observed. The imbalances between north and south continued to grow through the 2000s, fuelled by an out-of-control financial sector, so that when the volcanic explosion came, it was much bigger than it would have been at the beginning of the decade. Yet even the professional seismologists seem hardly to have noticed.

It is fascinating to go back and read the speech given in June 2008 by the president of the European Central Bank (ECB), Jean-Claude Trichet, on the tenth anniversary of its founding. After boldly claiming that 'it was the will of the democracies of Europe that led to the creation of the ECB', he declares: 'The euro has been a remarkable success. I don't intend to name and shame those who said that Europe's single currency would be impossible, or that its introduction would be a failure . . .' He goes on to articulate the political significance of the euro:

> The single currency is the most advanced feature of European unity and in many respects its emblem. We owe it to the lucidity of the founding fathers and to the determination of a series of visionary leaders.

Take your bow, Jean Monnet. After noting a few significant technical challenges, such as 'the lucid monitoring of national competitive indicators, including unit labour costs', Trichet concludes by addressing German chancellor Angela Merkel, who is there in Frankfurt alongside French president Nicolas Sarkozy. He recalls how earlier that year Merkel had quoted Konrad Adenauer to the effect that 'Europe today is a community of shared destiny'. This destiny is now shared, he concludes, 'with our fellow citizens, 320 million of them' in the eurozone. Cue Beethoven and 'Joy, spark of the Gods'.

The bankers should have known better. But this triumphalism was part of the spirit of the times. I shared it myself. I had earlier warned against the risks of the single currency, but now it all seemed to be going so well. Who was I, as a non-economist, to say otherwise? I liked pushing all those dirty old notes and coins to the back of my drawer and travelling around the continent without having to exchange a single franc, lire, schilling or tolar. I loved the sense of optimism in cities like Lisbon, Athens and Dublin, as the Union's promise of convergence between the continent's periphery and core was apparently coming true. The life chances of young Greeks, Portuguese and Irish seemed at last to be catching up with those of young Germans and Dutch, as were those of young Slovaks, Slovenians and Estonians. It was a time of great hope, and the euro was a symbol of that hope, from Tallin to Tenerife.

From 9/11 to 9/11

As our small group of European experts stood with President George W. Bush on the Truman balcony of the White House one fine May day in 2001, before our meeting to discuss his forthcoming trip to Europe, I casually noticed how planes from the nearby Reagan National Airport took off and climbed directly overhead. It never occurred to me that these planes could be used as terrorist weapons of mass destruction. In our subsequent discussion, the Iranian nuclear programme was briefly mentioned but Islamist terrorism did not feature. Instead, Bush identified China as the greatest challenge to the West: 'We'll all be fighting the darned Chinese one day.'

Less than four months later, Osama bin Laden's terrorists plunged hijacked civilian airliners into the twin towers of the World Trade Center in New York and the high-security walls of the Pentagon in Washington. Either the White House or the Capitol was the intended target for flight United 93, but they were spared thanks to the heroism of passengers. Several of them rushed forward along the narrow aircraft aisle to tackle the hijackers who then, with a last cry of 'Allahu akbar!' ('Allah is the greatest'), crashed the plane into a field in Shanksville, Pennsylvania. Bush was told that if a plane had been hijacked at Reagan National Airport it could have reached the White House in about forty seconds.

The moment a second plane crashed into the World Trade Center, at 9.03 a.m. on Tuesday 11 September 2001, immediately entered the collective memory log of humankind, alongside the moon landing and the fall of the Wall. The date, 9/11, written US-style, month before day, was the next great turning point in world history after 9/11, written

European-style – that is 9 November 1989, the day the Berlin Wall came down. Europe's 9/11 of hope was followed by America's 9/11 of fear.

The trauma of a direct assault on the heart of the American homeland, for the first time since the British torched the White House in 1814, transformed the United States, both at home and abroad. For Bush, China and Russia suddenly became partners in a 'war on terror' that took priority over everything else. Through the next decade, while China quietly continued its 'peaceful rise', the United States expended trillions of dollars, billions of political, bureaucratic and military hours, and much diplomatic and moral capital, on trying to defeat the Islamist enemy.

In December 2002, as the Bush administration prepared to invade Iraq, I had a background conversation with Vice President Dick Cheney in his heavily guarded residence in the grounds of the National Observatory in Washington.

'How does this war end?' I asked him.

'With the elimination of the terrorists.'

I was shocked not by the ruthlessness of Cheney's answer but by its stupidity. Get to number 267 on your list of terrorists and that would be the end of the war? Really?

He went on to explain that the administration had changed its mind about 'nation-building' since our meeting with the President in the White House a few months before, at which Cheney himself had been a brooding presence. Now, he said, they did intend to do nation-building and hoped that Iraq 'might become a beacon'.

In Cheney's every breath I sensed the hubris of a superpower that felt itself globally predominant and yet impudently defied, like the British Empire when it entered the Boer War at the end of the nineteenth century. Washington was 'drunk with sight of power', to recall the warning phrase that the English poet Rudyard Kipling addressed to his compatriots in his poem 'Recessional', just before the Empire was challenged by the Boers. America's imperial hubris was revealed in vainglorious phrases such as 'the new Rome', 'unipolar world' and 'Prometheus unbound'.

The 'war on terror' also changed US views of Europe and European views of the United States. I was now travelling to and fro every summer between Europe and a part-time post at Stanford University, so I clocked these changes, year on year, as in time-lapse photography. Europe largely disappeared from the front pages and even from the foreign pages of newspapers. It was all the Middle East and Afghanistan, plus some China and Russia. Europe led only in the Style pages. For some Americans, the Europeans were now a bunch of lily-livered appeasers. A partial exception was made for Tony Blair's Britain, but the French were 'cheese-eating surrender monkeys'. Jonah Goldberg, the journalist-provocateur who borrowed that phrase from an episode of *The Simpsons*, told me: 'Yes, I am anti-European.' Vice President Cheney insisted in our conversation that 'the Europeans' were 'a pain in the butt'.

Europeans repaid these compliments with interest. Immediately after 9/11, there had been an outburst of transatlantic solidarity. *Le Monde* carried a front-page editorial proclaiming 'We are all Americans'. The Brandenburg Gate in Berlin was draped with a banner saying '*Wir trauern* (we mourn) – our deepest sympathy'. In St Paul's Cathedral in London, the Queen joined in singing the Battle Hymn of the Republic with what the British press declared to be moist eyes. For the first time in its history, the NATO alliance invoked its Article 5: this attack on one was an attack on all. Although Washington did not take up the offer of making this formally a NATO response, European members of the Atlantic alliance supported the punitive invasion of Afghanistan, to root out Al Qaeda. But as the Bush administration turned from Afghanistan to Iraq, unity dissolved into bitter disarray.

Saturday 15 February 2003 saw millions of Europeans turn out on the streets of London, Madrid, Rome and other European capitals to oppose the invasion of Iraq. As the subsequent occupation turned into a disaster and photos were released of American soldiers torturing Iraqi detainees in Abu Ghraib prison, the United States' military, political and moral credibility suffered self-inflicted body blows. Yet Americans re-elected George W. Bush for a second term in November 2004. In Washington at the time, I noted how his defeated opponent John Kerry's voice broke with emotion as, in a gracious concession speech, he reaffirmed 'the truth that America is not only great but it is good'. That belief was shared only by a dwindling minority of Europeans.

This widening of the Atlantic was not simply a result of the American

9/11. It also followed from the European 9/11. The Cold War West in which I grew up was formed in the geopolitical struggle against a common enemy, the Soviet Union, which had soldiers and nuclear missiles in the heart of Europe. Once that common enemy had disappeared, it was always likely that the interests and priorities of the United States and Europe would diverge.

The continental drift was obscured during the 1990s by the Europeanism of President Bill Clinton and his colleagues, who spent a lot of time on the post-Wall issues of Russia, Germany, NATO enlargement and former Yugoslavia. They were also personally shaped by European experiences. Clinton's secretary of state, Madeleine Albright, actually was a European, born in Prague. The concluding section of the American diplomat Richard Holbrooke's account of his forceful peacemaking in Bosnia is headed 'America, still a European Power'. Clinton himself studied at Oxford, sharing a house with Strobe Talbott, who would become his administration's leading Russia expert, and travelled the continent on his vacations, soaking up impressions and ideas. As president, Clinton went so far as to say that 'since Europe is an idea as much as a place, America also is a part of Europe'.

That was bound to change sooner or later, but it did so with a bang under George W. Bush. The 'unvarnished Texan', as he introduced himself to us with charming self-deprecation, had been to Europe for only a few days in his life prior to the official visit in summer 2001 for which we were to prepare him. At one point he asked us: 'Do we want the European Union to succeed?' When Lionel Barber of the *Financial Times* and I replied most emphatically that we did and he should too, he rowed back: 'that was a provocation'. From the late 1940s until the 1960s, Washington had been instrumental in promoting west European integration, starting with the Marshall Plan which made American economic aid conditional on co-operation among the participating European states. Subsequent US presidents, including Bush's father, had often been ambivalent about this emerging 'Brussels', especially when it came with what they saw as a Gaullist, anti-American agenda. But throughout the Cold War, faced with that common enemy, the strategic conclusion had always been that European unity was in the American interest. Now it was a question.

The American 9/11 thus exposed and exacerbated a divergence whose deeper origins can be traced back to the European 9/11. Some Europeans welcomed this divergence. Referring to the 2003 European demonstrations against American-led war in Iraq, the French socialist politician Dominique Strauss-Kahn declared in *Le Monde*: 'On Saturday, 15 February, a new nation was born on the street. This new nation is the European nation.'

A similar vision of Europe as Not-America, defined and united by its differences with the United States, was articulated in a manifesto by Jürgen Habermas and the French philosopher Jacques Derrida. Rejection of Washington's unilateral militarism was rolled into a wider critique of the American social and economic model. German Chancellor Gerhard Schröder told a crowd in Hanover during the 2002 election that Germany would have no part in 'playing around with war and military intervention', and:

> The way things are in the United States, with bankruptcies and exploitation of the little people who now have to worry about who will take care of them when they are old – I say to you, that is not the German way that we want for our people.

Predictably, no European unity emerged on this basis. The Iraq war divided Europe as much as it did the transatlantic alliance. Tony Blair in Britain, José María Aznar in Spain, Silvio Berlusconi in Italy and José Manuel Barroso in Portugal effectively sided with Washington, together with a raft of central and east European leaders. Furious, French president Jacques Chirac lectured the central and east Europeans that they were 'not very well brought up' and would do better to stay silent. US defence secretary Donald Rumsfeld poured fuel on the flames by welcoming what he called 'new' Europe to counterbalance the 'old' Franco-German one.

I responded to this crisis with a book arguing that Europe would never unite against the United States, as Euro-Gaullists hoped. Instead, we Euro-Atlanticists should aim at a partnership not just with the United States but with all other liberal democracies in an increasingly post-Western world. This would no longer be '*the* free world', a Cold War phrase by now rarely used, and then often ironically. Rather, the aim should be a wider, not merely transatlantic community of closely co-operating free countries, also embracing the many people who live in unfree countries but yearn to breathe free. My title, *Free World*, programmatically dropped the definite article before the familiar two words. The book was far too optimistic, but the basic argument seems to me even more pertinent now than it was then.

Two decades on from 2001, a new US president called Joe Biden announced that US troops would finally leave Afghanistan on 11 September 2021, the twentieth anniversary of 9/11. America's precipitate withdrawal turned into a chaotic rout, as the Taliban stormed triumphantly into Kabul. This had been America's longest war. Few would pretend it had been a success. No one talked any more of the 'war on terror', except in history lessons. This turned out not to have been the defining geopolitical struggle of the twenty-first century.

Instead, the new occupant of the White House was right back to the central geopolitical challenge that George W. Bush had identified in our meeting shortly before the 9/11 attacks: China. I sometimes think the Chinese Communist Party should have posthumously awarded Osama bin Laden its highest medal, to thank him for launching the United States into more than a decade of strategic distraction. In response to the challenge from a China that in the meantime had become a superpower, but also from Russia and other autocracies, President Biden now articulated a bold vision. It was that of a wider, not merely transatlantic community of closely co-operating free countries, also embracing the many people who live in unfree countries but yearn to breathe free.

Muslims in Europe

Mohamed Atta, the Egyptian-born terrorist who piloted the first hijacked plane into the World Trade Center in New York on 11 September 2001, had been radicalised while living as a student in Hamburg. So had other members of what became known as the 'Hamburg cell' of the Al Qaeda conspiracy led from Afghanistan by Osama bin Laden. At the Quds mosque in Hamburg, Atta and his comrades were exhorted to wage violent jihad by an Islamist preacher who had spent time in Afghanistan. So the Islamist terrorist attack on America was partly made in Europe.

The 9/11 attacks illuminated, like a flare exploding over a landscape at night, the radicalisation of a small minority of the more than fifteen million Muslims of immigrant origin who were now living in western Europe. They were not the only Muslims in Europe. At least seven million Muslims had long been settled across the Balkans, most of them practising a quite relaxed version of Islam. In the Russian Federation there were an estimated fourteen million Muslims, some of whom would also make their way from the Caucasus or Central Asia to the city lights of non-Russian Europe. Turkey, a majority Muslim country with a population which had soared to sixty-five million, had recently been accepted as a candidate for membership of the European Union.

Nor were Muslims the only immigrants in western Europe. Far from it. The influx that had begun quite slowly with the arrival of people from former overseas colonies, like my east Oxford neighbours Laurie and Jeanette, and of those 'guest workers' from all around the Mediterranean, had by now resulted in foreign-born residents making up more than five per cent of the population in several west European countries. The proportion of immigrants was especially high in some cities, and dramatically so in particular quarters of those cities. Nearly half the population of Amsterdam in 1999 was of foreign origin, as were more than half of those living in the administrative region of Seine-Saint-Denis, just outside Paris.

The numbers would continue to grow through the 2000s, partly due to immigration, both legal and illegal, but also because immigrants – of all faiths and none – tended to have higher birth rates than post-Christian and post-68er Europeans. So a steadily increasing proportion of the Muslims living in Europe had actually been born there. They were, in the cumbersome but accurate wording adopted by German official-dom, 'people with a migration background'.

Most of those in the second generation were socialised into European ways through school and workplace, and spoke fluently the language of the country in which they lived. This did not necessarily mean they felt at home in Europe. In a pattern familiar from other migration histor-ies, while first-generation immigrant parents strove hard to fit in, their children sometimes wanted to rediscover their ancestral heritage and express their pride in it: 'What the father will forget, the son will remem-ber.' Often stuck in rundown housing estates, working in low-paid jobs or unemployed, they also resented the persistent discrimination that they faced because of their skin colour and foreign names.

Meanwhile, cheap air travel, the internet and mobile phones meant that people kept in much more intimate contact with their countries of origin than did the early-twentieth-century Irish or Italian lad who sailed the Atlantic to make a new life in the United States, returning only once in a blue moon to visit 'the old country'. This resulted in rich, multifaceted identities, but for some it also induced a kind of cultural schizophrenia, suspended between two worlds and not fully at home in either. These were the in-between people. Reading the life stories of young men who became terrorists, one often finds the same pattern: first they try out a more Western, secular lifestyle than their parents, then they take a sharp rejectionist turn towards a radical Islamist ver-sion of Islam that is almost equally alien to their traditional Muslim rel-atives. Further radicalisation follows contact with hardened extremists in places such as Algeria, Pakistan, Afghanistan or Iraq.

This dangerous alienation was already present in Europe before 9/11, but the 'war on terror' made it worse. One young Moroccan-Dutch woman explained that before the 11 September 2001 attacks 'I was just Nora. Then, all of a sudden, I was a Muslim.' Complex identities – Turkish or Kurd, Arab or Berber, Kashmiri or Bengali, Sunni or Shiite, Sufi or Salafi – were reduced to the single moniker of 'Muslim', and in tabloid newspapers, 'Muslim' was pretty much equated with violent extremist. Long overdue policies of active integration were now subsumed under the heading of 'counter-radicalisation', by which was sometimes crudely understood 'how do we stop them becoming terrorists'. Nervous citizens rang up the police in alarm just because people in the neighbouring apartment seemed to be speaking Arabic.

At the same time, the invasion of Iraq, accompanied by human rights abuses such as the torture perpetrated by Americans in Abu Ghraib prison, reinforced what was already a long-running Islamist narrative of Arab humiliation at the hands of the West. Add to this charge sheet the story of European indifference to the fate of Muslims in Bosnia. (No extremist preacher paused to mention that the West had intervened to protect the Muslims of Kosovo.) Compound that with a long-standing opposition to the very presence of Israel in what to many Arabs was simply Palestine, an opposition heightened by brutal actions of the Israeli state but also sometimes laced with outright anti-Semitism. Then watch as American-occupied Iraq, far from staunching the wellsprings of terror, became a new recruiting ground for Islamist terrorism. Palestine, Bosnia, Chechnya, Afghanistan and now Iraq were all rolled into a narrative of victimhood that could powerfully appeal to frustrated young Muslims in Europe – as did the notion of armed struggle and heroic martyrdom for your faith.

We can never know if terrorist attacks on European soil would anyway have resulted from the explosive mixture that was already present before 9/11 and the American invasion of Iraq; all we know is that a series of such attacks did follow. Over the next few years, country after country experienced its own version of 9/11. On 11 March 2004, Islamist terrorists bombed suburban trains travelling into Madrid, killing nearly 200 people. Spaniards called it 11M. In November that year, the Dutch filmmaker Theo van Gogh was brutally murdered on a quiet street in Amsterdam by a second-generation Moroccan-Dutchman called Mohammed Bouyeri. On 7 July 2005, it was London's turn, as commuters died horrible deaths on an underground train and in one of the capital's famous red buses. The British called it 7/7.

That same year the publication of cartoons of Muhammad in the Danish newspaper *Jyllands-Posten* resulted in death threats to the cartoonists. These became known as 'the Danish cartoons'. A decade after 9/11, in July 2011, the almost symmetrical far-right counterpart of Islamist terrorism arrived in the form of the Norwegian killer Anders Behring Breivik, who gunned down innocent teenagers at a youth camp on a holiday island, acting out his sick, internet-fuelled fantasy of a new 'crusade' against the infidels. His online manifesto called for the expulsion of all Muslims from Europe. And so the vicious spiral went on, down and down, each extreme reinforcing the other.

This was not my subject, my world, but I felt I must engage with it, so I read up on it, talked to experts, and went to see for myself. I started in Seine-Saint-Denis, one of the impoverished housing estates around Paris known as the *banlieues*. In the mediaeval cathedral of St Denis I contemplated the tomb of King Charles Martel, the 'hammer' of the newly Muslim Arabs at the battle of Tours in 732, then walked out across the Place Victor Hugo, now thronged with people from those very same Arab lands, many of the women wearing the hijab. The old France and the new. The old Europe – the one created, according to the historian Henri Pirenne, as a result of that first great confrontation with Islam ('without Muhammad, no Europe') – and the new, multicultural Europe.

Here, I experienced at first hand the anger of the *banlieues*. France was 'a hypocritical country', young Oussine told me. Try getting a job with a name like his. In France, he would always be an immigrant but back home in Morocco he was always an emigrant. Abdelaziz El Jaouhari, an Islamist activist born in France of Berber Moroccan parents, used almost identical words. The French Republic did not practise the equality it preached, he complained. Everything was fine if you were called Jean-Daniel and had blue eyes and blond hair, but not if you looked like him and were called Abdelaziz.

'What *égalité* is there for us? What *liberté*? What *fraternité*?'

The ban on the hijab introduced under President Nicolas Sarkozy was racist, he said. 'In Paris, Jews are still wearing their kippahs.' But

El Jaouhari had a message for the president: *'Moi, je suis la France!'* I'm France now.

In Clichy-sous-Bois, where rioters had set fire to cars a few months earlier, seventeen-year-old Muhammad – 'just call me Muhammad' – told me those riots were 'a way of making yourself heard'. Sixteen-year-old Souda said Algeria was so beautiful when they went back every year to stay with her grandparents. The people were so nice. Wearing a head-scarf caused her no problems there.

Another Muhammad said he and his mates would definitely support Algeria against France in football. 'Maghreb United!' he shouted, and the group of teenagers erupted in laughter.

'But what about Zinedine Zidane?' I asked, referring to the great midfielder in the French national team, whose parents were Berber Algerians.

'He's French,' chipped in Mehdi, 'but if he were burning cars, he'd suddenly be a foreigner.' Mehdi went on to explain that France had not come to terms with its colonial past.

In the desperately run-down Les Bosquets housing estate, once an award-winning example of 1960s modern architecture, a group of female community activists told me the reality of life there now: forty per cent unemployment, no police station, no shopping centre, hope-lessly inadequate transport links to any places where there might be work. People lived on welfare handouts, they explained, and if those payments were a few days late, the family had to borrow or go hungry. These eloquent, determined women summarised what their commu-nity needed in three crisp words: jobs, transport and respect. That word 'respect' kept recurring.

Zoulikha Jerrardi from Morocco wore a headscarf. She used not to, she told me with a smile, but when the hijab became stigmatised after 9/11, when Muslims were equated with terrorists, then she decided to wear it. People in government offices where she had business would gulp but say nothing.

'It doesn't impede me at all. I'm an emancipated woman.'

In Spain, I had visited the Lavapiés neighbourhood of Madrid less than a fortnight after the 9/11 attacks, and got a taste of the confused anger there. A young man from Tangier told me that he thought 9/11 was 'an attack on Islam', meaning his own moderate version of Islam, but added that his relatives in Morocco would think the Jews had a part in the attack. Even though he was a legal immigrant, with proper papers, he told me he had given up looking for a job and lived by petty thieving – 'like a wolf'.

Now, in 2005, I stood before the boarded-up Locutorio Nuevo Siglo, the 'New Century' call shop, one of those places where people with a migration background would keep in touch with their relatives and friends back home through the internet and long-distance phone calls. It was here that the Tangier-born Jamal Zougam had prepared the mobile phones that detonated the terrorist bombs on the commuter trains heading into Madrid's Atocha station on 11 March 2004. New century indeed. Zougam was subsequently sentenced to 42,922 years in prison.

Nearby, I talked to a sixteen-year-old who said Spain's former prime minister José María Aznar was to blame for the terrorist attacks because his government had supported the war in Iraq. Nineteen-year-old Muhammad Saïd told me the Atocha bombings were 'very bad', but the Spanish police treated Moroccans like him horribly. Just three days ago they had beaten him and taken his phone.

'Why?'

'Just because it had this photo on it!'

Then he showed me his phone screen. The photo was of Osama bin Laden.

Soon thereafter, in my first serious wrestling with the complex issues around the growing number of Muslims in Europe, I committed what was probably the worst mistake of my life as a political writer. In a review essay for the *New York Review of Books*, after expressing my 'enormous respect' for the 'courage, sincerity and clarity' of the Somali-born, Dutch writer and activist Ayaan Hirsi Ali, one of the authors whose work I was reviewing, I wrote that 'having in her youth been tempted by Islamist fundamentalism' she had now become a 'brave, outspoken, slightly simplistic Enlightenment fundamentalist'. I had picked up the last phrase from Ian Buruma's book *Murder in Amsterdam*, which I was also reviewing.

If there is one sentence I wish I had never written, that is it. What

I meant to convey was that the frontal, atheist critique of Islam she espoused was not the best way to win over European Muslims to accepting the values of a free European society, including free speech. As I went on to explain:

> A policy based on the expectation that millions of Muslims will so suddenly abandon the faith of their fathers and mothers is simply not realistic. If the message they hear from us is that the necessary condition for being European is to abandon their religion, then they will choose not to be European.

That was the core of an argument which still seems to me persuasive. But I compounded my error by mentioning, as an example of the kind of Muslim reformer who could persuade people with a migration background of the compatibility of Islam and a liberal, post-Enlightenment Europe, the controversial Islamist thinker Tariq Ramadan. This was a disastrous choice, for Ramadan turned out to be a fork-tongued, chameleon-like and deeply unsavoury character.

Friends objected to the phrase 'Enlightenment fundamentalist' and I soon realised that it was beyond the bounds of defensible literary provocation even implicitly to compare the stance of an exceptionally brave woman facing death threats from Islamist terrorists with the very fundamentalism that offered ideological justification for their violent acts. And did not I myself believe in the fundamentals of the Enlightenment? Rather, the issue was which strand of the Enlightenment legacy to pursue. Should it be the tradition of Voltaire, proposing freedom *from* religion in the public sphere? Or that of John Locke, proposing freedom *for* religion – which in our day means all religions and none – in that public sphere?

So I explicitly withdrew the ill-chosen phrase, at a public event in London with Ayaan Hirsi Ali herself. To no avail. For years thereafter, Ian Buruma and I were pilloried for our use of it. Whole books were written about this controversy. It was as if I had spent a decade writing a thick volume on The Principles of Enlightenment Fundamentalism, rather than two paragraphs in a book review. The French writer Pascal Bruckner even denounced me as 'an apostle of multiculturalism'.

The criticism nonetheless compelled me to think harder and dig deeper. I decided to concentrate on what seemed to me the central generic challenge for a secular, liberal European: how to defend and enhance the freedoms of an open society in conditions of growing diversity. It is a challenge with which our continent continues to wrestle and on which the future of freedom in Europe will depend. Increasingly, I focused on its sharpest edge: freedom of speech.

There had been a harbinger of the tension between free speech and what many Muslims saw as the absolute taboos of Islam as far back as 1989, when British Muslims burned copies of Salman Rushdie's novel *The Satanic Verses* and the subsequent Iranian fatwa forced the author to go into hiding with round-the-clock security guards. As Rushdie drily observed when we met later that year, his experience of 1989 was very different from the festival of liberation I had enjoyed in Warsaw and Prague. The tension seemed to subside for a time, but became acute again with the publication of the 'Danish cartoons' in 2005. Ten years after that, in 2015, it would flare up with even greater fury and a new name: Charlie Hebdo.

Cool Britannia

On Friday 27 July 2012, an estimated one billion people around the world watched an exuberant, humorous, poetic and warm-hearted celebration of modern Britain. Now I relive the experience thanks to a video of the London Olympics opening ceremony on YouTube. From a brief glimpse of the natural beauty of the Thames Valley we segue to the magical words of Caliban in Shakespeare's *Tempest*: 'Be not afeard; The isle is full of noises,/ Sounds and sweet airs, that give delight, and hurt not.' Giant factory chimneys emerge from the floor of the stadium, symbolising the raw, brutal energy of capitalism's first industrial revolution. The countervailing social democratic spirit of the welfare state is captured in a tribute to the NHS, with children jumping up and down on snow-white beds while nurses and doctors from the Great Ormond Street Children's Hospital dance joyfully around them.

On screen, we see James Bond – the actor Daniel Craig – arriving in a black cab at Buckingham Palace. One of Her Majesty's corgis does a full-body axial roll on the red carpet. Then the Queen – not an actor but the real Queen, playing herself – in a gorgeous peach-coloured dress, all silk, lace, beads and feathers, turns from her writing desk and says, 'Good evening, Mr Bond'. On the video recording, you hear a surge of applause from the stadium.

Sovereign and agent walk out together to the palace garden, step into a gleaming white helicopter and fly off across London, eventually coming to hover over the Olympic stadium. Bond opens the helicopter door. Will he jump? A long moment of suspense, with just the white underbelly of the helicopter illuminated against the night sky. Then *she* jumps, her peach-coloured dress billowing up above her knees as she swoops down to the stadium under the Union Jack canopy of her para-chute. Across the world, a billion viewers gasp. She is followed by Bond, on Her Majesty's Not-So-Secret Service, agent 007, licensed to enter-tain. As Her Majesty – a stunt double called Gary (not Sean) Connery – descends, we hear the famous throbbing dum-di-dum-dum theme tune of the Bond films. And the world and his aunt remark, in a hundred different languages, on *der berühmte britische Humor, le célèbre humour britannique, el famoso humor británico*.

Now a voice from the stadium loudspeakers asks in French – at the Olympics, announcements are still bilingual – that everyone stand for *Sa Majesté la Reine*, and there she is, the Queen, the one and only, in the same peach-coloured dress. In the sixtieth year of her reign, her 'diamond jubilee', she is still probably the world's most famous woman.

Every nation of her multinational kingdom is represented in the cel-ebration masterminded by film director Danny Boyle: England with a children's choir singing the great patriotic hymn 'Jerusalem' and archive footage of golden-haired rugby player Jonny Wilkinson kicking yet another goal; Northern Ireland with 'Danny Boy' and an Irish rugby try; Scotland with its rugby anthem 'Flower of Scotland' and a Scottish try; Wales with 'Guide Me, O Thou Great Redeemer' and a Welsh try. This is the complete 'home international', as rugby matches between the 'home nations' are called. Old and new are carefully mixed. Representa-tives of post-war Afro-Caribbean immigrants are immediately followed by pink-cheeked Chelsea pensioners in their scarlet uniforms.

As I watch the 2012 opening ceremony again, on a wet, windy morn-ing in 2021, I find my eyes filling with tears. Tears of love for this stir-ring, inclusive version of modern Britain but also tears of sadness for how we have lost it, through Brexit and the divisions that accompanied and followed Brexit. Back then, so many of us believed in this vision of a country at ease with itself and its place in the world, proud of its island story but also of the diversity that has come from immigration, open to both Europe and the Anglosphere, creative, inclusive, econom-ically dynamic but also socially caring, with Dickensian warmhearted-ness and a humour – perhaps Britain's greatest natural resource – that ranges from gentle irony to the outright lunacy of Monty Python. Was it just a piece of theatre, a fairy tale, a myth? But a myth that is shared by a sufficient number of people is also a reality. This is such stuff as nations are made on.

The national self-image captured in Boyle's show was a product of many hands, certainly including those of Winston Churchill and Margaret Thatcher. It continued to be burnished by the Conservative–Liberal coalition government of David Cameron and Nick Clegg, elected in 2010, under which the Olympics took place. But most of all, this attempted synthesis of the many different Britains reflected the spirit of the government which had won the Olympics for London, that of Tony Blair from 1997 to 2007. In the early years of the Blair government, the conscious blending of old and new was labelled Cool Britannia. A twenty-three-year-old whizz-kid called Mark Leonard, who had grown up in Brussels, came home and proposed 'rebranding Britain'. There was a lot of show business to this, as with much else in the Blair years, yet also substance.

A dynamic economy, flexible labour market and exceptional openness to immigration attracted millions of Europeans to Britain, as did the soft power of culture. The place really was cool. Some 300,000 French made their homes in the UK, especially in London, and perhaps as many Germans. At the highest point, there were probably close to one million Poles and well over a million other central and east Europeans. (My wife and I no longer had a secret language in which we could gossip about other people in the pub or restaurant, since wherever you went now, someone would understand Polish.)

In domestic as in foreign policy, Blairism tried to bridge the Atlantic and combine the best of American and European approaches. Much influenced by the example of Bill Clinton in the United States, Blairism also built on free-market foundations laid under Margaret Thatcher. It aimed to combine the dynamism of a Thatcherite market economy with the social protection of the welfare state created by a Labour government after the Second World War. The left should make its peace not merely with capitalism but with the globalised financialised capitalism symbolised by City of London skyscrapers such as 'the Gherkin' and 'the Shard'. Labour was rebranded New Labour.

Many on the continental European centre-left were fascinated by this New Labour mix. Italians talked admiringly of *Blairismo*. The German Social Democrat leader Gerhard Schröder campaigned on the idea of a 'new centre' and produced a joint paper with Blair entitled 'The Way Forward for Europe's Social Democrats'. When it came to fairness and equality, he told his party's annual conference in 1999:

> it really is as Tony Blair has put it. We are not about equal earnings. We are about real equality – equal chances for fulfilment, equal access to knowledge, equal opportunities to flourish.

The party's left wing initially put the kibosh on this un-socialist heresy. But when the German economy got into difficulties in the early 2000s, the German chancellor pushed through an 'Agenda 2010', embracing welfare and labour market reforms which, as he acknowledges in his memoirs, reflected the ideas of the Schröder–Blair paper. These reforms would prove to be essential to Germany's economic success inside the eurozone, massaging down German unit labour costs while those of south European eurozone members soared.

If ever there was a time when Britain seemed to be reasonably comfortable as a member of the European Union, it was in the early 2000s. True, Blair had, almost to the point of parody, the post-imperial British obsession with 'leadership'. The former West German Chancellor Willy Brandt recalled that in 1967 an earlier Labour politician, George Brown, asked him to help get Britain into the European Community, explaining: 'Willy, you must get us in so we can take the lead!' Now, at one of Blair's earliest international meetings, the New Labour leader told two of his closest advisers: 'Britain should be bigger!'

France and Germany, however, had no intention of giving up their divine right to lead, historically sanctioned by Charlemagne. Across a decade when Charles de Gaulle had kept the 'Anglo-Saxons' out of the club, saying '*Non*' to British membership twice, in 1963 and 1967, while signing and then building on the historic 1963 Élysée treaty with West Germany, the Franco-German 'couple' had grown accustomed to being the driving force of European integration. Just as Blair took up the reins, France and a now united Germany were preparing to take another decisive step forward, in the monetary union which was the central European political project of the 1990s. The first time Britain held the rotating presidency of the EU, in 1998, Blair found himself trying to umpire a furious Franco-German row about who should be the president of the

European Central Bank. Joining the euro therefore came to be seen as a litmus test of New Labour's commitment to the project called 'Europe', but Blair's own Chancellor of the Exchequer, Gordon Brown, in cahoots with the Eurosceptic press, made sure that would not happen any time soon.

Then came the great European bust-up over Iraq, from which Blair's reputation in Europe never recovered. Nonetheless, Britain was a major player in the European Union at this time, helping to move forward eastward enlargement, the 1999 opening to Turkey, cross-Channel military co-operation and a theoretically admirable 'Lisbon agenda' of economic reform. Kim Darroch, who arrived as Britain's permanent representative in Brussels at the end of the Blair years, sees that period as the high point of British influence inside the EU.

When I sit down to discuss this history with Tony Blair, in a cottage at the bottom of his garden on a blustery summer's day in 2021, he argues that while his relations with Schröder and Jacques Chirac were damaged by Iraq, the damage was not irreparable. Anyway, he got another chance with Angela Merkel and Nicolas Sarkozy. Moreover, Iraq did not cost him anything – rather the reverse – with other important member states. His pro-Americanism, combined with Britain's emphatic support for eastward enlargement, won him friends in Poland and all across central Europe. So also with his close allies, José María Aznar in Spain and Silvio Berlusconi in Italy – neither of them, let it be noted, exactly men of the left. Then he tells me how he won the 2012 Olympics for London. In the summer of 2004, Paris and Madrid seemed to be ahead of London in the competition to win votes in the International Olympic Committee. So he decided to take up an invitation to visit Berlusconi in the billionaire's palazzo of pleasures in Sardinia: 'the only man ever to take his wife there', Blair quips.

Berlusconi appeared with his head covered in a white bandana, apparently to hide some hair-implant surgery. The two leaders' offices had agreed that there would be no publicity, but the ebullient Italian said, 'Come for a little ride on my boat' and, hey presto, there at the quayside was a reception committee of paparazzi. (The very word derives from the name of an Italian press photographer, Paparazzo, in Federico Fellini's film *La Dolce Vita*.) They snapped photos of suntanned, bravely smiling Tony and incongruously headgeared Silvio which went around the world and are remembered to this day, especially because of the white bandana.

But Tony was able to make his ask: would Italy please support London's Olympic bid?

Silvio replied, 'You are my friend. I promise nothing but I see if I can help.'

The four Italian members of the International Olympic Committee were, of course, strictly independent – and doubtless unshakeable pillars of integrity. But one of them, Mario Pescante, did happen to be a junior minister in Berlusconi's government, and all of them somehow ended up voting for London, which beat Paris by four votes. The Italian votes. In this sense, too, the London Olympics can be seen as the last, best jive of *Blairismo*.

'Britain must overcome its ambivalence about Europe,' Blair declared in the German city of Aachen in 1999. The British ambassador to Germany saw the phrase in a draft of the speech and muttered 'Good luck with that!' From today's vantage point, one can obviously find things in the Blair years that helped pave the way for Brexit. There was the decision to open the door wide to central and east Europeans after their countries joined the European Union in 2004, without the transition period implemented in most other member states. The governor of the Bank of England said the economy could use the extra workers. Internal government projections put the numbers of those likely to seize the opportunity in the low tens of thousands. In fact, more than two million arrived in the next decade, according to official figures. The real numbers were probably even larger. Coming on top of immigration from outside the EU, this influx was a major reason many people voted for Brexit. I heard this often on the doorstep when campaigning in the 2016 referendum for Britain to remain in the EU.

Blair's metropolitan, cosmopolitan, left-liberal style was great for young university graduates in big cities, but not so great for the traditionally Labour-supporting working class in the post-industrial towns of northern England – nor, indeed, for traditional middle-class Conservatives like my parents. Compounding that cultural problem was New

Labour's closeness to the banks, hedge funds and venture capitalists of the booming City of London. Blair's close ally Peter Mandelson said he was 'intensely relaxed about people getting filthy rich', so long as they paid their taxes. In the financial year that ended in April 2008, London bankers received bonus packages amounting to about £16 billion, equivalent to more than forty per cent of the country's entire defence budget. My undergraduate friends who went into financial services in the run-up to London's 1986 'Big Bang' of deregulation were no more gifted than their contemporaries who became surgeons, musicians or diplomats, but they were quite disproportionately rewarded. It turned out that the most prophetic of the ABBA songs we sang in our student years was 'Money, Money, Money'. As its refrain insisted, this was a rich man's world.

The assets of the Bank of Scotland, which on the eve of the financial crisis claimed to be the biggest bank in the world, were valued at £2.2 trillion, more than one and a half times Britain's annual GDP. Gordon Brown boasted that Britain had achieved 'economic stability not boom and bust'. In fact there was an enormous financial boom and then an enormous bust. The Bank of Scotland lost nearly a third of its paper value and the British taxpayer had to bail it out, at a cost of £45 billion, or more than £700 for each man, woman and child in Britain. The bankers kept their bonuses while ordinary people had to bear the brunt of the subsequent recession and austerity. This was a disgrace seen across the entire democratic capitalist world, but Britain was an extreme case of it – and the worst excesses happened on New Labour's watch.

More directly paving the way for the 2016 referendum were two other features of the Blair years: his failure to make a stronger case for Europe at home in Britain, for fear of alienating the Eurosceptic press, and the way his government legitimated the idea of holding a big European referendum. 'I am a passionate pro-European,' Blair told the European Parliament in 2005. But he said that in Strasbourg, not in Britain. I helped him with a few of his European speeches at the time, including two he delivered in Warsaw. So when we meet now, I lay on his kitchen table the charge that he made the argument for Europe in Warsaw but not in Walsall – a town that voted sixty-eight per cent for Brexit.

Blair does not contest this but defends it as a pragmatic political judgement. He just did not think it was worth 'slapping people around the chops' with it and poking the beast in the eye. But, he insists, 'in Europe, I was pro-European'. This is an unintentionally revealing formulation, since it suggests that, like many other Brits, he instinctively thinks of Europe as somewhere else.

The beast in question was the Eurosceptic press, with the papers owned by Rupert Murdoch being joined by the *Daily Mail* under Paul Dacre, its aggressively Eurosceptic editor, the *Telegraph* group and the *Express* – whose proprietor Richard Desmond once cynically told Blair that *Express* readers were 'an old, sad group of people'. Of the nearly thirty-one million British daily newspaper readers in 2003, more than twenty-two million took a paper that could be classified as Eurosceptic. Their journalism was relentless, brutal and often mendacious. The propagation of fake news about the EU had been pioneered in the 1990s by a young Brussels correspondent for the *Daily Telegraph* called Boris Johnson, who 'reported' such invented stories as that the eurocrats proposed to ban crooked bananas and prawn cocktail-flavoured crisps. The tradition of Johnsonian fiction was continued by the *Sunday Express*, which headlined a 'news' story about the British government signing up to the proposed EU constitutional treaty in 2003: 'Queen: Is Blair Out to Axe Me?'

The *Sun*, proud of its famous 'Up Yours Delors' splash the day after Margaret Thatcher's Bruges speech in 1988, greeted the constitutional treaty with a front page headed 'Save our Country'. Under a wavy Union Jack, it declared '1588 – We Saw Off the Spanish Armada' (picture of Queen Elizabeth I), '1805 – We Saw Off the French' (picture of Admiral Nelson, victor of the Battle of Trafalgar), '1940 – We Saw Off the Germans' (picture of Churchill), '2003 – Blair Surrenders Britain to Europe' (unflattering photo of Blair).

'We saw the Eurosceptic press as something you had to *manage*,' Blair's press secretary, Alastair Campbell, tells me now. But the Blair circle had worked hard to get the support of Murdoch. As the new Labour leader in 1995, Blair travelled all the way to Hayman Island in Australia to address News Corporation executives. Campbell recalls that already in their conversations there, Murdoch made no secret of his anti-European views – 'those Europeans, you can never trust them' was the gist of it. At a crucial moment in the 1997 election campaign, Labour strategists felt they might be vulnerable to Conservative attacks over 'Europe'. So, as another key adviser records: 'We got the *Sun* to run an article by Blair the next day, promising that he would "slay the Euro-dragon".' Pretty active management, then. Subsequently, in the fateful psychodrama of the personal rivalry between Tony Blair and Gordon Brown, Brown would try to get the tabloids on his side as a critic of the euro. His press secretary even suggested to the *Sun* the headline 'Brown Saves the Pound'.

When I persuaded Blair to make one of his rare European speeches back home in Britain, in 2006, I urged him to take on the Eurosceptic press. All we got was this:

> Of course, the fevered frenzy of parts of the British media don't exactly help. I have long since given up trying to conduct a serious debate about Europe in certain quarters. But it's too easy just to blame it on the media.

In truth, he felt it was just too difficult to take them on. Only a year later did he finally denounce these papers as a 'feral beast'; but by then, he was about to leave office. His successors would continue to feed the beast, as he had done.

Looking back, Blair tells me the only substantive policy concessions they made to the Eurosceptic press were 'on the euro and the referendum'. But those were two decisive points. Britain had, of course, held a referendum on 'Europe' in 1975. Starting in the 1990s, pressure built from the right, including my old colleagues at the *Spectator*, to hold another. As Charles Moore records in his biography of Margaret Thatcher, she herself focused on the idea of a referendum soon after she was ejected from office in 1990. She wrote to a Eurosceptic MP in 1992:

> I have always felt that the best answer for us was to be a kind of free-trade and non-interventionist 'Singapore' off Europe, seeking contact and understanding with the growth areas of the world, but I have a feeling that such a scheme is perhaps too revolutionary even for my fellow Euro-sceptics here in the Commons.

She supported the Referendum Party founded by the billionaire James Goldsmith and near the end of her life privately told friends that she was in favour of leaving the EU.

Yet the Labour government itself legitimised the idea of a referendum by holding no fewer than five of them, on issues ranging from devolution in Scotland and Wales to a regional assembly for the north-east of England and even a proposed traffic congestion charge in Manchester. If a referendum was needed on a traffic congestion charge, how could one not be held on a question vital to the future of the nation? So Labour's 1997 election manifesto already promised a referendum on joining the euro. The eloquently pro-European *Guardian* columnist Hugo Young concluded the 1999 edition of his book about Britain and Europe by saying: 'The show would not be over before the people spoke.'

Then came the proposed constitution for Europe. Faced with a barrage of negative coverage, including the *Sun*'s charge of 'surrender', Blair again promised a referendum. 'I had to do it,' he tells me. He could never have got the treaty through the House of Lords without it. Thus two of the least democratically representative groups in Britain, unelected peers and unelected press barons, dictated this exercise in direct democracy. The French president Jacques Chirac was furious. So fearful was he of a likely rejection of the constitution by French voters that he had privately proposed to fellow European leaders, including Blair, a kind of no-referendum pact. His concern was justified. Once perfidious Albion set the precedent, Chirac had to have a referendum in France – and he lost it, decisively, by fifty-five per cent to forty-five per cent. That same summer of 2005, the Netherlands also held a referendum, and the majority there against the constitutional treaty was even larger: sixty-one per cent to thirty-nine per cent.

This let Blair off the hook. At the time, he told his Foreign Secretary, Robin Cook, that he had rather looked forward to a referendum battle, to which Cook replied: 'Then you're dafter than I thought.' In retrospect, Blair thinks Cook was right: 'We dodged a bullet.' Polling conducted for Britain in Europe, a pro-European pressure group, suggested that if all twenty-four other member states of the EU had ratified the constitutional treaty, fear of isolation might have produced a narrow majority in favour – but even then, the odds were against. And this was when almost everything in Europe still looked good.

The idea of another referendum on 'Europe' was now firmly established at the heart of British politics. Sooner or later, in one circumstance or another, the British people would be asked again. All three main political parties had gone into the 2005 election promising a referendum on the constitutional treaty. After the 2010 election, the Conservative–Liberal coalition government passed into law a 'referendum lock', committing itself to hold a popular vote on any further transfer of sovereignty to the EU. Even as he basked in the reflected glory of the London Olympics in the summer of 2012, the Conservative prime minister David Cameron had decided to go a step further. In a speech at Bloomberg's headquarters in London in January 2013, he committed himself to holding a decisive referendum on the basis of a negotiated 'new settlement' for British membership of the Union. I welcomed this, more fool me, as a chance to lance the boil at long last and overcome that paralysing British ambivalence about Europe.

Turning again to the speech Tony Blair delivered on my invitation, I read, with a very dry smile, his peroration:

> There is no other way for Britain. Britain won't leave Europe. No government would propose it. And despite what we are often told, the majority of the British people, in the end, would not vote for withdrawal.

History laughs.

Hubris

On 1 May 2009 I organised an eightieth birthday celebration for my friend and mentor Ralf Dahrendorf, the German-British liberal thinker. We both knew that he was dying. In his lifetime, he had seen the near-extinction of freedom in Europe and then its greatest ever advance.

As a fifteen-year-old boy, Ralf had spent the Christmas of 1944 in a Gestapo prison camp, where he had been incarcerated for distributing anti-Nazi flysheets with friends from school. He witnessed a prisoner dying a slow, terrible death by hanging in the freezing cold but also the courage of imprisoned German Social Democrats and Communists, who sang defiant marching songs of the labour movement over their Christmas meal of prison food. When he revisited the site of that Gestapo camp many years later, he picked up a small fragment of bluey-white smoked glass and kept it always on his writing desk. After his death, his widow gave it to me.

In 1946, Ralf was compelled to flee with his parents from occupied Berlin to Hamburg, in the safety of the British zone of occupation. His father, Gustav Dahrendorf, a Social Democratic politician, had just opposed the forced merger of the Social Democratic party with the Communist party in the Soviet-occupied zone that would soon become East Germany. As a result, he was likely to be arrested by Soviet security forces – and it was not only the father who was in peril. Working in the East German communist party archives in the early 1990s, I found a handwritten note. 'Young Ralf,' it said, '. . . 16 years [old], meant for the NKVD'. So the plan had been for the Soviet secret police to get Ralf to inform on his father. As Ralf recalled, two mysterious Russians had indeed visited the schoolboy when he was alone at home and started asking probing questions about his parents. Thus, before the age of seventeen, Ralf had the most direct, personal experience of both the totalitarian dictatorships, the Nazi and the Soviet, that brought Europe to its knees in the first half of the twentieth century.

Intellectually sharp as a razor, outwardly undemonstrative, even stiff, Ralf was not the Martin Luther type of intellectual, fiercely defying all the powers of this world: 'Here I stand, I cannot do otherwise.' He described himself as an Erasmian liberal, a man of dialogue, tolerance and moderation. At the end of his life he became a pillar of the British establishment. As a member of the House of Lords, he was not at all displeased when some verdigris-encrusted English hereditary peer took his arm and addressed him confidentially as 'Raif', an aristocratic pronunciation of the English 'Ralph'. But he had – and this, next to his brilliance and personal kindness, was what I loved in him – an unwavering, passionate, lifelong commitment to individual liberty.

Back in 1944, when the Gestapo arrested fifteen-year-old Ralf, just four major countries in Europe could be described as perilously free: Britain, Switzerland, Sweden and Ireland. In January 1974, the American think tank Freedom House counted seventeen free countries in Europe and just forty-one in the entire world. By 2004, however, it could tally an all-time record of thirty-five free countries in Europe and eighty-nine worldwide. As I talked to protesters during Ukraine's Orange Revolution at the end of that year, shivering in minus ten degrees centigrade on the snow-covered Maidan, the main square in Kyiv, I was convinced that we could advance further towards the goal articulated in the title of the book I published that year: *Free World*.

Four years later, in 2008, Freedom House reckoned that three billion people across the world now lived in free countries. Yet many hundreds of millions of people in those countries did not feel themselves to be free – and with good reason. Freedom House measured political rights and civil liberties, but not the achievement of those minimum social and economic conditions without which human beings can never truly be free. Dahrendorf called this the 'common floor' of healthcare, housing, education and opportunity. Without the common floor, people would not have the equal life chances essential to a mature, modern version of liberalism.

Persistent neglect of this imperative was one of the reasons why, as Ralf stoically faced the prospect of his own death in the summer of 2009, liberalism itself was descending towards a near-death experience. The immediate cause was the financial crisis of 2008. At our gathering for Ralf's eightieth, the economic commentator Martin Wolf argued that this financial crisis was even more severe than the one which had plunged Europe into the horrors of the 1930s. And so we sat around a table asking ourselves the question that liberal intellectuals would wrestle with for years to come: what went wrong?

If I had to summarise the answer to that question in a single word, it would be hubris – the tragic flaw of excessive self-confidence. The hubris of the American 'New Rome' marching into Iraq. The hubris of Cool Britannia and the hubris of my Polish friends, confident that fish soup had been turned back into an aquarium. The hubris of believing that the enlargement of the American-led geopolitical West into eastern Europe could continue smoothly without facing a fierce challenge from a revanchist Russia. The hubris of the eurozone, perfectly captured in Jean-Claude Trichet's 2008 speech of neo-Carolingian self-congratulation. The hubris of a European Union that, on the fiftieth anniversary of the Treaty of Rome, in 2007, saw itself as a model that the world might now respectfully emulate. Mark Leonard, he of 'rebranding Britain', had recently published a book entitled *Why Europe Will Run the 21st Century*. Several other books were written in that spirit at this time, often by admiring Americans.

The hubris, too, of a globalised, financialised capitalism which boasted that it had put an end to 'boom and bust' and found in free markets something like a universal panacea. And, yes, the hubris of liberals like me, who believed we could now advance from a free Europe towards a free world. There was nothing wrong with the goal. I embrace it to this day. The misjudgement was about how – and how fast – we could get there.

We linked our dream of spreading individual liberty much too closely to one particular model of capitalism. Globalised, financialised capitalism did bring major gains. The post-communist economies of central Europe grew dramatically, to the benefit of many. Hundreds of millions of people were lifted out of poverty in countries like China and India.

But a hypertrophied, unsustainable financial sector then plunged the entire economy of Western liberal democratic capitalism into crisis. This model also brought levels of inequality not seen in the West for a hundred years.

We liberal internationalists paid a lot of attention, quite rightly, to the other half of the world, but we neglected the other half of our own societies. The inequality was not only economic and social, it was also cultural: an inequality of attention and respect. How much sympathetic coverage of the hardships of white working-class life in poorer regions could readers find in liberal metropolitan newspapers such as the *New York Times* and the *Guardian*, until the populist backlash of the 2010s generated a wave of journalistic safaris to the Rust Belt in the United States and the post-industrial towns of northern England? Yet equality is an essential component of any liberalism worthy of the name. That means not just equal rights and equal opportunities but also what the legal philosopher Ronald Dworkin characterised as 'equal respect and concern' for all members of society.

Nowhere was the hubris of globalised, financialised capitalism more visible than at the annual meetings of the World Economic Forum in the Swiss ski resort of Davos, high on Thomas Mann's 'magic mountain'. After several days of substantive discussions there was a 'gala soirée' on the Saturday evening, a lavish extravaganza usually hosted by one country. The brutalist concrete congress centre was transformed into a palace of delights worthy of Versailles in 1788 or St Petersburg before the Russian revolution. One year, there was a Russian soirée for which the Davos municipal swimming pool was covered over and turned into an operetta fantasy of Orthodox onion domes, Cossack hats, vodka and caviar. Around these Potemkin pleasure palaces wandered the chief executives, bankers, hedge fund supremos and venture capitalists, arm in arm with their often younger, beautiful wives, wearing in jewellery alone the national income of a small African country. Here, I bumped into the Israeli trade minister Natan Sharansky, who in an earlier life had been the Soviet dissident Anatoly Sharansky and remembered a rather different Russia. Soon after the financial crash, these lavish soirées ceased. The word was they were now thought 'inappropriate'.

From Davos in 2009, my notebook records the following

advertisement for the investment bank Merrill Lynch: 'We make money the old-fashioned way – we earn it.' It would be hard to think of a slogan more ludicrously at odds with the facts of the recent past. Here was a bank that had just written off some $42 billion in reckless investments in sub-prime mortgages and only survived because it was bought by the Bank of America. Such wild risk-taking, which endangered the entire economy of the Western world, was directly, causally connected to the huge bonuses that bankers were creaming off. The development economist Paul Collier proposed a new crime of 'bankslaughter'. As with manslaughter in English law, malicious intent would not need to be proven, just utter recklessness. Yet when the crash came, most of the bankers walked away scot-free, replete with their undeserved gains.

Whether we liked it or not, we academics and journalists attending Davos were also part of the show. Although many of us thought of ourselves as spectators on the magic mountain, seen from outside we were as much members of a global liberal establishment as the bankers and hedge fund managers. One of the worst things that happened to liberalism in these years was that it came to be viewed as the ideology of the rich and powerful. The right-wing Catholic polemicist Patrick Deneen coined the usefully provocative term 'liberalocracy' – rule by liberals.

For some twenty years after 1989, it was quite reasonable to argue, as Francis Fukuyama did, that there was no credible, global ideological alternative to liberal democratic capitalism. Islamic fundamentalism could appeal to Muslims in many countries, also in Europe, but it could not attract adherents across cultures and continents, as both communism and fascism had done in the twentieth century. But that historical observation was then turned into a prediction and a prescription.

'The great struggles of the 20th century between liberty and totalitarianism', declared the US national security strategy in 2002, 'ended with a decisive victory for the forces of freedom – and a single sustainable model for national success: freedom, democracy, and free enterprise.' Alarm bells should ring whenever anyone says 'single sustainable model'. This was Margaret Thatcher's 'TINA': There Is No Alternative. Such thinking persisted into the 2010s in Angela Merkel's language of *alternativlos* (without alternative). Yet at the heart of liberalism, from John Stuart Mill to Ralf Dahrendorf, is the idea that our liberal proposals must always be tested against alternatives. This leads to a core paradox of liberalism: for liberalism to flourish, there must never only be liberalism. Western liberal democratic capitalism did so well in the second half of the twentieth century precisely because it was challenged by fierce ideological competition from fascism and communism. Liberated from such competition, it became lazy, self-indulgent and over-confident. Then the ideological competition finally re-emerged from a direction no one had anticipated in 1989. China's unprecedented combination of Leninism and capitalism created a model that had considerable appeal in many developing countries, especially when contrasted with the crisis of Western capitalism.

It's not that we liberal internationalists were blind. We saw many of the gathering problems and discontents, from Islamist terrorism to the disaster of Iraq, the overheating of financial capitalism and a citizens' revolt against the proposed European constitution. In one of my notebooks from 2006 I find the laconic entry 'Europe – whole, free and unhappy'. But after a quarter-century in which history had so unexpectedly, gloriously gone our way, we did tend to assume that these would be temporary setbacks, obstacles on an upward path, delaying but not reversing the larger course of historical development. In other words, deep down we somehow thought – or more accurately, *felt* – that we knew which way history was going. That is always a mistake and one that historians should be the last people on earth to make.

Faltering
(2008–2022)

Zweig and the downward turn

As we entered the second decade of the twenty-first century, people started talking about a book called *The World of Yesterday* by the Austrian writer Stefan Zweig. Subtitled *Memoirs of a European* and written in exile during the Second World War, this is an elegiac evocation of a Europe – 'the true homeland chosen by my heart' – that Zweig sees as lost forever. The epigraph to the last chapter, taken from Shakespeare's *Julius Caesar*, proclaims: 'The sun of Rome is set. Our day is gone.' Zweig ends his story with Britain declaring war on Nazi Germany, but the golden age he celebrates in lavish prose is not pre-1939 but pre-1914 Europe. That, for him, is Europe before the Fall.

> Never have I loved our old earth *more* than in those last years before the First World War, never *more* hoped for European unification, never *more* believed in its future than in this time, when we thought that we glimpsed a new dawn. But in truth, this was already the firelight of the approaching world conflagration.

Why did people go back to Zweig's book in the 2010s? Was it just because it was reissued in a new English translation in 2009? Or was it because they discerned, in his melancholy memoir, prophetic signs for a world once again on the brink of catastrophe? The Austrian-German novelist Daniel Kehlmann reflected that the book's popularity said 'much about our time, our fears, our feeling that perhaps something is just coming irretrievably to an end'.

When Zweig wrote his memoir in 1941–42, in exile first in the United States and then in Brazil, he was quite sure something had already come to an end. One title he proposed to his Spanish translator was 'The

Irretrievable Years'. Although only just turning sixty, this Jewish Austrian European was suffused with tragic fatalism. We cannot conclusively establish whether he was already contemplating suicide as he polished the manuscript in the final station of his exile, the leafy Brazilian town of Petrópolis. But certainly the knowledge that Zweig and his wife Lotte took their own lives by drinking poison in February 1942, just days after sending off the final typescript, adds a funereal edge to our reading of it.

As readers returned to Zweig's memoir, so Europe entered a 'time of troubles', to use a Russian phrase, or what some observers called a 'polycrisis'. Like the upward turn that began around 1985 and gathered speed from 1988 onwards, the downward turn that began around 2005 and gathered speed from 2008 onwards had many different elements. The French and Dutch votes against the European constitution in 2005, the financial crisis of 2008 that segued into the first of several waves of eurozone crisis, Russia's seizure of parts of Georgia in 2008 and of Crimea in 2014, the refugee crisis of 2015 and the *Charlie Hebdo* affair in the same year, the growth of populism in Hungary and Poland, Britain's Brexit referendum vote in 2016, the arrival of Donald Trump in the White House in 2017, the Covid pandemic that enveloped Europe in 2020 and the war of recolonisation that Putin launched against Ukraine in February 2022 – each had its own distinct causes. Yet as with the upward turn so now with the downward, the different elements were mutually reinforcing.

In the 1980s, the disparate policies and personalities of Gorbachev, Reagan, Thatcher and Kohl ultimately complemented each other. The push for a west European single market, led from Brussels by Jacques Delors, increased the magnetic attraction of 'Europe' to people behind the Iron Curtain. The liberation of central and eastern Europe and the unification of Germany gave a further powerful impulse to west European integration. An upward spiral resulted.

In the 2010s, the eurozone crisis spawned a Eurosceptic, populist party in Germany, the Alternative for Germany, that would then gain wider support through opposition to an influx of refugees in 2015. It exploited negative stereotypes of Muslims that had already been given wide circulation in response to post-9/11 Islamist terrorist attacks, of which the murder of journalists of the French satirical magazine *Charlie Hebdo* in early 2015 was another example. Putin supported anti-immigration west European populists and several of them expressed admiration for Putin. During the Brexit referendum, campaigners for 'Leave' highlighted both the state of the eurozone and the refugee crisis to explain why Britain should abandon a failing EU. Trump praised Brexit, Brexiters praised Trump. Economic difficulties caused by the Covid pandemic were redoubled by soaring energy and food prices resulting from the war in Ukraine. And so it went on, each negative development reinforcing the other.

The 2022 invasion of Ukraine by a nuclear-armed Russian dictatorship recalled to mind the apocalyptic darkness of Zweig's last chapters. Indeed, there were days in the early 2020s when I felt like my putative central European ancestor, Scholem Asch, who in the late 1930s wrote to his friend Zweig: 'It seems that we are entering a martyr period . . . we must take fate as it comes.' But that is not the spirit in which I write.

This last part of my book is headed 'Faltering', not 'Falling'. Many of the chapters that follow end in question marks. We simply do not know whether the descent of recent years will continue or be reversed, perhaps even becoming a story of full-scale recovery and further progress. What we do know is that the outcome will depend on us, the Europeans alive today. So the spirit we need is not Zweigish resignation but the resolute defiance shown by other writers of Zweig's time who continued to fight – with pen and voice – for what they believed in, for a dawn that would follow even the darkest night.

After all, if Stefan Zweig had held on for just another three years, he would have seen his native Austria liberated. Another twelve years and, at the age of seventy-five, he could have witnessed his beloved Vienna become, after the Austrian state treaty of 1955, the capital of an independent, democratic and peaceful republic, part of a Europe that would soon set out to remake the old movie *Rome* in a new way, by consent and in freedom.

Euro, crisis

In Brussels on the morning of Monday 10 May 2010 I watched a visibly sleep-deprived José Manuel Barroso, the former Portuguese student activist who was now European Commission President, and Herman van Rompuy, Belgian President of the European Council and occasional author of haikus, try to reassure an audience of business leaders that the euro had been saved. 'Any attempt to threaten the stability of the euro will fail,' said Barroso. This scene would be repeated many times over the next few years, in a Groundhog Day of narrowly averted Euro-geddon.

Their bold reassurances followed what was dubbed Europe's 'trillion dollar weekend', a frenzy of emergency meetings culminating in an announcement just after 2 a.m. on that Monday morning of a rescue package for Greece, and in effect for the whole eurozone, worth €750 billion. 'We shall defend the euro, whatever it takes,' said Olli Rehn, the usually phlegmatic Finnish European Commissioner for economic and monetary affairs. Why dub it 'trillion *dollar* weekend'? Because that would impress the largely anglophone and dollar-minded financial markets. Why make the announcement at 2 a.m.? Because it had to be done before the markets opened in Asia.

The previous autumn, a newly elected Greek government had revealed that the country's deficit was much larger than its predecessors had acknowledged. As Greece struggled to address the problem, the 'spread' had widened between the higher interest rates that investors demanded if they were to lend to the Greek government and the lower ones at which they were happy to lend to the German government. This opened the prospect of a 'doom loop', in which almost bankrupt banks would have to be saved by already debt-laden governments, which in turn would worsen the problems of those banks by cutting public spending or raising taxes to cover the interest burden on the soaring public debt, so that each insolvent partner would drag the other down until foreign investors came to believe that they must default – thus further widening the dreaded spreads and tightening the noose around the country's neck.

In April 2010, the Greek government announced that its budget deficit was now more than thirteen per cent of GDP and its public debt more than 120 per cent. (Recall that the Maastricht criteria were three per cent and sixty per cent respectively.) A new word entered the vocabulary, 'Grexit', meaning Greece exiting the eurozone. But Grexit would probably produce a domino effect, with markets moving on to the next weakest eurozone member. One senior German official remarked that this eurozone was a 'machine from hell'.

Hence the crisis meetings over that long weekend in May, with French President Nicolas Sarkozy, pale as a funeral shroud, instructing the then president of the European Central Bank, Jean-Claude Trichet – 'as a French citizen' – to do whatever was needed. But the Maastricht treaty had given the European Central Bank a mandate of absolute independence to guarantee monetary stability, like the Bundesbank. The treaty also had a 'no bailout clause', specifying that no eurozone national government would be responsible for another government's debts. That Sunday, 9 May, Angela Merkel faced regional elections in the important federal state of North Rhine-Westphalia and German public opinion was massively opposed to 'giving money to Greece'. Even the pro-European liberal weekly *Die Zeit* asked: 'What Will Happen to Our Money?'

In the end there was a big bailout which pretended not to be a bailout. But to assuage the Germans and other North European creditor countries, it came with harsh conditions imposed on Greece. The conditions were laid down in what Greeks called simply 'the Memorandum', enforced by what would come to be known as a 'Troika' of European Commission, European Central Bank and International Monetary Fund. Greece would have to slash its public spending on things like healthcare, education and pensions, in a draconian programme of austerity and reform. Meanwhile, most of the 'bailout' money went to pay off foreign creditors, including those German, French and other banks that had so imprudently lent to Greece in the locust years. 'Neither a borrower nor a lender be,' admonished Shakespeare's Polonius. But almost all the pain of adjustment fell on the irresponsible borrowers in the South, almost none on the irresponsible lenders in the North.

For the first but not the last time, European leaders rallied round to say that the euro had been saved once and for all. Merkel declared: 'If the euro fails, Europe fails.' Therefore it could not fail.

All the problems that economists had long predicted now emerged in the half-baked, over-extended monetary union, as well as some that had not been foreseen. Like an overweight bank manager with a weak heart, the eurozone staggered in and out of the doctor's surgery and the emergency room. The first, acute phase of the crisis ended in July 2012 when Mario Draghi, who had succeeded Trichet as president of the European Central Bank, made his famous statement that the bank would do 'whatever it takes' to preserve the euro. The patient survived, but in poor health. There was another acute emergency around Greece in 2015. This long-drawn-out crisis, or series of crises, was at once terrifying and extremely boring.

As some of us had feared, a currency union that was meant to strengthen and unite Europe actually weakened and divided it. Where northern and southern Europe had seemed to be converging in the early 2000s, now they diverged. The Greek economy shrank by roughly one quarter. In 2013, youth unemployment in Germany was just eight per cent but in Spain and Greece it was well over fifty per cent. Where a young German could be reasonably confident of finding a decent job in an economy that had flourished inside the eurozone, young Spanish, Portuguese and Greek university graduates were reduced to working as waiters in London and Berlin.

This not only impaired life chances; it endangered life itself. By early 2012, one in three Greeks lived below the poverty line. Suicides increased by a third between 2010 and 2013. Levels of medical care plummeted. Exhausted, working twenty hours a day to save patients' lives despite all kinds of shortages, Dr Theodoros Giannos, the head of the Elpis hospital in Athens, received the news in early summer 2015 that his twenty-six-year-old son, Patrick, had taken his own life by jumping in front of an underground train. 'There was just an emptiness in front of him,' he told a reporter, between wrenching sobs. 'The emptiness of the future they have taken away from us.'

The eurozone crisis both exposed and intensified a set of tensions that had built up inside the European system. In this age of globalised financialised capitalism, the European Union and all its governments walked in terror of 'the markets'. The American pundit James Carville joked that, if offered the chance of reincarnation, he would come back as the bond market: 'You can intimidate everybody.' Yet by decisive 'shock and awe' action, the US Treasury and the Federal Reserve, America's central bank, could (just) see off even the bond markets. Had the euro-zone had a common treasury, and a central bank with a wider mandate, it could have done the same. But the eurozone was this awkward halfway house of a common currency without a common treasury.

So the traders could speculate against the government bonds of the weakest member states, widening those spreads from German bonds. Bumping into Romano Prodi, the former Italian prime minister and European Commission president, at a moment of bond market attack on Italy, I asked him what he thought. Back in 2001 he had told me the euro would advance 'through crisis'; now he opened his arms wide and said: 'It seems my country is governed by *lo spread*.'

Markets dictating to democracies were soon followed by unelected international officials dictating to elected governments. This was a defect of technocratic liberalism in general and the European institutions in particular. Highly educated people often think the best form of government would be epistocracy: rule by the knowledgeable. Jean Rey, a former president of the European Commission, expressed this attitude perfectly in 1974, when confronted with the outrageous proposal that Britain should have a referendum on its membership of the European Community:

> I would deplore a situation in which the policy of this great country should be left to housewives. It should be decided instead by trained and informed people.

Now unelected officials of the 'Troika' in Brussels (European Commission), Frankfurt (European Central Bank) and Washington

(International Monetary Fund) would send emails instructing the Greeks to cut their pensions and health spending. At that meeting I attended in May 2010, Van Rompuy said the Greek government needed to 'change the culture and even the society in Greece'. A tall order, surely – and anyway, who was he to tell a democratically elected Greek government what to do with its own culture and society? The next year, European and international monetary institutions effectively compelled both Greece and Italy to remove their prime ministers, who were replaced by a former vice president of the European Central Bank and a former European Commissioner.

All this was done in the name of enforcing 'rules', a distinctively German economic approach embedded in the design of the eurozone. But policymakers bent those rules while pretending not to. Mario Draghi was a past master of the art of discreetly reinterpreting rules – and this reinterpretation was essential. If the eurozone had stuck strictly to the black letters of its treaties, Greece would have defaulted and the contagion might well have spread to other countries. But changing the rules by stealth left everyone unhappy: the indebted South because of the rigorous conditions being imposed upon it, the creditor North because the rules were being bent. In any case, those rules were never applied evenhandedly. Germany had exceeded the three per cent budget deficit limit for three successive years, 2001 to 2003, but had received barely a rap over the knuckles. How could an angry Greek not conclude that there was one rule for the weak and another for the strong, just as when the powerful Athenians confronted the much weaker Melians in 415 BCE? The Germans were the Athenians now.

In 1878, Otto von Bismarck told the German parliament that the recently united Germany should aspire to be only an 'honest broker' and not 'the schoolmaster' in Europe. In the 2010s, recently reunited Germany stepped into the very role that Bismarck had warned against: Europe's schoolmaster. Or perhaps one should say schoolmistress, for the personification of this role was Angela Merkel, the extraordinary woman who was German Chancellor for sixteen years from 2005 to 2021 – longer than Konrad Adenauer and only three years short of Bismarck. Again and again she repeated her schoolteacher's metaphor that every country in the eurozone must 'do its homework'.

The greatest irony was in the relationship between Germany and France, the greatest misery between Germany and Greece. In response to the fall of the Berlin Wall, François Mitterrand had pushed the project of European monetary union to ensure France maintained its political power when faced with a united Germany. But since money was Germany's strongest suit, the monetary union had precisely the opposite effect. Far from keeping France in the driving seat, it put Germany there. Germany was not the hegemon of the entire European Union but it was something very close to a hegemon of the European monetary union. Prodi sharply observed that 'the Lady [i.e. Merkel] takes the decisions and the French president then gives a press conference to explain the decisions'. Over dinner in Berlin, two senior German officials explained to me how they woke up every morning worrying how to make France *feel* that it was still Germany's equal.

Much worse was the impact on relations between Germany and Greece. Giorgos, my student roommate in rural Bavaria in 1974, told me how his uncle, the former communist partisan, could never forgive the Germans the atrocities perpetrated in occupied Greece during the Second World War. But Giorgos himself had a more positive image of Germany, doubtless influenced by his pleasant experiences with Bavarian girls in the local discotheque. As Greek students and workers flowed northwards and German investors and tourists came southwards; as the Federal Republic proved itself both a stable democracy and a friend of democracy in southern Europe; as both countries sat together as equals in the European Union, so attitudes gradually changed for the better.

Then the euro crisis broke and almost overnight the worst stereotypes returned on both sides. Merkel and her hardline finance minister Wolfgang Schäuble were bedecked with swastikas on Greek placards, Greeks pilloried as good-for-nothing 'swindlers' in Germany. 'Sell your islands, you bankrupt Greeks,' shrieked *Bild*, Germany's most widely read tabloid, 'and the Acropolis as well.'

This would have been bad enough if Germany and other north European creditor nations were administering the best medicine for the Greek economy. But the extreme harshness of the austerity cuts was counterproductive, making Greek economic recovery more difficult. In autumn 2012, I chaired a discussion with Schäuble – whose personal courage and European commitment I greatly admired – and an audience that included a deputy governor of the Bank of Greece, Eleni Louri-Dendrinou. She asked him about economists' professional assessment that the extreme austerity measures were dragging the Greek economy into a downward spiral. Schäuble replied that he didn't really set much store by economics; he believed in integrity, law and political will.

Yet the problem went deeper than the flawed economic judgement of individual German leaders. Rather, it was a structural clash of national democracy against national democracy. I wish Schäuble had taken a more pragmatic, economically enlightened approach. I wish Merkel had from the outset declared that Germany would do 'whatever it takes' to save the euro, rather than allowing a narrative of southern parasitism and northern virtue to establish itself in German public opinion. 'Whatever it took' would then have been significantly less, as markets recognised their master. I am sure that is what Helmut Kohl would have done – and a wheelchair-bound, eighty-year-old Kohl himself rebuked Merkel for not doing it, just days before the May 2010 Brussels summit. But there is no doubt that she was following the will of her own people, expressed through elections like that in North Rhine-Westphalia, parliamentary votes and public opinion polls, and reinforced by interventions from two of the most respected institutions in the country, the Bundesbank and the Constitutional Court.

'Today the German Bundestag will decide the fate of Greece,' the sociologist Ulrich Beck heard a German radio announcer declare in 2012. The parliament of one democracy would decide the fate of another. Here was the heart of the matter: the disjuncture between policies that were already European and politics that were still national. The logical solution was obvious: the politics must become European too. 'We can't have monetary union without some form of economic and political union,' said Van Rompuy in 2010. Yet a decade later, Europe was only a little closer to a genuine economic union, let alone to a full political one. The majority of Europeans did not support it and a democratic Europe that was created undemocratically would be a contradiction in terms. The peoples of Europe had not willed a United States of Europe even in the heady months after the fall of the Wall, when the course was set for a monetary union without economic or political union, and they willed it even less now.

Looking back in 2019, Schäuble reflected:

> We should have taken the bigger steps towards integration earlier on, and now, because we can't convince the member states to take them, they are unachievable.

Yet the logic of saving the eurozone pushed its members towards not just a banking union but also elements of a fiscal union, and hence towards the core political areas of taxation and public spending. For Kohl, monetary union had been a means to the end of political union; now, steps towards political union were justified by the need to secure the monetary union. At Maastricht, the cart had been put before the horse; now the cart was dragging the horse down a road it did not particularly want to take.

By the end of the 2010s, two things seemed clear: the eurozone was unlikely to collapse and it was unlikely to take another great leap forward, Maastricht-style, to a full economic and political union. Like the Holy Roman Empire of old, it would have to live with 'compromise and fudge'. The euro had become a strong, stable global reserve currency, outstripping the yen and pound. That was a great achievement; but at what a cost.

Clash of empires

In March 1994 I was half-asleep at a conference in St Petersburg when a short, thick-set man with an unpleasant, vaguely rat-like face – apparently some kind of sidekick of the city's mayor – made me wake up with a start. We must remember, he said, that there are territories now outside the frontiers of the Russian Federation 'that historically always belonged to Russia', and he mentioned Crimea. Some twenty-five million Russians had suddenly found themselves outside the motherland and Russia had a duty of care towards them. The international community must recognise such justified interests of the Russian state and 'of the Russian people as a great nation'.

Twenty years later, in March 2014, this man stood before an ecstatic audience in the Kremlin to celebrate Russia's annexation of Crimea, taken by force from the sovereign state of Ukraine. 'In people's hearts and minds,' said Vladimir Putin, 'Crimea has always been an inseparable part of Russia.' Inexplicably, it had been given to Ukraine by Nikita Khrushchev in 1954. Its inhabitants were therefore among the millions who, on the collapse of the Soviet Union,

> went to bed in one country and awoke in different ones, overnight becoming ethnic minorities in former Union republics, while the Russian nation became one of the biggest, if not the biggest ethnic group in the world to be divided by borders.

Years later he had heard residents of Crimea 'say that back in 1991 they were handed over like a sack of potatoes. This is hard to disagree with.'

With the forcible seizure of Crimea, Putin's Russia violated the most fundamental principle of Europe's post-1945 liberal order: that international frontiers should be changed only by peaceful means and with the consent of the states concerned. Putin had first broken this taboo in August 2008, when he sent his troops in to the Georgian territories of South Ossetia and Abkhazia, but this repeat offence in Crimea was larger and more consequential. It marked the return of an older, pre-1945 form of power politics. This action in 2014 recalled the world of 1914.

Putin said Crimea had 'always' belonged to Russia, but in fact it had been part of Russia only from 1783, when the formerly Tatar territory was annexed by Russia under Empress Catherine the Great, until the Bolshevik revolution in 1917. From the end of the Russian Civil War it belonged to the Soviet Union, for much of that time as an Autonomous Soviet Socialist Republic, until in 1954 Khrushchev gave it to the Ukrainian Soviet Socialist Republic, another part of the Soviet Union. If history justified Crimea's 'return' from Ukraine to Russia, then history could equally justify the 'return' of Silesia – most of which was under German rule between 1742 and 1945 – from today's Poland to Germany.

Putin's post-imperial yearnings were already clear when I met him in 1994, well before the first eastward enlargement of NATO in 1999, taking in Poland, the Czech Republic and Hungary. But much needed to happen before he would have the will, means and opportunity to seize Crimea. For a start, the seemingly insignificant forty-one-year-old deputy mayor of St Petersburg had to advance to become President Boris Yeltsin's prime minister in summer 1999 and then Yeltsin's chosen successor as president in 2000. Yeltsin considered several alternative candidates, including Boris Nemtsov, who later became an outspoken critic of Putin and was assassinated as a result. But after Russia's 1998 economic meltdown, Yeltsin settled on Putin, the man from the security apparatus who would also guarantee him immunity from prosecution. There were certainly deeper forces pushing Russia towards a confrontation with the West, but European history in the early twenty-first century would have looked different if the sick, erratic Yeltsin's choice had fallen on Nemtsov. Twice in our time, first with Gorbachev and then with Putin, Russia has demonstrated the importance of the individual in history.

In December 1999, just before he became president, Putin laid out his ideological stall in a 5,000-word manifesto that became known as his Millennium Message. Universal values such as individual liberty were all very well, he argued, but Russians had to go back to their core historical values of patriotism, collectivism, solidarity and a strong state. This was the 'Russian Idea'. Russia's destiny was to be always a great power, representing all Russians. In his first years as president, Putin maintained a relatively good relationship with the West. President George W. Bush welcomed him as 'a strong ally in the war against terror' – a cause to which Putin, who had turbocharged his own rise to power through a brutal war in Chechnya, happily subscribed. The new Russian leader was focused on consolidating his power at home and getting the country out of hock to the IMF and western banks. He enjoyed the recognition that came with Russia's inclusion in what was now the G8. But his anger at the West was steadily growing.

He had been infuriated by NATO's bombing of Belgrade and the way the West had wrested Kosovo away from Serbia. He saw the invasion of Iraq in 2003 as further evidence that the United States was on a rampage of regime change. Then came the second round of NATO's eastward enlargement in 2004, including the Baltic states, Estonia, Latvia and Lithuania. When he was just a KGB officer in Dresden, back in the 1980s, those had still been part of the Soviet Union. The collapse of the Soviet Union, he told Russia's Federal Assembly in 2005, was 'the greatest geopolitical catastrophe of the century'.

The last straw was the Orange Revolution in Ukraine in the winter of 2004, which began as a protest against a presidential election result being falsified in favour of the pro-Russian candidate, Viktor Yanukovych. With the conspiratorial mentality of a KGB officer, Putin believed that Western powers must be secretly masterminding any such popular protest, just as he had detected the secret hand of Washington behind Georgia's Rose Revolution the year before. By fomenting such 'colour revolutions', the West was now advancing into Russia's own front yard. Ukraine was, he insisted, 'a made-up country' which had always belonged with Russia as part of *russkiy mir,* the Russian world.

I arrived in Kyiv on Sunday 5 December 2004 and the first page of my notebook records a rather different view:

Nearly 25 years on. Another east European capital. Another revolutionary, pentecostal movement. Now *eastern* Europe proper, no longer 'central'.

Twenty-five years on, that is, from the 1980 Polish strikes that gave birth to Solidarity. For me, this was a further example of the peaceful, self-limiting type of revolution that had been pioneered in 1980 and triumphed in 1989. I located the Orange Revolution in an ongoing narrative of the quest for a Europe whole and free, as a bridge towards a more free world. History, I believed, was still going our way.

I talked to the people who were camping out in a sprawling 'tent city' on the Maidan, in temperatures as low as -10°C. A worker called Vova told me that as soon as he had heard of the protest against the falsified presidential election result the previous month, he had got on the road to Kyiv.

Who had asked him to come?

'The country summoned me.'

Anyone else?

'My conscience.'

And he raised both his giant, ham-sized hands in V-for-Victory signs.

I found that some of the student leaders had received training from veterans of earlier east European movements of civil resistance, notably the Serbian Otpor, which played a part in toppling Slobodan Milošević in 2000. But as I listened to people on the snow-covered Maidan – an engineer whose day job was to monitor radiation levels at the site of the Chernobyl nuclear power plant disaster, the owner of a beauty parlour from a small provincial town, a travel agent from the Carpathian mountains – I was left in no doubt that this was an authentic popular protest against the corruption, clientelism and gangsterism that had plagued the country ever since it gained its fragile independence in 1991.

With my former doctoral student, Timothy Snyder, who would go on to become one of the most celebrated east Europeanists of his generation, I looked into external influences on both sides. Significant funding and expert advice from some western countries, including the United States, and from activist philanthropists such as George Soros, had flowed to some who became 'orange revolutionaries'. But this was out-stripped by the scale of funding and expert advice coming from Russia to help the campaign of Moscow's favoured candidate, Viktor Yanu-kovych. There were outside influences from all sides, but the Orange Revolution was made in Ukraine.

From 2005 onwards, the dial began to turn towards a frontal confron-tation between Putin's Russia and the West. One could describe this as yet another clash of empires in the perennially contested borderlands of eastern Europe, but the empires involved were different from those of the past – and from each other. The West was not a single, coherent geopolit-ical actor in this neighbourhood. At NATO's 2008 Bucharest summit, the George W. Bush administration pushed for a 'Membership Action Plan' for Ukraine and Georgia, but France and Germany strongly opposed this. In a fateful compromise, the concluding communiqué said 'these coun-tries will become members of NATO' but without specifying any signifi-cant concrete steps to make it happen. This was the worst of both worlds: increasing Putin's sense of threat without guaranteeing Ukraine's security.

For its part, the EU was the most reluctant empire in history. Many Europeans refused to think of the EU as an empire at all, associating the term with coercive colonial rule. But if an empire is a system of supra-national law, authority and power, then the EU is as much an empire as the Holy Roman Empire was. Sometimes things can be seen more clearly from the outside. Dmytro Kuleba, who was successively Ukraine's ambassador to the EU, Europe minister and foreign minister, described the European Union as 'the first ever attempt to build a liberal empire', contrasting it with Putin's attempt to restore Russia's colonial empire by force. He explained:

> I understand that people do not like the word empire, but this is how
> history is written. You have to show that different things of a similar
> scale can be built on different principles: those of liberalism, democ-
> racy, respect for human rights, and not on the principle of imposition
> of the will of one on the rest.

In the wake of the eastward enlargements of the Union in 2004 and 2007, Brussels developed what was called an Eastern Partnership with countries including Ukraine, Georgia, Belarus and Moldova. Some Europeans, notably in Sweden, Poland and the Baltic states, saw this as a stepping stone towards those countries becoming members of the EU. That is certainly what the Ukrainians I stood among on the freezing Maidan wanted, as they waved their European flags. They roared their approval when their presidential candidate, Viktor Yushchenko, his face horribly pockmarked from an attempt to murder him by poisoning, declared: 'I'm sure the world will recognise us as a civilised European nation.'

Many leaders of west and south European states, however, saw the Eastern Partnership as a long-term alternative to membership, or at best the kind of glorified waiting room that François Mitterrand had intended for countries like Poland and Hungary with his project of a European Confederation. When I pressed the then president of the European Commission, José Manuel Barroso, to state publicly that the European Union wished Ukraine to become a member one day, he replied: 'If I did that, I would immediately be slapped down by two major member states.' (He meant France and Germany.)

Putin's Russia, by contrast, now became a revisionist great power. It wanted to regain dominance over territories that had been part of its empire, its 'Russian world', and was prepared to use any available means to do so. In response to the Orange Revolution, Putin established a department to promote Russia's influence in its 'near abroad'. Headed by a 'political technologist' – the Russian version of spin doctor – it deployed a whole panoply of techniques, some of which made Western spin doctoring look like a genteel game of bridge. If the West supported NGOs, Moscow would create its own. Critical wits dubbed them GONGOS: government-organised non-governmental organisations. Soundbites, media narratives, partisan radio and television stations, 'alternative facts', covert funding, social movements – anything the West could do, they could do better.

The Russian president announced his confrontation with the West at the Munich Security Conference in February 2007, denouncing the 'unipolar model' of a world dominated by the United States. Action followed the next year. If the West could take Kosovo away from Serbia and invade Iraq, without explicit UN approval, then Putin would take

South Ossetia and Abkhazia from Georgia. And he got away with it. Russian officials told Fiona Hill, a leading British-American specialist on Russia, that as Putin contemplated seizing South Ossetia and Abkhazia in August 2008 they had reckoned with a possible NATO military response. Nothing of the kind happened. French President Nicolas Sarkozy brokered a ceasefire, partly blaming the impetuous Georgian president who had actually started the military exchanges. There was no more decisive Western response, not even economic sanctions on Russian leaders and officials. The suspension of the NATO–Russian Council was hardly a terrible blow to Putin. Soon, the Obama administration was proposing a 'reset' in Russian–American relations.

Over the next five years, we can detect in Putin's behaviour a growing sense of both threat and opportunity, fear of the West mingling with contempt for it. Seeing the Arab Spring and large opposition demonstrations in major Russian cities in 2011 and 2012, he feared that Western-masterminded 'colour revolutions' were coming to bite him. Yet as the West struggled with the impact of the financial crisis, while authoritarian states like China were flourishing, the wider global 'correlation of forces' seemed to be shifting to Russia's advantage. Maybe history was now going his way. As Syria descended into a terrible civil war, unchecked by either the United States or Europe, he deployed his military to turn the tide in favour of President Bashar al-Assad, thus becoming an indispensable player in any subsequent negotiations. Putin bombed his way to the head of the peacemakers' table.

Yet still there was this irritating, post-modern empire called the EU. Pursuing a Brussels-style bureaucratic, regulatory implementation of the vague political mandate of Eastern Partnership, the EU came to Ukraine in 2013 with a proposed association agreement, including significant advantages for trade and investment. Few in Brussels thought hard about the geopolitical implications, let alone prepared for a strong Russian reaction. If Moscow had earlier differentiated between NATO, the US-led military alliance, and the softer, civilian EU, Putin now considered both unacceptable. Kyiv must choose between the European Union and his Eurasian Economic Union: EU or EEU. President Viktor Yanukovych, who had been elected in a reasonably free and fair election in 2010, after the administration of our Orange Revolution hero

Viktor Yushchenko had descended into a corrupt mess, had promised that he would sign the EU association agreement. At the last minute, confronted by Moscow with both a hefty stick and a large carrot, he reneged on his promise.

Now something extraordinary happened. Ukrainians came again to the Maidan, insisting that their country remain on its European course. This time they christened their mass protest 'the Euromaidan'. Ten years after the Orange Revolution of 2004, this was the second Ukrainian attempt to make a peaceful revolution. Its supporters called it 'the revolution of dignity'.

Putin's initial hope was still to retain his influence over all of Ukraine, through Yanukovych. That was Plan A. Covert intelligence, military and other preparations were made for the seizure of Crimea, but by Putin's own account it was only on 23 February 2014, after Yanukovych had fled from Kyiv, that he finally and definitely turned to Plan B. Back home in Russia, Putin's popularity soared as a result of the annexation of Crimea, helping him to win election as president for a fourth time in 2018.

Unlike Georgia in 2008, this did provoke a Western reaction. Russia was booted out of the G8, which reverted to the original G7 of industrial democracies. NATO deployed small multinational battle groups in Poland and the Baltic states, on a rotating basis, arguing somewhat Jesuitically that this did not violate its commitment in the 1997 NATO–Russia Founding Act to avoid 'additional permanent stationing of substantial combat forces' and more realistically that Russia's behaviour had changed the entire security context. The EU and the United States imposed economic sanctions on the Putin regime. Yet Germany, already heavily dependent on Russian energy supplies, went ahead with the Nord Stream 2 gas pipeline, bypassing Ukraine and Poland to bring Russian gas directly to Germany. The chairman of the board was the former German Chancellor Gerhard Schröder, by now a close friend of Putin's, and its chief executive was a former Stasi officer called Matthias Warnig.

Meanwhile, Putin had moved on from Crimea to the large parts of southern and eastern Ukraine which he described as Novorossiya, New Russia, a terminology that harked back to the area's eighteenth-century colonisation under Catherine the Great. Separatist fighters in the Donbas region were not just equipped and armed by Russia but commanded by special forces soldiers and paramilitary adventurers from Russia. When a counteroffensive by Ukrainian forces had some success, Putin sent his own forces in to push them back. On a visit to Kyiv in 2015, I saw volunteers rattling collection tins for the Ukrainian army and for the now more than one million internally displaced people. This was a country at war. A low-intensity armed conflict in eastern Ukraine continued for eight years. By the end of 2021, it had already claimed over 14,000 lives. Yet European leaders still blithely talked of 'seventy years of peace in Europe'.

Putin's Russia was a danger not just to its immediate neighbours but to all the democracies of Europe and North America. When summer holidaymakers boarded Malaysia Airlines flight MH17 to Kuala Lumpur at Amsterdam airport on Sunday 17 July 2014, the last thing on their minds was the east European countries over which their plane would fly. Then a missile launched by Russian-led insurgents from a Russian Buk missile launcher in eastern Ukraine, probably in the mistaken belief that the thing in the sky was an enemy aircraft, tore flight MH17 apart in mid-air and ended the lives of all those innocent passengers. When Russian operatives poisoned a former Russian spy and his daughter with the nerve agent Novichok in the English cathedral town of Salisbury in 2018, a British woman called Dawn Sturgess died and a British police sergeant, Nick Bailey, suffered life-changing health damage after both came into accidental contact with the poison. Those east European countries were not so far away after all.

West Europeans might view the corrupt, chaotic politics of Ukraine as some exotic east European peculiarity, but then it turned out that Moscow was actively supporting far right, populist parties in western Europe, while sowing disinformation through media outlets such as RT and false accounts on social media. Although the geopolitical orientation to which Putin subscribed was generally described as 'Eurasianist', his supporters did not hesitate to suggest that he represented a better Europe – patriotic, Christian, martial, carnivorous, heterosexual, philoprogenitive – against the decadent, post-national, multicultural, LGBTQ-hugging, Muslim-welcoming, vegetarian, pacifist Europe of the EU. A commentary on the Tsargrad.tv website argued that 'the

European Union is the main enemy of Europe today – more and more west Europeans recognise this'. Nationalist populists from Viktor Orbán in Hungary to Marine le Pen in France embraced this Putinesque vision of Europe. The Italian populist Matteo Salvini praised the Russian leader and wore a T-shirt bearing his image.

Americans might think this was just a European affair, but then it turned out that Russia had made a covert attempt to swing the 2016 US presidential election to Donald Trump, using agents of influence, extensive social media disinformation and hacked emails from the Democratic campaign. When motorists on the East Coast of the United States found themselves queueing for petrol in the early summer of 2021, it was due to a cyberattack on an American oil pipeline that almost certainly originated in Russia.

We had thus been warned, again and again, ever since 2008 and most violently since 2014. Yet it was not until Vladimir Putin launched a full-scale invasion of Ukraine in February 2022 that Europe and the entire transatlantic West woke up to the threat he posed.

Charlie Hebdo

The debate at the *Guardian* lasted all day. This was Thursday 8 January 2015, and the previous morning journalists of the French magazine *Charlie Hebdo* had been murdered by Islamist extremists. The assassins said they were taking revenge for the magazine's publication of satirical cartoons of Muhammad. As they left the blood-drenched editorial office in Paris, they shouted: 'We have avenged the Prophet Muhammad!' Staff and contributors of Britain's leading left-liberal newspaper were now wrestling with the question of whether it should reprint some of the cartoons.

I argued that it should. Whether you liked or hated those undoubtedly offensive cartoons, they were now front-page news. Readers should have a chance to make up their own minds about them. By the symbolic act of republication, the *Guardian* would manifest solidarity with the murdered French journalists and their surviving colleagues. Above all, we would show that violent intimidation would not succeed. Ever since the fatwa on Salman Rushdie in 1989 we had been faced with what my work on free speech had led me to call 'the assassin's veto'. It declared: 'If you say, draw, write or publish that, you will be killed.' We must demonstrate that the assassin's veto would not prevail.

Marshalling these arguments, I launched an online appeal for a 'week of solidarity' in which a wide range of newspapers, broadcasters and bloggers would republish a selection of the *Charlie Hebdo* cartoons – not just those of Muhammad, but also equally outrageous ones of Jews and Christians – with an introduction explaining why they were being republished now. There would be safety in numbers. If just one or two papers reprinted the cartoons, they would themselves become the object of violent attacks. My appeal was published in newspapers from *El País* and *La Repubblica* to *Gazeta Wyborcza* and *The Hindu*. It failed comprehensively. Editors everywhere agonised over republication. Dean Baquet, the executive editor of the *New York Times*, said he spent 'about half of my day' going to and fro on it. Then each publication did its own thing in its own time: some reprinting, some not.

Since journalism is an intensely competitive business, I should have known better. But I was not wrong to identify the need for collective action. The editor of the *Independent* gave this revealing explanation of his decision not to follow his instinctive wish to republish: 'I think it would have been too much of a risk to unilaterally decide in Britain to be the only newspaper that went ahead and published.' The offices of the *Hamburger Morgenpost* were firebombed the day after it did, unilaterally, reprint some of the cartoons.

The *Guardian* decided not to reproduce the original cartoons. Alan Rusbridger, its long-time editor, argued that the imperative of solidarity should not compel you to depart from your own editorial standards of taste and civility. That would itself be a victory for the assassins. Most striking was the case of *Jyllands-Posten*, the paper that had published what became known as the 'Danish cartoons' in 2005. While several Danish papers reprinted the *Charlie Hebdo* drawings, *Jyllands-Posten* did not, citing its 'unique position' and fears for the safety of its staff. The editor who had commissioned the original cartoons in 2005, Flemming Rose, told the BBC: 'We caved in.' 'Violence works,' he said. 'Sometimes the sword is mightier than the pen.'

Meanwhile, the Twitter hashtag #JeSuisCharlie (I am Charlie) started whizzing around the world's social media. I used it at once. The next Sunday, thousands of home-made banners and placards proclaimed *'Je Suis Charlie'* in a huge demonstration in Paris that started, with conscious symbolism, from the Place de la République. The values of the French Republic were at stake. German chancellor Angela Merkel, British prime minister David Cameron and Israeli prime minister Benjamin Netanyahu joined French leaders at the front of the Paris march, and so did King Abdullah II of Jordan.

The next week, *Charlie Hebdo*'s front page showed a weeping Muhammad holding a sign saying *'Je Suis Charlie'*. Above his head were the words *'Tout Est Pardonné'* ('everything is forgiven'). In a moving press conference, the man who had drawn it, Renald Luzier, one of the magazine's few surviving regular cartoonists, revealed that he himself had wept after drawing it. 'At last,' he explained, 'we had the fucking front page. It wasn't the front page the terrorists wanted us to do, because there are no terrorists [on it]. There's just a man who cries. A man called Muhammad.'

This image the *Guardian* did reproduce online, with a warning that some readers might find it offensive. Meanwhile, a nagging little counter-hashtag had appeared on social media: #JeNeSuisPasCharlie (I am not Charlie). Just a few years later, you could fill a small library with texts interpreting and disputing the meaning of these two apparently simple phrases: I am Charlie, I am not Charlie.

'Charlie Hebdo' was not just an extreme case and a single event. The magazine had reprinted the Danish cartoons in 2006, its offices had been firebombed in 2011 and it had published its most outrageous cartoons of Muhammad in 2012. One showed a rear view of the sacred figure of all Muslims squatting on all fours, naked, testicles and penis dangling, with a star over his arsehole and the words 'A star is born!' The 2015 New Year's issue of the magazine, which was lying around when the assassins broke into the editorial meeting, had a cover cartoon of a bearded jihadist with an AK-47 beneath the words 'Still no attacks in France'. Irony upon irony.

Five years later, in 2020, the trial of some of those involved in this atrocity, and in a related attack on a Jewish supermarket, would spark a further round of violence. A schoolteacher called Samuel Paty was beheaded by a lone assassin just because he had shown his school class a couple of the *Charlie Hebdo* cartoons of Muhammad. Paty had done this only to invite a discussion about the legitimate limits to free expression. Before showing the cartoons, he had invited any child who might be offended to look away or leave the room. President Emmanuel Macron honoured the schoolteacher's memory in a ceremony at the Sorbonne, standing before his coffin and defiantly proclaiming:

> We will defend the freedom that you taught so well and we will proudly proclaim the value of secularism. We will not renounce cartoons and

drawings, even if others retreat. We will provide all the opportunities the Republic owes its youth, without any discrimination.

Most obviously, 'Charlie' highlighted the question of violence. While George W. Bush's 'war on terror' seemed almost ancient history to a United States that now lived largely free from attacks by Islamist terrorists, Europe continued to be hit by them. A Christmas market in Berlin; the metro and airport in Brussels; London's Westminster bridge and a concert arena in Manchester; Stockholm, St Petersburg, Barcelona. France was assaulted again and again. After *Charlie Hebdo*, it was the turn of the Bataclan theatre in Paris, the seafront at Nice, the town of Trèbes, an eighty-five-year-old priest in Normandy and the schoolteacher Samuel Paty. The French lived with the everyday danger of terror attacks as, in the 1970s and 80s, the British had with repeated bombings by the Irish Republican Army.

Almost all these atrocities were committed by young men who had spent most of their lives in Europe and had often been born there. As after 9/11, Spain's 11M and Britain's 7/7, Europeans asked themselves: Why do they do it? Some analysts pointed to social causes in the disadvantaged neighbourhoods in which many of these young men grew up. Polemicists blamed a single, undifferentiated 'Islam'. Those who studied the phenomenon of second-generation radicalisation replied: but *which* Islam? Salafi or Sufi? Wahabi or Barelvi? Europe had encouraged the 'guest worker' generation of immigrants to come to work in Europe and then carelessly left too many of them living off welfare handouts in areas like Seine-Saint-Denis, the *banlieue* on the outskirts of Paris.

With equal carelessness, Europe had allowed many of its new mosques to be led by imams trained in countries such as Turkey and Saudi Arabia, propagating highly conservative or militant radical versions of Islam. Worse still were the self-appointed pseudo-imams, with no formal position, whose pivotal role you encounter in many life stories of European Islamic terrorists. When the already-radicalised young man was sent to prison for a first offence, that prison became a schoolhouse of further radicalisation at the hands of hardened Islamist extremists among the inmates. The wider Middle East – Iraq, Palestine, Afghanistan, Algeria, Yemen, Libya – furnished arguments for holy war and, to cap it all, locations for terrorist training when the new recruit got out of jail.

All these elements were present in the biographies of the *Charlie Hebdo* assassins, the brothers Chérif and Saïd Kouachi. They were of Algerian immigrant parentage and had an impoverished and disturbed early childhood. Their father died of cancer when they were still young and their mother succumbed to alcohol, drugs and perhaps suicidal despair, so the teenage orphans were taken into care. After the American invasion of Iraq, the young men started paying more attention to Islam. A self-appointed pseudo-imam began their radicalisation. Under his influence, Chérif, the younger brother, planned to fly to Syria, but instead was arrested and spent twenty months in pre-trial detention in a notorious French prison. There, where the state was supposed to be keeping him safe, he was groomed to become a terrorist by an Al Qaeda recruiter. Both Saïd and Chérif attended an Islamist camp in Yemen, where they received weapons training. After murdering the *Charlie Hebdo* journalists, the brothers identified themselves as 'Al Qaeda in Yemen'. Anti-Semitism was another familiar ingredient of the mix. 'It is because of the Jews,' said Chérif.

A year later, a study by the Institut Montaigne, a French think tank, showed that a large majority of French Muslims felt reasonably at home in France and would never endorse radical Islamist views, let alone reach for a gun. Some thirty per cent of those surveyed said they never attended mosque and another thirty per cent did so only on special occasions such as Eid. But it was the actions of the violent minority that shaped a burgeoning debate about European identity.

When Turkey's Islamist president Recep Tayyip Erdoğan was still trying to make the case for Turkey to be admitted to the EU, he urged Europe to demonstrate that it was not a 'Christian club'. A Christian club was exactly how many Europeans had thought of their civilisation in relation to Islam for more than a thousand years. Europe was the home of Christendom, to be defended against the 'infidel', the 'Turk', the 'Moor'. Echoes of that older version of European identity could still be heard in the debate around Turkey's possible EU membership, even as contemporary Europeans could not agree to mention Christianity in the preamble to their Union's proposed constitution. The language of 'crusade' was revived by anti-Muslim, far-right terrorists such as the Norwegian Anders Behring Breivik.

This was not, however, the main meaning of 'Charlie'. 'Charlie' stood for many different things to different people, but for few, if any, did he stand for Christianity against Islam. For everyone who marched under banners proclaiming 'I am Charlie', including King Abdullah II of Jordan, 'Charlie' certainly represented the basic proposition that we should not murder people just for what they say or write. For most Europeans, 'Charlie' stood in some general sense for the defence of the values of the Enlightenment, including free speech, tolerance and secularism. For many in France, he stood for the specific French version of secularism known as *laïcité*, which President Macron vowed to uphold. First put into law in 1905, following more than a century of fierce conflict between the Catholic Church and the anti-clerical heirs of the French Revolution, *laïcité* required not merely the separation of church and state, but a rigorous exclusion of religion from any part of public life.

Beyond this, however, there were more particular meanings. For the cartoonists, 'I am Charlie' was a defence of a distinctively French tradition of outrageous caricature stretching back at least to depictions of King Louis Philippe as a pear and gross Gargantua, which earned nineteenth-century cartoonists such as Honoré Daumier a stretch in prison. For most of the magazine's journalists, and many of their contemporaries, 'Charlie' was also about the legacy of 1968: not just secularism but atheism, extensive freedom of expression, sexual and other lifestyle freedoms. In short, a 68er's version of the Enlightenment.

In his book *Murder in Amsterdam*, Ian Buruma captured the particular alarm of Dutch 68ers who in their youth had finally shaken off the influence of the Christian churches which they felt had stifled Dutch life, only to see what they regarded as an even more intolerant religion returning through the back door. It was the atheist, free-living, liberal lifestyle of these 68ers and post-68ers that induced the most acute cultural schizophrenia in some second-generation European Muslims – the in-between people. The traditional, socially conservative, practising Christian, now more often found in the United States than in western

Europe, was much less of a problem for them. It was especially these more radical, atheist, socially liberal versions of #IamCharlie that some European Muslims rejected with #IamNotCharlie.

I tweeted #IamCharlie without hesitation. But to dig deeper into the many meanings of #IamCharlie was to ask nothing less than what it meant to be a European in the twenty-first century.

'Invaders'

Still shaken by the *Charlie Hebdo* attacks, Europe soon faced its next shock – the refugee crisis which became acute in the summer of 2015 and lasted into 2016. The EU frontier control agency Frontex registered some 1.4 million 'irregular' arrivals in those two years, but the real number was probably closer to two million. Some preferred to talk of a 'migration crisis', indicating that among the newcomers were economic migrants as well as refugees. Yet very many of them were fleeing war and persecution – the classic case of the refugee – in countries such as Syria, Libya and Afghanistan.

Europe did not cause the terrible civil war into which Syria had descended after the Syrians' initially peaceful version of the Arab Spring had failed to overthrow Bashar Al-Assad and Vladimir Putin rode to his fellow dictator's aid. But the European Union and its member states, preoccupied with the eurozone crisis and having no coherent European policy towards the Middle East, had done almost nothing to prevent the Syrian catastrophe or prepare for its consequences. In Libya, France and Britain led a military intervention to topple the dictator Muammar Gaddafi but left behind a failed state which rapidly became a paradise for people smugglers transporting refugees and migrants from Africa to the nearby Italian island of Lampedusa.

Coming hard on the heels of *Charlie Hebdo*, and all the other terrorist attacks across Europe, the refugee crisis reinforced in many minds an equation that tabloid journalists had long promoted: Immigrant = Muslim = Terrorist. This was, of course, deeply misleading. Many immigrants to Europe were not Muslims. Most European Muslims were not immigrants. The vast majority of Muslims were not terrorists. Yet this crude, mendacious but emotive equation accelerated the rise of new political forces in Europe, usually described by the shorthand label of populists. Populism came in many shapes and colours, but right-wing nationalist populism built its narrative around the demagogic conflation of alleged threats from immigration and Islam.

In a striking example of the power of narrative over reality, populist leaders in Hungary and Poland successfully exploited fears of Muslim immigration in countries that had virtually no Muslims. According to estimates by the Pew Research Centre, Muslims comprised 6.9 per cent of the population of Austria in 2016 but only 0.4 per cent in next-door Hungary. In Poland, the figure was just 0.1 per cent, compared with 6.1 per cent in Germany. Nonetheless, it was Viktor Orbán in Hungary and Jarosław Kaczyński in Poland who launched some of the most lurid rhetorical attacks on Muslim migrants. They were 'invaders', said Orbán. They brought dangerous 'parasites and protozoa', cried Kaczyński. Both their governments refused to take in even a minimal quota of refugees. Orbán built a razor-wire fence along Hungary's frontier with Serbia to keep out the infidel 'invaders', earning effusive praise from Donald Trump. Islamophobia without Muslims resonated with socially conservative societies unused both to large-scale immigration and to Islam.

Yet the boost to nationalist populism was equally apparent in west European countries that did have both many Muslims and large populations with a migration background. In Germany, with close to five million Muslims and more than twelve per cent of its population being foreign-born in 2016, the Alternative for Germany (AfD) swiftly morphed from an anti-euro protest party into an anti-immigration one. Fears stoked by a large, seemingly uncontrolled influx of refugees and migrants now helped the far-right, xenophobic AfD to national electoral success. Following the 2017 general election, it became the largest opposition party in the Bundestag. Germany's mainstream parties refused to recognise it as a legitimate partner in the country's democratic politics, insisting that its presence must not be 'normalised'; but somehow it was.

In Italy, with nearly three million Muslims and some ten per cent of its population foreign-born by 2016, the issue – coming on top of the pain caused by the eurozone crisis – catapulted the militantly anti-immigrant populist Matteo Salvini into government for more than a year. France was home to perhaps six million Muslims, while around twelve per cent of its population was foreign-born. The demagogically compounded issues of immigration, Islam and terrorism, along with the socio-economic discontents of the 'France of the periphery', helped the leader of the National Front, Marine le Pen, to secure more than one third of the vote in the second round of the 2017 presidential election, which pitted her against Emmanuel Macron. Liberal Europeans breathed a sigh of relief when the far-right candidate received the support of 'only' 10.6 million French voters.

Influenced by populist rhetoric and sensationalist media coverage, people across the continent vastly overestimated the size of the Muslim minority in their country. In a poll conducted in late 2016, French respondents said that thirty-one out of every hundred people in France were Muslim. The true figure was around a quarter of that. The Italians, Germans, Belgians, Dutch, Danes and Spanish gave answers between three and six times the actual numbers. Fresh from the anti-immigration narrative that contributed significantly to the vote for Brexit in June 2016, British respondents said fifteen out of every hundred people in Britain were Muslim. The real figure was under five.

Faced with the dramatic political impact of the refugee crisis, European leaders concluded that Europe must do more to 'manage' – that is, limit – immigration. Donald Tusk, the former Polish prime minister who was then president of the European Council, argued forcefully that Europe could not continue with both deliberately open internal borders and unintentionally open external ones. It had to secure the external frontier. By the beginning of the 2020s, the result would be a new Iron Curtain, this time running around the edges of Europe rather than down its middle.

The political upheaval was accompanied by a wave of cultural pessimism, verging on what the historian Fritz Stern once called 'the politics of cultural despair'. In Germany, it produced books with titles such as *Germany Abolishes Itself*, by Thilo Sarrazin, a former Bundesbank director, and *Finis Germania* (ungrammatical Latin for 'The End of Germany'), by Rolf Peter Sieferle. These were significant not for their intellectual quality but for their sales. Sarrazin's book was Germany's biggest political bestseller since unification: 1.2 million copies in less than nine months. *Finis Germania* featured in *Der Spiegel*'s bestseller list, until *Der Spiegel*'s editors decided that such a distasteful tract must not be a bestseller – for what should not be, could not be – and silently removed it from the list.

France offered strong competition to Germany in this business of cultural pessimism. 'France is dead,' declared the journalist Éric Zemmour in a bestselling book called *The French Suicide*. Renaud Camus argued in successive editions of his *The Great Replacement* that the native population in Europe was deliberately being replaced by an alien, Muslim one. 'Immigration has become an invasion,' he declared. Europe faced 'demographic colonisation by population transfer'. There were no more 'terrorists' but 'an occupier who from time to time executes a few hostages, us, as occupiers always have'.

The celebrated French writer Michel Houellebecq captured this sense of civilisational panic in his novel *Submission*, published by grim coincidence on the very day of the *Charlie Hebdo* murders, 7 January 2015. His protagonist, a middle-aged academic at the Sorbonne, sees change and decay in all around him, from 'literature, the *major art form* of Western civilisation, now ending before our very eyes' to 'the last vestiges of a dying welfare state'. Between bouts of casual sex, he reflects that the phrase *Après moi, le déluge* had long summarised his own state of mind, 'but now, for the first time, I had a troubling thought: What if the deluge came before I died?'

Which it then does. In Houellebecq's satirical narrative of an imagined 2022 presidential election, artfully peppered with real figures from French political and cultural life, the country's socialist and centre-right parties cut a deal with the charismatic Muhammad Ben Abbes, a (fictional) Muslim Brotherhood candidate, to keep out Marine le Pen in the second round. The Sorbonne then becomes an Islamic university. French women start wearing baggy smocks, with the result that 'the contemplation of women's arses, that small, dreamy consolation, had also become impossible'. In the end, our hero 'submits' to Islam, is given back his teaching post with a much higher salary at the now Saudi-funded

Sorbonne, and pleasures himself with the thought that he can possess three nubile young wives.

Houellebecq leaves you guessing how much of this he means seriously. As the real 2022 election drew near, however, twenty retired French generals were definitely not joking when, in the wake of yet another terrorist atrocity, they wrote an open letter to a right-wing magazine claiming that France was falling apart because 'Islamism and the *banlieue* hordes' were 'detaching large parts of the nation so as to turn them into territories subject to dogmas contrary to our constitution'. If nothing was done, they threatened, there would be 'an explosion and then intervention by our comrades on active service in a dangerous mission to protect our civilisational values and the safety of our compatriots'. Marine le Pen replied on the magazine's website, inviting them 'to join our action so as take part in the battle that is opening, which is certainly a political and peaceful battle, but is above all the battle of France'. Facing Macron again in the second round of the 2022 presidential election, Le Pen secured more than forty-one per cent of the vote, well up on her 2017 performance. The result was less dramatic, to be sure, than that in Houellebecq's satire, but still alarming enough.

The Pew Research Centre estimated that, even in the very unlikely event of there being no further immigration to Europe at all, Muslims could be nearly thirteen per cent of the population of France by 2050 and around one in every ten inhabitants of Belgium, Britain, the Netherlands and Germany. These were just projections, with a wide margin of error, but the basic demographic facts were plain. An extremist like Zemmour might call his political party Reconquête, invoking the Christian Reconquista (reconquest) of Muslim territory in Spain in the Middle Ages, and articulate dark fantasies of mass repatriation. But unless Europe descended into full-fledged fascism they would remain just that – fantasies. What is more, as the outsize cohort of baby boomers moved into retirement, zero migration would not provide enough people of working age to fund their pensions and sustain the level of social care expected from a contemporary European welfare state. Europe would need more immigrants, as well as the millions of men, women and children with a migration background who were already here.

There was only one good way forward. Europe had to remain true to its own essential freedoms and values while at the same time being a place where people with a migration background, including many of the Muslim faith, could feel at home. It had to sustain freedom in diversity. This was, without question, one of the biggest challenges Europe had bequeathed itself over the half-century since I sat with what my youthful diary called a 'volatile Turk' delivering his late-night harangue against imperialism in an overnight train to Berlin.

Brexit

For several days after my compatriots had voted for Brexit in the referendum on 23 June 2016, continental European friends embraced me with heartfelt words of consolation, as if I had just lost a loved one. It felt like that too. For someone who had spent a lifetime deeply engaged with Europe, this was a great defeat – and one with personal consequences. When individuals are deprived of their citizenship against their will, it is usually because they are victims of a particularly nasty regime or have committed some heinous act. I and the many British Europeans who felt like me were now to be stripped of our European citizenship thanks to a democratic vote of our own people.

'History to the defeated/ May say Alas but cannot help or pardon,' wrote W. H. Auden of the Spanish Civil War, which ended with the defeat of the Republican side he supported. I was, needless to say, a passionate Remainer – a term that did not exist until the word 'remain' was chosen for the wording of the referendum question in 2016 and has only historical and biographical meaning since Britain left the EU at the end of January 2020. In the 2020s, it would be futile for us ex-Remainers to sit around like old Jacobites in the novels of Walter Scott, brooding over our wine and whisky on the dastardly tricks of our opponents and the blunders of our own side. Rather, people on both sides of the Channel and the Atlantic need to understand what happened and learn the lessons of Brexit for the rest of Europe.

'The British never really felt at home in Europe.' 'They were bound to leave sooner or later.' Such assertions, now often heard, contain two fallacies: that Brexit was inevitable and that its causes were unique to Britain. The way the history of Brexit is already being written offers a perfect example of what the philosopher Henri Bergson called 'the illu-sions of retrospective determinism' – the almost irresistible temptation to believe that what actually happened somehow had to happen.

Not true. The result was close: just under fifty-two per cent for Leave, just over forty-eight per cent for Remain. So 650,000 votes would have swung it the other way. What if the Conservatives had delivered on their 2015 manifesto promise to enfranchise British citizens who had resided abroad for more than fifteen years? Many of those who now lived in Spain, Portugal and France would surely have turned out for Remain. What if EU citizens who had lived in Britain for as long had been allowed to vote? What if the voting age had been reduced to sixteen, as it was in the 2014 referendum on Scottish independence? The younger the person, the more likely to vote Remain, and there were potentially some 1.2 million voters between the ages of sixteen and eighteen.

What if a different Labour leader had campaigned for Remain with a conviction that the socialist Eurosceptic Jeremy Corbyn could never muster? What if the silver-tongued Conservative debater Michael Gove had put personal loyalty to Cameron before his own Eurosceptic convic-tions? What if the opportunist Boris Johnson had stuck with Remain? Johnson himself told us that he was undecided, 'veering around like a shopping trolley', until the last minute. We even have the text of the newspaper column he wrote trying out the arguments for Remain: 'Think of the rest of the EU. Think of the future.' But he thought of his own future.

Careful analysis of survey data found statistically significant evi-dence of a 'Boris effect'. His gamble eventually took him into No. 10 Downing Street, succeeding Theresa May as Conservative leader and hence as prime minister in July 2019. It was then Johnson and his adviser Dominic Cummings who correctly calculated that he could win an elec-tion in December 2019 by echoing the four-syllable referendum slogan 'Take Back Control' with the equally catchy four-syllable election slogan 'Get Brexit Done'. Then, and only then, did Brexit become inevitable – and a hard Brexit at that.

If any one or two of these individual or group choices had gone the other way, historians would even now be writing learned chapters explaining why the pragmatic British – 'a nation of shopkeepers', as

Napoleon supposedly called us – had put economic self-interest before concerns about immigration, identity and sovereignty.

Equally mistaken is the notion that the underlying causes of Brexit were unique to Britain. Some elements were distinctively British and, more specifically, English. Long-time Conservative Eurosceptics were obsessed with the fact that European law and judgements of the European Court of Justice took precedence over English law and courts. This English preoccupation with legal sovereignty can be traced all the way back to Henry VIII's 1532 Act in Restraint of Appeals to Rome, which declared 'this realm of England is an empire' – meaning by 'empire' not rule over others but complete legal authority over your own territory. Memories of Empire in the more familiar sense – empire with a capital E – also fed the idea that Britain might have a bright future across the seas, and buttressed a self-confidence that Britain could go it alone. 'We used to run the biggest empire the world has ever seen,' Johnson wrote in early 2016, 'and with a much smaller domestic population and a relatively tiny Civil Service. Are we really unable to do trade deals?'

Since Britain had only joined the European Community in the early 1970s, after France and Germany had set the terms on which it operated, a British political elite obsessed with 'leadership' always had a nagging feeling that others were calling the shots. The British relationship with 'Europe' was more coolly transactional than that of most other member states, for which Europe's history and mystique also counted. The influence of Margaret Thatcher on two generations of Conservative politicians, journalists, think-tankers and academics cannot be overstated. Thatcherism formed a whole world – the world of the *Spectator*. No other European country had anything like the British Eurosceptic press, relentlessly pushing negative stories about Brussels, strung together in a powerful meta-narrative of plucky freedom-loving Brits being pushed about by beastly bureaucratic Belgians, French and Germans.

More immediately, David Cameron, the prime minister who called the referendum, made some fateful mistakes. It was folly for Cameron to make the vote hinge on a renegotiation of the terms of Britain's EU membership, which was always likely to end with slim pickings. Even more than his predecessors as prime minister, he failed to make a positive case for Britain being in the EU, well in advance of the actual referendum.

'You can't fatten a pig on market day,' said his own election guru, Lynton Crosby. Cameron acknowledges in his memoirs that he should have done more to 'mix criticisms of the EU with talking about its very real achievements'. In truth, being himself a Eurosceptic – 'I want *less* Europe,' he exclaimed to aides, when people in Brussels called for 'more Europe' – and having persistently trimmed to more radically Eurosceptic sections of his party, the last-minute case he made to the British public amounted to little more than 'the alternative to EU membership is worse'.

Significant though these specifically British causes were, many of the discontents that impelled more than seventeen million people to vote for Britain to leave the EU were shared in several other European countries. In a survey conducted earlier in 2016, seventy-one per cent of the Greek respondents, sixty-one per cent of the French and forty-nine per cent of the Spanish said they felt unfavourably towards the EU – all more than the forty-eight per cent of the Brits who expressed the same view. True, when it came to agreeing with the statement that your country 'could better face the future outside the EU', the British (forty-seven per cent at the last asking before the referendum) were outdone only by Cypriots (fifty-five per cent). But in two other countries, Austria and Slovakia, the figure exceeded forty-five per cent, and the average across the entire EU was about one out of every three people asked. The British were not a uniquely anti-European outlier.

The novelist Robert Musil wrote that early-twentieth-century Austria was just 'an especially clear case of the modern world'. Britain was an especially clear case of contemporary Europe. After treading in George Orwell's footsteps to Wigan and hearing people explain how they felt ignored and disrespected by a remote metropolitan elite, the Dutch journalist Geert Mak reflected 'had I not seen something similar all over western Europe?' So had I, not just in western Europe but also in eastern Germany and south-eastern Poland. People thought they were treated like second-class citizens and exclaimed, 'I don't recognise my country any more.'

'It's about democracy,' my father would always tell me, explaining his hostility to the EU. Although the EU had a directly elected European Parliament, and no major decisions were taken in Brussels without the involvement of elected representatives of member states, many Europeans felt this did not add up to real democratic self-government. 'I know this is partly an illusion,' a Swiss student once confided in me, explaining why he didn't want Switzerland to join the EU, 'but I like the *feeling* that we govern ourselves.' Many in Britain wanted that feeling back.

Shortly before the Brexit vote, the British Election Study asked a representative sample of interviewees an open-ended question: 'What matters most to you when deciding how to vote in the EU referendum?' They processed the responses into word clouds. The biggest word for Remain voters was 'economy', followed by terms like 'rights', 'trade' and 'security'; the biggest for Leave voters was 'immigration', followed by 'sovereignty', 'country' and 'control'.

Cameron and his entourage concentrated almost exclusively on the economic case, a strategy they believed had defeated Scottish nationalists' push for independence in the 2014 referendum in Scotland. They tried to avoid the issue of immigration. But the financial crisis of 2008 and subsequent Great Recession had fed profound discontent with the existing version of capitalism among the many who were struggling as a result. It also undermined the credibility of metropolitan experts making abstract arguments about economic consequences. When the political scientist Anand Menon explained to an audience in the northern city of Newcastle that modelling of the likely effects of Brexit suggested it would lead to a reduction in GDP, a lady in the crowd shouted: 'That's your bloody GDP, not mine.'

The ongoing crisis of the eurozone made the cross-Channel economic comparison very different from that at the time of the 1975 referendum, which confirmed Britain's membership in the European Community. That came at the end of a long period in which the main west European economies had done better than the British economy. They didn't look so good in 2016. A *Daily Mail* editorial on the eve of the referendum declared:

> As for the 19 countries locked into the catastrophic, one-size-fits-all single currency – the very apotheosis of the European dream of ever closer political and economic union – just ask the jobless young people of Greece, Spain or France if the euro has underpinned their prosperity.

One of Britain's leading experts on survey evidence, John Curtice, concludes that the economic argument broke much less decisively for Remain than No. 10 had hoped. In Curtice's view, Leave was carried over the wire by a combination of doubts about the globalised economic model represented by EU membership, fears that the EU undermined British identity, and hopes that Brexit would reduce immigration.

Immigration, in this context, meant both a lived reality and a populist narrative spun around it. Unlike in Poland or Hungary, immigration to Britain was a large-scale phenomenon. The migrants came from both inside and outside the EU and the impact was cumulative. By 2016, around thirteen per cent of Britain's population was foreign-born. Since the EU's big eastward enlargement in 2004, millions of central and east Europeans had taken advantage of the EU's freedom of movement to come to Britain. They were followed by south Europeans seeking work in the wake of the eurozone crisis. The number of (non-British) EU citizens living in the UK jumped from around one million in 2004 to at least 3.5 million in 2016. Less than a month before the Brexit vote, the official figure for net migration to Britain in 2015 was published. At 333,000, it made a mockery of Cameron's promise to reduce net migration to less than 100,000 a year.

Whatever the precise numbers, the Asian-British shopkeepers and white working-class residents I spoke to while campaigning for Remain in east Oxford knew from everyday experience that there were a lot of 'east Europeans' placing a strain on schools, hospitals, social services and housing, as well as taking some low-paid jobs. For the most part, they just honestly felt that too many people had come into the country too fast and Britain's welfare state was creaking under the strain.

On top of this true experience and honest feeling, however, was overlaid a political narrative that was far from true or honest. The Leave campaign played on all the leitmotifs familiar from the libretto of populism in other European countries: nation versus Europe, democracy versus liberalism, 'the people' versus the elite, with 'the people' being defined ethno-nationally, against people from elsewhere. And contempt for expert knowledge: 'I think the people in this country have had enough of experts,' said Michael Gove, as a leader of the Leave campaign. The three key themes that Curtice identified – globalised European economy,

identity and immigration – were woven into a single narrative and distilled into the brilliantly effective slogan 'Take Back Control'.

The side of a red Brexit battlebus carrying Johnson and Gove around
the country brazenly claimed that ending Britain's budget contributions
to the EU would liberate '£350 million a week' for the National Health
Service. This was combined with an even more spurious claim that,
since Turkey was going to join the EU along with some countries in
the western Balkans, millions more people would come flooding into
Britain, exploiting the welfare state. The UKIP leader Nigel Farage's
Leave.EU campaign tweeted: 'Dave [Cameron] wants to give 75 million
Turks access to your #NHS!' The mainstream Vote Leave campaign was
scarcely less misleading, as in this message from one of its co-chairs, the
Labour MP Gisela Stuart:

> Instead of giving an extra 88 million people – more than our entire
> population – access to the NHS, I believe it would be safer to take
> back control. We should give our struggling NHS the £350 million
> we send to the EU every week.

Britain's net contribution to the EU budget in 2016, taking account of
the money it got back from Brussels in various ways, was actually about
£185 million a week. The notion that eighty-eight million people from
Turkey and south-eastern Europe were suddenly going to gain access
to the NHS was beyond ridiculous.

As elsewhere in Europe, immigration was linked to Islam and terrorism. Thus the egregious Gove a fortnight before the vote:

> With the terrorism threat that we face only growing, it is hard to see
> how it could possibly be in our security interests to open visa-free
> travel to 77 million Turkish citizens and to create a border-free zone
> from Iraq, Iran and Syria to the English Channel. It is even harder to
> see how such a course is wise when extremists everywhere will
> believe that the West is opening its borders to appease an Islamist
> government.

These messages were magnified by the country's predominantly
Eurosceptic press. 'Yet Another Load of Migrants Arrives in UK declaring We're from Europe – Let Us In', the *Daily Mail* splashed over a

photograph on its front page just days before the vote. A small correction on page two subsequently admitted that they came from Iraq and Kuwait. On social media, viral misinformation and some Russian disinformation heightened the alarm. To cap it all, a Brexit-supporting government minister, Penny Mordaunt, made the completely false claim that Britain could not veto Turkey's accession to the EU. 'Leave were lying,' Cameron remarks indignantly in his memoirs. While he fought a gentlemanly campaign, like some late Victorian toff boxing according to the Marquess of Queensberry's rules, his opponents were kicking him six inches below the belt.

It's important to say clearly that many millions of those who voted for Britain to leave the EU knew exactly what they were doing. They included my oldest friend, Richard Pertwee, and would certainly have included my father. It's insulting to claim otherwise. But it's not misleading to suggest that this no-holds-barred campaign made all the difference to the final result, by swinging a last block of voters over the line. Some six months after the vote, Dominic Cummings, the mastermind of the Vote Leave campaign, reflected in a blog post:

> If Boris [Johnson], [Michael] Gove and Gisela [Stuart] had not supported us and picked up the baseball bat marked 'Turkey/NHS/£350 million' with five weeks to go, then 650,000 votes might have been lost.

Baseball bat, indeed. Yet also crucial to Leave's success was the fact that the baseball bat was wielded by, so to speak, gentlemen cricketers. Sophisticated, cultured, well spoken, they appealed to a middle-class electorate that would not have gone for Nigel Farage and the bovver boys of Brexit. This was populism with an Oxford accent.

When we say 'Brexit', we mean not only the actual vote but also the three and a half years of furious political argument that followed. For all its Etonian and Oxonian polish, British populism, like other populisms of the 2010s, threatened the customary practices and institutional balances on which liberal democracy depends. But the threat was less severe than in Hungary, Poland or the United States. There was no British equivalent of the 6 January 2021 mob invasion of the Capitol in

Washington. Perhaps the most serious challenge was the Johnson government's attempt to prorogue (i.e. suspend) parliament for five weeks in autumn 2019, at a crucial moment of decision about Brexit. The attempt was struck down by Britain's Supreme Court, in a crisp, muscular, unanimous judgement. Having cited precedent going back to 1611 ('the King hath no prerogative but that which the law of the land allows him') and noted that the proposed prorogation's 'effect on our democracy was extreme', it marched briskly to this magnificent conclusion:

> This Court has already concluded that the Prime Minister's advice to Her Majesty was unlawful, void and of no effect. This means that the Order in Council to which it led was also unlawful, void and of no effect and should be quashed. This means that when the Royal Commissioners walked into the House of Lords it was as if they walked in with a blank sheet of paper. The prorogation was also void and of no effect. Parliament has not been prorogued.

The government immediately accepted the verdict. Democracy resumed.

My continental European friends laughed with disbelief at the archaic practices of the Westminster parliament, some of which were indeed ridiculous. But every mature democracy has its foibles and weaknesses. In 2017, it took Germany six months to form a government. Belgium once took more than a year. Old-fashioned and ramshackle though it was, this was still a genuine parliamentary democracy at work. I sat on the sagging green leather benches of the Strangers' Gallery in the Commons chamber during several dramatic debates, including that on 15 January 2019 in which Theresa May's proposed deal with the EU went down to the biggest defeat in modern British parliamentary history. In the spring of 2019, the House of Commons voted to take back control of its own order of business, which was usually set by the government. It then held a series of 'indicative votes' to see if a majority could be found for any way forward on Brexit. The proposal for a 'confirmatory public vote' failed by just twelve votes.

'Confirmatory public vote' meant a second referendum, now rebranded as a 'People's Vote'. I marched in several demonstrations for a People's Vote, the largest of which probably gathered around one million people in central London. In the end, these failed utterly, as had the million-strong London march against British participation in the Iraq war. But they also showed how a sense of personal identity had come to be attached to the European Union and how strongly people felt about that identity.

I find it telling that the biggest pro-European demonstrations I witnessed anywhere in Europe in the first two decades of the twenty-first-century were not in Paris, Berlin or Rome, but in Kyiv and London. The former gathered people who wanted to join the EU; the latter, those who did not want to leave it. British demonstrators now displayed the same spontaneous creativity that I had seen in Prague, Kyiv, Belgrade and East Berlin. Handwritten placards proclaimed: 'Don't Blame the Bulgarians or Romanians, Blame the Etonians', 'My Grandfather Died for EU' and 'Freedom, I Will Not Give EU Up'. A T-shirt read: 'I am a Citizen of Europe'. The Duke of Wellington's house at Hyde Park Corner was wreathed in European flags.

In London, at least, these were pretty middle-class affairs. 'I Can Get a Better Deal at Waitrose' was how one placard dismissed the deal that Theresa May had negotiated with the EU. The word I heard most often at these rallies was 'sorry', spoken as people tried to avoid stepping on each other's toes. I also heard a fair smattering of French, Italian and German, which suggested that alongside us British Europeans there marched not a few of the millions of continental Europeans who had come to live in Britain. By the end of 2021, more than five million EU citizens would be granted permanent settled status in post-Brexit Britain. Whether or not Britain was in Europe, Europe was in Britain.

Some of my friends denounced a second referendum as profoundly undemocratic. You couldn't demand a replay of the match just because you lost. I won't pretend I did not feel the force of this objection. Against it, one could argue that this decision was so momentous, for Britain and for Europe, that we must be quite sure we had thought it through. The Leave side had won the referendum by highlighting everything wrong with EU membership while remaining inspirationally vague about the alternative. It then emerged that parliament could not agree which version of Brexit to choose. Surely it made sense to have a confirmatory public vote on the actual exit deal negotiated with the EU? At the heart of the British constitutional tradition is the sovereignty of parliament, which Brexit was supposed to restore in all its pristine glory. If, therefore, our sovereign parliament had decided to hold a second, confirmatory referendum on the real Brexit deal, that would have been constitutionally legitimate.

But what would Britain have looked like if a second referendum had reversed the verdict of the first? Unlike a vote for Remain in the 2016 referendum, which is what most leading Brexiters expected, the legitimacy of this result would have been widely questioned. The country might have become more bitterly divided than it appeared to be at the beginning of the 2020s. To be sure, deep wounds remained, but Britain was not a hyperpolarised country like the United States or Poland, torn between two warring political tribes, each with its own version of reality. Representatives of all sides still met on the airwaves of the BBC for robust but civilised debate, conducted on the basis of shared facts. There were neither Remainers nor Leavers when we all united around the National Health Service – the closest thing modern Britain has to a national religion – in the battle against Covid.

These years of political struggle over Brexit carried a heavy price, abroad as well as at home. Since my political connections were strongest on the continent rather than in Britain, I concentrated my efforts there. I went to Brussels to speak with Donald Tusk and to Berlin to bend the ears of leading politicians. In newspaper commentaries, I pleaded with our European friends to allow us more time to get to the right decision. Today, I read these increasingly desperate pleas with melancholy irony. For decades, I had watched with a mixture of deep sympathy and mild amusement how Polish, Czech, Bosnian and Ukrainian friends made their pitches to the powerful in Europe, who then still included the British. Our particular national crisis is crucial for the future of the continent, the petitioners would explain. We are standing up for your European values. It is in *your own* interest, Europe, to help us. Now I myself became that petitioning European from the periphery, deploying identical arguments to persuade the powerholders in Berlin, Paris, Brussels and – since the central Europeans' earlier petitions had finally succeeded – also in Warsaw and Prague.

Initially, I encountered sympathy and sadness, expressed in those warm, consoling embraces. But as the weeks turned to months, the months to years, and the British simply could not agree what they wanted, that turned to irritation and contempt. The antics of the barking Speaker of the House of Commons, John Bercow, might be good entertainment – 'better than anything on Netflix' said the former Polish president Aleksander Kwaśniewski – but the UK was wasting everyone's time and distracting Europe from its other major challenges. 'We have come to dread seeing old British friends, now so obsessed with Brexit that it is all but impossible to talk of anything else,' wrote Sylvie Kauffmann, editorial director of *Le Monde*, in 2019. A German columnist said Britain had made itself a laughing stock.

In the spring of 2019, the BBC aired a fly-on-the-wall documentary showing how the Brexit steering group in the European Parliament had followed the seemingly endless, infuriating cross-Channel negotiations. At one point, two aides in the office of Guy Verhofstadt, the former Belgian prime minister and chair of that steering group, jokingly exulted: 'We got rid of them! We kicked them out! We finally turned them into a colony . . . !' More soberly, Danuta Huebner, a Polish member of the European Parliament and former European Commissioner, remarked: 'We have a common objective to get rid of them in March 2019.' Get rid of them! For a quarter-century, from 1979 until Poland entered the EU in 2004, I had argued passionately in the capitals of Europe that the Poles were not Them, to be kept outside in the cold, but Us, as much Europeans as we British, French and Germans. Now here was one of my Polish friends saying that we Brits were no longer Us. We had become Them, to be got rid of.

Since Brexit was such a major event it was obviously too soon to say, at the beginning of the 2020s, what all the consequences would be. As Britain emerged blinking from the simultaneous impact of Brexit and the Covid pandemic, a coincidence which made it more difficult to disentangle the one from the other, we did not even know whether the state formally known as the United Kingdom of Great Britain and Northern Ireland would survive in its current form. Would the Scots vote to leave the British union and then rejoin the European one? That would be the end of Great Britain. Might the majority of the Northern Irish one day vote to join Ireland? That would be the end of the United Kingdom.

All living former British prime ministers argued that the country would be poorer, weaker and less influential outside the EU. Most of the country's friends abroad agreed. In opinion polls, a large majority of younger Brits said they thought the country had been wrong to leave the EU. Perhaps in some respects, such as jobs for British people without a university education, things could actually get better. The economic consequences of Brexit would make the post-Brexit goal of 'levelling up' more difficult to finance. But 'levelling up' was precisely what British society needed, as did other capitalist democracies, and in that sense the voice of one important group of Brexit voters had been heard.

Deeply worrying though the impacts of Brexit on Britain were, I was, unusually among British opponents of Brexit, even more concerned about the damage it would do to Europe. Many continental Europeans took the contrary view, saying Brexit enabled the EU to achieve more progress than it could have with the troublesome Brits still on board. Travelling around the continent in the early 2020s, I was struck by how seldom Britain was mentioned at all.

Yet consider what the negative consequences for Europe could be. For decades, the European project drew strength from a sense that it represented the future, the direction that history was going. It had a nimbus of irreversibility. Losing a major member state must, at the very least, take the shine off that nimbus. Roughly half the factors that caused Brexit could also be found elsewhere in Europe. At the beginning of the 2020s, many were still there: for example, the complex of fears around immigration, Islam, terrorism, sovereignty and control, and the way these were woven together into a populist, Eurosceptic narrative.

Princess Diana famously observed that 'there were three of us' in her marriage, which made it 'a little crowded'. With the threesome of France, Germany and Britain inside the EU, almost the opposite was true. It was the ménage à trois that helped the union to work, allowing all sorts of compensating balances for the other member states. If you disliked a Franco-German initiative, you could look to Britain; if you had reservations about a British-German policy, turn to France. It remained to be seen how happy the family would be with only France and Germany in the master bedroom. Or could Italy or Spain take Britain's place? Self-evidently, losing one of the Union's leading military, diplomatic and intelligence powers weakened the EU's foreign policy clout. A much-trumpeted security alliance between Australia, the UK and the US (Aukus), elbowing out an existing arrangement between Australia and France, suggested tensions that might lie ahead.

Already, there appeared to be a dynamic of competition between the UK and the EU. Where Brexiters said the point of Brexit was to show that a country could be 'better off out', leaders like French president Emmanuel Macron insisted the EU must ensure Britain was visibly worse off out. This objective logic of competition was compounded by the subjective process of Othering. With shocking speed, what had for more than forty years been a common, if fractious, Us was becoming Us versus Them. For a British European like me, this divergence created a painful dilemma. I could not want my own country to do badly. Yet if post-Brexit Britain did too well relative to the EU, that would encourage tendencies of disintegration in the European Union. The best formula I could come up with is that I wanted Britain to do very well and the EU to do even better. But it still felt like doing the splits.

In the short term, Brexit discouraged continental nationalist populists from calling for Frexit, Italexit, Nexit, Hungexit or Polexit. But how long would that remain true? In the last Eurobarometer poll conducted before the Brexit vote, the overall average proportion of EU citizens who said their country would be better off outside the Union was thirty-four per cent. In 2021, in an EU without Britain, it was still twenty-eight per cent. If Britain somehow muddled through to an alternative business model, nationalists elsewhere in Europe might sooner or later be tempted to follow suit. The probability of such an option prevailing in any continental country was still small, but it was not negligible.

'And why shouldn't they do what we did?' my old friend Richard, who voted for Brexit, might ask. What is wrong with a continent of free-trading, peacefully co-operating, sovereign, democratic nation states? The question deserves an answer. Here is mine. It's one thing to have a Europe in which a few semi-detached mature democracies, such as Switzerland, Norway and now Britain, are grouped around a central commonwealth of closely integrated countries. It's quite another to have a Europe in which all the member states of the European Union have gone their own ways, after a traumatic disintegration. Only the most naive historical optimist would count on them all remaining liberal democracies and continuing to co-operate peacefully with each other.

Even if European countries did not actually come to blows, as they had throughout pre-1945 history and still were doing in Ukraine, they would be competing fiercely with each other, as Britain was now competing with the EU. Europe would be weaker and more divided. And this was not the world of the nineteenth century, in which Europe was the most powerful continent. Since the United States was preoccupied with its own domestic problems and its new challenges in Asia, twenty-first-century Europe would be a standing invitation for outside powers such as China to divide and rule, as Europeans had once done in Africa and Asia.

The European Union might survive one Brexit. It could not survive many more.

Demolition

Democracy endured in Britain but the country ceased to be a member of the EU. Hungary remained a member of the EU but ceased to be a democracy. Poland's populist government tried to follow Hungary's example. Since the liberation and transformation of central Europe had been a central political experience of my life, I lived this erosion of democracy in Poland and Hungary almost as intensely as Brexit.

In September 2021, I received a letter from Viktor Orbán, the Hungarian prime minister, which began: 'I recently had the opportunity to see an interview that you gave to Euronews, where you stated that my illiberalism is "without question, a real threat to the European Union".' In response, he enclosed a copy of one of his recent speeches 'partly inspired by your thoughts'. Simultaneously, he posted a longer, public version of this missive on his website, in a series which he outrageously described as Samizdat. (Samizdat was underground self-publishing by Soviet bloc dissidents like Václav Havel who had no other means of reaching the public and risked imprisonment as a result, whereas Orbán now controlled most of the mass media in Hungary and would be quoted even in the few that still opposed him.) His Samizdat No.12 said his speech attempted 'to spell out – in categories comprehensible for Western audiences – the intellectual essence of today's European debates, as we see them'.

I first met Orbán in Budapest in June 1988, when he was a fiery twenty-five-year-old student leader of a recently founded youth movement opposed to the country's already fast decaying communist regime. My notebook records the movement's name, Fidesz, meaning Alliance of Young Democrats, and some of the aims that he and his fellow students excitedly explained to me: 'Rule of law & human rights, new constitution, freedom of association, freedom of the press.' A year later, in June 1989, I watched this short, intense, raven-haired young man deliver an electrifying speech during the ceremony on Heroes Square in Budapest to mark the reburial of Imre Nagy, the leader of the 1956 Hungarian revolution. That autumn, he turned up at Oxford, on a student scholarship funded by the Hungarian-American billionaire philanthropist George Soros. He didn't stay long, but I can still see him standing in front of me, lean, bright-eyed and dynamic, explaining how he and his friends were going to build a normal Western liberal democracy on the Danube.

Three decades later he was the politician who had demonstrated that a country could demolish liberal democracy while remaining a full member of the European Union. He no longer even pretended that Hungary was a liberal state. In a speech to an ethnic Hungarian audience in Romania in 2014, he said: 'I don't think that our European Union membership precludes us from building an illiberal new state based on national foundations.' His Alliance of Young Democrats, whose original statutes specified that members had to be younger than thirty-five, had become a ruling party of middle-aged anti-democrats. Corruption by power and money was written all over his face. It might not be strictly accurate to call him a dictator, but he certainly had a dictator's jowl.

Like Brexit, the demolition of democracy in Hungary resulted from a combination of deeper causes, contingent events and the role of individuals. Deeper causes included the authoritarian legacy of Hungary's pre-war past and the trauma of losing two thirds of its pre-1914 territory in the 1920 Trianon treaty. If you visit Budapest today, you can see a large Trianon monument erected by the Orbán regime in front of the magnificent nineteenth-century parliament building, with the Hungarian names of all the 'lost' towns and villages engraved on the memorial's largely subterranean stone walls. More recently, the global financial crisis had hit Hungarians hard. In his 2014 speech announcing his turn to illiberalism, Orbán said the financial crisis had showed that 'liberal democratic states cannot remain globally competitive'.

Contingent events included the mess made by socialist–liberal coalition governments between 2002 and 2010. At one point, the socialist prime minister told an internal party meeting: 'We've been lying morning, noon and night.' Fidesz played the leaked clip over and over again. A peculiar electoral system meant that in the 2010 election Fidesz got more than two-thirds of the seats in parliament on just fifty-three per cent of the popular vote. A post-1989 revision of the 1949 communist constitution meant that this two-thirds majority could be used to change the constitution. Then Orbán, with the streetfighter instincts formed in his tough childhood, pounced.

He described this fortuitous election result as 'a revolution in the polling booth' and claimed that it represented the deep will of the Hungarian nation. Soon the country would have a new constitution. The new political dispensation was officially described as a System of National Cooperation. One by one, Fidesz neutralised all the liberal democratic checks and balances: the judiciary, the public prosecutors' office, the tax administration, the national audit office, the electoral commission, the public service media. It gerrrymandered constituencies, favouring the rural and small-town Hungary where the party had done best since it took a sharp turn to the right in the 1990s. It granted citizenship rights to close to half a million of the ethnic Hungarians living in neighbouring states such as Romania and Slovakia, and allowed them to vote by post. Their votes went overwhelmingly to Fidesz. Hungarians living in the West, who tended to be more liberal, had to travel to a consulate in person to vote. So much for equal suffrage.

Not content with subordinating public media, Orbán gradually secured effective control of most of the commercial media, through friendly oligarchs who were often rewarded with state contracts in other parts of their businesses. The state advertising budget was pumped up and steered to supportive media outlets. At election time, much of the state apparatus swung into action behind Fidesz. Outside Budapest, your chance of getting a public service job or public contract increasingly depended on proven loyalty to the ruling party. Civil society organisations were harassed and some of them closed down.

Using these and other more 'informal' methods, Orbán won supermajorities in parliament three more times, in 2014, 2018 and 2022. He seized the opportunity of the refugee crisis in 2015 to become a cheerleader for the anti-immigrant populist right across Europe, building the razor-wire fence on Hungary's border to Serbia and refusing a request from Angela Merkel and the EU to take just a small quota of the migrants generously accepted by countries like Germany and Sweden.

In the 2018 election, he campaigned against both 'Brussels' and his sometime Oxford scholarship funder, George Soros. Fidesz ludicrously alleged that there was a 'Soros plan' to supplant Europe's native-born, Christian population with mainly Muslim 'invaders', thus going one step further than Renaud Camus' 'great replacement' theory by attributing the conspiracy to a Jewish billionaire. Orbán welcomed the election of Donald Trump, who responded by inviting him to the White House and exclaiming: 'It's like we're twins.' In a move that looked like a personal vendetta against Soros but also had an element of political calculation, he expelled the Soros-funded Central European University, the region's best university, from Budapest. 'Stop Soros!' declared Fidesz campaign posters, and 'Stop Brussels!'

Such democratic backsliding was meant to be impossible for a member of the European Union. From the 1970s onwards, starting with the former dictatorships in Spain, Portugal and Greece, joining the European Community had been seen as securing the transition to democracy at home. In central and eastern Europe, the linkage was even stronger. The twin processes of building new democracies and preparing for accession to the EU were inseparable. This was member-state-building as much as nation-state-building. The Union's accession requirements, laid out in what were called the Copenhagen criteria, demanded the consolidation of democracy, media freedom, the rule of law and respect for minority rights. Many, myself included, believed this effect would endure. How wrong we were. For all the noble words in the opening articles of the Treaty on European Union, it turned out that the EU lacked any effective mechanisms to defend democracy inside a member state.

Hungary was not like Russia, where Putin's critics were locked up or poisoned – and that was partly thanks to its EU membership. But the EU sustained the Orbán regime at least as much as it constrained it. Well-educated Fidesz lawyers were expert at finding legal constructions that seemed compliant with European law, mirroring arrangements in some other European country, when the reality behind the facade was very different. Hungary became a Potemkin state. Given the

security provided by the European single market, the German car indus-
try located a significant part of its production in this nearby, high-skill
and relatively low-wage country, which rewarded it with generous subsidies. At one point, close to one third of the country's industrial exports
consisted of German cars and their parts.

Freedom of movement, a core achievement of the EU, had the unintended consequence that Hungarians who did not like Orbán's illiberal
regime could simply go and live in another European country. As the
Bulgarian political writer Ivan Krastev observed, it was easier to change
countries than to change your own country. Between 2010 and 2018,
there was a nearly 200 per cent increase in the number of Hungarians
residing in other member states. 'You know,' a Hungarian friend matter-
of-factly explained, 'they don't want to live in a fascist country.'

Throughout the 2010s, the European People's Party (EPP), the alliance of centre-right parties in the EU, kept Fidesz as a member, despite
ample evidence that it violated the EPP's proudly proclaimed democratic
principles. Fidesz votes helped maintain the EPP as the largest grouping
in the European parliament and Orbán retained top-level influence in
the Union. Germany's Christian Democrats, and especially the Bavarian
Christian Social Union, were his most influential protectors. Thus the
institutional empowerment of Europe-wide parties, which was intended
to make the EU itself more democratic, ended up facilitating the erosion of democracy inside a member state.

The biggest benefit to the Orbán regime came from very large direct
transfers of EU funds. In 2017, these amounted to some 3.5 per cent of
gross national income, almost equalling Hungary's total annual growth
that year, which was 4.1 per cent. Virtually all these funds went directly
to the central government, providing Fidesz with the means for extensive patronage. EU funds financed the renovation of roads, buildings
and facilities in Fidesz-supporting towns and villages, while also providing handsome spin-offs for local businesses, officials and supportive
media-owners. According to one analysis, more than ninety-five per
cent of public investments in Hungary were co-financed by the EU. A
nice sprinkling of this largesse reportedly ended up in the pockets of
some of Orbán's friends and family.

Orbán thanked his most generous supporter by denouncing it. On

Saturday 23 October 2021, the sixty-fifth anniversary of the outbreak of the Hungarian revolution in 1956, I stood in a large crowd at the bottom of Andrássy avenue in Budapest. What was described to me as a national rock band, dressed all in black, performed a song about the 'five million Hungarians' who were left outside Hungary after the 1920 Treaty of Trianon. 'We are of one blood!' was the refrain. Then Orbán strode onto the stage and gave this reading of history:

> Just as in 1849, 1920, 1945 and 1956, Europe's high dignitaries are once again trying to go over our heads to make decisions about our fate, but without our consent. They would force us to be European, sensitive and liberal – even if it kills us. Today the words and actions that Brussels directs at us and the Poles are like those usually reserved for enemies. We have a feeling of déja vù, as throughout Europe we hear echoes of the Brezhnev Doctrine.

He thus equated the European Union with the Soviet Union. Then came a dose of conspiracy theory about the political opposition at home. Opposition leaders, he said,

> have been competing to see which of them could rule over Hungarians by the grace of Brussels and George Soros as their governor in Hungary: who could be the new pasha [Ottoman governor] of Buda . . . They openly say that to regain power they will even join forces with the devil. Their aim is to take Hungary from the hands of [the Virgin] Mary and put it at the feet of Brussels.

Boris Johnson liked to talk of having his cake and eating it but Orbán successfully practised the 'cakeism' that Johnson merely preached. His regime was funded by the EU and he got re-elected by attacking the EU. Yet the EU continued to feed the mouth that bit it.

Not confining himself to criticism, the Hungarian leader advocated an alternative vision for Europe: anti-liberal, socially conservative, pro-natalist, professedly Christian and ethno-nationalist. In July 2022, he told an ethnic Hungarian audience in Romania that Hungary did not want to join the 'mixed race' world of Western Europe, where 'European peoples are mixed together with those arriving from outside Europe'. He thus continued a long tradition of reactionary visions for Europe. The British fascist Oswald Mosley, for example, campaigned after the

Second World War for what he called 'Europe as a Nation'. His wife
Diana spent several years editing a magazine called *The European*. Now
Orbán, although only the prime minister of a small central European
country, became one of the most influential figures promoting the latest
iteration of anti-liberal Europe. 'We used to think that Europe was our
future,' he said. 'Today we know that we are Europe's future.'

The speech he sent me laid out this European vision. In front of a student audience at the Mathias Corvinus Collegium, an educational institution lavishly endowed by his government, Orbán argued that while the
United States had fallen prey to 'Neo-Marxism – referred to as "woke"
over there', leaders in Europe

> have induced a Muslim demographic, political and economic flood,
> thereby creating a new situation in France, Italy, the Netherlands,
> Belgium, Germany and Austria. This means that for the first time in
> European history, they managed to break into Europe even north of
> Spain.

'They'. The invaders. Meanwhile, 'the concept of open society has
deprived the West of faith in its own values and historical mission'. The
West was now 'rich and weak'. The mission of central Europe – in whose
name he presumed to speak – was to stiffen the West's backbone. Europe
should be Christian, national, proud of its traditions. The Hungarians,
in particular, had for a thousand years had the specific national mission of 'organising life in the Carpathian basin'. (The Slovaks, Romanians and Serbs who shared this basin should presumably be happy to
be 'organised' by the Hungarians.) The young men and women of the
Mathias Corvinus Collegium must be the intellectual vanguard of this
heroic fight for our culture. Orbán even quoted St Matthew: 'Go, and
make disciples of all nations.'

In that evangelical spirit, Orbán received both Éric Zemmour and
Marine le Pen as honoured guests in the Hungarian capital. Tucker
Carlson of Fox News came to Hungary as a disciple, praising Orbán
effusively and informing his viewers that 'BLM [Black Lives Matter]
is not allowed to torch entire neighbourhoods in Budapest'. After the
European People's Party had finally screwed up the courage to suggest
that Fidesz did not belong with Europe's democratic centre-right, the

Hungarian leader was instrumental in forming a loose alliance of six-teen far-right Eurosceptic parties, including Marine le Pen's Rassemblement National (the re-named National Front) in France, Matteo Salvini's Lega and the post-fascist Fratelli d'Italia in Italy, Vox in Spain and the Freedom Party of Austria. But his closest ally was the Polish Law and Justice party, PiS.

In Poland, the demolition began five years later than in Hungary. In May 2015, the PiS candidate, Andrzej Duda, won the presidential election with one of those narrow majorities of fifty-two per cent to forty-eight per cent that kept recurring in post-Wall Europe. In a parliamentary election that autumn, PiS gained an absolute majority in parliament. Although they had won with just 37.5 per cent of the vote – amounting to only eighteen per cent of those eligible to vote, since the Polish abstention rate remained high – PiS politicians talked as if they represented the general will of the entire nation.

Jarosław Kaczyński, the party's boss and master strategist, now started following the Hungarian playbook. Unlike Orbán, Kaczyński had not won a supermajority that would enable him to change the constitution, so de-democratisation in Poland went more slowly, but the direction of travel, and many of the tactics, were the same. Here too, the still fragile checks and balances of a recently constructed liberal democracy were assaulted one by one. The independence of the judiciary was largely destroyed, despite protests from the EU.

The supposedly public service television, TVP, became an organ of aggressive propaganda for the ruling party. It is hard to convey just how crude, manipulative and paranoid its coverage became. All the historic Polish resentments against Germany were revived, as those about the Treaty of Trianon were in Hungary. Merely speaking German was presented as a kind of treachery. Again and again, a clip was played of Donald Tusk, the president of the European Council who in 2021 returned to Polish politics as an opposition leader, saying just two words in German: '*für Deutschland*' ('for Germany'). The government's resistance to EU attempts to uphold the rule of law in Poland was presented with the strapline: 'The Polish constitution against the German hegemon'. Other straplines included: 'Brussels wants to forbid eating meat?', 'The opposition wants to Islamicise Poland?' and the magnificent 'Poles are not soulless'. At worst, the channel stooped to playing on the anti-Semitism still present in parts of Polish society. In a hard-fought presidential election in 2020, which the opposition candidate Rafał Trzaskowski came close to winning, one news bulletin reported:

> Experts have no doubt [that] the stream of money that currently flows from the state budget into the pockets of Polish families will dry up if Trzaskowski, after his possible victory in the presidential election, seeks to satisfy Jewish demands.

Meanwhile, critical media were starved of state advertising and belaboured with numerous lawsuits. One of the main groups of provincial newspapers was bought by a state-controlled energy company whose boss was very close to the ruling party. Aggressive efforts were made to push out foreign owners of independent media, in the name of 'repolonisation'. The most dangerous of these efforts was a law targeted at the widely watched independent television news channel, TVN, which was American-owned. In sharp contrast to an ineffective European Union, the United States intervened decisively to block what would have been a deadly blow to media freedom and therefore to any prospect of the next election being fair as well as free. Subsidies from the government and foundations connected with state-owned enterprises were slashed for liberal, independent NGOs and publications, but showered on cultural and educational institutions supportive of the ruling party.

What the political scientist Richard Hofstadter once called 'the paranoid style in politics' was manifested in a conspiracy theory around the tragic death in 2010 of President Lech Kaczyński, Jarosław's twin brother, in a plane accident at a Russian military airfield in Smolensk, when he was on his way to mark the anniversary of the Soviet murder of Polish officers at Katyn in 1940. On every front, PiS advanced a simplistic, one-dimensional narrative in which Poland appeared only as the martyred victim of foreign powers and heroic defender of European freedom. Decades of careful work by historians illuminating the darker sides of Poland's record in the twentieth century – and which European nation does not have such darker sides? – were denounced as a 'pedagogy of shame'. In the little village of Przysieczyn and the nearby town of

Wągrowiec, schoolteachers confided to me their fears of a new, mandatory history and civics curriculum, under which they would no longer be able to explore the historical truth freely and critically.

The ruling party benefited from the disarray of the left and significant failings of the liberal governments that had ruled from 2007 to 2015, headed by Donald Tusk and his successor. PiS skilfully exploited all the many discontents that had grown out of the post-communist transition and a quarter-century of liberalisation, Europeanisation and globalisation. As I had seen when revisiting the sad remains of the Gdańsk shipyard, deep unhappiness with economic inequality was exacerbated by a sense of historical injustice. Many felt that the transition had been good for those in the big cities but not for the other Poland, on which the metropolitan liberal elites looked down. In a society more profoundly revolutionised by capitalism than it had ever been by communism, people harked back to the old certainties of family, church and nation.

Helped by a growing economy and large EU transfers, the PiS government did materially support the poorer half of Polish society. Its flagship policies included a monthly payment of 500 zloties for each child, snappily marketed as '500 plus', and an additional '13th month' pension payment. 'PiS has done something for the worse off,' the former mayor of Przysieczyn, a sturdy, pink-faced, thoroughly decent man, told me. His own grandson had got the '500 plus' and it had made a big difference to the whole family. Rafał Trzaskowski, the opposition candidate who narrowly lost the 2020 presidential election, recalled an encounter with a voter in south-eastern Poland. This young mother said she really disliked Kaczyński, his party and his ideology, but she would still vote for Duda, the PiS candidate, 'because they gave my son his first vacation'. A Warsaw student insisted to me that this was not just cash being redistributed, it was also dignity. Polish populism combined right-wing rhetoric and cultural policy with economic and social measures usually associated with the left.

If PiS had not been demolishing the foundations of liberal democracy, all this could have been regarded as a legitimate change of political course. One might not like the party's programme, just as one might dislike the policies of any governing party anywhere, but one could work to change it at the next election. Like Orbán in his letter to me,

Poland's populist leaders would enjoy nothing more than a lofty intellectual debate with liberals about the future of Western civilisation. But this was not the point. The point was that they were changing the rules of the game so the next election would not be free and fair.

Poland was not as far gone as Hungary. It still had major independent media and opposition parties, a vibrant civil society capable of mobilising large popular protests, strong local government, including big cities in opposition hands, an upper house of parliament with an opposition majority and an independent ombudsman, as prescribed in the constitution. Yet the erosion was serious enough. On a properly ambitious definition of what democracy should be, 'illiberal democracy' is a contradiction in terms. Democracy is liberal or it is not democracy. The term is nonetheless useful to describe a liberal democracy in a perilous state of decay, and in that sense, Poland was an illiberal democracy.

All this was profoundly depressing. Poland and Hungary had led the charge out of communism in 1989. On the twentieth anniversary of the velvet revolutions, in 2009, they had seemed still to be in the vanguard, as two of central Europe's consolidated post-communist democracies. Yet by the thirtieth anniversary of 1989, Poland and Hungary were leading the charge away from democracy. Other central European countries exhibited similar tendencies. The Czech Republic with its oligarch premier Andrej Babiš, Slovakia with its populist ruling party long led by Robert Fico, Slovenia under its right-wing populist premier Janez Janša – all had softer versions of the same phenomenon. Even Austria had a government in which the slick young chancellor Sebastian Kurz, himself no stranger to opportunistic populism, was in coalition with the Freedom Party, which would subsequently join Orbán's network of sixteen far-right parties.

In the years leading up to 1989 we used to talk of the 'democratic opposition' in the Soviet bloc. By this we meant not the opposition in a democracy, like Labour against Conservatives or Christian Democrats against Social Democrats, but an extra-parliamentary opposition that was committed to creating a democracy. I had supported that 'democratic opposition'. Now I found myself supporting those who were trying to restore democracy. Fortunately, there were many of them and their possibilities were much larger than they had been before 1989.

In June 2019, Slovakia elected a new president, Zuzana Čaputová, a lawyer and environmental activist from a fresh young party called Progressive Slovakia. She was deeply committed to democracy, human rights and the project of European Union – in short, as she happily acknowledged, an heir to the tradition of Václav Havel. Two days later, I stood with a large crowd in Prague's Letná park, where I had witnessed the largest rally of the Velvet Revolution in November 1989. One of the organisers this time round, a twenty-four-year old theology student called Benjamin Roll, told me his father had been an acoustic engineer for the 1989 rally. References to Havel were everywhere. A large banner carried his injunction: 'Truth and love must prevail over lies and hatred!' Roll told the crowd that they were not trying to make a new revolution but to save the existing democracy:

> We are warning against the course of change in our country under Babiš and [president Miloš] Zeman. We are warning against the taming of justice and the media, and the usurpation of power by a few oligarchs. We are warning against democracy being stealthily stolen away from us.

Two years later, a combination of two opposition coalitions managed narrowly to defeat Babiš in a parliamentary election in the Czech Republic. It was an important signal for the whole region.

In Hungary, a united opposition had regained control of the city government of Budapest and a coalition of six parties backed a single candidate to defeat Orbán in parliamentary elections in April 2022. On the edge of Heroes Square, the very place where Orbán had delivered his revolutionary speech in 1989, I heard that candidate, a conservative, Christian provincial mayor called Péter Márki-Zay, demand the restoration of democracy in front of an enthusiastic crowd waving European flags. Alas, the opposition was not as united as it needed to be. In an election that was largely free but definitely not fair, Orbán used state-funded billboards, public television and paid advertising on Facebook to tell Hungarians he would keep them out of the war in Ukraine and keep cheap Russian gas flowing to Hungary from Vladimir Putin, whom he visited for that purpose in Moscow. But at least the opposition was still there and the war in Ukraine had driven a wedge between Orbán and his Polish allies.

In Poland, some of my old friends were once again on the barricades for democracy, although the lead was now sometimes taken by our children's generation. Tens of thousands of young women, dressed in black, filled streets and squares to protest against one of the most severe tightenings of abortion law in Europe. Back in the 1990s, people had accepted the new constitution and the new institutions of liberal democracy with little debate. Adopting them was just what you had to do to be a 'normal' country, to 'return to Europe' and fulfil the Copenhagen criteria for joining the EU. Now, as Poles had to fight for the independence of the judiciary and the separation of powers, they made them their own.

For the first time in a very long while – some might say since 3 May 1791, when the country had adopted its first modern constitution – Polish patriotism became focused on the defence of the constitution. In 2018, portly Lech Wałęsa baffled people in Washington by turning up for the funeral of President George H. W. Bush wearing, under his sober suit, a T-shirt decorated with what seemed to be a miscellaneous jumble of letters. Had the old trooper forgotten his shirt and tie? No, the letters on the T-shirt spelt out *konstytucja* (constitution) – with the *ty* (meaning 'you') and the *ja* (meaning 'me') picked out in red, as if to say 'the constitution is you and me'. A founding father of Polish democracy was standing up for its constitution and Americans, of all people, should have got the point.

Even the slow-moving European Union seemed at last to be waking up to the erosion of democracy in Hungary and Poland and the threat it posed to its own legal and political order. The entire fabric of the single market depended on the supremacy of European law, which was challenged by Poland's politically subordinated constitutional court. European unity in the face of Putin's invasion of Ukraine was jeopardised by the presence of the illiberal, Putin-friendly Hungarian prime minister in the highest decision-making body of the Union, the European Council, which required unanimity for such decisions.

The question mark hanging over the future of central Europe at the beginning of the 2020s was thus as large as any in Europe. I was not impartial on this issue. I knew what I wanted for the region, with all my heart, and who I would support, with pen and voice. But I knew no more than anyone else how things would turn out. It was possible that, on the fortieth anniversary of the velvet revolutions, in 2029, central Europe would be suffering from more authoritarianism, nationalism, corruption and conflict. It was also possible that it would have returned to the paths of freedom and democracy with a richer understanding of what was needed for both to endure.

A new Iron Curtain

I am standing inside the frontier crossing to Morocco in Ceuta, the Spanish enclave on the northern tip of Africa, just across the Straits of Gibraltar from the continent of Europe. On each side of me are metal gates, freshly painted blue on the Spanish side, rather shabbier on the Moroccan. Behind me, a high fence on a thick concrete base stretches out into the shallows of the Mediterranean Sea. Looking inland, an even more formidable modern double fence snakes across the hilly country-side. The part facing Morocco is well over six metres high at this point, with a cylindrical fortification along its top to make it more difficult to cross, a sandy strip too wide to jump, a second fence, video cameras and alarm sensors. Here is Europe's new Iron Curtain.

The Spanish Civil Guard commander tells me that almost every day young men from sub-Saharan Africa try to clamber over the double fence, using hooks to help them scale the wire mesh. Some succeed, despite the Spanish guards racing to apprehend them along a specially built road that runs the length of the frontier. The lucky ones melt into the dense housing settlements at the outer edges of the city. Then they apply for legal asylum or try their luck at getting illegally across the Straits to the promised land of Europe.

As I inspect the fortifications around Ceuta on a blustery winter's day in 2021, I'm irresistibly reminded of viewing those around West Berlin more than forty years earlier. The Berlin Wall was topped with the same kind of cylindrical obstacle. The Iron Curtain that divided Europe from Europe was a double fence for much of its length. There is, of course, a fundamental difference: that Iron Curtain was erected by the dictatorships of the Soviet bloc to keep their own people in, this one is built by the democracies of the European Union to keep other people out.

Yet there is the same sense of being at the frontier between two worlds. West Berlin was a barricaded enclave of the West in the East; Ceuta is a barricaded enclave of Europe in Africa. There you had the front line between geopolitical West and East; here is the front line between global North and South. By night, looking down from a helicopter, you see bright lights on one side and near-darkness on the other. I am helped to understand the situation here by Suleika Ahmed, a young Spanish woman of Moroccan origin who grew up in one of Ceuta's poorer neighbourhoods, close to the fence. 'If I'd been born just a few metres away,' she tells me, 'I would have a completely different life.'

Nor is the difference between Europe's old bad Wall (for keeping people in) and its new walls (for keeping people out) as clear-cut as most Europeans might like to believe. By the early 2020s, the EU increasingly relied on neighbouring authoritarian states to keep would-be migrants away. This gave those states what has been called the weapon of mass migration. On Monday 17 May 2021, the King of Morocco, angry that Spain was giving health treatment to a leader of the Polisario, Morocco's enemy in a bitter conflict over Western Sahara, apparently decided to try out this weapon. The chosen target was this enclave, the oldest European colony on the mainland of Africa, originally conquered by the Portuguese in 1415 and in Spanish hands since the late sixteenth century.

Over the next twenty-four hours, a multitude of men, women and children crossed the beach on the Moroccan side and approached the frontier fence that stretched only a little way into the Mediterranean. At low tide they waded around the barrier, at high tide they paddled or swam, carrying small children and even holding babies above their heads. Moroccan frontier guards stood by, doing nothing. Spanish guards were overwhelmed.

The Moroccan authorities clearly encouraged people to go. A Spanish police officer who was on duty that day tells me he saw buses lined up on the other side of the border post. Moroccan kids were told at school that this was a chance to see the footballer Lionel Messi in Ceuta. Some arrived with just their school satchels. Word swiftly spread by mobile phone. In total, it is estimated that at least 12,000 people came across in the course of that day and night. 'That is fifteen per cent of the population of our city,' the mayor of Ceuta told me, adding 'I cried that night.' Fifteen per cent of the population of London would be 1.3 million people. Imagine 1.3 million migrants entering London in a single day. A photograph went around the world of the crowd approaching the fence on the beach. It encapsulated, in a single image, the fears about immigration that had roiled European politics for a decade.

The next day, Spanish soldiers and armoured personnel carriers lined up on the beach, guarding the fence, while urgent representations were made to the Moroccan authorities by the Spanish government, with support from the EU. Within a few days, the Moroccan frontier guards were back to being the gendarmes of Europe. Most of the people who had come across would gradually return to Morocco. Some made their way onwards to 'the Peninsular', as Ceutis refer to mainland Spain. But when I visited the city, six months on from the event that most Ceutis call the *entrada masiva*, 'the mass entry', several hundred unaccompanied minors were still housed there.

I sit with a group of these Moroccan teenagers in a hostel called 'Esperanza' – that is, Hope. Yahya, a bright, lanky sixteen-year-old in red puff jacket and sneakers, tells his story. When he woke up that morning, he thought it would be a normal school day. Then he heard the incredible news: the frontier is open! At once he jumped into a taxi and drove the 40 km to Ceuta, where he managed to get through the fence.

Didn't he hesitate to abandon family, friends and homeland just like that?

'No. I had no doubts. I had thought about it beforehand.'

Why did he come?

For a better life in Europe. The situation in Morocco was just so hopeless.

All these young men tell the same story about the life they have left behind. No jobs, no prospects. Poverty. Desperate families. Teachers who hardly bothered to teach.

Yahya says he originally wanted to be a footballer. Now he likes the idea of becoming a writer. He has already written some things, in Arabic, on Facebook.

What does Europe mean to them?

'They consider you a human being there,' says fifteen-year-old Ilyas. He wants to be a pilot.

And what's the worst thing about Europe? A long pause, then Ayman replies: 'Being sent back to Morocco!'

All laugh, but actually this is their worst fear. When the Ceuta authorities repatriated fifty-five unaccompanied minors to Morocco, some of the kids I'm talking to immediately left their hostels, to go and live on the streets. That was horrible, they say, but anything was better than being sent back. One of them has a heavily bandaged arm. I am told he injured it while trying to stow away on a boat to Europe.

As I listen to Yahya, Ilyas and Ayman, I realise that for them, 17 May 2021 was what 9 November 1989 was for a young East German. 'The frontier is open!' Unbelievable. The chance to flee a dictatorship. The hope of a better life.

But for Juan Sergio Redondo, the local leader of Vox, the Spanish populist party, this was something very different: not just 'the mass entry' but 'the invasion'.

'Yes, it is correctly defined as an invasion orchestrated by the Moroccan government,' the sharp-nosed politician and part-time history teacher tells me, when we meet the next day. Redondo's party is a significant force here: the member of the national parliament for Ceuta is from Vox.

What should Spain do about the 'invasion'?

It should totally close the frontier until Morocco unconditionally recognises Spanish sovereignty over Ceuta. And it should turn the frontier fence into a proper wall.

'We want a real wall, a concrete wall.'

So for Yahya, 17 May was like the fall of the Wall, but for Redondo, it's the occasion to demand a new Wall.

The EU, he goes on, should accept the proposal to build walls, 'as the Polish government is doing with Belarus'. He is referring to another migration drama that is playing out as we speak. The Belarusian dictator

Alexander Lukashenko is using the misery of innocent people even more cynically than did the Moroccan king, to destabilise neighbouring European countries and, through them, the entire EU.

Whereas King Mohammed VI just allowed some of his own people to cross to a nearby city many of them already knew, Lukashenko actively encouraged people from distant Syria and Iraq to fly to Minsk, a city most of them had probably never heard of, in the hope of getting into the EU. Each traveller paid a high price to regime-connected Belarusian travel agencies. On arrival in the Belarusian capital, they were transported to the Polish frontier and incited by Belarusian border guards to make an illegal crossing. Sometimes the guards themselves cut the razor wire that had been hastily laid by Polish forces along the previously unfenced rural frontier. Lukashenko personally told a group of migrants at the border that if they wanted to go westwards: 'It's up to you. Go through. Go.'

Poland's ruling PiS party – a partner of Vox in Viktor Orbán's gang of sixteen far-right parties – closed the frontier to Belarus as best it could, and said it would not let anyone in. Despite the party's loudly proclaimed Christian principles, for many days it did not allow basic humanitarian aid to reach the freezing, weak and hungry migrants who were languishing under the ancient oaks and pine trees of Białowieża, one of the last large areas of primaeval forest in Europe. At least twenty of them died of cold, hunger, thirst and disease. No Good Samaritans please, we're Christians. Then the ruling party rushed through a law that permitted Polish forces to push migrants back into Belarus, in contravention of European and international law. 'The guards were kicking people like footballs,' reported Dzhavad Asgari, a thirty-two-year-old lawyer who had fled from the Afghan capital of Kabul, together with his pregnant wife and five-year-old son.

The rest of the EU joined Poland in denouncing Lukashenko's action as a 'hybrid attack' and helped the country – and neighbouring Lithuania – secure the Union's eastern frontier. This was indeed a hybrid attack, aimed at harming the EU, but it was also a genuine humanitarian crisis – and one to which Europe and the United States had inadvertently contributed. Dzhavad Asgari was there only because the West's precipitate withdrawal from Afghanistan earlier in 2021 had brought the Taliban back to power in Kabul. Others on the Polish–Belarusian border were Kurdish refugees from the civil war in Syria, or from Iraq, a state torn apart by internecine strife following a Western military occupation in which European states, including Poland, had participated. Aka, a Kurd in his mid-twenties, summed up why they were risking their lives in the freezing dark of a primaeval forest in Europe's borderlands. 'It's Europe or death,' he said.

The Iron Curtain of the Cold War was a land frontier, dividing Europeans from other Europeans. This new one ran across water as well as land. The Mediterranean, once the Mare Nostrum uniting the Graeco-Roman world around its shores, now divided Europe from the Middle East and global South. On perilous crossings from Turkey to the Greek islands of Lesvos and Kos, or from Libya to the Italian island of Lampedusa, death came not by freezing in a forest or falling from a high fence but by drowning. According to the International Organization for Migration, more than 21,000 people drowned while trying to cross the Mediterranean between 2014 and 2021. We have transcripts of some of the desperate phone calls that migrants made as their flimsy vessels sank:

> 12.39: The boat is sinking. I swear to you, there's about two metres of water in the boat . . . My name is Mohammad Jamo. Call a doctor.
> 13.48: We are dying. 300 people are dying . . . My telephone credit is up. If you cut the connection, you have my number, please call me.

Mohammad Jamo was a Syrian doctor. He drowned with his two sons.

Although a central claim for Brexit was that it would enable Britain to control immigration, in 2021 an unprecedented number of people risked their lives to cross the Channel in flimsy boats. Many succeeded, but in the early hours of 24 November 2021 at least 27 men, women and children died when their narrow, unseaworthy rubber dinghy sank in a freezing sea. One of only two survivors of this tragedy was a twenty-one-year-old construction worker called Mohammed Sheka. Originally from the Kurdish region of Iran, his family had moved to Iraqi Kurdistan in search of work. With the aid of people smugglers, his migration odyssey had taken him from Iraq via Syria to Belarus, thence crossing the frontier to Poland, on through the open border to Germany and then France, in order to try his luck across the Channel. Despite his ordeal, he told his brother: 'I'm going to try again.'

'We are an example of Fortress Europe,' a Spanish journalist told me as we sat outside a nice bar in Ceuta's elegant central pedestrian zone, the frontier fence seeming almost as far away as the Wall once did to drinkers in the trendy bars of West Berlin. The fall of that Wall symbolised the highest hopes of Europe in our time. Young Europeans would come to regard freedom of movement as the defining achievement of post-Wall Europe. Yet three decades later, Europe was busy building new walls around its edges. For European citizens, Europe meant openness and freedom; for those outside, it meant long visa queues, high metal fences and death in a cruel sea.

The internal opening of Europe drove its external closing. While 'freedom of movement' in the technical sense of the freedom to work, study and live in another member state was secured by the treaties of the EU, the freedom to travel around the continent without frontier controls was provided by the Schengen area. Initiated in 1985 as an agreement between five founding members of the European Community – Germany, France and the Benelux countries – the Schengen area became fully operational only in the mid-1990s. Colloquially known as 'Schengenland', this was later joined by many southern, northern and east European member states, as well as non-EU members such as Switzerland and Norway. The first major external barriers to go up as a result of the Schengen opening of the internal ones were the metal fences around Ceuta and the other Spanish North African enclave of Melilla. Until then, the perimeter of Ceuta had frontier posts but no effective physical barrier. Construction of today's formidable modern fortification started in 2005, largely in response to increased immigration from sub-Saharan Africa.

The main wave of new European wall-building began later, with the 2015 refugee crisis. Hungary had pioneered the tearing down of the old Iron Curtain in 1989, the barbed wire fence at its frontier to Austria being symbolically cut with giant wire cutters by the two countries' foreign ministers. Now Viktor Orbán's Hungary pioneered the erection of a new Iron Curtain and other countries followed suit. At the time, I called this a 'reverse 1989'. In the 2018 Hungarian election campaign, an Orbán-supporting tabloid even put the famous giant wire cutters into a photomontage of George Soros and opposition leaders. So the wire cutters that had been the great symbol of liberation were now used to convey a fabricated threat of Jewish-facilitated Muslim invasion.

After the 2021 crisis, both Poland and Lithuania said they would build physical barriers on their frontier to Belarus, adding some 700 km to the new Iron Curtain. Yet these terrestrial walls were less than half the story. The EU of twenty-seven member states, after Brexit and before any further enlargement, had external land frontiers of more than 13,000 km, but its coastline, including all the Greek, Italian and other islands, exceeded 53,000 km, of which more than 31,000 km was in the Mediterranean. You could not build walls down the middle of the Mediterranean or the English Channel.

So what would Europe do? An important precedent was set in March 2016 when, on the eve of an EU summit, Angela Merkel and the Dutch prime minister Mark Rutte agreed with the Turkish prime minister Ahmet Davutoğlu that the EU would give Turkey €6 billion over six years to help it look after the millions of refugees it was already hosting – so long as the Turkish government would prevent any more of them from crossing to the nearby Greek islands. Together with the subsequent closure of borders along a land route through the Balkans, Merkel's Turkish deal ended the acute phase of the refugee crisis. But paying this enormous Danegeld to Turkey increased the temptation for other neighbours to try some migration blackmail, as we then saw in Ceuta and on the Belarusian frontier.

Most European governments were petrified that any new flare-up of illegal immigration would strengthen support for populist parties like Vox, which had flourished off the back of the refugee crisis. ('Wouldn't it be in your interest politically to have the frontier open in Ceuta?' I asked the sharp-nosed Redondo of Vox. 'Of course!' he replied, with a quick, cynical smile.) Ironically, European leaders now had to worry about the very thing they had worked for decades to enhance: Europe's attractiveness, its soft power. Yet they also wanted Europe to remain law-abiding, respectful of human rights and humane.

By the early 2020s, they seemed to have settled on an uncomfortable mix of measures. They would strongly urge refugees and migrants to use legal channels of asylum-seeking and immigration – although these were often not easily accessible and sometimes not available at all. They would step up intelligence and police operations to go after the people smugglers and strengthen the barriers on external land frontiers. The EU's own frontier control organisation, Frontex, was scheduled to expand to 10,000 employees, which would make it the largest EU agency. Beyond this, they would cajole, train, incentivise and simply pay neighbouring countries, as well as states closer to crisis-torn countries like Syria, to hold the refugees and migrants there. In Britain, Boris Johnson's government even announced a policy of deporting asylum-seekers to Rwanda, claiming this would deter people smugglers.

All this led Europe into extremely dubious moral territory. One of the basic principles of international refugee law is called non-refoulement. In plain English, this means that you must not send people back into danger. Yet there were multiple reports of Greek and other coastguards turning refugee boats back towards the shores from which they came, just as Polish frontier guards had pushed migrants back into the freezing forest on the Belarusian frontier. The EU also funded the Libyan coastguard and encouraged it to catch those who set out across the Mediterranean towards Europe, which they did in large numbers. But in the anarchy that followed the European-led military intervention to topple Muammar Gaddafi, much of Libya had fallen under the control of gangster warlords and militias. Many of the would-be migrants, along with others who never made it to the sea, were incarcerated in inhumane detention camps which recalled the camps of Europe during the Second World War. Overcrowding, disease, malnutrition, beatings and rapes – all were reliably reported by UN observers. Pope Francis called these Libyan detention camps 'places of ignoble torture and slavery'. So Europe was complicit in sending people back into danger.

To salve their consciences, Europeans blamed all the evils on criminal people smugglers, adding that Europe was always open to 'genuine refugees' but not to mere 'economic migrants'. These were inadequate half-truths. More co-ordinated European action was certainly needed to catch and punish the people smugglers who took thousands of euros off each individual, before sending many to their deaths. But so long as legal channels did not meet the demand for migration, there would always be a supply of illegal ones. That continuing demand resulted from the condition of the wider Middle East, exacerbated by the consequences of Western military interventions and the failure of the Arab Spring, but also from the existential misery of many in sub-Saharan Africa. Bad governance, civil wars, pandemics, rapid population growth and climate change would increase this misery.

Even if border forces did not physically turn migrants back, merely to leave them to the mercy of the high seas was to condemn some to death. Mohammed Sheka, the survivor of the November 2021 tragedy in the Channel, told a Kurdish news website that someone on the boat rang the French police, gave their location and was told: 'You're in British waters.' Someone else phoned the British side, he said, and was told: 'Call the French police.' And so most of them drowned. Their bodies were found close to the invisible maritime border between France and Britain. In autumn 2013, shocked by a migrant boat sinking off Lampedusa with the loss of at least 339 lives, Italy launched a large, effective search and rescue operation, fittingly called Mare Nostrum. It secured safe arrival for more than 150,000 migrants in one year. But in 2014 it was closed down and succeeded by more limited EU operations called first Triton and then Sophia. The inevitable result was that more people drowned, or were picked up by the Libyan coastguard and sent to those terrible camps. In 2019, under pressure from the Italian populist Matteo Salvini, the EU stopped all sea patrols in the central Mediterranean.

Occasionally, the bodies of the dead washed up on Europe's shores. In September 2015, photographs of the tiny body of a three-year-old Kurdish boy Alan Kurdi lying face down in shallow water on a beach near Bodrum in Turkey helped galvanise an initially generous response to the refugee crisis in countries such as Germany. Fifteen years earlier, the Spanish newspaper *La Vanguardia* had published a photo that was still more eloquent of Europe's moral quandary. It shows a young couple in swimsuit and bikini sitting under a floral umbrella, drinks cooler to hand, on a sunlit beach at Tarifa, an Andalusian coastal town just 13 km across the Straits of Gibraltar from the closest point in Morocco. The couple have their eyes turned towards a man dressed in jeans and yellow T-shirt who is lying motionless on the beach near them. Perhaps this is the exact moment the sunbathing couple realise this is not a drowsy fellow sunbather but the dead body of a migrant, washed up on the coast of Eutopia.

Does it matter whether the man in the yellow T-shirt was an 'economic migrant' or a 'genuine refugee'? The most remarkable sentence in the coalition agreement of the German government that took office in 2021 read simply: 'It is a civilisational and legal duty not to let human beings drown.'

In May 2016, less than a month before the Brexit vote, the *Daily Mail* ran a thundering headline: 'The Tragic but Brutal Truth: They Are Not Real Refugees! Despite Drowning Tragedy Thousands of Economic Migrants Are Still Trying to Reach Europe.' In fact, many of them were refugees according to the standard definition derived from the 1951 Geneva Convention on refugees: someone having a 'well-founded fear of being persecuted for reasons of race, religion, nationality, membership of a particular social group or political opinion'. On average, around fifty per cent of asylum requests in the UK in the late 2010s were granted. Most of the people coming across the Channel in small boats between 2018 and 2020 were from Iran, Iraq, Syria and Afghanistan, and the asylum approval rates for migrants from those countries were even higher. Millions of Ukrainians fled the war that engulfed their country in 2022 and no one doubted they were genuine refugees.

How sustainable anyway was that binary distinction, born of the circumstances of post-1945 Europe? Back then it seemed clear enough. The refugee – a Jewish Communist fleeing Nazi Germany or a bourgeois Christian fleeing the Soviet Union. The economic migrant – a poor farmer's son from Sicily or Ireland, seeking a better life in America. But now? We must surely accept that extreme poverty, disease and illiteracy in sub-Saharan Africa constitute constraints on individual liberty that can be every bit as life-deforming as political or religious persecution. There is a continuum, not a bright line, between the categories of refugee and migrant. In any case, with its rapidly ageing population, most of Europe needed more migrants to sustain its welfare states. At the beginning of the 2020s, Germany's economic need for immigrants was calculated at some 400,000 a year.

European reactions also varied according to the skin colour, religion and culture of the arrivals. There was a telling contrast between Poland and Hungary refusing to take in even a few thousand refugees from the Middle East in the refugee crisis and throwing open their doors to millions of white European refugees from Putin's war of terror in Ukraine. Yet what seems to have unsettled even unprejudiced Europeans most of all was a sense that immigration was uncontrolled. Hence the extreme reaction, swiftly translated into votes for populists, to photos of the crowd of refugees (or migrants, if you will) walking up train lines from the Balkans towards Germany, and those of the Moroccan crowd running towards that fence on the beach at Ceuta. Hence the impact of the Brexit slogan 'Take Back Control'.

In Ceuta, there are two enormous statues of Hercules, each of them standing between two pillars. The allusion is to the mythical 'pillars of Hercules', the rocky peaks of Calpe and Abyla which Hercules is said to have pushed apart to create a western opening from the Mediterranean to the unknown beyond. Calpe is generally identified with the Rock of Gibraltar and Ceutis see Abyla in their own Monte Hacho, although the nearby Moroccan peak of Jebel Musa also claims that ancient title. The statues, created by the Ceuta-born artist Ginés Serrán-Pagán, differ from each other in a thought-provoking way. The first, located on the waterfront downtown, shows a giant Hercules pushing two pillars apart, but the second, located at the entrance to the harbour, unconventionally shows Hercules pulling the two pillars together.

These statutes are a perfect metaphor for the twin Herculean tasks that Europe now faced. On the one hand, it did have to secure its external frontiers, and in that sense to keep Europe and the rest of the world apart. In theory, one might argue that liberal, open societies should have open borders. In practice, that would rapidly spell the end of liberalism in most such societies, especially those with a high standard of living and a generous welfare state. Just look how some two million unscheduled newcomers over the years 2015–16 – only 0.4 per cent of a (pre-Brexit) EU population of about 500 million – had catapulted xenophobic populists to unprecedented political heights and set European nations against each other. Europe could not be barrier-free both internally and externally. To ensure, without being radically inhumane, that more than 13,000 km of land border and 53,000 km of waterfront were secure was in itself already a Herculean task.

At the same time, Europe had to pull the pillars together. In its own self-interest, and to remain true to its professed values, it had to provide safe, legal routes for refugees – and migrants in extreme need – to seek a new life. The processing should be fair and swift, wherever it was done. Those who had no genuine case could legitimately be repatriated to countries where they were not at risk. Those who were accepted, however, should be given every opportunity, and active assistance, to integrate as full citizens in European societies.

Insecure frontiers contributed to inflammatory populist rhetoric about 'invaders', which in turn made the integration of people with a migration background, especially those of the Muslim faith, more difficult. That was a vicious spiral. But there was a potential benign cycle. As geographically blessed Canada showed, managed immigration and active integration could be mutually reinforcing. 'We can do it,' said Angela Merkel, trying to radiate Obama-like optimism. The intellectual and commercial history of Europe, as of North America, demonstrated the exceptional contributions that refugees from adversity could make to free societies. In the bright eyes of young Yahya, Ayman and Ilyas, sitting in the Ceuta refugee centre called Hope, I saw that possibility. But I glimpsed also the anger that could be unleashed if Europeans were foolish enough not to enable such newcomers to feel at home in Europe.

Beyond this, Serrán-Pagán's heroic image of Hercules pulling the pillars together evoked an even larger task. If the gulf between global North and South widened further as a result of climate change, population growth and bad governance, no defensive fortifications would suffice. Ever more people would clamber over those fences, however high, and launch themselves onto the high seas, however rough, crying 'Europe or death'. What would Europe do then? Build even higher walls? Add death strips? Just let them drown? Europe's own interests and values demanded that it strive to close the huge gap between North and South. That was the most Herculean task of all.

War in Ukraine

In an earlier draft of this book I asked: 'Are we fated to go all the way back?' I never imagined my question would be answered before I had finished the last chapter. After Vladimir Putin's armies invaded Ukraine on Thursday 24 February 2022, Europe went all the way back. On the very soil where the Wehrmacht and SS had waged a war of terror between 1941 and 1944, a war of terror was now prosecuted by Russian forces: indiscriminate shelling of cities, torture and execution of civilians, rape. The same cities, towns and villages suffered again, the same nation, sometimes even the same individual men and women.

Boris Romanchenko, a ninety-six-year-old Ukrainian who had survived four Nazi concentration camps, including Buchenwald and Bergen-Belsen, was killed by a Russian shell in his home city of Kharkiv. A Russian missile struck close to Babyn Yar, the site of a notorious Nazi mass murder of Jews. Ukrainian journalists reported that old people in villages around Kyiv referred to the Russian invaders as *nimtsi*. 'Germans'.

Once again, millions of innocent men, women and children had to flee their homes with 'just three suitcases'. Among the crowd of desperate mothers and screaming children trying to board a train at Kyiv's central station, Tanya Novgorodskaya, an art historian accompanied by her fifteen-year-old daughter, told the *Guardian* correspondent Shaun Walker: 'Look at these faces around us. They are exactly the same as in the photographs from the Second World War.' Nearly eight million Ukrainians were internally displaced; more than six million became refugees outside the country. They included numerous members of the country's Jewish community, some of whom found safe refuge in a very different Germany. Burnt-out tanks and armoured personnel carriers littered the roadside in half-destroyed villages – scenes from Normandy after D-Day. Mariupol, the port city on the Sea of Azov which Russia targeted to complete its 'land bridge' from Crimea to the Donbas, was so pulverised by Russian artillery that it looked like Warsaw in 1945, a city of ruins.

When Russian troops retreated from the Kyiv suburb of Bucha, the bodies of local residents were found sprawled on the streets with their hands tied behind their backs and gunshot holes in their skulls. Putin honoured the unit that was almost certainly responsible for these atrocities, the 64th Separate Guards Motor Rifle Brigade, as 'a role model in fulfilling its military duty, valour, dedication and professionalism'. There were numerous reported cases of rape and sexual violence. Amnesty International summarised the testimony of one woman in a village east of Kyiv: 'Two Russian soldiers had entered her house, killed her husband, then repeatedly raped her at gunpoint while her young son hid in a boiler room nearby.'

Draw a black-and-white filter across the colour photographs of these scenes, and you are in 1942, not 2022. But look more closely at a photograph of the corpse of a Ukrainian woman lying on a street in Irpin, another Russian-occupied suburb of Kyiv. What is that symbol on the fob of the key ring lying beside her? Restore the colour and you see it clearly: the yellow stars and blue background of the European flag.

For seventy-seven years since 1945, people had compared this or that European villain to Adolf Hitler. For seventy-seven years, this had been indefensible hyperbole. Even the genocidal war crimes in former Yugoslavia, although comparable in brutality to those of the Nazis, did not have the same scale or geopolitical implications. But now, for the first time, a comparison with Hitler seemed appropriate. There were not the gas chambers of extermination camps. There was not (yet) a world war directly involving the armed forces of multiple countries across the planet. But we Europeans had declared 'Never again!' and what we saw in Ukraine, after February 2022, was what was meant never to happen again.

Back in 1978, when I went to have lunch with the old British fascist Oswald Mosley in his Temple de la Gloire near Paris, I was convinced that fascism was finished, never to return. Fascism was a phenomenon of a particular epoch. But now a credible argument could be made that

Putin's regime was indeed fascist. There was the cult of a single leader, an aesthetic of martial violence and heroic death, the cultivation of a sense of historical resentment, the indoctrination of youth, ruthless persecution of dissenting minorities, an ideology of domination by one *Volk* over others, the demonisation of the enemy. In a long essay he published in summer 2021, Putin repeated his view that there was no separate Ukrainian nation. Ukrainians were just a version of Russians. Outside powers were trying to turn Ukraine into an 'anti-Moscow Russia'.

Of course there were novel elements in Putin's regime, and not all the features of 1930s fascism. But that's the case with all recurrent historical phenomena: nationalism, chauvinism and utopianism also never recur in exactly the same form. This was post-Soviet fascism for the internet age. Ukrainians called it 'ruscism'. The old East German political balladeer Wolf Biermann sardonically observed that 'Putin speaks truth: Ukraine *is* full of fascists – for the real fascists there are his Russian occupation armies.'

Central to both German fascism and Soviet communism was the big lie. Putin's big lie was to claim that it was his enemies who were the fascists. He said that Ukraine was run by neo-Nazis and the purpose of his war was to 'de-Nazify Ukraine'. Ukraine's Jewish president, Volodymyr Zelensky, replied: 'How can I be a Nazi? Tell that to my grandfather, who spent the whole war in the Soviet infantry.' In Kremlin usage, 'Nazi' became just a synonym for Ukrainians who opposed Russia's invasion or fell victim to its unguided missiles. When a Russian airstrike hit a concert hall in the central Ukrainian city of Vinnytsia, killing numerous civilians, the chief editor of the Kremlin-funded news channel RT, Margarita Simonyan, repeated a Russian defence ministry claim that the concert hall had housed a 'temporary Nazi deployment'. So the definition of a 'Nazi' was someone Russia had just killed. Ukrainian 'fascists' were whoever Russian fascists said they were. Orwellianism in our time.

Before 24 February, almost everybody outside Ukraine had believed that if Putin launched a full-scale invasion, his military victory would be swift, even if Russia then found the occupied country ungovernable. With an extraordinary feat of sustained military and civil resistance, Ukrainians proved almost everybody wrong. Once again, we saw the pivotal role of the individual in history. On the first day of the invasion, as Russian advance forces attempted to penetrate the Ukrainian president's compound in Kyiv, the United States offered to evacuate Zelensky. He refused. Whether or not he actually said 'I need ammunition, not a ride,' that widely reported response captured the impact of his decision to stay. The effect was electrifying, both abroad and at home. A frontline Ukrainian soldier would later tell the British journalist Lindsey Hilsum: 'Our president is still in Kyiv and it's like a beacon . . . that he's still here. President Biden said to him, we can take you from Ukraine, but he is still in Ukraine and he protects our land alongside us. . . . It makes us feel strong.'

When Russia's Black Sea flagship, the *Moskva*, ordered a small contingent of Ukrainians to surrender the tiny but strategically placed Snake Island, they replied: 'Russian warship, go fuck yourself'. Soon, that 'go fuck yourself' was seen on roadway signs and billboards all over the country. Meanwhile, the mighty *Moskva* was sunk by missiles fired from the Ukrainian shore. More than once, Ukrainian farmers towed away crippled Russian tanks with their tractors. The country's anti-corruption agency issued a tongue-in-cheek communiqué stating that captured Russian tanks need not be declared as assets.

The professional Ukrainian army, battle-hardened because it had been fighting Russian and Russian-backed separatist forces in eastern Ukraine since 2014, was supported by an entire society. The farming town of Voznesensk, for example, fought for two days and nights to prevent Russian forces getting a strategic bridgehead across the Southern Buh river, which would open the way westward towards Odesa. Professional soldiers blew up two bridges and fired British anti-tank missiles to cripple Russian tanks and armoured cars. Local construction workers blocked off streets, channelling the Russian advance towards the Ukrainian line of fire. Everyone else pitched in. 'We used hunting rifles,' said Alexander, a local shopkeeper. 'People threw bricks and jars. Old women loaded heavy sandbags.'

'They are big, but we are brave,' explained a Ukrainian MP, now wearing territorial defence force uniform. Russia's power was vertical but Ukraine's was horizontal. Ukrainians could draw on traditions of social co-operation and improvisation going all the way back to the seventeenth-century Cossacks, who fought on horseback for their right to govern themselves. If ever there was a 'people's war', this was it.

It may have looked like a mid-twentieth-century war, with tanks, heavy artillery and ruined cities, but it was also a twenty-first-century war, fought with drones, satellite imagery and cybertools. The fact that Russia had nuclear weapons – and Putin threatened the West with 'consequences you have never encountered in your history' – meant the United States and other Western powers calibrated the kinds of weapons they sent to Ukraine, aiming to avoid escalation to nuclear war. Ukraine had given up its nuclear weapons in 1994 in return for security assurances from Russia, the UK and the United States that had proved worthless. Countries around the world might reasonably draw this conclusion: 'If you have nuclear weapons, don't give them up; if you don't, try to acquire them.'

Beside the battles of weapons, technology and morale, there was a battle of narratives. With audiences in Europe and North America, Ukraine effortlessly won this contest. Zelensky had pursued a successful career as both actor and television producer before going into politics. He and his production team were expert at telling their story. Dressed not in a commander-in-chief's grand uniform but in plain military olive-green T-shirt, trousers and sneakers, an outfit skilfully suggestive of a people's self-defence army, Zelensky spoke punchily and passionately through video link to parliaments and international meetings around the world. Again and again, he asked European leaders for three things: more weapons, more sanctions on Russia and a path to EU membership. The prospect of joining Europe's liberal empire, instead of Russia's anti-liberal one, was that important to him and his compatriots. 'Do prove that you are indeed Europeans,' he admonished members of the European Parliament.

Outside the West, it was a different story. Not only did Xi Jinping's China, the world's new superpower, line up with Putin. The other members of the so-called BRICS group, Brazil, South Africa and India, sat on the fence or effectively sided with Russia. When food prices soared in the Middle East and Africa because Ukrainian and Russian grain exports had been halted by Putin's war, the West was blamed for prolonging the war and imposing sanctions. Russian foreign minister Sergey Lavrov was warmly received in several African countries. The West might celebrate the restored transatlantic unity of NATO – an alliance now joined, as a direct reaction to Putin's aggression, by formerly neutral Sweden and Finland – but the global balance was much less favourable.

In this book, I set out to cover the 'overlapping timeframes of post-war and post-Wall'. There are important ways in which both periods may be said to end in 2022, with the beginning of the Russo-Ukrainian war.

First, post-Wall. Recall the finale of the Cold War. All the way from spring 1989, through the fall of the Wall in November 1989 and until the final collapse of the Soviet Union at the end of 1991, we feared the violent reaction of an authoritarian imperial centre that was losing its empire. That reaction came in August 1991, with a putsch against Gorbachev which, had it succeeded, would have ushered in a very different post-Wall period. Instead, the failed putsch only hastened the end of the Soviet Union. The last major empire in Europe seemed to have softly and suddenly vanished away. Lulled into a false sense of security, we came to regard a post-imperial and even post-national politics of peaceful international co-operation and globalised economic interdependence as the new normal.

Yet the old normal of nations and empires pursuing their ends through all available means never went away – and certainly not from the mind of Vladimir Putin. His yearning to restore a lost Russian greatness, which I glimpsed in St Petersburg already in 1994, was translated into military action, first in Chechnya, then in Georgia in 2008, and most consequentially in Ukraine from 2014 onwards, with the annexation of Crimea – the turning point at which the West failed to turn – followed by an ongoing war in the Donbas. Partly because the West failed to turn, what had miraculously *not* happened in 1989–91 happened in 2022: the empire struck back with all the force at its disposal. Recalling the 'unbelievably peaceful' end of communism in 1989, Wolf Biermann commented, 'Now, thirty years later, comes the reckoning.' In this sense, the war in Ukraine can be described as the end of the post-Wall period and its illusions.

The story of the post-war period is more complicated. For the European state system, the post-war period ended in 1990–91, with the treaty settlements at the end of the Cold War. Yet what happened then was not the creation of a set of entirely new institutions but an enlargement of the existing West, extending its post-1945 institutions eastwards. Many of today's key organisations, such as NATO, the European Economic Community that became the EU, the World Bank and the International Monetary Fund, not to mention the United Nations, trace their origins to the aftermath of the Second World War. In that sense, we still live in the post-war world, although these Western institutions are increasingly challenged by powers such as China, Russia and India.

There is, however, an important sense in which the post-war time-frame, like the post-Wall one, came to a close in 2022. When Tony Judt called his seminal history of post-1945 Europe *Postwar*, his title had both an obvious and a less obvious meaning. Obviously, it meant after the war. Less obviously, it meant after war. Crying 'Never again!', Europe now defined itself against its own multi-millennial history of armed conflict and resolved to remain at peace. The anti-war generation of 68ers and post-68ers, politically ascendant in the post-Wall period, was even more determined than the 39ers and post-39ers had been to keep our continent that way.

That post-war Europe abjured and abhorred war would have been surprising news to the many parts of the world, from Vietnam to Kenya and Angola to Algeria, where European states continued to fight brutal wars in an attempt to hang on to their colonies. It would also have been news to Hungarians during the Soviet invasion in 1956, Czechs and Slovaks in 1968, and the peoples of former Yugoslavia in the 1990s. But by the early 2000s, many Europeans thought they were finally approaching Immanuel Kant's dream of perpetual peace.

Most European countries took a handsome 'peace dividend' after the end of the Cold War, cut their defence spending to below NATO's target of two per cent of GDP, ran down their supplies of weapons and ammunition, and reconfigured their forces to face threats from 'non-state actors'. After all, no one in Europe was going to start a major inter-state war, were they? Much of Europe, and especially its central power, Germany, became heavily dependent on Russian gas and oil. Economic interdependence would only reinforce peace, wouldn't it? Few recalled an old Russian proverb: 'Perpetual peace lasts until the next war.'

Now war was back. As I took the newly built underground railway connection from Unter den Linden to the Federal Chancellery in central

Berlin in July 2022, passing under the line of the former Wall, a news-flash on a screen in the carriage showed tanks and heavy artillery fire in Ukraine. It looked like a scene from the Second World War. Chancellor Olaf Scholz called 24 February 2022 a *Zeitenwende*, an epochal turning point, and announced a big increase in German defence spending. With sustained expenditure of two per cent of its GDP, Germany would have the third-largest defence budget in the world.

Most other European countries also promised to increase their defence spending. Poland declared an ambition to have the largest army in the European Union. The EU itself spent billions of euros from a so-called European Peace Facility on ammunition and arms for Ukraine. Shedding the illusions of the post-Wall period, this 'peace project' recognised that military power would be needed to restore and keep that peace. As previously neutral Finland and Sweden hurried to enter NATO, the EU and NATO were linked more closely than ever before. Ukraine, Moldova and Georgia joined the countries of the western Balkans as candidates for the embrace of these two strong arms of the geopolitical West.

I travelled to Ukraine four times in the first year and a half of what Ukrainians always carefully called 'the *full-scale* war'. In Bucha – that near-rhyme for 'butcher' – I met a woman whose nephew had been murdered by Russian forces simply because he had some photos of destroyed Russian tanks on his phone. In Irpin, I saw the ruins of a Ukrainian cultural centre that had been deliberately targeted by the Russian occupiers, and in Borodyanka, a statue of Ukraine's great nineteenth-century poet, Taras Shevchenko, shot several times through his large metal head by Russian soldiers. Ukraine was not just to be reincorporated into the Russian empire; its culture and identity were to be destroyed. Thousands of Ukrainian children were separated from their parents and forcibly deported to Russia, where they would be raised as Russians. In March 2023, the International Criminal Court issued an arrest warrant for Vladimir Putin, holding him directly responsible for this war crime. 'We cannot allow children to be treated as the spoils of war,' the court's prosecutor explained.

But Ukraine would not be brought low. Tetiana, a young activist I met in the western Ukrainian city of Lviv, worked part-time as a tattoo-ist. She told me that people often asked for tattoos of the Ukrainian flag or the country's trident symbol, but since the full-scale invasion one of the most popular was the single word *volia*. A rallying cry in Ukrainians' struggle to be masters of their own fate ever since Shevchenko's time, *volia* means freedom, but also the will to fight for it.

The courage to live and die for liberty was most obviously apparent in the men and women of the Ukrainian armed forces. Take Yevhen Hulevych, for example, a tall, lean, fine-featured man whom I met over an evening drink in early December 2022. An editor, philosopher and essayist, he had started to help refugees from eastern Ukraine imme-diately after the invasion but soon concluded that this volunteer work 'was not enough for me'. Despite being in his mid-forties, Yevhen signed up for active service, was trained as a machine gunner, and fought for many months in the grinding ground campaign to recapture the city of Kherson. He lived much of the time in foxholes that he himself dug out with a spade. This usually took between thirty minutes and an hour, he told me. You had to be quick; your life depended on it.

As we sat in the elegant Grand Café Leopolis in the heart of beauti-ful Lviv, he showed me the line of their slow advance on the map appli-cation on his phone. He singled out a particularly bloody spot where he remembered strangely shaped acacia trees. In one action, two-thirds of his company had been injured: 'also the fields and trees are wounded'. When he finally caught a bullet himself, he was sent to a hospital in Odesa, but as soon as he recovered he went back to the front. The more combat experience you have, he explained, the greater your value as a soldier. His younger comrades had need of him.

In October 2022, he was wounded again, in the back and legs, and crawled 700 metres in extreme pain – dragging his precious weapon with him – before reaching a point from which he could be evacuated. Now, two months later, he was determined to return to the front yet again: 'I have this feeling that I haven't finished my job.' We talked at length about death. He had seen many dead bodies at the front, he said, and after a time 'you get accustomed to the prospect of death, you're less afraid of dying'. Yevhen told his story in an unnerving, quiet monotone, as if all the emotion had been burned out of him by months of shellfire.

His eyes, too, were strangely expressionless. But with a rare flicker of visible feeling he added 'I really want to see if I will be lucky . . . to see what this country will be like after the war.'

This conversation made a deep impression on me and I wrote about it in the *New York Review of Books*. Responding to that essay, a novelist in Lviv emailed me to say that Yevhen had been killed on New Year's Eve, just twenty-three days after we spoke, in the murderous fighting around Bakhmut. He would never see what his country would be like after the war. 'You know, it really is our best people who are dying,' reflected the indomitable investigative journalist Nataliya Gumenyuk, as we talked over lunch in Kyiv. The bravest and the best.

Visiting Lviv's military cemetery, which is called the Field of Mars, on that visit in December 2022, I had walked up a gentle slope through a small forest of new graves, each bedecked with flowers, flags and a photograph of the dead soldier. At the top of the slope there were fresh rectangular holes dug in the frozen earth, awaiting the next of the fallen. When I returned ten months later, there was a second forest on the other side of the path. Already there were 520 fallen from this one city, including three women, all medics. I laid flowers on the grave of Yevhen Hulevych.

According to American estimates, Ukraine, a country of fewer than 40 million people, suffered more than 70,000 war-related fatalities in just a year and a half. In an opinion poll conducted in summer 2023, four out of every five Ukrainians said someone among their close family and friends had been killed or injured.

At Lviv's 'Unbroken' rehabilitation centre in autumn 2023, I talked to wounded soldiers. In every corridor, men without a leg, an arm, a foot, waited for the artificial limbs being crafted in a workshop downstairs. Maksym, a career soldier and specialist sniper, had lost most of his foot to a hidden mine in what was supposed to be a cleared minefield on the southern front. He was determined to rejoin his unit: 'they're waiting, my people'. But he offered a sober first-hand assessment of how difficult it would be to get the Russian-occupied territories back. The Russian defensive lines were formidable and 'the Russians have more men'. Only the fall of Putin would end this for good.

Vasyl, a burly, tattooed front-line infantry commander and part-time boxer, had recently lost a leg to a mine on the eastern front, in Kupiansk. He told me he had been inside the Russian trenches 'about fifty times'. His T-shirt proclaimed: 'No sacrifice, no victory'. He, too, wanted to rejoin his comrades, although he did reluctantly acknowledge that with an artificial leg he would no longer be storming into the Russian trenches. I asked him what was needed to achieve Ukrainian victory, expecting an answer about arms supplies from the West, but he replied with just two words: 'motivated people'. Did Ukraine have enough of them? He worried about that. After we shook hands and I wished him luck, he suddenly jumped from the treatment table on which he had been sitting and started skipping incredibly fast, his blue skipping rope whizzing around under his single foot. As he did so, he looked at me with a broad grin on his face, as if to say, 'here's your answer'.

The seafaring ancient Greeks were well acquainted with the shores of what is today Ukraine. Myth had it that the spirit of Achilles went to live on what is now Snake Island but is marked on a sixteenth-century map I have at home as Achilles Island. While Achilles might not quite have said to his Trojan adversary, 'Hector, go fuck yourself!', there's little doubt that his spirit was there with the defenders of Ukraine. In the mud-filled trenches around Bakhmut, so uncannily reminiscent of those in the 1917 battle of Passchendaele, soldiers like Yevhen might have repeated the words of the British First World War poet Patrick Shaw-Stewart:

> Stand in the trench, Achilles,
> Flame-capped, and shout for me.

Ukrainians routinely referred to their soldiers as 'warriors'. The ritual response to the patriotic incantation 'Glory to Ukraine!' was 'To the Heroes, Glory!'.

It was not just those bearing arms who exhibited such a will to fight for freedom, such *volia*. An entire society was mobilised in this war. Far from the front line, I watched a group of volunteers making improvised paraffin candles for the troops. Take an empty metal food can. Cut and roll up a narrow double-strip of corrugated cardboard to fit neatly inside. Insert two small rectangles of cardboard as wicks. Dig some white paraffin powder from a sack, melt in a saucepan over an electric ring and pour carefully over the cardboard in the can. Send to our boys in the east. Iryna, in everyday life a sales assistant in a shoe shop, was an especially quick and dexterous maker of these trench candles, which gave both light and heat. On her phone, she showed me a video of one flickering in the trenches, sent by a grateful soldier. Everyone I encountered seemed to be doing something: sending food, clothes or equipment, helping internally displaced people or travelling to the battle zones in the east and south to rescue the old and sick from villages in the line of fire.

I sought out refugees from the pulverised city of Mariupol. Tetiana, a sturdy, middle-aged city official, told me through repeated bursts of tears how her best friend, Luda, had been killed, together with a soldier son, by a Russian missile hitting their ninth-floor apartment. 'Their screams were heard for hours, but no one could help.'

Sitting opposite me in a coffee shop, Dmitry described how, when he was just seventeen, his childhood world had fallen apart as Russian forces took Mariupol. Suddenly, his family had no electricity, heating or running water. They hunted for firewood in nearby spinneys, cooked what little food they could find over an open fire and washed in puddles. He saw a mother and child lying dead on the ground, a man who had lost a leg, a father burying his own child in the yard. Now a first-year student at the Taras Shevchenko National University in Kyiv, Dmitry took pains to tell his story precisely, without exaggeration. If he lives to be ninety, he will still remember his youthful experience of war, as those sturdy old farmers in Westen and Przysieczyn always remembered theirs. That will be 2095. The memory engine again.

Dmitry's family was Russian-speaking. His uncle was a Russian citizen who lived in the city of Stavropol. He used to come visiting every year. When these horrors started to unfold, they messaged this uncle to tell him what was happening. They even sent photographs. His response: 'It's not true.' He denied it all, and then went silent. Since then, no contact. What future was there, I asked Dmitry, for Ukraine's relations with Russia? 'No future.'

Utter rejection of all things Russian was now to be heard from every Ukrainian. According to regular opinion polling conducted by the Kyiv International Institute of Sociology, in May 2013 some eighty per cent of Ukrainians still had a positive attitude towards Russia; by May 2022 that figure was down to two per cent. I lost count of the number of people who told me they could no longer bear to read or speak Russian. 'My mother tongue tastes like ashes,' wrote the Ukrainian scholar Sasha Dovzhyk. An academic mentioned to me that his students now wrote 'russia' and 'russian' with a small r. 'I don't correct them.'

In the Syayvo ('Radiance') bookshop in central Kyiv, the staff collected Russian-language books to be recycled, with the proceeds going to the Ukrainian army. Lydia, a young English-speaking shop assistant, told me that in less than nine months they had pulped more than 111,000 books and purchased a military support vehicle which grateful soldiers called the Syayvomobile. In the cellar, she showed me a large pile of neatly bundled books, including Dostoevsky's *The Brothers Karamazov* and a Russian-language edition of Kafka, waiting to be destroyed. While I was there, a man wandered in with a couple of new bundles and asked diffidently, 'Could you take fifty-five volumes of Lenin?' Of course!

Nearby, Pushkin Street had been renamed after an early twentieth-century champion of Ukrainian nationhood, Yevhen Chykalenko. 'Surely Pushkin is not to blame for Putin!' horrified booklovers around the world might exclaim. For Ukrainians, however, engaged in an existential struggle for their independence against Russia's war of recolonisation, Pushkin was a symbol of the imperialism that had long denied Ukraine's right to a separate national existence. And Putin's Russia made this connection explicit. When Russian forces occupied Kherson, billboards featuring the great Russian poet were deployed in a propaganda campaign that proclaimed Russia was 'here for ever'. Small wonder some Ukrainians now referred on social media to 'Pushkinists' launching missile attacks on their cities. For example: 'Pushkinists didn't allow us to sleep properly – it was very loud in Kyiv.' So it was Putin who had done for Pushkin.

As Ukrainians saw it, they had now embarked on deep decolonisation. The country wanted to get out from under the Russian bear, once and for all, as far away as possible from everything Russian – and as close as possible to everything European.

Every second word in Ukraine was now 'Europe'. 'Europe' resounded from President Zelensky, in countless meetings with visiting European leaders; from foreign minister Dmytro Kuleba, who explained to me, as we sat in the heavily sandbagged foreign ministry in Kyiv, why the EU is a 'liberal empire'; from Olha Stefanishyna, the supremely competent and confident thirty-seven-year-old minister for Euro-Atlantic integration; and from Lydia, the Syayvo shop assistant, who told me she wanted to make their bookshop more 'European-like', which she explained as 'beautiful, interesting and cool'. If Russia – or 'russia' – had become a word of hate, Europe was the word of hope. Here, as in Spain, Portugal and Greece in the 1970s, as in Poland, Czechoslovakia and Hungary in the 1980s, as in the Baltic states in the 1990s, as in south-eastern Europe after the wars in former Yugoslavia, I saw the dreams of Europe and freedom marching together, arm in arm.

2022 was to Ukraine what 1940 was to Britain: a moment of national peril and trauma, but also of unity, courage and resolution. A year that would define the nation, to itself and to the rest of the world, for generations to come. Young Tetiana, the activist and tattooist, told me that when she had travelled abroad previously, she had been shocked to discover that foreigners 'thought Ukraine is, like, part of Russia'. But now 'finally, the world finds out what Ukraine is'.

In the autumn of 2023, after more than 600 days of the largest war in Europe since 1945, there was still no end in sight. No one knew when Ukraine's new 'year zero' would be. No one could credibly predict the final shape – economic, political, military, territorial, demographic – in which the country would emerge from such a terrible conflict. The European Union had accepted Ukraine as a candidate for membership and it was now unthinkable that NATO would simply let it be gobbled up by Russian aggression. But as other east European countries could testify, that yearned-for integration into the Euro-Atlantic West could still prove a long, slow and uncertain process. This much, however, was clear: with their *volia*, Ukrainians were writing an extraordinary new chapter of European history. Everyone now knew Ukraine.

Delphi

I treasure a photograph of my wife, Danuta, whispering an existential question into the ear of an ancient stone on the slopes of Mount Parnassus, one sunny day in 2018. She is consulting the oracle at Delphi. Half of the large rectangular stone has three holes arranged in a triangle, as for the legs of a tripod, and the other half has a larger hole cut right through it. We had just been told by our guide that the Pythia, the woman who was the voice of the oracle, sat on that tripod while intoxicating vapours came up through the larger hole, inspiring her to utter words that were thought to come directly from Apollo. These ecstatic utterances were written down and interpreted by a priest sitting nearby. Since the priests at Delphi had long experience of being consulted by individuals and governments from all over the Mediterranean world, the priestly interpreter doubtless infused some of his own worldly wisdom into the finished oracular judgement.

On further investigation, it turns out that the holes and grooves in the stone to which Danuta whispered her question were probably made much later, to convert it into an olive press. But the rest is mostly true. Although a verified tripod base and vapour hole have never been found, recent research shows that the local geology would encourage gases to seep up through the fissured bedrock, and traces of ethylene, a gas that can induce a trancelike state, have been detected. So the Pythia may well have been high.

For more than ten centuries, people came to consult the oracle here, endowing the hillside sanctuary with precious gifts – altars, statues, sacred vessels, small temples – arranged along the zigzag Sacred Way up to the temple of Apollo, where the Pythia spoke and priests interpreted.

Viewing the still impressive remains, set against the magnificent green and grey backdrop of Mount Parnassus, you need only a little imagination to recreate the scene at ancient Delphi.

Here, for example, comes the fabulously rich King Croesus of Lydia, sometime around 580 BCE. He has prepared the way with lavish offerings including a mighty gold statue of a lion, a gold statue of a woman and ceremonial vessels wrought in both gold and silver. He asks with unusual directness – for questions to the oracle were traditionally more exploratory – whether he would win if he waged war against King Cyrus of Persia. The oracle responds: 'Croesus, having crossed the Halys, will destroy a great empire.' Taking that as a yes, Croesus crossed the river Halys and destroyed a great empire – his own. (The Halys is today's Kizilirmak river in central Turkey.) Later, he despatched chains symbolising his new servitude under Cyrus of Persia to the oracle at Delphi and complained about its bad advice. According to Herodotus, the oracle tartly replied that Croesus 'did not understand what was spoken or make further enquiry: for which now let him blame himself'.

Delphi carried on even after Christianity became the official religion of the Roman Empire in the fourth century CE, but by the seventh century the sanctuary had fallen into disuse. Landslides partly covered its glorious monuments and a humble agricultural village called Castri was built on top of it, using some of the ancient stones. For more than a thousand years, the oracle slumbered underground. Only at the end of the nineteenth century was the village moved to a nearby location so that excavations could gradually reveal this wonderful corner of Europe's kaleidotapestry.

But the yearning to know the future never died. The rich and powerful consulted the entrails of sacrificed animals, palm lines in the human hand, tea leaves, predictive almanacs and the alignments of the stars. They sought advice from astrologers, high priests, mystics, shamans and economists. The fourteenth Dalai Lama fled Tibet in 1959 on the advice of the Tibetan State Oracle. Contemporary Europeans often liked to regard themselves as rational heirs of the Enlightenment, but in one survey more than fifty per cent of respondents in France, Germany and Britain said they took astrology seriously. Economists were professionally ennobled with the creation of a new Nobel Prize in 1969, almost as if they were scientists in the way that physicists and chemists are scientists. Historians, too, were invited to tell the future.

And this is how, in 2018, Danuta and I came to be at Delphi, participating in the Delphi Economic Forum. This is a kind of Hellenic mini-Davos at which economists, political scientists and other experts are asked to help politicians and business leaders make smart choices for the future. So far as I can recall, no one predicted – even delphically – that the world would soon be in the grip of a pandemic, let alone that we would have a major war in Europe within four years.

Our deep human desire to anticipate the future has aspects of both folly and wisdom. It is folly to imagine we can know what will happen tomorrow, let alone farther into the future. It is wisdom to try to make the most informed, intelligent guesses possible about the challenges we are likely to face, in order to prepare for them. Immanuel Kant describes the faculty of foresight as 'of greater interest than anything else because it is a condition of all possible practice and all possible purposes to which human beings relate the use of their powers'. Political scientists, economists, risk analysts, commentators and historians can all contribute to this foresight – so long as they recognise the limits of their crafts.

In some fields, such as physics and weather forecasting, prediction has become more accurate, but on the larger canvas of human affairs it has become more difficult. The complexity of our globalised, hyper-connected world means that an unprecedented variety of factors and events, some of them seemingly small, can rapidly have a large impact on the other side of the globe. A new virus emerges in China, for example, and soon we have a pandemic sending most of Europe into lockdown.

The coronavirus pandemic that swept across our continent in the spring of 2020 has been characterised as a 'grey swan' event – long regarded by experts as probable but still a complete shock when it came. A 2004 US National Intelligence Council assessment judged that 'it is only a matter of time before a new pandemic appears, such as the 1918–19 influenza virus that killed an estimated twenty million worldwide' and this could 'put a halt to global travel and trade during an extended period'. Other experts issued similar warnings. The wisdom that should flow from such warnings does not consist in trying to predict the exact nature, time and place of an event, which is impossible, but in making better contingency plans.

By 2020, freedom of movement across the continent had become one of the defining features of being European. That was the promise of the maroon passport common to all EU member states. Overnight, with the arrival of Covid, this freedom was gone. Ever since I turned eighteen in 1973, there had not been a single year when I did not travel on the continent. Now it was a full year and a half before I would once again set foot in my other homelands. When I did, the combination of Covid and Brexit made travelling to the continent more like my stressful experience in 1969 than the blithe freedom of 2019. Entry restrictions, Covid test certificates, multiple forms, border control stamps once again filling up the pages of my once again dark blue British passport.

For me, working from home like so many others, Covid lockdown had the advantage that I could get on with writing this book, surrounded by stacks of other books about Europe piled high on the floor of a spare bedroom. For millions of less privileged Europeans, it was a different story. Death, bereavement and long Covid were accompanied by bankruptcy, unemployment and loss of schooling. Demographers may someday identify a Generation C whose lives were permanently changed by the pandemic.

You have to go back a long way, perhaps as far as 1945, to find an event that was directly experienced by so many Europeans at the same time. Even the fall of the Berlin Wall was not a direct personal experience for most Europeans. Yet the first response to this pan-European event was that Europeans turned to their national governments, with different national responses and the return of hard national frontiers. On 15 March 2020, Germany announced that it would unilaterally close its borders to France, Austria, Switzerland, Denmark and Luxembourg the next morning. 'Goodbye Schengen' declared an Italian newspaper. Initially, the EU was almost invisible. The European Commission's first tender for personal protection equipment received not a single application. Meanwhile, China was sending face masks to Italy, Serbia and several other European countries.

Four months later, however, Europe was back, with an agreement to disburse a total of €750 billion to help EU member states recover from the economic consequences of the pandemic. At a stroke, Germany and other north European creditor nations broke not just one but two of their long-standing eurozone taboos. Roughly half the money would take the form of grants, not loans, and the funds for this package would be raised on the money markets as shared European debt. The significance of this breakthrough lay particularly in what it promised to the hard-pressed economies of southern Europe, which had suffered inside the eurozone.

Most spectacularly, Mario Draghi, the saviour of the euro a decade before, would now, as Italian prime minister, have some €200 billion to spend on a recovery that was also supposed to make the Italian economy more productive and more green. By the autumn of 2022, however, Italy's right-wing populists were in power and the future of that transformative recovery was in question. It was important for the whole continent that a founding member of the EU, with its third-largest economy and Europe's 'eternal city' of Rome, should see a strong economic and political future for itself at the heart of the Union. But that was uncertain, as the future always is.

In an essay on 'The Unknown Future and the Art of Prognosis', the historian Reinhart Koselleck suggests that the more our historically informed foresight can draw on *recurrent* experience, the more accurate it is likely to be. Thus the prediction 'you will die' is one hundred per cent accurate. In a vast historical dataset, there are no examples to the contrary. Koselleck also argues that proverbs are repositories of accumulated wisdom, not to be lightly dismissed. Take 'pride comes before a fall', for example: so true of Europe, of the entire West, in the Croesus-like hubris of its financialised globalised capitalism in the early 2000s.

Then there are recurrent phenomena such as wars, revolutions, empires and indeed pandemics, of which we have sufficient historical instances to detect typical patterns and make careful statements about probabilities. To view the Soviet bloc in the 1980s as an empire, for example, rather than as something entirely new, was to recognise an empire in decay and know that decaying empires eventually fall. We could not predict when it would fall, but we could see where it was headed.

This kind of historically informed guesswork, based on the careful study of repeated experience, is doubly useful when the findings are shared, reflected upon and vigorously debated. The classical scholar Michael Scott argues that this is how the oracle at Delphi helped decision-makers in the ancient world. The very process of making your way to the slopes of Parnassus, waiting your turn with others who faced similar dilemmas and then consulting the Pythia gave people an opportunity to reflect. The oracular judgements, with all their ambiguities, were carried back and debated in what, at least in city-states such as fifth century BCE Athens, was a genuine process of deliberative democracy. Only then was a course of action decided upon. Decision-makers, if they were wise, would revise this policy as they went along, monitoring its efficacy and taking account of new circumstances as they arose.

Ancient wisdom – and still wise today. It was not wrong, after the collapse of the Soviet Union in 1991, to seek a strategic partnership with Russia, invest in helping the country to modernise, bring it into the G7 group of advanced industrial countries and try to enhance European security through pan-European organisations like the OSCE and a NATO–Russia partnership. But, alert to recurrent historical patterns of imperial and post-imperial behaviour, we should have foreseen that, after a centuries-old empire had collapsed in just three years with hardly a shot fired in anger, there was likely, sooner or later, to be a reaction from the former colonial power. When the violent backlash started, in Georgia in 2008 and, at the latest, with the seizure of Crimea and the start of an ongoing war in eastern Ukraine in 2014, we should have made a stronger response, reduced our energy dependence on Russia, and anticipated worse to come. We could not predict exactly what Putin would do, nor when he would do it. He did not know himself. But if we had learned from the history of empires, we would have been better prepared to meet the challenge of his invasion of Ukraine in 2022.

So what should we anticipate and prepare for now? Europe has descended from one crisis to another since 2008. As I write, nobody knows whether that trend will continue. But the descent started from a high place and much of the post-war and post-Wall European achievement endures. If you're a citizen of the European Union today, with enough money to travel, you can wake up on a Friday morning and decide to take a budget airline flight to the other end of the continent, without needing a visa, a passport, or to change currency. If you fall in love with the place, or with someone you meet, you can settle down to live, work or study there. From Helsinki to Athens and Tallinn to Lisbon, you'll find yourself in the largest area of relative freedom, prosperity and security achieved in European history. This is not yet 'Europe whole and free', but it's closer to that goal than our continent has ever come before. If we simply manage to defend and extend this achievement for another few decades, we will be doing very well.

Yet the challenges inside and all around Europe are daunting. The wonderful European freedom I've just evoked is not enjoyed by many millions of people inside the EU who face poverty and social exclusion or belong to oppressed minorities. In several countries, the integration of people with a migration background is not going well. The worldwide economic disruption caused by the Covid pandemic has been redoubled by the impact of the war in Ukraine. Inflation is back with a vengeance. Levels of public and private debt have soared. Recession looms. The eurozone may again be tested. Such bad times can be good for populists. Hungary is no longer a democracy. Poland's democracy is seriously threatened.

That's before we even get to the large parts of Europe that are not in this Union – places where some 400 million Europeans live, if we use the broad definition of Europe I suggested at the beginning of this book, compared with some 450 million inside the EU. Post-Brexit Britain is still far away from a constructive new relationship with the continental commonwealth. People in Kosovo, Bosnia and Serbia still don't know whether the Union really wants them. Ukraine is at war, Moldova and Georgia threatened, Belarus bleak. Putin's Russia is a fascist dictatorship. Turkey suffers under an authoritarian regime which condemns even peaceful, moderate civil society activists to long jail terms.

Europe doesn't end at any clear line; it merely fades away across the Mediterranean, Eurasia and even, in an important sense, across the Atlantic. (Canada would be a perfect EU member.) Over the next decades, what Europe does at its periphery will be as important as anything at its core. In the Middle East, the promise of the Arab Spring has long since given way to renewed authoritarian rule. Even in Tunisia, the last surviving flowers of that spring seem to be withering. How things look to young Moroccans, I learned in Ceuta.

Pressing in on Europe and our troubled neighbourhood are large forces, such as demography, climate and technology, and great powers, old and new. When I started travelling around Europe just over fifty years ago, the world's population was less than four billion. Now it's more than eight billion. Africa's population is projected to double again by 2050, adding another 1.2 billion people. What can we Europeans do to enable a sustainable, let alone a dignified life for all these men, women and children on earth? Or shall we simply surround our continent with a new Iron Curtain, salve our consciences by giving less than one per cent of our GDP in development aid, and turn Europe into a fortress of the privileged? That's the direction Europe is heading at the moment, but it seems to me neither morally tolerable nor politically feasible.

Climate change knows no frontiers. Over the last fifty years, the earth's temperature has increased by about 0.5 degrees – more than in the entire 11,000 years from the end of the last ice age until 1900. The climate emergency is the great political cause for Europe's post-89er generation; not to have addressed global warming when it would have been easier do so is the greatest failure of my generation. Are today's democracies capable of making the necessary radical and rapid changes? In a 2020 survey, fifty-three per cent of young Europeans said they think authoritarian states are better equipped than democracies to tackle the climate crisis.

Or will technology come to the rescue? This same half-century has seen one of the most extraordinary technological leaps in history. If you plucked someone straight from the early 1970s into today's world, put into their hands the magic box we now call simply 'my phone' and showed them everything it can do, they would think this was science fiction. But technological advance is often double-edged. The internet has given us unparalleled access to the world's knowledge; it has also facilitated a poisonous politics of disinformation and tribalism. Artificial intelligence will do some wonderful things, but some experts think it could become an existential threat to humankind. It may well increase the danger of war, allowing the development of weapons whose inner functioning even those who supposedly control them do not fully understand, let alone their adversaries, be it the United States looking at China or vice versa.

This matters because these large forces will play out in a world of sharp competition between great powers. In the early 2000s, many Europeans (and some Americans) believed that late-twentieth-century Europe might pre-figure the future of the world: post-national, economically interdependent, co-operative, law-abiding, peaceful. In the 2020s, the world seems more likely to resemble late-nineteenth-century Europe, full of suspicious, mutually antagonistic great powers that see war as the continuation of politics by other means. Increasingly, the shots will be called by non-Western powers.

The story of Europe I've told in this book would have been impossible without the massive post-1945 contribution of the United States. Yet hubris at home and abroad has done terrible harm to the 'land of the free'. With the storming of the US Capitol on 6 January 2021, we saw a violent attempt to subvert the result of a free and fair election. Europeans must hope that the United States recovers as it did after Watergate and Vietnam, but we will not be able to rely on it as much as we could, for the most part, in the post-war and post-Wall periods.

For as long as Vladimir Putin is in the Kremlin, we shall have to deal with an aggressive, ruthless Russia. Strategically, the bigger challenge is China. We may not like its model of developmental authoritarianism, an unprecedented amalgam of Leninism and capitalism, but it looks quite attractive to many in the global South. China already leverages its wealth into significant influence inside Europe, especially in southeastern Europe. Meanwhile, Xi Jinping hungrily eyes Taiwan, as Putin eyed Crimea. Sober analysts put a high probability on some kind of military confrontation between the United States and China over Taiwan within the next five years.

What about the non-Western democracies in which I placed such hopes in my 2004 vision of a free world, and in which President Joe Biden apparently still places some of his? Surely we can look to India, the world's largest democracy, to Brazil and to South Africa? But as those three countries' active or passive support for Russia during the Ukraine war has shown, we can't assume states will line up with the West just because they are democracies. There are specific reasons in each country, but common to most of them is the historical memory, and resentment, of domination by the West. After some 600 years of European colonialism (recall that Ceuta was first taken in 1415), and some two centuries of Western global ascendancy, with the hegemonic baton passing from Britain to the United States, it's payback time.

Faced with this daunting world of the 2020s, let's remember both lessons of Delphi. First, we don't know what will happen this afternoon, far less in a few years' time. Second, we need intelligent, historically informed guesswork to prepare for the challenges we seem likely to face. Already by the time you read this, something unexpected will have happened. Decades make fools of the most sagaciously farsighted. Weighty predictions made back in 1973 look hilarious in 2023. (Remember: the Soviet Union was going to overtake the United States.) Any we make now will suffer the same fate in 2073. Readers fifty years hence will laugh out loud at my pencil-flashlight attempts to penetrate the darkness of the future. 'How absurdly optimistic' they may exclaim, from their nuclear shelter or desert cave; or 'How absurdly pessimistic', from some technologically wizard Muskville or Zuckerdrome. Meanwhile, the twenty-somethings of 2073 will be confronting elderly post-89ers with the big things they missed or messed up in their time, as the post-89ers have recently confronted my generation.

If any one of several plausible worst-case scenarios comes true, from a US–China war over Taiwan to a collective failure to stop global warming soaring beyond 2° above pre-industrial levels, then sometime in this decade a new Stefan Zweig might well sit down to write a threnody to an irretrievably lost 'World of Yesterday'. But I repeat, with emphasis, that Zweigish fatalism is not the spirit called for today.

Rather, we need 'pessimism of the intellect, optimism of the will', to use the great motto coined by the French writer Romain Rolland and popularised by the Italian Marxist thinker and activist Antonio Gramsci. Intellectual pessimism can be something positive. The strongest case for the European Union is based not on naïve Panglossian optimism but on constructive pessimism. It's precisely because we understand Europe's chronic tendency to fall back into its bad old ways that we value every European structure of law, co-operation and peaceful conflict resolution. The intellectual pessimism of the 1970s laid the foundations for the upward turn of the late 1980s, which opened one of the most hopeful periods in European history. Ill-founded intellectual optimism in the early 2000s paved the way for the downward turn that began in the second half of that decade.

The wisdom of this motto is not just intellectual and political; it's also psychological. As Gramsci explained in 1929, in a letter from a fascist prison to his brother Carlo:

> My own state of mind synthesises these two feelings and transcends them: my mind is pessimistic, but my will is optimistic. Whatever the situation, I imagine the worst that could happen in order to summon up all my reserves of willpower to overcome each and every obstacle. Since I never build up illusions, I am seldom disappointed.

In short, this is a prescription for mental strength. Anticipate the worst, work for the best.

Emerging from a communist prison in the 1980s, Václav Havel expressed a similar thought in a slightly different way. 'Hope is not prognostication,' he said. 'It is an orientation of the spirit, an orientation of the heart.' Hope is 'an ability to work for something because it is good, not just because it stands a chance to succeed . . . It is not the conviction that something will turn out well, but the certainty that something makes sense, regardless of how it turns out.'

Today's Europe, for all its faults, limits and hypocrisies, for all the setbacks of recent years, is still far better than the one I set out to explore in the early 1970s, let alone the hell my father encountered as a young man. It's also better than those of earlier centuries, including the pre-1914 Europe idealised by Stefan Zweig. In fact, adapting Churchill's famous remark about democracy, we might say that this is the worst possible Europe, apart from all the other Europes that have been tried from time to time. To defend, improve and extend a free Europe makes sense. It's a cause worthy of hope.

Epilogue: On a Normandy Beach

I am on the beach at Ver-sur-Mer, where my father landed with the first wave on D-Day in 1944. It is 7.30 in the morning, the time at which he landed. A cloudy sky is flecked by pink touches of dawn. The wind propels a strong, tangy smell of salt water and seaweed. Where once this green-grey sea was filled with the landing craft, amphibious tanks and earsplitting gunfire of the greatest armada the world has seen, all is now empty and calm, save for two early morning fishermen in waders, trying their luck in the shallows of the advancing tide. Somewhere over the horizon is England.

Standing on this windswept Normandy beach, I think of everything that Europe has been through in the nearly eighty years since my father landed here and especially across the half-century of European history I have witnessed myself. People, places, events. A shipyard in Gdańsk, a theatre in Prague, a wall in Berlin, a killing field in the Krajina. Ralf, Václav, Bronek and Pierre. Annegret, Róża and all those young Europeans on whom the future of Europe will depend. The triumphs and disasters, patient achievements and foolish mistakes – including my own. The great men who turned out to be so small and the 'ordinary' men and women who proved great. Those once exotic lands that have become homelands.

After a while, I turn away from the green-grey sea and take the narrow track up which my father advanced on 6 June 1944, under fire, sharing the weight of a heavy army radio with his signaller, Bombardier Croxford. A few days later, the bombardier would show off his tea mug, with a hole drilled straight through it by a sniper's bullet. A movie cliché, but this time true. On the high bluff at the top of the sharp rise ahead I can still make out their first orientation point, the villa they called 'lavatory pan house', although the circular drive that gave it that nickname has now been built over with modern houses. So has the German battery just behind it, part of Hitler's 'Atlantic Wall'. Perhaps the father of Jan Osmers, the local historian in the village of Westen, visited friends here when he served in one of the Waffen-SS regiments tasked with resisting the Allied invasion.

Casting my eye along the bluff to the west, I see, in the dawn's early light, the British and French flags, Union Jack and Tricolore, flying high above what looks at first sight like a kind of Acropolis. This is the British Normandy Memorial, inaugurated only in 2021. Its central monument is flanked by a giant rectangle of double rows of pale Burgundian limestone columns, like a cloister but open to the skies, the columns linked at the top by wooden beams, as in a pergola. From the seaward side of the memorial, you have a perfect view, down across well-tilled fields and marshy ground, to mile upon mile of the Normandy landing beaches. One face of the central monument is given over to the words in which Charles de Gaulle announced to his compatriots that the liberation force had been launched *'des rivages de la vieille Angleterre'* – from the shores of old England.

On the limestone columns are engraved the names of 22,442 people from more than thirty countries who died while serving under British command in the Normandy campaign between 6 June 1944 and the liberation of Paris at the end of August. They are grouped by day of death and very simply recorded: surname, initials, rank and age. I look particularly for the names of two men who were killed doing exactly the same dangerous job as my father did, in the same regiment. Here they are. 14 June: Hall, EWC, Capt[ain], 24. 20 June: Swann, KG, Maj[or], 28. To Dad, they were 'Ted' Hall and 'Ken' Swann: brother officers, friends. 'The lads that will never be old.' I study their faces on his wartime photos.

It could so easily have been him. The casualty rate for forward observation officers in his artillery regiment was more than fifty per cent in the first three months of the Normandy campaign. Another of them, Stephen Perry – my godfather, Uncle Stephen – once told me, as we sailed together across the Channel, how the shrapnel was still moving around inside his body thirty years later. Robert Kiln – my brother's godfather, Uncle Robert – lost a leg in the Battle of Arnhem. Who dares to claim it can never happen again? It already has, in Yugoslavia, in Ukraine. 'Ah, but it couldn't happen here,' they say. They always say.

Remembrance is about the past but for the future. Like the German village of Westen and the Polish hamlet of Przysieczyn, this small French town understands that well. The good work of remembering has been going on for many years here and not just because it attracts tourists. An aviation enthusiast called Jean-Pierre Dupont spent part of the war as a child in 'lavatory pan house' – or rather, to give it the dignity of its proper name, Villa Salvador. Fortunately, he was no longer there when the guns commanded by Robert Kiln inadvertently blew an enormous hole through the middle of the villa on D-Day, while trying to hit the German battery behind. Towards the end of the last century, M. Dupont set out to create a small museum documenting the local D-Day. Now his successor as curator shows me their photographs and model reconstructions of the landing, of which he knows every detail. That German battery just behind the Villa Salvador had Russian Red Army guns captured on the Eastern front and transported all the way to Normandy. The Wehrmacht troops at Ver included soldiers recruited from German annexed territories in western Poland, the Sudetenland and Alsace. There are Polish names on the British Normandy Memorial. All Europe was here.

After the liberation, Dietrich Habeck was among the German prisoners of war kept in Ver-sur-Mer to de-mine the area. As a fifteen-year-old, he had been interrogated by the Gestapo because he belonged to a Bible circle. At eighteen, he was conscripted into the Wehrmacht, where he served as a radio operator. During his time in Ver, where he was held until 1948, he became friendly with two of his French guards and subsequently came back regularly to visit. In 1973, now a distinguished medic in Münster, Professor Habeck saw a 'For Sale' sign outside the Villa Salvador and bought it as a holiday home. On the fiftieth anniversary of D-Day, in 1994, Jean-Pierre and Jeannine Dupont took four English guests – my mother and father, Uncle Robert and his wife – up for lunch with the Habecks, in the villa with which their personal histories were all so curiously intertwined. Frau Habeck laughingly thanked the British veterans for having blown such a big hole in the wall, since it gave her the idea of putting in a lovely large window. Here's a photo from that day: the English, French and Germans standing side by side, all smiling in front of the handsomely restored, half-timbered house. Europe.

The mayor of Ver-sur-Mer talks with passion of his community's *devoir de mémoire,* its obligation to remember. He has just inaugurated a 'memory walk' which consists of nine memorial tablets, mounted on waist-high pedestals along a pedestrian route around the town. Beside photographs and descriptions of what happened locally, there is some world history – Churchill and Roosevelt, for example – along with a few carefully chosen quotations. I like particularly this message to the future from Charles de Gaulle: 'Patriotism is to love your own country; nationalism, to detest that of the others.' And this from Konrad Adenauer: 'History is the sum total of things that could have been avoided.'

The local council has also created a shadow 'youth council' with a titular 'youth mayor' and deputies. Some of the youngsters are to make presentations beside the memorial pedestals. At the Sexton Côté Mer (Sexton-on-sea) bistrot, its curious name explained by a Second World War British Sexton tank placed on a pedestal in the middle of the Espace Robert Kiln, a small, triangular public space just across the road, I meet thirteen-year-old deputy youth mayor Léandre: curly hair, freckles, bright eyes above his anti-Covid facemask. He is to do Churchill and Roosevelt. After a slightly shaky start, in which Churchill appears to be President of the United States, he talks rather well – reading from notes on his phone – about the reasons behind the founding of the United Nations. I try a little memory transfusion.

Nothing could be more intensely, quintessentially European than this Normandy countryside with its rich fields, copses and hedgerows, winding lanes through higgledy-piggledy villages, and mediaeval churches with descriptive noticeboards recalling the time of Guillaume le Conquérant (William the Conqueror to English-speaking readers). Its large manor-farms have great, thick stone walls and, in the cool interiors behind those walls, the good food and wine that is also a part of European culture. Prosperity. Peace. Freedom. No direct experience of the problems that torment the *banlieues* of large French cities. Here, surely, in this place that has so much of Europe, support for the political project that we call 'Europe' should be at its height.

Yet in the second round of the presidential elections in 2017, more than a third of the votes cast in Ver-sur-Mer went to Marine le Pen, the leader of the National Front, who had praised Brexit and called for France to leave the eurozone. Such were the doubts and resentments that had grown around the European project since it began to falter in the first decade of the twenty-first century. Analysing the detailed election figures for Ver, this means that 359 people voted for the far-right nationalist candidate. (In the 2022 election, it would be eighty-two more.)

'Few of them will admit to it,' a local councillor warns me. But I do find one.

On a glorious, sunny Saturday, he and I sit down to a trencherman's platter of *tête de veau* (calf's head) and root vegetables at the Sexton Côté Mer bistrot. Monsieur M., as I shall call him, is a cheerful, intelligent, bibulous retired dentist in his mid-eighties, full of anecdotes and joie de vivre. I drink a glass of wine, he downs four. Born in 1936, he has vivid childhood memories of the German occupation: a German soldier coming to supper while a deserter hid in the loft; listening secretly to Radio Londres, the BBC's wartime French service; being liberated by the Canadians. But he thinks Europe has gone wrong in more recent times. He will vote for le Pen again, 'because of immigration'. He is very clear about that.

'I support Brexit. And for France today: out of the euro, out of the EU.'

'Brussels' – he uses that shorthand – keeps telling us what to do, even how to prepare our Normandy cheeses. And what about democracy?

Then I, the English European stripped of my European citizenship by the vote of my compatriots, set out to persuade him otherwise. The Union has many faults, but does he really want to take the risk of its disintegration? Surely he remembers a much worse Europe?

After a few rounds of this curious role reversal – the Englishman trying to persuade the Frenchman of the virtues of Europe – I resolve that we should at least share a toast to Europe.

'*Alors*,' I say, lifting my glass, '*quand même et malgré tout* (all the same and in spite of everything), *l'Europe!*'

No, he won't join me. He picks up his third glass of wine and proposes that we drink instead to '*la viticulture!*' The cultivation of the grape.

But I'm not giving up. Over dessert, I try again. Again, Monsieur M.

demurs, this time suggesting that we drink to '*nous!*' To us. Which, I think to myself, could almost be construed as the same thing, although he doesn't mean it that way.

Finally, after long resistance, he yields, raising his last glass with a half-reluctant, half-cheerful shrug.

'*L'Europe!*'

A note from the author

Thank you for travelling this far with me. On www.timothygartonash. com I give my sources for all quotations in this book, apart from those that come from my own notebooks, as well as for many of the facts and figures.

On the same website, you can find a selection of illustrative material, from my father's photos of cricket in Westen in 1945, a covert Stasi photo of me and my friends taken in 1980, and the bottle of 'Stalin's Tears' vodka given me by Bronisław Geremek when he was Polish foreign minister in the late 1990s, all the way to a 2021 letter from Viktor Orbán, glimpses of the new Iron Curtain that I saw in Ceuta, and images from the war in Ukraine.

The story continues. If you're interested in following subsequent developments, you might enjoy my Substack newsletter, 'History of the Present', at timothygartonash.substack.com.

Many people helped me in the writing of this book. For conversations, reminiscences, guidance on particular points and much more I am most grateful to Gian-Paolo Accardo, Suleika Ahmed, Corinne Ailleret, Suzanne Ailleret, Othon Anastasakis, Carol Atack, Erica Benner, Jarosław Berendt, Paul Betts, Carl Bildt, Tony Blair, Koussay Boulaich, Hugo Brady, Archie Brown, Helen Buchanan, David Cameron, Alastair Campbell, Paul Chaisty, Sebastian Chosiński, Cathryn Costello, Jean-François le Cuziat, Pat Cummings-Winter, Kim Darroch, Florian Dirks, Weronika Dorociak, Jean-Philippe Dupont, Charles Enoch, Tula Fernández, Irena Grosfeld, Margret Herbst, Judith Herrin, Fiona Hill, Lindsey Hilsum, Harold James, Jan Kaniewski, Jonathan Keates, Matthew Kiln, Kostis Kornetis, Kamila Kłos, Małgorzata Kranc-Rybczyńska, Joachim Krätschell, Werner Krätschell, Jarosław Kurski, Oliver Letwin, Edward Llewellyn, Eleni Louri-Dendrinou, Noel Malcolm, Hartmut Mayer,

Michael McFaul, Franziska Meifort, Michael Mertes, Charles Moore, Wolfgang Münchau, Norman Naimark, Mattia Nelles, Kalypso Nico-laïdis, Peter Nippert, Pablo Núñez Díaz, Philippe Onillon, Zbigniew Orywał, Jan Osmers, Richard Pertwee, Maria Polachowska, Charles Powell (London), Charles Powell (Madrid), Jonathan Powell, Stuart Proffitt, Condoleezza Rice, Andrew Riley, George Robertson, Jacques Rupnik, Michael Scott, Jean Seaton, James Sheehan, Aleksander Smolar, Róża Thun, José Ignacio Torreblanca, Ivan Vejvoda, Jean-Luc Véret, Stephen Wall, Kieran Williams, Peter Wilson, Joachim Woock, Mark Wood, Martin Wolf, Michael Žantovský and Philip Zelikow.

For invaluable research assistance and feedback, special thanks to Marilena Anastasopoulou, Sonia Cuesta Maniar, Lukas Dovern, Jan Farfal, Olivier de France, Kristijan Fidanovski, Daniel Kovarek, Josef Lolacher, Ana Martins, Jonathan Raspe, Adriana Riganová, Olena Shumska, Alexandra Solovyev, Lucas Tse, Achille Versaevel, Reja Wyss – and not least to my successive Dahrendorf Programme research managers, Maxime Dargaud-Fons, Selma Kropp, Jana Bühler, Luisa Melloh and Adele Curness.

Georges Borchardt, Natasha Fairweather, Stuart Williams, Bill Frucht, Ana Fletcher and Graeme Hall made the editorial process enjoyable at every stage. I am particularly grateful to Daniel Judt, Ian McEwan, Michael Taylor, Tobias Wolff and Robert Zoellick for their close readings of earlier drafts. My greatest debt is concealed in the dedication.

Index of people and places

Individual place names are generally listed under the country in which that place is now located

Belgium 3, 6, 16, 35, 38, 68, 120, 204, 207,
  208, 275, 277, 281, 287, 290, 300
  Bruges 124–6, 232
  Brussels 22, 32, 37, 55, 56, 63, 65, 123, 125,
    126, 168, 175, 214, 227, 229, 232, 246,
    248, 251–2, 254, 260–1, 262, 269, 281,
    282–3, 285, 289, 297, 299, 301–2, 350
Belunek, Jan 7
Bercow, John 290
Bergson, Henri 280
Berlusconi, Silvio 194, 215, 229–30
Biden, Joe 216, 324, 343
Biermann, Wolf 323, 326
Bildt, Carl 36
bin Laden, Osama 211, 216, 217, 222
Bismarck, Otto von 36, 252
Blair, Tony 124, 125–6, 166, 196, 213, 215,
  227–35
Bloch, Ernst 46
Boleslaus, King 62
Bonaparte, Napoleon 63, 64, 70, 144,
  280–1
Bosnia 39, 49–50, 166, 179, 180–2, 184, 185,
  186, 187–8, 203, 214, 219, 289, 341
  Sarajevo 17, 49–50, 102, 166, 178, 180,
    188, 208
  Srebrenica 39, 166, 179, 184–8
  Tuzla 179, 180, 186
Bouyeri, Mohammed 220
Boyle, Danny 226, 227
Brandt, Willy 18, 35, 69, 133, 135–6, 168,
  228
Breivik, Anders Behring 220, 271
Breslau. See Poland, Wrocław
Brewster Jr, Kingman 121
Britain xv, xvi, xvii, 3, 5, 6–7, 9, 10, 16,
  18–23, 27, 28, 29–30, 33–4, 41, 44, 47,
  51, 52, 53, 54, 55, 63, 64–5, 67, 68, 71,
  72, 73, 75, 76, 80, 90, 95, 97, 103, 107,
  112, 113, 114–15, 116, 121–7, 132, 133–4,
  135, 137, 155, 159, 166, 182, 190, 199,
  206–7, 212, 213, 215, 220, 224, 225–35,
  236, 237, 238, 245, 246, 247, 251, 264,
  266, 267, 269, 275, 277, 279–93, 294,
  299–300, 313, 315, 316, 317, 318, 319,

322, 324, 325, 331, 334, 336, 338, 341,
  344, 347–51
Cambridge 106
England xvi, xvii, 33, 46, 52, 54, 63, 68,
  113, 121–7, 197, 225–7, 230–1, 234, 239,
  281, 346, 347
London 20, 81, 96, 104, 173, 186, 213, 220,
  223, 225, 227, 229, 230, 231, 235, 250,
  269, 287, 288, 310
Manchester 234, 269
Northern Ireland 166, 182–3, 184, 185,
  226, 290
Oxford xvi, 74, 77, 100, 114, 116, 123–4,
  164, 180, 214, 217, 284, 286, 295, 297
Scotland xviii, 68, 183, 226, 234, 280, 283
Wales 226, 234
Westminster 129, 269, 287
Brown, George 228
Brown, Gordon 229, 231, 233
Browning, Christopher 186
Buchanan, Helen 44
Bulgaria 52, 62, 119, 158, 159, 288, 298
Burma. See Myanmar
Buruma, Ian 122–3, 222–3, 271
Bush, George H. W. 132, 138–9, 147, 148,
  155–6, 157, 306
Bush, George W. 161–3, 183, 196, 211, 212,
  213, 214, 216, 258, 260, 269
Byron, George Gordon 88, 92

Cameron, David 124, 227, 235, 267, 280, 281,
  282, 283, 284, 285, 286
Campbell, Alastair 232
Campbell, Colin 182, 185
Camus, Renaud 276, 297
Čaputová, Zuzana 305
Carlson, Tucker 300
Carville, James 251
Catherine the Great, Tsarina 257, 263
Ceaușescu, Nicolae 99, 115, 135
Celan, Paul 78
Chancellor, Alexander 121, 122, 128
Charlemagne, Emperor 37, 43, 61, 62, 63,
  64, 65, 166, 228
Chechnya 219, 258, 326